POPULATION AND PROGRESS IN A YORUBA TOWN

POPULATION AND PROGRESS IN A YORUBA TOWN

ELISHA P. RENNE

The University of Michigan Press
Ann Arbor

In memory of Adé Mobain-re Ọbáyẹ́mi

Ká s'òótọ́ ká kú, ó sàn ju ká ṣ'ẹ̀bi ká bá wà láàyè
Better to tell the truth and die, than to lie and live

© Elisha P. Renne, 2003
All rights reserved
Published in the United States of America by
The University of Michigan Press
First published in the UK by Edinburgh
University Press, as part of the International
African Library series

No part of this publication may be
reproduced, stored in a retrieval system, or
transmitted in any form or by any means,
electronic, mechanical, or otherwise, without
the written permission of the publisher.

Typeset in Plantin
by Koinonia, Bury, and
printed and bound in Great Britain
by Bell & Bain Ltd, Glasgow

Library of Congress Cataloging-in-Publication
Data applied for.
ISBN 0-472-08983-8

The right of Elisha P. Renne to be
identified as author of this work has been
asserted in accordance with the Copyright,
Designs and Patents Act 1988.

CONTENTS

List of Figures and Tables vi
Preface ix
Acknowledgements xi

PART I ANTHROPOLOGICAL AND DEMOGRAPHIC CONCERNS

1 Introduction: Paradoxes of Progress 3
2 Historical and Anthropological Aspects of Ìtàpá: Centripetal and Centrifugal Tendencies 19
3 Demographic Dimensions of Ìtàpá-Èkìtì 42

PART II BODIES, PERSONS AND SOCIAL RELATIONS

4 Women's Bodies, Virginity and Marriage 71
5 Child-fostering, Blood Ties and Parenthood 89
6 Burial, Rebirth and Relations with the Dead 111

PART III POPULATION, DEVELOPMENT AND THE STATE

7 Personal Hygiene, Public Sanitation and Western Education 135
8 Houses, Descendants and Land Tenure 155
9 Counting Bodies: Censuses, Vital Registration and the Creation of Ekiti State 175
10 Conclusion: Local Development, Politics and Two Funerals 197

Appendix I Research Methods and Materials 211
Appendix II Important Dates in Ìtàpá and Nigerian History 228
Appendix III Contraception Ever Used by Ìtàpá-Èkìtì Women, based on 1992, 1997 Surveys 232

Notes 234
Bibliography 252
Index 269

LIST OF FIGURES AND TABLES

FIGURES

1.1	Ẹgbẹ́ (club) launching, Ìtàpá-Èkìtì, December 1991	8
1.2	Old Methodist Church building, Ìtàpá-Èkìtì, September 1991	9
1.3	Federal government family planning promotional poster/logo	12
2.1	Map of Ìtàpá-Èkìtì, showing eight major quarters	20
2.2a	Map of Nigeria, showing Ekiti State	22
2.2b	Map of Ekiti State	23
2.3	Main road through Ìtàpá-Èkìtì, 1992	24
2.4	Women from the three houses of Ẹbí Ọmọba at àjà mùta, Ìtàpá-Èkìtì, January 1992	32
2.5	Envelope used for collecting funds for Rẹ́mọ Day	38
2.6	Reo, the type of truck first seen in Ìtàpá	40
3.1	Population pyramid for Ìtàpá-Èkìtì, 1991	45
3.2a, b	Marriage types and husbands' residence, women aged 15–39, and 40–65	50
3.3	Divorce and marriage patterns, Ìtàpá-Èkìtì, 1997	52
3.4	Median ideal number of children wanted, by sex and age group, Ìtàpá-Èkìtì, 1992, 1997	53
3.5	Women's experience of infant/child mortality, 1992, 1997	57
3.6a	Children born, July 1992–June 1997, where delivered, by age of mother	59
3.6b	Children born, January 1987–December 1991, where delivered, by age of mother	59
3.7	Women (n=294) from 1992 Ìtàpá survey in 1997	61
3.8	Card for attending Methodist Maternity Hospital, Ìkọ̀lé-Èkìtì	63
3.9	Ìtàpá Maternity Centre	64
4.1	Illustration of ovulation cycle, from health textbook (Usua and Dada 1987: 129)	80
4.2	Educational levels of women who discuss childbearing with spouses	87
5.1a, b	In-fostering by age of foster-mother, Ìtàpá-Èkìtì, 1992, 1997	107
5.1c, d	Out-fostering by age of foster-mother, Ìtàpá-Èkìtì, 1992, 1997	108
6.1	Funeral observances for the Ọbalókè, Ìtàpá-Èkìtì, February 1992	112

LIST OF FIGURES AND TABLES vii

6.2	House with fish on door with grave (*oróri*) on front stoop, Rẹ́mọ, Ìtàpá-Èkìtì, December 1992	115
6.3	African Church grave, Ìtàpá-Èkìtì, July 1997	117
6.4	Ìtàlè festivities, Ìtàpá-Èkìtì, February 1992	123
7.1	Children showing hands to teacher during school inspection	141
7.2	Incinerator near main market, Ìtàpá-Èkìtì, July 2000	149
7.3	Fetching water from Ọ̀sun Stream, Ìtàpá-Èkìtì, 1997	150
8.1	Old house with iron roof, Ìtàpá-Èkìtì, August 1997	156
8.2	House interior with shelf, Ìtàpá-Èkìtì, 1992	158
8.3	Transaction types by date of land transfer	163
8.4	Houseplot boundary with *ọ̀dàn* tree, Rẹ́mọ, Ìtàpá-Èkìtì, 1999	165
9.1	Birth dates written on house wall, Oròkè Quarter, Ìtàpá-Èkìtì, 1997	176
9.2	Èkìtì Kete bumper sticker, 1996	189
10.1	Sawmill, Ìtàpá-Èkìtì, July 2000	198
10.2	Programme cover for an earlier Ìtàpá Day, 1996	202
10.3	Town hall named in honour of the late Chief S. A. Dada, Ìtàpá-Èkìtì, July 2000	204
App.1.1	Age heaping by survey women's age, Ìtàpá-Èkìtì, 1997	212
App.1.2	Comparison of ages reported in 1992 and 1997 surveys	214
App.3.1	Comparison of contraception ever used, women's survey, 1992, 1997, Ìtàpá-Èkìtì	233

TABLES

3.1	Population of Ìtàpá-Èkìtì	44
3.2	Household composition: per cent distribution by households by sex of head of household, household size, and presence of foster children, Ìtàpá-Èkìtì, 1991	46
3.3a–c	Characteristics of survey men (1992) and women (1992, 1997), Ìtàpá-Èkìtì	47
3.4a, b	Total fertility rate, Ìtàpá-Èkìtì, 1992, 1997	55
4.1	Early sexual experience of Ìtàpá-Èkìtì women, aged 35–70+	75
4.2	Early sexual experiences of Ìtàpá-Èkìtì women, aged 15–34	76
4.3	Diseases associated with virginity, Ìtàpá-Èkìtì, 1992	82
5.1a	Relationship of in-foster children to foster parents, Ìtàpá-Èkìtì, 1991	93
5.1b	Relationship of out-foster children to foster parents, Ìtàpá-Èkìtì, 1991	93
5.2	Foster parents' experience of being fostered, Ìtàpá-Èkìtì, 1991	94
5.3a	Reason for child being in-fostered, Ìtàpá-Èkìtì, 1991	96
5.3b	Reason for child being out-fostered, Ìtàpá-Èkìtì, 1991	97

5.4a	Comparison of time spent on school, work, and leisure by pairs of fostered and non-fostered children, Ìtàpá-Èkìtì, 1991	101
5.4b	Comparison of time working by fostered and non-fostered children, Ìtàpá-Èkìtì, 1991	102
8.1	Houseplot land transfers and household characteristics	162
8.2	Houseplot boundaries by land transaction types	166
8.3	Family type and household composition, by houseplot transaction type	168

PREFACE

> The ... message 'Family planning for the progress of parents and children' assumes an unusual ability on the part of the masses to make inference from ... a vague word such as 'progress' (*Ìlọ́síwájú*). This message should have been broken down to specific and familiar items of everyday life.
>
> P. O. Olúsànyà 1989a: 445

This book was written partly in response to a question raised by a prominent Belgian demographer at a seminar on culture and fertility. 'Why was it,' he asked, 'that Nigeria, with its abundant resources, including its vast oil wealth and its well-educated population, was lagging behind countries such as Kenya and Botswana in fertility decline?' In the chapters that follow, I attempt to answer this question, based on ethnographic and survey research in one Èkìtì Yoruba town in south-western Nigeria. While the specifics of this case study do not apply uniformly throughout Nigeria, the most populous country in sub-Saharan Africa, the more general conclusions do. Influenced by the work of the Nigerian demographer, P. O. Olúsànyà, whose extraordinary insights into population dynamics in Nigeria remain relevant, I have organised this book around an examination of two related questions. First, what did people mean by the term 'progress', *ìlọ́síwájú* (or development, *ìdàgbàsókè*, as it is more commonly referred to in Èkìtì)? Secondly, how did people's thinking about having children relate to their ideas about progress? Focusing on 'specific and familiar items of everyday life' associated in some way with reproduction, I examined the processes whereby people's ideas and practices concerning childbearing were changing. While I found that some younger people were re-evaluating their thinking about what constituted a large family, it soon became clear to me that state policies and programmes – in other words, politics – were a fundamental part of the picture. The Nigerian government's adoption of a National Population Policy in 1988, which made 'family planning' contraceptives available in government clinics, influenced people's ideas about family size and progress. But so did more indirect government projects such as the implementation of a federal land law and a national census.

This research took place during a particular period of time (1991–2000) that situated these local reassessments of 'the progress of parents and children' within a specific political and economic context. This was a time of uncertainty, not only in terms of transportation, water and government services; it was also a time of a federal Structural Adjustment Programme, national strikes and political violence. This political uncertainty, along with a declining infrastructure, unemployment and rising infant mortality, hardly provided the situation in which people living in a small rural town would consider having significantly fewer children, despite the concurrent economic constraints.

So in response to the Belgian demographer, I would say that the particularities of national politics, along with the cultural and socio-economic specifics of thinking about family size and progress, explain continuing high fertility in Nigeria. Politics, of course, is also a factor in the demographies of Kenya and Botswana, although these countries' histories and political circumstances differ considerably. During the period 1991–2000, for example, Kenya had one national leader, Botswana two, and Nigeria five. To present an analysis of the historical, political and social bases for demographic differences among sub-Saharan African countries would require another book, at least. Here, rather more modestly, I have attempted to show how women and men in one small south-western Nigerian town are rethinking ideas about family size, and how their re-assessments relate both to progress as they see it and to the actions of the State. Such demographic and anthropological studies are critically important if collaborative approaches to population issues, as suggested by Amartya Sen, are to succeed. By focusing on the accomplishments of people living in one Yoruba town as well as the obstacles they face at the local and national level, the ways toward solving their town and country's political and socio-economic problems may more clearly be seen.

ACKNOWLEDGEMENTS

This study began its circuitous path from the United States, to Australia, and to Nigeria and back, when I took up a postdoctoral fellowship at Health Transition Centre at the Australian National University, Canberra. I am grateful to John C. Caldwell, Pat Caldwell and I. P. Orùbuloyè, who advised me on this project and helped me to get settled in the small Èkìtì Yoruba town of Ìtàpá-Èkìtì. Through the assistance of Dr Michael Òjó, I was introduced to members of the community, including His Royal Highness, Ọba Adéyẹyẹ Àmùdá Alli, Oguguleso II, the Ọwátàpá of Ìtàpá, and his council of chiefs as well as women's groups such as Ẹgbẹ́ Bọmọlayọ̀, and the many men and women of Ìtàpá whose kindness and consideration contributed immensely to my research. I thank them all for their hospitality and patience in allowing a stranger who asks incessant questions to live, intermittently, in their town since 1991.

I have been affiliated with several universities during the course of this study, including the Australian National University, Ekiti State University-Adó-Èkìtì, Emory University, Princeton University and the University of Michigan, and I am most grateful to colleagues and friends at these institutions: Gigi Santow, David Crawford, Jenny Porteous, Judith Littleton, Jennifer Braid, Wendy Cosford, Jacob Adétúnji, Abíọ́dún Arikenbi, S. O. A. Akínbulumọ, James Trussell, Akín Bánkọlé, Tom Hanson, Rena Lederman, Gillian Feeley-Harnik, Tom Fricke, Stuart Kirsch and Ann Biddlecom, among many others. Those in Nigeria who provided advice and moral support include J. A. Ebigbọ́lá, J. F. A. Àjàyí, A. O. Àkànle, the late S. A. Dada, the late I. A. Ókè, Ọláide Adédòkun, Chris Bánkọlé and members of the Ọbasaju Family.

I would also like to thank the many people who have assisted in this research project over the years, including Káyọ̀dé Owóẹyẹ, Comfort Àjàyí, Adénìkẹ́ Ọṣọ, Sunday Fálọdún, Kẹ́hìndé Àjàyí, Fẹ́mi Òjó, Olaóyè Ìdòwú, Tóyin Owóẹyẹ, Ìyábọ̀ Arọ́ṣọ, Bọ́ṣẹ̀ Ayẹni, and Bísí Ògúnṣakin. I owe a special debt to the Owóẹyẹ family, particularly to the late Felicia Owóẹyẹ, who generously allowed me to stay in the family home. Without her help, and that of her son Káyọ̀dé, his wife Tóyin, and their children, this research would not have been possible.

Research funding for this study was provided by several sources, including the Andrew W. Mellon Foundation, administered first through the Health Transition Centre, Australian National University, and then through the Office of Population Research, Princeton University, as well as the Wenner-Gren Foundation for Anthropological Research, and the Office of the Vice President for Research, University of Michigan. The College of Literature, Science, and Arts, and the Department of Anthropology, University of Michigan generously provided subvention funds for illustrations in this volume.

This book represents research conducted over a nine-year period and earlier versions of some chapters have been presented as seminar papers and have been published, although all previously written work has been significantly revised. Many thanks go to readers of these seminar papers and manuscript chapters, including LaRay Denzer, Stephen Kunitz, Susan Watkins, Carolyn Makinson, Anthony Carter, Etienne van de Walle, Charles Westoff, Akín Bánkọlé, Jane Guyer, Karen Hansen, J. D. Y. Peel, Karin Barber, Murray Last, Misty Bastian, Judith Byfield, Olúfúnke Okome, Susan Bergh and Julius Scott, as well as two anonymous readers for the International African Institute. In addition, Karin Barber's expert advice on Yoruba language questions was greatly appreciated. Finally, J. D. Y. Peel, of the International African Institute, helpfully assisted with publication logistics and Julie Isaac kindly provided maps. James Dale, of Edinburgh University Press, and Sarah Burnett gave excellent editorial advice, making the publication process a pleasure.

This manuscript is dedicated to the memory of Professor Adé Ọbáyẹmi, whose knowledge of the north-eastern Yoruba area and dedication to the study of Nigerian history made him the best of mentors. *Sun re o!*

PART I

ANTHROPOLOGICAL AND DEMOGRAPHIC CONCERNS

1

INTRODUCTION: PARADOXES OF PROGRESS

Tí èníyàn kò bá lè tẹ̀síwájú, a tẹ̀sẹ́hìn
If anyone cannot go forward, they will go backward.

Yoruba proverb

This book is about local perceptions of fertility and progress. These terms, fertility and progress (or as they are more often referred to in the literature, population and development) are so closely linked in present-day Western thinking – the idea being that (high) fertility impedes (economic) development – that it is difficult to imagine them in any other way. Yet it is also possible to envision fertility as something desirable for the development of a town, from a moral as well as an economic perspective (Olúsànyà 1989b). Indeed, one of the terms for development in Yoruba – *ìdàgbàsókè* – refers to the 'raising up' of a moral community, in a way similar to that in which children are 'raised up' to become responsible adults. This interpretation of development, conceptualised as a type of growth that conflates economic and human development (Peel 1978: 141), has particular implications for local perceptions of fertility and progress. These perceptions and how they are changing in the small Èkìtì Yoruba town of Ìtàpá-Èkìtì in south-western Nigeria are the focus of this study.

PARADOXES OF PROGRESS

In order for a town to grow – to develop – into a large, prosperous community, it must have people: *ọmọ ìlú*, 'children of the town'. This corresponds with the idea that an individual man or woman aspiring to 'bigness' as an 'owner' of wealth and power (that is, to be a patron) must have people as clients: *ọmọ ẹ̀hìn*, followers (literally, 'children of the back'). As many who have written on Yoruba social life have observed (for example Apter 1992; Barber 1991; Barnes 1986; Berry 1985; Guyer 1997; Peel 1983), this dynamic form of patron–client relations operates similarly on ever-wider levels of society. From the compound head and familial followers of wives, children, and assorted extended family members and friends, to town quarters' heads and chiefs, and to local government officials with their entourage of supporters and hangers-on; all these heads must have a body of followers.

In the case of family compounds and towns, the wisdom of this need for people is dramatically evident when a house, for reasons of death, disease, or infertility, is abandoned and physically decays, literally portraying the demise of the family that once inhabited it. Towns that lose population – through out-migration caused by misfortune or lack of opportunities or amenities – likewise may dwindle and be ultimately abandoned as well. It is not only for prestige and comfort that rural townspeople seek progress. Rather, these developments also keep people from leaving, increase the town's population, and attract others to it. Indeed, having many people is viewed as one of the characteristics of a well-developed town, as one woman, a retired schoolteacher, explained:

> When people are many in the town, it brings more development than when they are few. A single finger can't pick a louse in the hair (*ìka kan kò lè mú iná l'órí*) – unless there are two or three fingers [it can't be done]. So where there are many people, developments will be many and more rapid than in a place where the population is small.
> (DI97-3, Ìtàpá-Èkìtì, 1997)

Yet certain aspects of development may limit population growth, undermining the very vitality of small towns such as Ìtàpá-Èkìtì. Townspeople face three fundamental paradoxes in keeping, increasing and attracting people and in 'raising up' their town.

One of these paradoxes of progress has to do with the pervasive dynamic of Èkìtì social life alluded to above, namely the divisive tendencies of individuals and groups to competitively separate from others, in search of headship and followers of their own (Barber 1991; Lloyd 1968b: 42). Referred to as centrifugal tendencies in Chapter 2, this competitive drive for leadership and followers counters the centripetal actions necessary for those coming together to develop a town or community. Consequently, Ìtàpá townspeople have spoken of 'a lack of love' or 'lack of unity' when asked to explain what was impeding progress in their town (cf. Peel 1978: 158). While the social dynamic of striving for followers – of which having many children is part – has brought certain improvements such as better housing, the continual hiving-off of groups at all levels of society fosters a lack of cooperation that undermines the very development so fervently desired (Berry 1985: 194).

A second and related paradox pertaining to population directly concerns the town's population, specifically its fertility. In Ìtàpá-Èkìtì, a primary means of developing the town and its children in this century has been associated with Western education. Yet a significant relationship between education and lower fertility – namely that increased education, particularly for women, is related to fewer births – has been shown in numerous demographic studies (Castro Martin 1995; Diamond et al. 1999; Jeffery and Basu

1996), although the exact reasons for this relationship may vary (Bledsoe et al. 1999). In Ìtàpá-Èkìtì, educating one's children and having relatively fewer children so as to be able to educate all of them well seems to have widespread support, as discussed in Chapter 6. Nonetheless, this practice undermines levels of fertility associated with an increase in people, an important dimension in developing the town. Additionally, many of these educated sons and daughters seeking employment opportunities migrate to larger cities elsewhere in Nigeria (see Chapter 3), further diminishing the town's population (see Peel 1983: 258). Ideally, this migration should serve the town well, as these educated children are able to attract resources from outside the town for its development, which in turn should attract more people to it. However, this has not happened to any large extent.

The third paradox relating to fertility and progress concerns various contradictory practices, policies, and development programmes of the Nigerian state. Rather than routinising government services, the ambiguous functioning of government programmes (Chabal and Daloz 1999) reinforces the need for an extended network of people – some who can stay in the town to maintain land holdings, for example, and others who have privileged access to local sources of political power. Furthermore, population has become a principal form of evidence used in arguments for greater access to state resources, both in terms of numbers of elected federal representatives and in the allocation of federal funds for development.[1] Hence, the importance of 'getting out the people' in the 1991 census as part of a village effort to enhance its position in local government politics and also part of a longstanding Èkìtì effort to establish an independent Ekiti State, created in 1996 (see Chapter 9). Ìtàpá residents generally viewed the creation of Ekiti State as a victory for the development of the Èkìtì area. It has attracted many Èkìtì indigenes to move back home and at the same time has brought Èkìtì residents closer to government resources, giving the 'politics of numbers' (Alonso and Starr 1987) a particular cogency in late twentieth-century Nigeria.

An examination of these three paradoxes helps to explain why fertility in this south-western Nigerian town – despite the presence of factors associated with its decline such as widespread literacy, knowledge of contraceptives and their availability, and economic concerns associated with childbearing (Coale 1973) – remains relatively high.[2] It is not that these factors are unimportant or that they do not have predictive value under certain conditions. Rather, the problem with thinking about population and development in ways that assume a universal explanation of fertility decline is that these terms may have different meanings for people in particular places and under particular political and economic circumstances (Greenhalgh 1990). This study argues for the need to include larger political and economic factors in explanations of fertility behaviour. It also argues for the importance of considering the local point of view, in other words, how Ìtàpá townspeople themselves understand their fertility and see their own progress. Let us begin with fertility.

CONCEPTIONS OF FERTILITY

The meaning of some words seems so transparent that they go without further probing. This tendency to accept 'the one most in evidence', as Feeley-Harnik (1991) citing Hocart (1937: 345) puts it, would seem to apply to the word 'fertility', which is often associated, at least in the demographic literature, with the number of children an individual has borne. Yet, as Townsend (1997: 108–9) has observed, 'A person's fertility is a description of a place in a web of relationships with offspring, with other kin, and with a range of social groups and institutions.' The clarification of these relationships is crucial for an understanding of what fertility means in a particular social context. For example, in many West African societies, the ubiquity of certain forms of child fostering underscores the involvement of those other than the biological parents in fertility behaviour (see Chapter 5). Such an analysis of social relationships and fertility, however, might usefully include a consideration of the ways that social structure intersects with specific interpretations of fertility in terms of broader cosmological beliefs. In Èkìtì, for example, fertility is evidenced by the birth of a child, whose being is believed to be brought about, in part, through the sexual congress of a woman and a man. Yet fertility is also believed to be affected by otherworldly forces including ancestral spirits and God as well as by the worldly machinations of others. Those in structurally equivocal social positions (such as jealous co-wives) and those whose behaviour subverts social life more generally (referred to as witches) may seek to delay or end another's pregnancy.[3] In other words, fertility has a particular biological, cultural, and social cast for Èkìtì women and men that can be further understood by a close reading of the word itself.

Fertility, fecundity and giving birth to children

Actually, there is no one word in Yoruba that coincides in meaning with the English word fertility. Some words used refer specifically to things associated with fertility, such as fruit, soil, or particularly fecund animals. For example, *eléso*, fertility or fruitfulness, is derived from the word *èso*, fruit. Thus a new bride might be saluted, '*Á so èso àsogbó!*', May the bride be fruitful! (Abraham 1962: 592). Similarly, the term *olọ́ọ̀rá*, literally owner of fertile earth, derived from *ọ̀rá* (Abraham 1962: 525), may be used to convey the idea of fertility. The term *ẹlẹ́dẹ̀*, pig, is also used to describe certain women who are 'full of children', referring to the pig's birth of multiple piglets. Another word, sometimes translated as 'fertility', is *iṣeabiamọ*, the act of being the mother of a child.

While the first three terms associated with fertility make reference to God-given aspects of the natural world – fruit, soil, and animals – the word ìṣeabiamọ implies a certain agency on the part of women. Ìṣeabiamọ, literally 'the act of being the owner of a small child', consists of three words (ìṣe, an act of being, abí, the owner of, and ọmọ, child) which capture three elements critical to its meaning. First, fertility is something that is done, not simply something that happens as a natural event. The act of fertility refers most obviously to the labour of childbirth, but there is a battery of things social, spiritual, and medicinal (Adétúnjí 1996) that must be attended to in order to ensure a successful delivery. Secondly, the culmination of the physiological act of fertility, being the owner (abí) or mother of a child (ọmọ), not only provides concrete evidence of fertility but also serves as a marker of a new social status for the mother and child (Fortes 1978), with both receiving new names. It also refers to the child's crossing of boundaries: from inside the body to outside, from another world to this one, and from private to public space.[4] Thirdly, this child, ọmọ, for whom extensive things are done – in prenatal preliminaries, in the labour of birth, and in postpartum social positioning – represents a particular dialectical relationship of support and dependency, of domination and subordination, of leaders and followers that underwrites many aspects of Èkìtì Yoruba social life. Indeed, kinship and political relations are often couched in terms of a parent-child metaphor in Èkìtì. For example, the king's descendants are referred to as ọmọba (children of the king), the residents of Rẹ́mọ Quarter are called Àwa Ọmọ Rẹ́mọ (we children of Rẹ́mọ), and those born in Ìtàpá are known as ọmọ Ìtàpá. Heads of households are referred to as baálé (bàbá ilé, literally 'father of the house') and group leaders are called father and mother (bàbá ẹgbẹ́ and ìyá ẹgbẹ́ respectively; see Figure 1.1). This classification of relationships in terms of dominant and subordinate positions may also be seen in several different contexts, including bodily ones. Toes are referred to as ọmọọ̀kasẹ̀ (literally, 'children of the foot'), fingertips as ọmọnríìka (children of the finger), and the eye's pupil as ọmọlójú (child of the eye).

Yet there is a particular quality to such relationships that is sometimes overlooked. While one group may be physically, economically or politically dominant, a relationship with the physically weak, the poor or the disenfranchised nonetheless exists (Simmel 1950). For it is through their relationships with dependants, subordinates and followers that these dominant groups are partly defined. Thus while Èkìtì Yoruba women and men may be dominant – they are bigger, have worldly experience and are capable of moral judgment – they nonetheless need these tiny beings – children – to define themselves as adults. The proverb Ọmọ kò ní àyọ̀lé, ẹni ọmọ sin ló bímọ ('there is no joy having children, until a child buries the one who gave birth') alludes to this dependence of the dominant. The child is dependent on

Figure 1.1 Ẹgbẹ́ (club) launching, Ìtàpá-Èkìtì, December, 1991. Such meetings are a common form of raising money for group projects, such as farming and buying commodities in bulk for sale. Ẹgbẹ́ members often emphasise their group affiliation by wearing identical outfits ('uniforms'), while the group's patron and patroness wear distinctive dress. (photograph by the author)

parents (including an army of extended family members on both the mother's and father's sides) for sustenance and protection, yet people must do many things not only to have children but also to maintain the ties that bind children to them and to this world.

Developing children, developing the town

One critical change in the relationship between parents and children concerns what constitutes the proper way of 'raising a child up to be good, to become a responsible adult (or elder)'. In the past, an etiquette of observing hierarchies of age and gender, ideals of generous responsibility to subordinates, and the amassing of closely guarded oral knowledge were learned through children's everyday experiences on the farm, in the house and in annual festivals and rituals; through apprenticeships in trades; and through initiation into *imọlẹ̀* cults and other specialist medico-religious instruction. Such activities related to a cosmology based on belief in distinctive deities and spirits, associated with specific geographical sites and family

Figure 1.2 Old Methodist Church building, Ìtàpá-Èkìtì, September 1991. This structure, built in 1922, was on one of the earliest sites of the earliest schools in Ìtàpá. It has been replaced by a larger concrete-block church building, which was dedicated in April 1995. (photograph by the author)

groupings, whose worship sustained a particular system of social and political organisation (see Chapter 2).

During the 1920s, a small number of children began to attend specially constructed schools where a particular type of knowledge, initially Biblical knowledge acquired through reading and writing, was taught in a certain way; children were seated and used books and chalkboards (see Figure 1.2). Associated with the introduction of Christianity and Islam to Ìtàpá and the idea of ọ̀làjú ('enlightenment', literally derived from the word lajú, to open the eyes)[5] that led returning townsmen to introduce these new religions to their community in the first place, schools were started by various churches in Ìtàpá in order to further 'open the eyes' of children to this new knowledge. These innovations in belief, in the attainment and constitution of knowledge and in dress associated with ọ̀làjú (that is, with 'civilisation, enlightenment') contributed to a radical shift in intergenerational social relations and local political organisation in Ìtàpá, as it did in many Yoruba towns (see, for example, Apter 1992; Matory 1994; Peel 1983).

The perseverance of early church leaders in establishing and maintaining these schools suggests that at least some of these men understood, as did

Durkheim (1961), the powerfully persuasive support for their views which could be provided by changes in the moral bases and concrete practices of education. In promoting a shift from a belief in localised *imǫlę̀* to a universal God (and Jesus Christ, his son), these men sought not only to introduce a form of education based on openly available knowledge, they further reinforced their claims of efficacious powers with concrete improvements brought to the town by the economic successes of its educated sons and daughters. In this sense, then, thinking about the proper 'raising up of a child to be an elder', of which Western education has become a critical element, has merged with developing the town, associated with infrastructural improvements such as buildings of various sorts: schools, a bank, a post office and a clinic. Being properly raised themselves, having acquired *ǫ̀lájú* – 'enlightenment' – through education, these educated Ǫmǫ Ìtàpá ('children of Ìtàpá') are themselves in a position to 'raise up' or develop the town. Indeed, the fact that the word for this type of town development is *ìdàgbàsókè*, literally 'the fact of growing up (*sí òkè*) to become an elder (*di àgbà*)' suggests this connection.

These overlapping ways of thinking about 'raising' a child, *ǫmǫ*, and a town, *ìlú*, 'to become an elder', (that is, to maturity), parallel the things that should properly be part of this process: education (for the development of children) and buildings (for the development of the town). They also intersect with ideas about the need of families for children and the need of the town for citizens and political support, which have implications for changing interpretations of fertility and development.

REASSESSING FERTILITY AND DEVELOPMENT

Some townspeople have come to consider the difficulties of raising many children up well. The decline of the Nigerian economy associated with falling oil prices and beginning in the early 1980s, the institution of a Structural Adjustment Programme in 1986, and the implementation (often unsuccessful) of various economic revitalisation schemes and political programmes in the 1990s have contributed to this reconsideration.[6] Indeed, the national political and economic uncertainty of the period from 1980 through the 1990s is reflected in there having been seven different heads of state,[7] the decline in the naira-dollar rate of exchange from ₦1=US$1.54 in 1982 to ₦120=US$1 in 1999. Furthermore, during the years of the two military regimes headed by Ibrahim Babangida (1985–93) and the late Sani Abacha (1993–8) which spanned most of this period, one of the primary tactics used to maintain a semblance of political stability (aside from threats of arrest and sheer terrorism) was to create new states and local governments (cf. Smith 1981: 360). Efforts were also made to curry favour with traditional rulers who were given various stipends to ensure their loyalty and support (Akinkuotu 1998; Vaughan 2000). Through their attempts to maintain political power and economic access by favouring one group and then another, these former political leaders fostered disunity in the country. Their efforts were met with considerable indirect and direct political resistance, reflected in strikes, mass prayer meetings, assassinations and bombings (see Appendix II).

This situation of increasing political and economic uncertainty has led some to reinterpret fertility as something that one continues to need but with increasing limits. Aside from earlier patterns of postpartum abstinence and child-spacing (Orùbùloyè 1981a), limiting the number of children has been made possible by the use of modern contraception, referred to as family planning or *fètò s'ọmọ bíbí* (literally 'planning the child that is born'). Specifically, the devaluation of the naira associated with the implementation of a federal Structural Adjustment Programme (Adépòjù 1993) has made educating children extremely expensive. This is, in part, because of the increasing cost of materials (books, paper, pens, uniform material and so on) and, in part, because of the withdrawal of government support for primary education.[8] Together, changing ideas about social relations, political uncertainties and economic considerations have provided the impetus for having fewer children so as to raise them well.

In addition to the increasing cost of education, the federal government introduced a national population policy in 1988 that supported limiting population growth as a way to better develop the nation (Federal Republic of Nigeria 1988). In the same year, the former President Babangida proposed the idea of 'Four [children]-is-enough'. Women, it was suggested, should have no more than four children each, lending official legitimacy to those who were thinking of having fewer children (see Figure 1.3).[9] This proposal generated considerable debate in terms of the soundness of its underlying assumptions (e.g. Ọbaléké 1988), in terms of national north-south tensions, and in terms of gender inequality. Nonetheless, some, but not all, women and men in Ìtàpá have come to see the proposal as an aspect of 'development' (*idàgbàsókè*), primarily because of the economic difficulties of educating many children well, as one woman explained:

> To me personally, I strongly believe that the policy is quite good. In the past, people used to give birth to about seven or eight children. But the question that worries me is what will they eat? Can we have children without giving them an education? This won't be appropriate. Because of this, I will say the policy is good. [And] I pray to God that if the policy is accepted in Ìtàpá, it will still bring development.
> (DI97-35, Ìtàpá-Èkìtì, 1997)

For this elderly Ìtàpá woman (with no formal education herself), the town will be improved if people have fewer children who can be cared for and well educated.[10]

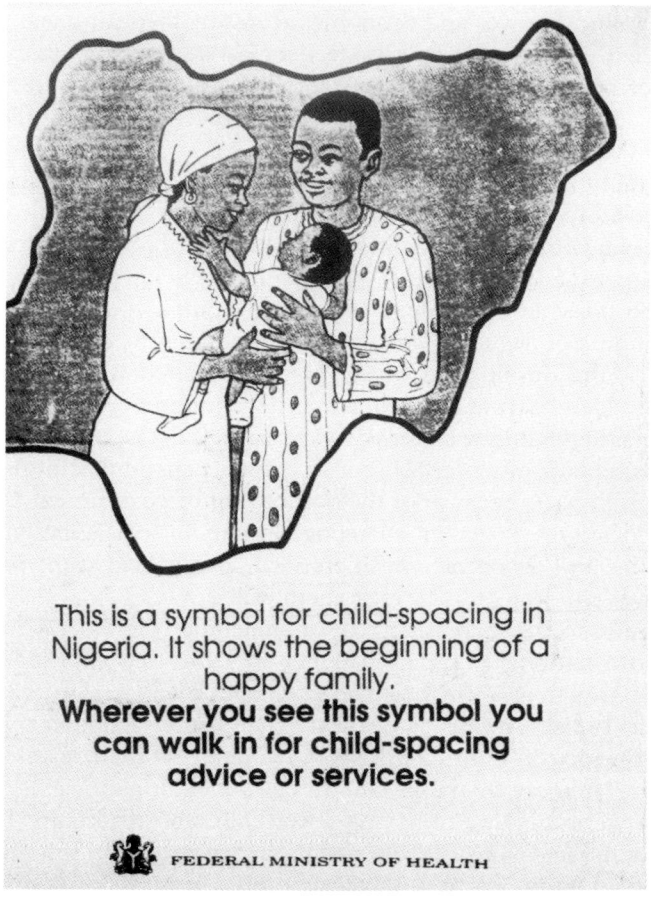

Figure 1.3 On 1 April 1998, the Nigerian Federal Government introduced the National Population Commission Decree, which was officially launched on 20 October 1989 (PAN 1990: 8; see Federal Republic of Nigeria 1988), along with a promotional logo, emphasising child-spacing (*The Guardian on Sunday*, 10 May 1992: B6).

However, if some are reassessing the benefits of having many children, others are sceptical of government pronouncements:

> The government of the day is heralding that policy in order to further reduce its responsibilities for people. The government screams of the woeful economic condition, no money, no food, they want to use that to create fear in the minds of people. But I wonder if a farmer having about five thousand heaps of yam, five thousand heaps of cassava, will

ever listen to the policy. We see farmers in our town who used to load a '911' lorry to transport produce to Lagos to sell every year. The policy is for government workers who have nothing [other] than staying in the office daily, whose children couldn't identify yam leaves from cocoa leaves. They couldn't know whether yams come from the soil or from the top of the tree. Government officials buy from the market, that is why they are bitter. They can't easily feed their children; they measure before they cook and farmers just cook as much as they like. The farmers believe strongly that having many children is helpful, especially on the farm, from which others are given education.

(DI97-14, Ìtàpá-Èkìtì, 1997)

The man quoted here is referring to the practice of senior children, having graduated and secured employment, providing school fees for junior siblings (Caldwell 1977a: 20).[11] For farmers, these educational benefits constitute a mixed blessing as few of the children whose parents have so desperately worked to educate them in the hope of future individual success and community improvement can find office jobs in the town. This dearth of employment opportunities deemed suitable by secondary school and university graduates has led to an exodus of young people to cities such as Ìbàdàn and Lagos in search of jobs (see Chapter 3). The need to educate the young thus conflicts with the need to keep at least some of them at home where their labour is required to work on farms and in local schools and businesses, to care for elderly relations, to maintain family houses and to attend to local political affairs.

This situation puts families in something of a double bind regarding fertility. On the one hand, there are economic, as well as cultural, social, and political, considerations that encourage some people to reassess fertility and to think about limiting it in certain ways. On the other hand, the fact that educated children are likely to live and work outside the town means that they leave elderly parents to manage alone in family houses and to relegate farm work to tenants and shopkeeping to outsiders. This dilemma is exacerbated by a decline in government infrastructural services in the town (for example, no electricity for months on end, no piped water for over five years, no telephone service). This dearth of services has made it difficult both for people to establish businesses and for those without children, since children are needed to fetch water, to deliver messages, and to queue for kerosene for lighting. The effects of this dilemma may be seen in the comments of two older women, one the retired schoolteacher quoted earlier, the other a midwife, both with successful children living outside the town:

> I have only four children ... None of them stay with me, they are all away in far places. But if I had had six, at least when four of them are away, the remaining two will live with me. It is good in one way if we

are able to give them education; [but] my children are all away, nobody is remaining at home to help.

(DI97-3, Ìtàpá-Èkìtì, 1997)

Look at the water supply, there is nothing like that again – where we have not seen pipeborne water for the past seven years. If not because of the fact that I have some foster children, I would have been facing a very big problem. I don't have a well in the house and I need to drink water.

(DI97-16, Ìtàpá-Èkìtì, 1997)

Educated and well-off children living outside may help parents directly with remittances (Adépòjù 1974) and the community indirectly through privileged access to government development programmes; however, in the short term their absence neither addresses the problem of providing water on an everyday basis for elderly parents nor does it provide for the growth in an occupationally diverse population associated with *idàgbàsókè*, the building-up of the town.

The problem for Ìtàpá residents, then, is how to attract people amid competing demands for the labour and loyalty of their children (Feeley-Harnik 1991: 13). For those remaining in Ìtàpá, various strategies for doing this have emerged. These include the establishment of an annual 'Ìtàpá Day' (see Chapters 2 and 10) and a local development association with branches in many south-western Nigerian cities (Chapter 2; see also Rea 1998), as well as alternative visions of 'development' that differ somewhat from that advocated by the state and educated government officials. Rather than having the 'four who are enough' advocated by the government, some residents may opt to have five children, sending them to primary and possibly secondary school but training them in farm work or craft apprenticeships as well. Thus while the town's total fertility rate appears to have declined from 6.2 to 5.3 live births in the period from 1992 to 1997 (see Chapter 3), women continue to bear around five children. As will be seen, this alternative strategy – having more children rather than fewer as advocated by the government – makes sense in the light of particular government programmes that further complicate the everyday lives of small town residents.

DEMOGRAPHIC–ANTHROPOLOGICAL STUDIES OF FERTILITY

This demographic–anthropological study of fertility and development focuses on everyday things and practices associated with changing ideas about individuals, their bodies and social relations in one small rural Èkìtì Yoruba town, in the context of contemporary government policies and programmes. This approach treats interpretations of fertility and progress as part of a historical process (Vincent 1986; Moore 1987), reflected in a range of practices including body techniques, kinship relations and programmes initiated by the state. It emphasises the improvisational quality of social life, in which cultural beliefs and associated individual and institutional actions are continually being constructed and reinterpreted in relation to changing economic and political interests by different social actors (for example young and old, women and men, farmers and government officials) who may have different stakes in how fertility is interpreted, 'proper' social relations are constituted, and moral meanings are defined.[12]

The insistence on considering the contextual bases – cultural, social, political, economic and historical – of fertility has characterised demographic–anthropological research in recent years. A demographic–anthropological literature, summarised in two excellent introductory chapters by Greenhalgh (1995) and Kertzer and Fricke (1997),[13] has grown with the recognition of the mutual benefits that such an interdisciplinary approach could bring to the study of particular aspects of social life – namely fertility (or reproduction), marriage and death (or mortality) – interests historically shared by demographers and anthropologists (Caldwell et al. 1987). While the distinctive disciplinary approaches and beliefs about what constitutes evidence – demographers insist on numbers while anthropologists utilise ethnographic (and historical) narratives – sometimes strain relations between the two disciplines (see Hill 1997), collaboration between anthropologists and demographers has illustrated the benefits of integrating both quantitative and qualitative approaches to the study of birth, procreation and death.

One of the primary aims of demographic anthropologists has been to contextualise the study of demographic phenomena, incorporating cultural, historical and political aspects of social life that are not easily assessed through quantitative analysis. Schneider and Schneider (1996), for example, have examined the distinctive ways in which fertility decline reflected the political economy of increasing industrial production and wage labour among unequal socio-economic groups in one town in twentieth-century Sicily. In discussing the use of *coitus interruptus* among certain social classes (the landed gentry, artisans and well-off peasants), and not others (landless poor), they also consider the moral aspects of this historical process whereby 'the phenomenon of reproductive stigma' (Schneider and Schneider 1996: 11) has been used as a way of discrediting those who continue to have large families. Other anthropologists have also taken a political economic perspective. Greenhalgh's (1988) study of Chinese fertility decline focuses on institutions and mobility goals as critical components of fertility dynamics, while Kertzer (1995) has related fertility decline to historical processes of economic change – particularly industrialisation – and shifts in social organisation and associated social norms in late nineteenth- and early twentieth-century Northern Italy.

The micropolitics of kinship and gender relations is the focus of other recent demographic–anthropological studies of fertility along with analysis of the cultural meanings of particular aspects of these social processes and economic changes. Thus, Fricke (1997) examines marriage timing, land pressure and inheritance rules for Nepali villagers and the implications of their reinterpretations for fertility change. Bledsoe (2002) focuses on the meaning of the term 'natural fertility' for a group of Gambian women who use Western contraceptives to regulate birth intervals that support better health for mothers and the regular birth of many children. While the specific focus of these studies of fertility varies according to the particular social and historical contexts of place and theoretical perspectives of the researcher, all of these demographic–anthropological studies of fertility use qualitative and quantitative data in their analyses.

In this book, I take a similar approach to the study of fertility, combining a cultural analysis with a 'political economy' perspective. As in the demographic–anthropological studies described above, this study of population and progress questions some of the underlying assumptions of the demographic theory of fertility transition, namely that once certain conditions approximating industrial Western societies are attained (such as nuclear family formation, Western education, and biomedical healthcare), fertility will decline. Fertility transition theory, along with the modernisation theory from which it derives (Greenhalgh 1995: 11), has not explained why fertility remains high despite the fact that some Westernising preconditions have been met, nor why development, despite a plethora of projects, has failed to 'take off' particularly in sub-Saharan Africa. As this study demonstrates, neither fertility change nor development follows a universal trajectory. Whether lower fertility or Western models of development are viewed as possible or advantageous reflects cultural ideas about proper social relations as well as political–economic conditions, which hinder or facilitate these changes.

However, my approach to these topics differs somewhat from other demographic–anthropological studies of fertility in my close attention to the cultural meanings attributed to specific things, which provide a way of understanding 'the underlying cultural formations concerned with how people classify and order and symbolise their worlds' (Cohn 1980: 215). For the purposes of this study I have focused on things closely related to human bodies – such as houses and graves, hymens, blood and bones – which have implications for demographic studies: namely, birth, marriage and death. The reinterpretations of such things provide a concrete means for understanding changes in the moral evaluation of fertility-related practices and consequently in reinterpretations of fertility, particularly in relation to ideas about development and to state programmes and policies. By amassing 'data of very varying types, collected by different methods' (Richards 1941: 48), certain 'diagnostic things' stand out in the course of research on areas of demographic interest such as marriage, childbirth and death as best capturing this sense of significant change.[14]

One benefit of this approach is that people can specifically describe things and relate them to particular practices and experiences. They can also describe how their changes in thinking about them may be given a particular moral cast. By examining the ways in which things and ideas are interconnected and are continually being reinforced and reassessed by the use of things in the course of everyday life, changes in fertility-related thinking and practices may more clearly be seen from people's own perspectives. Thus in the chapters in Part II, quantitative and qualitative data are integrated by relating them to particular things and events concerning arranged marriage, child-fostering and burial practices, all of which have implications for thinking about fertility, about the growth of children and of the town and about what constitutes progress. Yet these changes do not take place in a political and economic vacuum, since they are influenced by state institutions such as schools, federal policies regarding land law, and government efforts to win political support. In Part III, these local reassessments and contested visions are then related to larger political and economic forces, both in the colonial era and the independence era, underscoring how past beliefs and practices concerning population and progress are being differentially interpreted, reinterpreted and reproduced in the present. These local and national interconnections underscore the fact that the fertility and the development of individual bodies and of towns as well as the programmes and policies of the body politic are related matters.

SUMMARY OF CHAPTERS

This study of fertility in one Èkìtì Yoruba town, Ìtàpá-Èkìtì, in Ekiti State, Nigeria, is based on material (interviews, surveys, newspaper articles, archival documents and written local histories) collected from mid-1991 to mid-2000. Participant observation in everyday affairs, celebrations and ritual events, as well as photographic research, also informs this study. Questions about fertility, gender relations, houseplots, local development projects, burial and health education, among other topics, were asked in informal and structured interviews, and in survey questionnaires (see Appendix I).

The remaining chapters in Part I focus on the study setting. In Chapter 2, the physical aspects of this Èkìtì Yoruba town are described, followed by a discussion of the town's social and political organisation. Chapter 3 consists of an examination of the demographic dimensions of the town, based on censuses and fertility surveys and the history of one local development project directly relating to fertility, the establishment of the Ìtàpá Maternity Centre.

The three chapters that constitute Part II focus on the interpretation of individual bodies and substances closely associated with fertility, examining how their reassessments reflect changing perceptions of kinship and social relations. In Chapter 4, the decline in the importance of the hymen is related to changing perceptions of virginity, arranged marriage, marital fertility and the social and spatial boundaries circumscribing the actions of women. Chapter 5 examines the ways that blood, that 'juice with curious properties', is used as a symbolic barometer defining the boundaries of kinship. Redefinitions of 'blood relations' may reflect changing assessments of child-fostering and of who is considered 'a good parent'. Finally, the redefinition of boundaries marking the domains of the living and the dead is examined in Chapter 6 in relation to changing perceptions about how and where individuals are born and buried.

The chapters in Part III consider the intersection of practices of individual townspeople, kin groups and the Nigerian state. In Chapter 7, the personal and public hygiene taught in primary school health classes, which has contributed to different perceptions of cleanliness and of proper childcare, is considered in the context of a dearth of state infrastructural support. In Chapter 8, the effects of the introduction of a national land tenure scheme on village houseplot ownership, land boundaries and fertility are examined. The explicitly political dimension of fertility as population relating to the census and its importance in local arguments for the constitution of an Ekiti State are the subjects of Chapter 9. In the book's conclusion (Chapter 10), the ambiguous relationship of population and development is considered. While local perceptions of bodies, social relations and economic exigencies have contributed to reinterpretations of fertility and a reassessment, by some, of the connection between many people and development, they are nonetheless part of a broader political–economic context. A longing for 'Life More Abundant' and for the concrete improvements of *idàgbàsókè* is tempered by a disillusionment with government programmes and policies, leading some to pursue alternative interpretations of population and progress and ways for attaining these ends.[15]

2

HISTORICAL AND ANTHROPOLOGICAL ASPECTS OF ÌTÀPÁ: CENTRIPETAL AND CENTRIFUGAL TENDENCIES

> Unity is strength
> Ìtàpá club motto

Èṣọ́ orúta ègìrì òkè, 'Ìtàpá, the gem of the rock', so the praise poem for Ìtàpá-Èkìtì begins. The town is situated at the base of a rocky expanse, itself located on an escarpment that extends from Osín to the east to Ìlúpéjú to the west (Òjó 1966), which then dramatically descends as one approaches the town of Ọyẹ́. The uninhabited area surrounding Ìtàpá consists of cultivated farmland, virgin forest, bushy undergrowth and barren rock ledges, all criss-crossed by numerous footpaths. The inhabited area of the town is largely cleared of vegetation with the exception of shade trees, boundary-marking plants and occasional ornamental flowers.

The main road that transects Ìtàpá and also links it to other Èkìtì towns was started and partially completed in 1923 (Ògúntúyì 1979: 148). The paved version of this road, finished in 1976 and referred to as 'Express' by Ìtàpá residents, passes by many of the main institutions in the town and is intersected by smaller unpaved feeder roads leading to the eight different town quarters (ekù or àdúgbò; see Figure 2.1). Approaching Ìtàpá on this road from the town of Ìlúpéjú to the west (see Figure 2.2b), one first sees the Total petroleum station on the left with a two-storey modern house built to the rear by its owner. Further up the road there are other modern, cement-sided houses with louvred glass windows, some surrounded by concrete block walls. Then one comes upon the large, warehouse-like Redeemed Church of Christ and the long, low, pink and green building that houses the Maternity Centre (see Figure 3.9). This newer area of the town includes several houses built by children of Ìtàpá (ọmọ Ìtàpá) who are living in cities and towns throughout south-western Nigeria. A short distance further along the road one comes to the centre of the town with its older-style houses – some built with mud-bricks, many of which are plastered over with cement, and others left plain (see Figure 2.3). A small covered market, a shrine (ojúbọ) for Èṣù (the Yoruba trickster deity), stenciled signs for the Cherubim & Seraphim Church and the Ìtàpá Ìféyẹwá Cooperative Union, and a row of concrete storefronts constitute an informal town square. About fifty feet further along the road on the left are the old and new Methodist

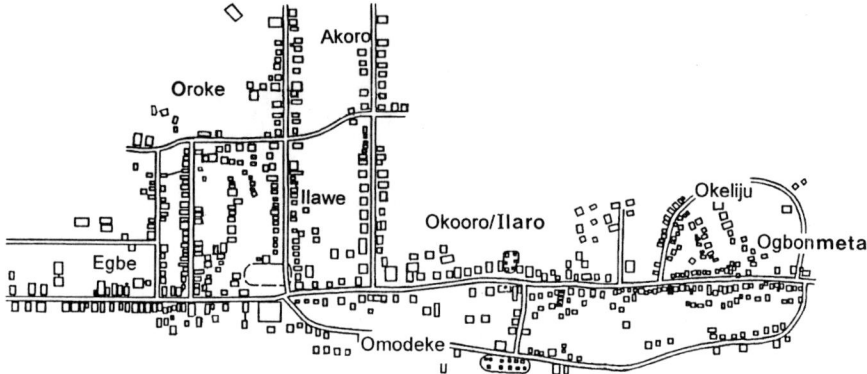

Figure 2.1 Schematic map of Ìtàpá-Èkìtì, showing the eight major quarters that make up Ẹgẹ̀tún (Òkòòrò/Ìláró, Akòró, Ìlawẹ̀, and Oròkè) and Rẹ́mọ (Òkèlìjù, Egbè, Ògbọ́nmẹ́ta, and Ọmọdékè).

Church buildings, the Town Hall and the new Ekiti State Judicial Customary Courthouse. The road bends slightly to the right where one sees the palace of the Ọwátàpá, with the Ansar-Ud-Deen Mosque in front and the official Ìtàpá market, behind.[1] Thereafter, other buildings – the Post Office, the African Church, St Philomena's Catholic Church and a newly reopened petroleum station – line the road. One then approaches a sort of liminal space known as Igbó Afà, where buildings are less common.[2] It is only when one enters the area primarily associated with Rẹ́mọ that houses are once again densely clustered around either side of the road. These dwellings diminish as one approaches the Ìtàpá-Osín Secondary School on the left and the Aiyédọgbọ́n Hotel on the right. The road curves as it approaches Àorogún Hill, with its bare expanses of black striated rock, and then descends toward the village of Osín.[3]

BOUNDARIES AND ROADS

This view of Ìtàpá was very different at the beginning of the twentieth century. Then, the town consisted of uncleared forest and undergrowth, with rocky escarpments offering the only large clearings. The town now known as Ìtàpá consisted of groups of small settlements linked by narrow paths. Because of the luxuriant growth of grasses, bushes and trees, people living in compounds in one quarter of the town could not see those living in others, as the educator and local historian Chief S. A. Dada explained:

> All these places you pass small bushes, the town was not one, it was a single town of many habitations ... For example, my own part, Ìláró, was still separated from Isao which was the same thing as my own, the same habitation now only separated by the road. But in those days, my

mother even told me of a story where one night they were passing from one part of that small habitation to another part and they met some spirits in the bush in between. And charms had to be offered before the spirits disappeared. It shows just the belief of the people then and how they [were] separated. There were just many habitations in one small town...
> (Interview: S. A. Dada, Ìbàdàn, August 1997)

These small settlement groups constituted the early quarters of the town but they were distinct in their identities. This was, in part, because of the difficulties of mobility and visibility caused by the bushy undergrowth and, in part, because they consisted of different groups of people who had earlier migrated to Ìtàpá from the east and west.

Two things altered this picture. The first was the building of the main road. The first phase of this undertaking involved the entire town in months of strenuous labour (Renne 2000a). Clearing space for the road enabled residents of compounds in neighbouring quarters to see each other as part of one community, rather than as separate groups. The road also provided access for men to seek wage labour elsewhere in south-western Nigeria, where they worked as labourers on farms and building sites.

The second thing that changed the appearance of the town was that when these men returned, they built new houses, separate from their family compounds, with the proceeds of their labour. As the settlements grew in numbers, family land in their respective quarters became scarce. People began asking for houseplots in other quarters of the town, particularly in quarters adjoining the road which were seen, as one chief put it, 'to be a centre of civilisation' (LTS-102, Ìtàpá-Èkìtì, January 1992). By 1960, the informal eastern boundary (*ilà oòrùn*, literally the place of sunrise) and western boundary (*ìwọ̀ oòrùn*, place of sunset) of the town were expanded to accommodate this growth:

> There was a [belief] in those days that is you don't go beyond the boundary on the way to Ìkọ̀lé or the way to Ìlúpéjú but now, that [rule] has been broken [for a] long time ... When I was young, [it was] not that [these] boundaries are marked but people just didn't go beyond their domain. But since 1960 I can say, people have been building on where land [is] available.
> You know, Dr Òjó's house, it's now very far from what we can say Ọbasálú's house, I think you know Ọbasálú? Those used to be the boundary of the town at that time and the paternal grandfather of this boy used to be the end at Ìkọ̀lé, that's Solomon ... Laṣebikan, that used to be the end of the town then. But now the town has grown even to include the grammar school and about one mile after that house ...
> (Interview: S. A. Dada, Ìbàdàn, August 1997)

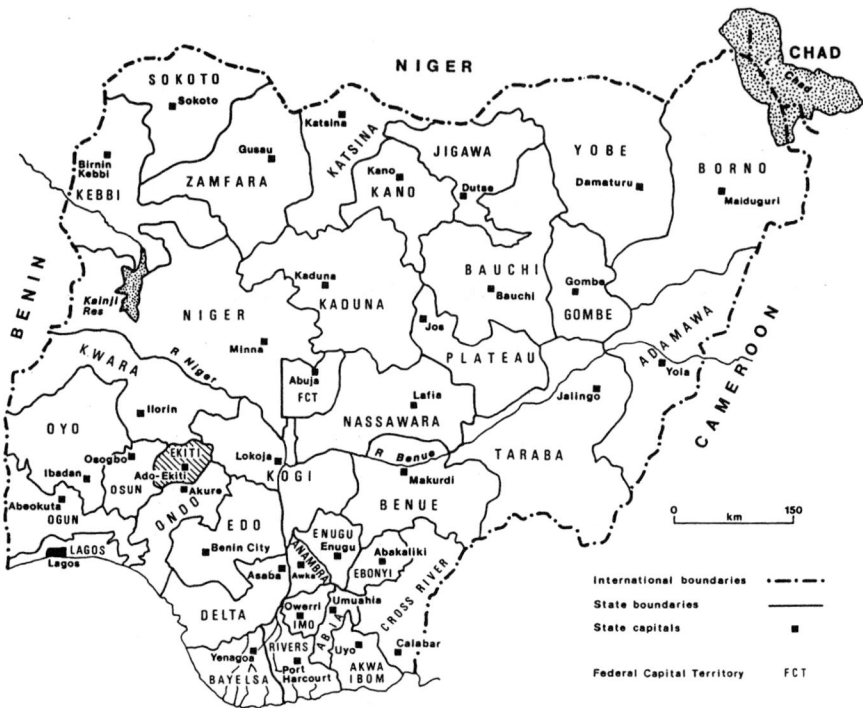

Figure 2.2a Map of Nigeria, showing Ekiti State.

The expansion of boundaries reflects both the increasing population and prosperity of the town, particularly the new construction outside the old town borders by successful *ọmọ Ìtàpá* ('children of Ìtàpá') who returned to build modern houses in their home town in the 1970s and 1980s (Barber 1991; Berry 1985; Peel 1983; Rea 1998).

This growth provided redress of sorts for the town's past: its population was dispersed during the nineteenth century Yoruba wars (Johnson 1921: 423; Ògúntúyì 1979: 75–7), when some from Ìtàpá fled to the town of Aiyédé to the north-west for protection.[4] While many people returned after the Èkìtì wars ended in 1886, kidnapping raids persisted up until 1900 (Ògúntúyì 1979: 77). It was people, not property, who were the principal objects of these raids.[5]

Because of this background, some have a different translation for the phrase that begins the Ìtàpá *oríkì*, '*Èṣọ́ ọrúta ègìrì òkè*'. Rather than emphasising the beautiful gem-like quality of this small town nestled among the rocks, some translate it as 'Ìtàpá, sentry post on the rock', stressing the town's vulnerability and its need for vigilance:

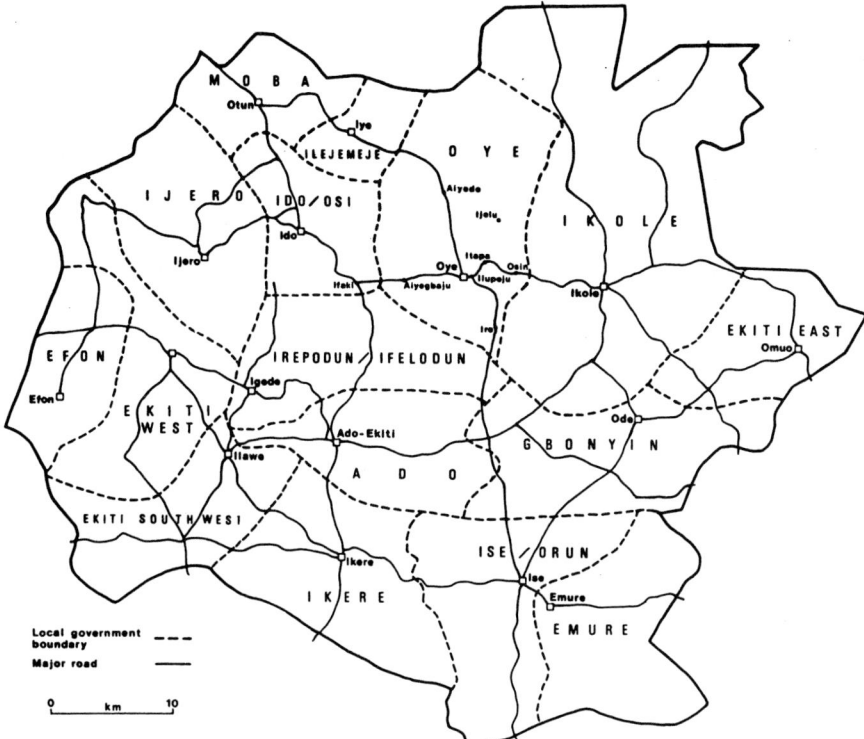

Figure 2.2b Ekiti State.

During the wars, people always prepared routes for escape. In Ìlárò my own quarter, you could escape to the Ijétí Stream, from there you go around the hill, from there you go to hilly farmland and before you do that, no other stranger could follow you. You see, in general these are just escape routes, everybody prepares for any invasion to be able to escape without looking, without wading through an open space where an enemy can catch them.

(Interview: S. A. Dada, Ìbàdàn, 1997)

The need to manage the centripetal and centrifugal movements of people – toward or away from Ìtàpá – characterises many aspects of the town's social and political history.

ÌTÀPÁ ORIGINS AND DYNAMICS

The area now known as Ìtàpá, according to one version of the origins of Ìtàpá (Láyẹni, cited in Ayẹni 1991; Owóèyẹ 1999), is said to have been settled by three sons, their mother and two hunter–friends who came from

Figure 2.3 Main road through Ìtàpá-Èkìtì, September 1991. (photograph by the author)

Ilé-Ifẹ̀ (Ayẹni 1991; Láyẹni 1935; Owóèyẹ 1999).[6] The three sons – Amọ́wá, Ọlósín, and Ẹléjẹ̀lú – of this unnamed mother are referred to as Ọmọ Èyé Mẹ́ta ('three children of one mother' (Ayẹni 1991: 4)) and became the founding heads of the three towns of Ìtàpá, Osín and Ìjẹ̀lú (see Figure 2.2b), while the two friends, Ẹlẹ́mọ and Ọbaárò, established the two main sections of the town, known as Rẹ́mọ and Ẹgẹ̀tún. Another variation on this theme of origins describes two hunters, Ẹlẹ́mọ and Ọbaárò, from Ilé-Ifẹ̀ who first settled Rẹ́mọ and Ẹgẹ̀tún respectively, but who subsequently returned to Ifẹ̀ to bring with them additional followers, including the three sons who became the rulers of the towns of Ìtàpá, Osín and Ìjẹ̀lú. On this second trip, the first Ọwátàpá, Amọ́wá, brought with him the paraphernalia of kingship including the òrìṣà Elútàpá, which was worshipped in Ifẹ̀ and later in Ìtàpá, and from which the town of Ìtàpá took its name. In yet another version, Amọ́wá and his two friends who originally migrated from Ifẹ̀ went back to bring their òrìṣà, the Òrìṣà Ìtàpá, and its attending babaláwo priest with them. The wife of this priest gave birth on the trip to Ìtàpá and it was their offspring who subsequently settled one of the quarters in Ẹgẹ̀tún. Despite these variations, the authenticity of the settlement of Ìtàpá and the neighbouring towns of Osín and Ìjẹ̀lú by three brothers is confirmed by the presence of a gravesite, said to be that of the brothers' mother, situated between Osín and Ìtàpá known as Ojú Èyé Osín.[7]

Seven of the eight quarters were said to be settled by these successive groups of migrants from Ifẹ̀ coming to join people living in Ìtàpá.[8] The expansion of Ìtàpá from these original settlements resulted, in some cases, from children of these early migrants establishing their own family houses, referred to as ẹbí, or streets within the original àdúgbò. These ẹbí sub-groups within particular àdúgbò quarters continued to think of themselves as a single unit when it came to the performance of certain rituals such as funerals, group farmwork, chieftaincy affairs (such as installations and representation on the council of chiefs) and the recitation of common oríkì praise poems. For example, the oríkì for Òkèlìjù Quarter begins with a reference to a geographical feature of the entire quarter, Ọ̀tẹ̀lẹ́ Stream: 'Ọmọ olómi ọ̀tẹ̀lẹ́ àmulóyún' ('children who are the owners of Ọ̀tẹ̀lẹ́ Stream, which gives pregnancy to women who drink from it'). Other quarter oríkì refer to particular crops associated with the area, with a quarter's well-fed inhabitants, or describe the strength of a quarter's army.

Yet groupings of families (ẹbí) within particular quarters may also distinguish themselves in certain ways. Some have individual deities (imọlẹ̀ or umọlẹ̀ [Èkìtì dialect] and òrìṣà), which they worship. Furthermore, these sub-quarters may be divided in turn into lower and upper parts of the street. Thus, Akòró Quarter is divided into three sub-quarters – Ìlísà, Ìlójò, and Ìmìlà – with the latter divided into Ẹbí Òkè (up) Ìmìlà and Ẹbí Odò (down) Ìmìlà. Nonetheless, these distinctions are overridden when larger quarter concerns take precedence, as when an important political leader for the entire quarter dies. In addition, particular quarters are said to have especially close relationships, some stemming from relations between early migrants and some resulting from specific historical circumstances. Orókè and Egbè Quarters, for example, jointly observe funeral rituals and chieftaincy installations as a result of their coming together during the nineteenth-century Yoruba wars (probably because of their westernmost position in the town) to form a special group of warriors referred to as Ogún Òsì.

The various explanations of the founding of Ìtàpá, sometimes called 'charter myths' (Bohannan 1952), and the evidentiary emblems – such as praise poems, deities and material objects – used to support them reflect the political positions of those recounting them, as well as memories passed down. Some versions stress the seniority, by virtue of those who founded it, of one settlement over another, legitimating the ranking of Ìtàpá chiefs. Others stress a particular deity brought by one group or another that was subsequently owned by that group, although worshipped by all in early Ìtàpá, stressing another form of authority and ranking. Such interpretations of the past are of some importance as different versions have had consequences for present-day political organisation, including the position of the Ọwátàpá and the constitution of the town's council of chiefs (ibodè), their ranking and remuneration. For example, in the history of Ìtàpá written by

Julius Láyẹni, he stresses the Ọwátàpá's authority in all matters: 'Many people came to stay with them and they gave each sect quarter to live, and appoint head for each sect and through this head they approach Owatapa.' These origins stories underscore the ways that quarters grow by attracting people to settle in them, while at the same time the distinctive cultural identities that have developed for sub-groups within these quarters also suggest a countervailing tendency of division from them. Indeed, as Láyẹni (1935) observed, when the settlement of Ìtàpá grew in numbers and became 'too overcrowded', both through natural increase and through in-migration, some people moved away to neighboring Ìlúpéjú (earlier known as Egòsì) west of Ìtàpá.

Turner (1957) has referred to these centrifugal and centripetal patterns of population movements as schism and continuity. In his study of Ndembu village, he used 'social dramas' to illustrate the ways in which population, particularly groups of followers and their leaders, plays an important part in forging these separations and continuities.[9] In Ìtàpá-Èkìtì, these alliances and separations have been played out in several forms over the last century. Despite the changes that have taken place in the town, the importance of people as followers – those won over by political leaders, lineage elders and wealthy patrons through political alliances, religious movements, or through kinship ties – persists. As in other Yoruba towns in south-western Nigeria,[10] the ebb and flow of population has strengthened or weakened the powers of this community,[11] its vitality literally associated with the vital demographic events of birth, death and migration. For it is through people that these strategies of alliance and separation have been perpetuated.

A POLITICAL HISTORY OF ÌTÀPÁ

Much of Ìtàpá's political history is remembered in terms of the reigns of successive kings (ọwá) of Ìtàpá, the traditional rulers of the town and its high-ranking chiefs who have sought strategic alliances with neighbouring kingdoms. Indeed, Ìtàpá's geographical location, at the intersecting boundaries of two traditional kingdoms – Ìkọ̀lé-Èkìtì to the east and Ọyẹ́-Èkìtì to the west (see Figure 2.2b) – further underscores the wisdom of strength in numbers.[12] When necessary, alliances were forged; when this protection was deemed disadvantageous, independence was asserted. For example, during the precolonial period, Ìtàpá first allied itself with the kingdom of Ìkọ̀lé as a way of countering aggressive moves by the kingdom of Ọyẹ́, which had allied itself with the kingdoms of Adó and Ìjẹ̀ṣà:

> During the reign of this Owa [Owa Arawamokunrin] the country was too overcrowded and many Itapa people went to settle at Egosi at a place called Odo-Illa and some of them went to another place called Ewo … Owa Ogogun next succeeded and soon sent for his people at

Egosi and Ewo. This repeated call led to war with Oye; Ado and Ijesha came to assist Oyo people and Ikole came to assist Itapa.

(Láyẹni 1935: 2–3)

Ironically, this war fought over the repatriation of Ìtàpá emigrants led to a loss of population as Ìkọ̀lé soldiers kidnapped Ìtàpá children in the absence of Ìtàpá soldiers:

> This war was afterwards called Ogun Yinmiomo (give me a child war) because when the people of Itapa went to war with Oye, Ikole people who came as an auxiliary for Itapa took their young folks which they left at home and sell them, and when Itapa people returned, they could not get their children which they left at home, so they got annoyed with the action of the Ikole people and refused their aid again and drove them away.

(Láyẹni 1935: 3)

Consequently Ìtàpá, under the leadership of Ọwátàpá Amèrìjoyè, disengaged itself from its alliance with Ìkọ̀lé and joined forces with the nearby kingdom of Aiyédé during the Ariba [Ìlọrin] War in 1875:

> Amerijoye was a great friend to the then Ata of Aiyede who was then known and called Esu Atangora and he came from Iye, so that when Amerijoye got to the throne they made an agreement that they would be living together and their people, in order to defend themselves against their enemies from constant tribal wars which his late brother Ogogun had underwent during the previous reign. So they both settled together at a place now called Aiyede at the same time, Esu Atangora came with forty-five people from Iye. This Owa stayed with his people at Aiyede for a number of years until when Ibadan war broke out against Aiyede, this war necessitated Itapa people returning back to their land.

(Láyẹni 1935: 3)

This oscillating pattern, particularly of alliance with and separation from Ìkọ̀lé, continued into the colonial period. The desire to separate from Ìkọ̀lé largely characterised Ìtàpá-Ìkọ̀lé relations during this period. This friction was exacerbated by the historian–letter writer Julius Láyẹni who contributed to a 'war of words' between the Ọwátàpá, the Ẹlẹ́kọ̀lé (the king of Ìkọ̀lé), and A. C. C. Swayne, the District Officer for Èkìtì District in 1932 and again in 1934.

A political historian for Ìtàpá

During the colonial period, when Ìtàpá was once again in a political alliance with the Kingdom of Ìkọ̀lé, the reigning Ọwátàpá, Alli (Sanni) Atọ́batẹ̀lẹ̀ I (1929–42), and his chiefs sought to assert their rights to be considered a separate kingdom independent from Ìkọ̀lé's control, with its own beaded-crown king under British colonial rule. One of the attractions, apart from the authority and prestige of being named a beaded-crown ọba (and hence a direct descendant from Ilé-Ifẹ̀), was the possibility of acquiring the salary and some of the accoutrements of a Native Authority chief, such as a native court. One strategy attempted to attain this end was the commissioning of a written 'History Researches on Itapa' from an Ẹ̀gbá man, Julius B. Láyẹni.[13] Several excerpts from this work are cited above. Láyẹni's letterhead describes him as an 'Author & Historical Researcher' and he also signed himself as a 'public writer' in his numerous letters to the District Officer, A. C. C. Swayne, in Adó-Èkìtì in the mid-1930s.

The ten-page, handwritten history, completed in 1935, is a fascinating document, both in its interpretation of Ìtàpá's past and a piece of evidence commissioned to promote the Ọwátàpá's political agenda. It begins with a description of the origin of Ìtàpá with a migration from Ilé-Ifẹ̀ and concludes with a confirmation of the power of Ọwá of Ìtàpá, his direct descent from King Odùduwà of Ifẹ̀, and the sovereign independence of Ìtàpá, whose citizens are 'not subject to any neighbouring chiefs or state'(Láyẹni 1935: 10). The following discussion considers the ways in which this document played a part in the attempts of the reigning Ọwá of Ìtàpá, Alli Sanni, to convince British colonial officials that Ìtàpá should be considered separately from Ìkọ̀lé, and in the subsequent responses of the King of Ìkọ̀lé and the colonial administration who sought to keep Ìtàpá in its place.

In his narrative about the origins of Ìtàpá, Láyẹni (1935: 4) stresses not only the independence of the Ìtàpá Kingdom but its sovereignty over neighbouring groups:

> At this period *before the advent of the British Government* Owa Itapa was a paramount ruler and all other chiefs of the neighbouring countries were subordinate to him and they form chief advisers, executive and privy council to Owa of Itapa [my emphasis].

However, with the advent of colonial rule in Èkìtì enforced after 1886 (Ògúntúyì 1979: 77), the British did not view the Ọwá (King) of Ìtàpá in this way; rather they considered him as a Bale [sic] (village head) and Ìtàpá as a 'sub-town of Ikole' (Swayne, Ekiti Division, 1934, NNAI).[14]

The written evidence and the Ọwátàpá's requests

In District Officer A. C. C. Swayne's letter, dated 27 November 1934, to the Ondo Provincial Resident at Akúrẹ́, he mentions Julius Láyẹni's request to write a history of Èkìtì, noting in a handwritten postscript that 'I have just received a second letter from Mr Láyẹni which suggests that his object [is] to prove the independence of the Bale of Itapa. We still have no power to stop him.' In this letter, Láyẹni was requesting that the Ọwátàpá be granted a messenger, a native court and a seat on the Ekiti Judicial Council (Láyẹni, 11 November 1934, p. 4). This letter was followed up with several reminders, including one complaining about taxation and the payment of court fees without benefits for Ìtàpá (Láyẹni, 1 December 1934, p. 15). The correspondence between Láyẹni and District Officer Swayne continued with the submission of the 'Historical Researches on Itapa' in February 1935. In the case of the history as well as the earlier requests for a native court, Láyẹni was told to await an upcoming intelligence report for Ìkọ̀lé District that would set matters straight. The district officer was also under pressure from the King of Ìkọ̀lé 'to see to the matter of the Owatapa for me and to warn him to be in peace' (The Elékọ̀lé, 24 April 1935). District Officer Swayne replied that the Ọwátàpá had been told 'that his town is at present regarded by Government as part of Ìkọ̀lé District and he should conduct himself accordingly' (3 May 1935, p. 50).

Láyẹni and Ọwátàpá Alli Sanni were ultimately unsuccessful in their bid for separation from Ìkọ̀lé. Subsequent Ọwátàpá and district officers continued to spar over this Ìtàpá-Ìkọ̀lé leadership issue. For example in 1950, the Acting District Officer, William Simpson, wrote in his 'Touring Notes': 'I believe that it might be necessary to remove or suspend Owatapa from office. He is the arch conspirator who [,] still hankering after his independence [,] is disturbing relations between Itapa and Ikole' (Simpson, Ikole Touring Notes, 11–15 March 1950; NNAI). It was not until 1989, when Ìtàpá became part of the newly formed Oye Local Government Area (see Figure 2.2b) after the division of Èkìtì North Local Government (interview with Prince Alóngé, Ìrè-Èkìtì, August 1997), that Ìtàpá was able to extricate itself from Ìkọ̀lé overrule. However, this move did not end Ìtàpá leaders' quest for their own local government during the time from its transfer to Oye Local Government.

The formation of Oye Local Government Area

Since independence in 1960, the political prerogatives of some Èkìtì Yoruba kingdoms have been subsumed under national, state and local governmental organisations. For example, the kingdom of Ìtàpá is now part of Oye Local Government Area (LGA), Oye LGA is under the jurisdiction of Ekiti State, and Ekiti State is part of Nigeria. Ìtàpá's position with respect to these three centres of power is remarkably similar to its situation during the colonial period when it attempted to leave Ìkọ̀lé. Having joined the newly formed Oye LGA in 1989, some are now lobbying for a local government separate from Ọyẹ́, tentatively named Ifeyewa LGA, with Ìtàpá as its headquarters. The earlier hopes for a more equal distribution of power among the relatively smaller towns of Ọyẹ́, Ìlúpéjú, Ìrè, Aiyédé and Ìtàpá has been disappointed on several occasions.[15] Some of this discontent also stems from the feeling that the population of Ìtàpá (and of neighbouring

Ìjẹ̀lú and Osín) is not adequately represented in local government affairs. Only a separate local government, with Ìtàpá as its headquarters, would set these matters right.[16] As some see it, a separate local government would result in the building of a new secretariat (or in the expansion of the local town hall) and the employment of many townspeople directly and indirectly in its operations, not only revitalising the community through local efforts but also by attracting strangers to come and stay.

ORGANISATION OF THE TOWN

Sitting under the square, concrete-block and iron-roofed bus shelter (provided by the Ẹ̀ṣọ́ Orúta men's club) in the centre of town, one is surrounded by three of the eight different quarters (*ekù* or *àdúgbò*) of the town. These quarters adjoin one another and are undistinguishable, except for the occasional street signs indicating their names. Unlike in the past, when these quarters were separated by bushy undergrowth, open roads link the different quarters of the town. Since house frontages are mostly devoid of vegetation, one can see in a glance the houses of Egbè Quarter to the left, those of Ìlawẹ̀ Quarter across the main road to the right, and those of Ẹgẹ̀nà Street to the immediate right. When the sun is setting, one can even see glimpses of the small hill town of Ìjẹ̀lú, shimmering in the distance.

Each of the main quarters of the town has its head and council, mirroring the organisation of the town with its Ọwátàpá and council of seven ruling chiefs (known as the Ìràfà chiefs).[17] The two main sub-divisions of the town, Rẹ́mọ (Ìtàpá Odò, 'lower Ìtàpá') and Ẹgẹ̀tún (Ìtàpá Òkè, 'upper Ìtàpá'), are each divided into four major quarters (see Figure 2.1). In Rẹ́mọ, these include Òkèlìjù, Egbè, Ògbọ́nmẹ́ta, Ọmọdékè, and in Ẹgẹ̀tún, they include Òkòòrò/Ìláró, Akòró, Ìlawẹ̀, and Oròkè, although the two sets of quarters are not necessarily geographically contiguous nor is the particular constitution of the sets unchanging.[18]

These major quarters, in turn, have minor quarters within them. For example, Ọmọdékè, a quarter of Rẹ́mọ, includes the sub-quarters Ààfin, Ìsálú, Ìlọrọ̀, and Isao, each of which are associated with particular family divisions or in-migrating groups who were given land in different parts of the town, as was earlier discussed. These sub-quarters are further divided by constituent families (*ẹbí*, or houses (*ilé*) used here in a dynastic sense; see Barber 1991: 155) which in turn have their heads and family councils. These councils are made up of the respective compound heads (or *baálé*, literally *bàbá ilé*, 'father of the house'). Compound heads, descendants from original founders of the quarter where they are living, ideally live in these quarters. However, with the building of the main road and the movements of many households to the roadside, some of the newer quarters may consist of residents with different family and quarter affiliations. Nonetheless, compound heads belonging to particular families and quarters are responsible for participating in family meetings, and if they are members of a quarter council, they are expected to attend these meetings as well.

QUARTERS AND HOUSES

Quarters are generally constituted by several sub-groups, referred to as *ẹbí* (families), and within each *ẹbí* group there are individual houses (*ilé*). These groups and sub-groups – quarters, families and houses – come together to celebrate certain religious observances, such as annual offerings to a specific quarter deity, each with its own local shrine.[19] Quarter members also contribute to fund-raising events for quarter work projects (such as road maintenance, for which each quarter is responsible), to the performance of funeral observances and to the selection of a new quarter head and chiefs. In order to see how the dynamics of centripetry and centrifugality operate at the level of a quarter and its families and houses, the death in 1995 of one quarter head and the subsequent dispute over his replacement is considered.

A local dispute

The Oròkè Quarter, situated on a hilly rise on the north-western edge of town, commands a dramatic view of the town as it descends toward the main road below.[20] However, as lovely as this landscape is, several local sons and daughters have built new houses in quarters closer to the main road. The concrete-block house built by the late Ọbalókè, Judge I. A. Ọkẹ́, located on Dèmí Street, is one such house. It consists of a massive, single-storey structure with a broad veranda decorated with ornamental fretwork concrete-blocks in the front, and two long corridors on either side off which two small parlours with adjacent bedrooms are found. Between these two corridors, in the centre of the house, there is a massive sitting-room with two large bedrooms in the back, one each for the house-head and the senior wife. Behind the main house structure there is a large courtyard, with several small rooms and a sheltered kitchen situated along its periphery that essentially enclose the space, as is commonly found in Yoruba house design (Dmochowski 1990: 2.54).

Shortly after the Ọbalókè died on 27 January 1992 (see Chapter 6), the wide veranda of this house was filled with people from all quarters of the town who came to greet the deceased who had been seated in his sitting-room. The corpse had been washed and dressed in regal finery by men from two *ẹbí* sections, Dèmí and Òwà, of Oròkè Quarter, who were also responsible for digging the grave and for burial. The Ọbalókè's immediate burial was followed by several quarter-wide and town events, emphasising the disruption within the quarter that this death had caused and the unity of the quarter's houses in mourning their loss. For example, for the next seven days, women from the third section, Ẹbí Ọmọba (from which Ọbalókè

Figure 2.4 Women from the three houses of Ẹbí Ọmọba at *àjà mùta*, January 1992. (photograph by the author)

came), joined women from Dẹ̀mí and Ọ̀wà to dance around the quarter, singing war songs. Some were dressed as men, wearing *agbádá* and caps (see Figure 2.4).[21] When they came to Ọbalókè's house, they took sides, the Dẹ̀mí and Ọ̀wà women on the left, the Ẹbí Ọmọba women on the right. Both sang songs of abuse (Apter 1998), threatening each other with sticks (known as *tẹ̀tẹ̀rẹ̀gún*) and blaming the other side for the death.[22] In this ritual confrontation known as *àjà mùta*, the three main houses of the quarter dramatise their distinctive identities and competing distrust as a prelude to reconciling their respective differences and shared loss. This unity was displayed at the funeral party (*ìje*) held on 3 February 1992, sponsored by the Ẹbí Ọmọba section and attended by others in the quarter and town.

Nonetheless, this unity was also undermined by the competitive drive for distinction associated with the centrifugal trends of Ìtàpá social life, contributing to the considerable conflict and delay in naming a new Ọbalókè. Once again, there were three competing groups, all within the Ẹbí Ọmọba section of Orókè Quarter that provides candidates for the position of Ọbalókè.[23] Within this section there are three royal houses – Òjó/Òké, Àkọmu, and Olókundé – from which candidates could theoretically be selected. Yet the practical realities of available candidates and historical consequences of prior selections have led to a 'tradition' of candidates coming from the Òjó/Òkẹ́ house alone. In 1999, a new candidate was selected although he was not from the Òjó/Òkẹ́ house but rather from another: Àkọmú. His selection and installation were immediately disputed by prominent members of the Òjó/Òkẹ́ house and at the time of writing, a stalemate exists. Until this argument is resolved through the successful lobbying of higher-ranking political officials by members of one of the disputing families, the quarter will remain leaderless and disunified.

FAMILY COMPOUNDS: THE DYNAMICS OF SEPARATION AND REUNION

These centrifugal and centripetal tendencies toward separation and unity, seen within the town and its various quarters, also operate within individual family compounds. For example, they characterise the actions of compound residents, many of whom frequently come and go to the extent that the meaning of the term 'residence' is somewhat unclear (Feeley-Harnik 1991: 11). These tendencies are also concretely embodied in the physical layout of the compound itself. A main sitting-room and adjoining bedroom, located at the front of the house, is associated with the house-head (*baálé*), while adjoining corridors lead to the rooms, hiving off in many directions, that belong to various wives, children and other family members. Each room has its own lockable door and may be empty for a few days to several months during the year, depending on its owners' outside interests. Behind the house and often in a separate shed can be found the kitchen, marking in a symbolic way wives' subordinate but vital relationships with their husbands' family compounds. In other words, the physical layout of the compound expresses an ideal of extended (and extensive) kinship relations while revealing the considerable mobility of its occupants. The structure of these family houses is also associated with the configuration of the human body in various ways, mirroring the fate of the bodies of many family members who will ultimately be buried within the house or at its periphery.

A concrete slab (a grave, *orórì*) with the name of the deceased and date of death is often the first structure one encounters when approaching the stoop (*gbàgede*) that adjoins the front (*ojúde*, literally 'face of the outside') of a family compound. One then usually steps up to a doorstep (*ìmésèlè ẹnu ọ̀nà*), through a central doorway (*ojúulé*, literally 'eye of the house'; Abraham 1962: 463), and into a main corridor (or passage, *upèpé*). In older houses, mud benches (*orí upèpé*) were built at the end (*orí*, head) of a passageway (*upèpé*). Often one of the two rooms adjacent to the front door serves as a parlour (*palò*), where family portraits are hung and heavy armchairs provide seating for visiting guests (see Frontispiece). Other rooms (*yàrá*) are used as bedrooms, sometimes with a small window opening (*ojú fèrèsé*). Houses currently have iron roofs (*àjà*) although in the past they were made of *gbòrògì* leaves (DI97-9, Ìtàpá-Èkìtì, 1997), specially grown for thatching the top of the house (*òrùùlé*, literally head (*orí*) of the house (*ulé*)). Cooking areas (*àdìrò* or *kisinni*) are generally located at the back of the house (*èyìnkùlé*), and often consist of open covered sheds.

While a large family compound, populated by many members and generations of patrilineally-related kin is the ideal, many of the compounds in Ìtàpá consist of a single house-head (*baálé*), his wife (or wives) and children, and possibly an elderly mother and grandchildren, as will be seen in the following chapter. Only 13 per cent (n=52) of the households in 1991 had two or more adult brothers living together. In Ìtàpá, as elsewhere in Yorubaland, 'the dynamic of individual aggrandisement ... fired ... other men, at the domestic level, who strove to break away from their seniors' control' (Barber 1991: 242).

Despite this separation of sons within families, each of whom is striving to build his own house to be populated by his immediate and extended kin, a seasonal unity is attained when many *ọmọ Ìtàpá* return home to participate in family meetings, usually over the Christmas holidays. At these meetings, family members assemble to discuss issues pertaining to the immediate family compound including maintenance of the family house, school fees for children and division of property on the death of a family member. For example, in the case of an important chief who recently died, family members met to decide on the division of his property. The house was divided into sets of bedroom and parlour, with one set for each of the three 'maternal lines', and one set reserved for the general use of all of his children. While these meetings preserve an ideal of family unity, they also provide an avenue for private interest and conflicts over these divisions. Thus, despite the difficulties of maintaining these family meetings and for outsiders mustering the time, money and energy to attend them, most family members cannot afford to miss them.

The division along maternal lines in this chief's family compound, described above and discussed in several studies of Yoruba kinship and marriage (Bender 1970, 1972; Eades 1980; Lloyd 1966, 1970), constitutes an essential building block from which yet another dynamic of separation and unity derives. The unit of mother and uterine children, the *ọmọ ìyá kan*, constitutes the smallest family unit. Celebrated in song, proverbs, stories, novels, and more recently in memoirs (for example, Ṣóyinká 1988, 1989), the image of a mother nursing or carrying her child on her back is frequently seen in Yoruba sculpture (Drewal et al. 1989). This close physical connection between mother and child is also reflected in the Yoruba proverb, *Ọmọ t'ó bá dára ti bàbá ni, ọmọ t'ó bá burú ti ìyá ni* ('The child that is good is for the father, the child that is bad is for the mother'). It suggests that if a child is a failure, only its mother will love and remember it, stressing the 'unofficial' but nonetheless strong emotional ties between mother and child (Barber 1991: 171). In contrast, fathers, who may stress their 'official' (legal) authority over their children in this patrilineal society, may nonetheless have more distant relations with them, in part because they may have several different wives. While the proverb ostensibly supports an ideology of patriarchal authority over children ('good children are for the father'), it also implicitly criticises fathers who may only recognise successful children whereas mothers love their children regardless. It thus reflects the tension between the structural positions of fathers and mothers to children, the former relationship stressing legal obligation and the latter stressing emotion and affection. Both have distinctive reasons for wanting children, relating to ideals of patrilineal organisation and marriage practices in the town.

KINSHIP AND MARRIAGE

In Ìtàpá, people claim patrilineal identities based on descent, through men, from a male ancestor. For a man, this identity is concretely made by continued residence in a patrilineal compound after marriage, through claims to patrilineal land, titles and names, and through legal custody of children in cases of divorce. For a woman, this patrilineal identity is blurred by patrilocal residence (when she moves to her husband's house after marriage or after bearing a child; see Chapter 3), by matrilateral claims to property (property such as clothes and jewellery tend to be given by mothers to their daughters), and by affective relations with her children (belonging to their father's patrilineage) described above. While women maintain their place within their own fathers' patrilineage and may return to their family compound for more or less extended stays in case of divorce or illness, their physical departure puts them at something of a disadvantage in lineage affairs. Similarly, their lack of membership in their husbands' patrilineage puts them at a disadvantage in their marital homes, as does the prevailing ideology reflected in the proverb 'The husband is the head of the wife' (Ọkọ ni olórí aya). The possibility of a monogamous marriage being transformed into a polygynous one may also reinforce a husband's position of being one among many.

However, this depiction of kinship and marriage in Ìtàpá is somewhat fluid and subject to alteration, depending on circumstances and on the individuals and families involved. For example, ọmọ Ìtàpá living outside the town would live as tenants in houses neither associated with the husband's or the wife's family nor owned by either spouse. Furthermore, within Ìtàpá women as well as men aspire to building their own family houses. While more men succeed in doing this, they may need to get houseplots for building from matrilateral family ties or through their wives' families. Finally, while many women uphold an ideology that supports men's authority (Omídèyí 1987), some do not. A woman who has become wealthy through her independent economic activity (such as formal sector employment or informal trading) may improve her subordinate position in her husband's house by building her own house and heading it. By playing upon the ideal of the 'big man', whose authority is constituted by wealth and followers (Barber 1991), women may acquire authority in their own right, owning houses where they, their children and other kin may live. Indeed, the fact that some women may become wealthier and more powerful than their husbands is acknowledged, if disapprovingly, by men who refer to such women as belonging to the 'club' called *Ẹgbẹ́ kíni ọkọ yóò ṣe* (the club whose husbands cannot control them). As one man observed, 'in some homes, women are husbands and husbands, wives.' The contradictory fact that there are 'women who are husbands' does not deny that male authority persists but rather suggests that there are women who have been successful in playing the system for their own ends.

Thus, while the relationships between men, women, and children in Ìtàpá have a specific cast based on ideals of patrilineal social organisation, patrilocal residence and polygyny, the centripetal tendencies that encourage fathers to marry several wives to ensure lineage growth and continuity, and the centrifugal tendencies that encourage sons and sometimes their mothers to establish separate households, all contribute to the need for children. Both men and women have reasons to persuade at least some of their children to remain in the town, amid the many enticements that encourage them to leave.

ÌTÀPÁ DAY

One of the ways that townspeople have devised to attract their far-flung family members to return to the town was the establishment of Ìtàpá Day, first held in 1988. Like other such town festivals held throughout southwestern Nigeria (Berry 1985; Trager 2001), it was held to provide a non-ecumenical but neo-traditional means for bringing Ìtàpá sons and daughters back to the town to support its development and to maintain ties with family and friends.[24] Ìtàpá Day derived from the earlier celebration of Harvest Day, which was itself a Christian innovation derived from earlier festivals to celebrate various deities in the town, such as the Ògún Festival which is still celebrated every September.

Ìtàpá Day festivities take place on the first weekend of October, after months of preparation by two of the town's *ẹgbẹ́* social clubs (one men's and one women's) in conjunction with the Ìtàpá Day Planning Committee, the Ọwátàpá, the council of chiefs, and members of the Ìtàpá Progressive Union. The 1996 event, organised with the motto 'Coming Together for Development' took place at the newly constructed town hall (see Figure 10.2).[25] In addition to the launch of a ten-million naira development fund, there were prayers, speeches by the chairman, the keynote speaker, the Ọwátàpá and club sponsor–representatives. Cultural entertainment interludes included traditional dances, a 'cultural show' and the singing of the newly created Ìtàpá-Èkìtì anthem. The printed programme listing these events and their scheduled times fails to capture the excitement, tedium, and chaos of these festivities. People constantly come and go and small children run about, while at the same time careful calculations are made of the cost of the finery worn by dignitaries occupying the seats of honour and the reasons for the absence of those who were invited but did not come. Wealthy ọmọ Ìtàpá living in Lagos and Ìbàdàn who have returned for the event stun the crowd with cheques for thousands of naira and are showered with applause in exchange for their donations. After the contributions of these individuals have been announced, time is allotted for group donations. The names of the myriad ẹgbẹ́ – town-wide men's and women's groups or clubs, organised by common interests and age and thus cross-cutting quarter and family loyalties – are read.[26] In 1996, their representatives, along with those of the various branches of the Ìtàpá Progressive Union, came up to the stage to make their contributions. Following this, donations were made by individual quarters' representatives while those with 'Sundry Donations', as the programme puts it, completed the official fundraising portion of the day. Final remarks, a prayer and a last rendition of the Ìtàpá anthem brought the celebration to a close in the early afternoon, in time for visitors from nearby towns such as Adó-Èkìtì to return to more modern accommodation to which they had become accustomed.[27]

Several things stand out in the 1996 celebration and its programme. First, among the successful ọmọ Ìtàpá living outside the town, many are used to urban amenities such as electricity, running water and flush toilets. In seeking to draw these people back to a town which currently lacks these comforts, the Ìtàpá Day Committee decided to depict the town as a tourist nature spot in its printed programme ('You Need to Visit ... The Jeti spring with its ever sparkling waters ... And Perceive the Beauty of Nature'). This representation of picturesque nature contrasts with older images portraying nature as the dangerous abode of spirits and illicit power. Secondly, unity among ọmọ Ìtàpá in the development of town was stressed in several aspects of the programme. Members of the educated elite constituting the Ìtàpá Progressive Union, traditional chiefs and Christian and Muslim religious leaders were equally involved. Furthermore, expressions of both national and local identities were expressed in the singing of the Nigerian anthem and its recently formulated counterpart, the Ìtàpá-Èkìtì anthem. Finally, while soliciting development funds from individuals and groups living outside Ìtàpá as well as from community sources was a prominent part of the programme, little was said about exactly how the ten-million naira development fund was going to be accounted for and spent.

It is this latter point that contributed to a certain scepticism among townspeople as to whether the funds would be used to develop the town or whether they merely constituted a source of funds for the 'development' of the Ọwátàpá and his chiefs (see Chapter 10). Partly as a consequence of these suspicions and partly to ensure that development funds were directed to their own quarter, more individual quarters began to hold their own Quarter Day events.

QUARTER DAYS

The first quarter day, Ẹgẹ̀tún Day, held in 1984, began a process whereby individual quarters in the town organised their own 'days', using the framework of the larger town festivals. These quarter festivals, such as Rẹ́mọ Day, Egbè Day, Oròkè Day, Òkèlìjù Day and Ẹgẹ̀tún Day, are held in the second half of the year. For example, the first celebration of a Rẹ́mọ Day for all four quarters was held at the Town Hall on 19 October 1998. It was advertised through preliminary meetings and by the distribution of small, printed envelopes (see Figure 2.5) addressed to 'Ọmọ Rẹ́mọ' (descendants of Rẹ́mọ) and inviting them to come and also to contribute money for developing their quarter. The 1998 event was sponsored by a chairman and four other men from the quarter who were responsible for collecting money (₦60 for men, ₦30 for women) and two large yams from quarter residents. The programme followed the usual sequence of speeches, collections and a 'cultural display' of local dancers, after which all were served a meal of pounded yam and soup. The money raised at this event, approximately ₦14,000, will be used to build a Rẹ́mọ Quarter Hall.[28] Rẹ́mọ Day

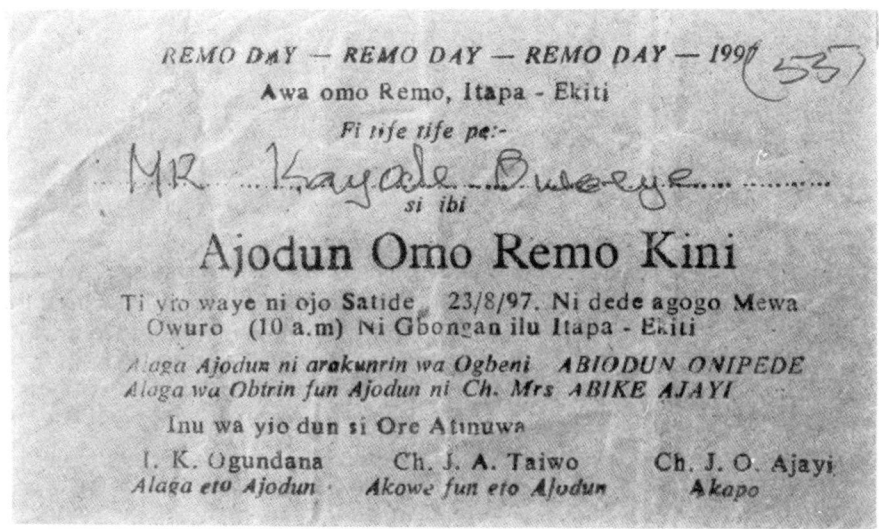

Figure 2.5 Envelope used for collecting funds from *Awa omo Remo* ('we children of Remo') for Rẹ́mọ Day, Ìtàpá-Èkìtì, 1997. (photograph by the author)

Committee members set up a bank account in which to keep the money until sufficient funds to begin building have been collected.

CENTRIPETRY AND CENTRIFUGALITY IN ÌTÀPÁ

The tendencies toward unity – as expressed in the celebration of Ìtàpá Day and in the Ìtàpá Town Hall – and separation – as seen in the performance of individual quarter days and in the building of individual quarter halls – reflects a particular form of competition. This competition is characterised by ever-higher levels of sub-groupings vying for resources at the next higher level, beginning at the family level, on through the level of the quarter, the town, the local government, and on up to the state and national level (Peel 1983: 222). Thus, in calculating the success of Ìtàpá Day, townspeople are also comparing themselves – in terms of money raised, attendance figures and numbers of prestigious visitors – with neighbouring communities with their own 'days'. This competition with other towns in Oye Local Government Area is also seen in other town-wide fundraising events, such as funds contributed to the newly formed Ekiti State in 1996. When their contribution was compared with funds given by other towns, it was used as evidence for greater local government and state recognition of and benefits for Ìtàpá. And just as towns compete among themselves for local government and state funds, so sub-units within the towns – the quarters – compete for town development funds. The establishment of quarter days is part of this process in which sub-units compete at the next higher political level for resources with which to develop their town and attract people to stay in it.

Yet people are aware that there are dangers for the development of the town in this sort of competition. For example, in the first Ìtàpá Day speech (in 1988), Chief S. A. Dada decried 'the unfortunate situation in which an Ìtàpá man now prefers to claim that he is from Rẹ́mọ or Ẹgẹ̀tún [subsections of the town, rather than as a single entity, Ìtàpá]. This is a backward step if we match this with our immediate neighbours …' (see Chapter 10). He was referring to the town of Ìlúpéjú, which formerly consisted of individual villages that have come together under a single king, the Apéjú. Their subsequent strength in numbers, both in terms of revenues raised for the local government coffers and of population, has increased the town's standing so that the Apéjú's rank was upgraded from Grade D to Grade B.[29]

This comparison with Ìlúpéjú is instructive in other ways as well. Several factors have contributed to the successful unification of Ìlúpéjú. Historically, the large market held in the crossroads linked this rich agricultural area with other parts of Yorubaland to the south and west. Johnson (1921), for example, mentions traders from Ìlọrin coming to Ìlúpéjú (Egòsì) market in the nineteenth century. During the colonial period, when the five villages now known as Ìlúpéjú were under the political control of the King of Ọyẹ́, their prosperous market gave them a certain autonomy. Several government-

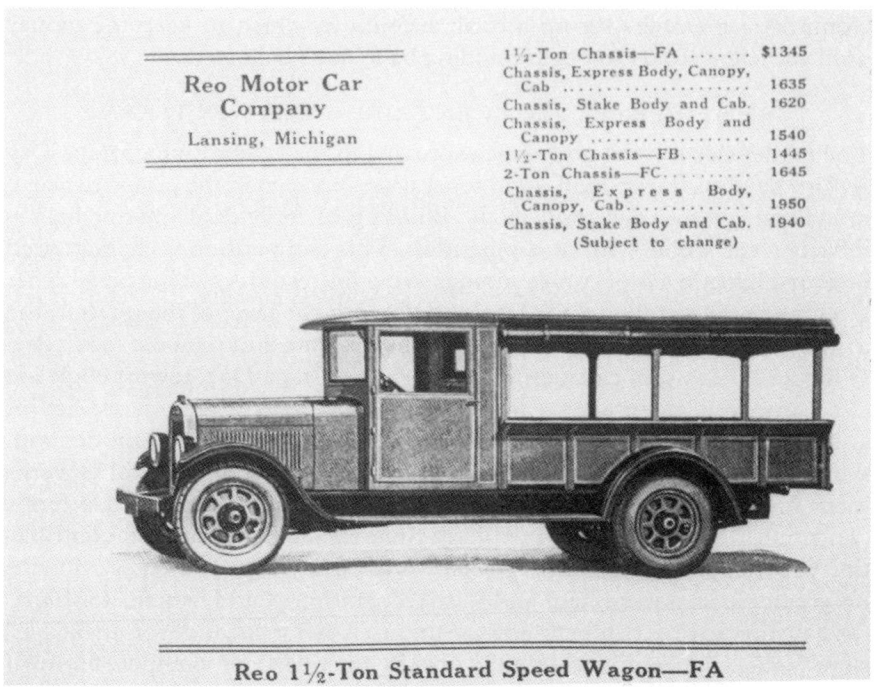

Figure 2.6 Reo, first motor vehicle seen in Ìtàpá, manufactured by the Reo Motor Company, Lansing, Michigan, USA. (National Automobile Chamber of Commerce, *Handbook of Automobiles*, New York: National Automobile Chamber of Commerce, 1928, p. 160)

sponsored structures were built during this period near the market, including a postal agency, a health centre and a transport depot. More recently, one of the prominent sons of the town, S. A. Ajíbóyè, a former member of the Ondo State House of Assembly representing Èkìtì North 3, helped the town acquire various development projects such as a commercial bank and sub-post office. In contrast, Ìtàpá's rocky location, limited arable land and small market, as well as its subordination to the King of Ìkọ̀lé and the subsequent difficulties faced by its residents in obtaining development funds during the colonial period, historically help to explain its limited resources and have contributed to its present difficulties. Thus despite the presence of a road which brought commerce to Ìlúpéjú with the coming of motor vehicles (see Figure 2.6),[30] Ìtàpá has no major market or industries.[31] This relative lack of development in Ìtàpá compared with Ìlúpéjú was attributed to a lack of love by several people, as one man explained:

For example, when I see something I feel is good for development at
Ìlúpéjú, I bring this home telling my people that it would assist
development of our town. But because we don't love ourselves, it will
be difficult for you to accept my idea, we will disagree on the issue.
(DI97-36, Ìtàpá-Èkìtì, 1997)

In some ways, this road may be undermining people's efforts to come together. For example, in the past, although Ìtàpá townspeople walked long distances to work in towns such as Iléṣà, Ìbàdàn and Lagos, they soon after returned to build houses where they continued to reside in the town. Presently, the educated sons and daughters of the town working in southern cities come back on this road to build their own houses but do not reside in them. For them, the presence of the main road has led to easier access to the town and also out of it. And for the townspeople remaining, long-distance taxis that serve southern cities leave Ìtàpá every morning and return in the late afternoon, providing the opportunity for young people to look elsewhere for work. The local taxis that ply this road have made it easier for women to take their kola and other produce to sell in the larger markets at Ìlúpéjú or Ìkọlé, rather than focusing their trade on Ìtàpá's small market.[32]

This ease of mobility, as well as a lack of local opportunities, has fostered an intensification of comings and goings. It has both undermined the reasons for staying in Ìtàpá and heightened the need for centripetal strategies used to attract people to the town. Some of these centripetal strategies include the establishment of Ìtàpá Day and efforts to establish a local government with Ìtàpá as its headquarters. Yet another strategy for attracting and keeping people in the town is to have a certain number of children. Some may resist the centrifugal pull toward southern cities, staying at home while others, working outside, will contribute generously to the town's development. The demographic dimensions of fertility and mortality as well as migratory population movements have vital implications for the people and progress of Ìtàpá. They are the subject of the following chapter.

3

DEMOGRAPHIC DIMENSIONS OF ÌTÀPÁ-ÈKÌTÌ

Were we led all that way for Birth or Death?
T. S. Eliot

The numbers pour down like dry hail ...
Italo Calvino

The demographic dimensions of Ìtàpá-Èkìtì considered in this chapter expand on the ideas of centripetry and centrifugality discussed in Chapter 2. More specifically, it examines what people do to increase, acquire or attract followers, particularly children, from a demographic perspective. These things include strategies of fertility and the in-fostering of children. Alternately, things that result in a loss of population, including infant mortality and the out-migration of young people, are also considered. Documenting the comings and goings of people is at the heart of demography.

This demographic documentation is considered in the context of one local development project directly related to these trends: the Ìtàpá Maternity Centre. The Centre was built, in part, to address problems of infant and maternal mortality and of pregnant women needing to travel to neighbouring towns (Ìkọ̀lé, Ìrè and Ìlúpéjú) for clinic deliveries. It has nonetheless encountered some of the same constraints faced by the town at large, namely finding funds amid a decline in federal support for social services. The fact that some younger women are now giving birth at home, in church-sponsored maternities and in hospitals outside Ìtàpá highlights one of the difficulties of local development projects. In this case it is the difficulty of maintaining community support and services in order to retain existing clients and to attract new ones who might, for a range of reasons, prefer giving birth elsewhere.

Before discussing these aspects of demography and development, I give some of the basic dimensions of the town's population. This information not only sets the stage, so to speak, for understanding generational and gender dynamics in the town but also for clarifying how certain configurations of fertility, infant mortality, child-bearing and migration have changed over time.

SURVEYING ÌTÀPÁ

Two surveys were conducted in early 1992 and mid-1997, along with a village-wide census in late 1991 (see Appendix I on research methods). In the process of conducting the 1991 census, a map of the town was made (see Figure 2.1). This map was used to select a sample of women and men to survey, using standard demographic interview forms that had been modified to reflect local language use and social practices. In the surveys conducted from January–March 1992, 294 women (aged fifteen to forty-nine) and 302 men (aged twenty to fifty-four) were interviewed. In June 1997, a follow-up survey using an identical format was carried out: 305 women were interviewed, of whom 152 had been interviewed in the 1992 survey.[1] Interviews based on several smaller topic-specific questionnaires on child-fostering, burial practices, houseplot transactions, local development and census-taking were also conducted with both women and men during this five-year period. Their responses will be discussed in detail in later chapters. Additionally, the Ìtàpá material will be compared with data from the 1990 Nigerian Demographic and Health Survey (Nigeria, Federal Office of Statistics 1992) and the 1986 Ondo State Demographic and Health Survey (Ondo State, Ministry of Health 1989), and supplemented with information from a 1991 demographic survey of urban Adó-Èkìtì (Caldwell et al. 1992: 221). By comparing these different sources of data, Ìtàpá-Èkìtì's demographic dimensions are placed within the wider context of south-western Nigeria.

THE POPULATION PARAMETERS OF ÌTÀPÁ

The exact number of people living in Ìtàpá is difficult to assess, as several factors come into play. One of the most important factors is the way that population is conceptualised. According to demographic conventions, a distinction is made when conducting a census as to whether people are residents in principle or in fact, that is, whether they are *de jure* or *de facto* residents. The former category consists of individuals who by right or birth live there or can claim it as their home, the latter comprises those who are actually present at the time when a census is taken. Most national calculations of population are based on *de facto* censuses. When speaking of population in Ìtàpá, however, people tend to think in terms of the town's *de jure* population, reflected in 1991 national census results (see Chapter 9). In other words, all *ọmọ Ìtàpá* ('children of Ìtàpá') whether or not they are resident are considered part of the town's population. Their absence is perceived as temporary since it is considered likely that they will eventually come home to be buried: as one Ìtàpá man living in Àkúrẹ́ explained, 'No matter how rich and important you may be in another town, one day – dead or alive – you will return home' (OI-23, Àkúrẹ́, 1991). Indeed, in my 1991 census, household members sometimes included in their lists of household

Table 3.1 Population of Ìtàpá-Èkìtì

1991 Town Census, National Population Commission (De jure population)		1991 Town Census, Renne (De facto population)			
Men	Women	Age group	Men	Women	Total
5,449	5,943	0–14	701	680	1,381
		15–29	428	449	877
		30–59	295	536	831
		60+	217	268	485
TOTAL 11,392			1,641	1,933	3,574[a]

a During my census, I tried to get an idea of *de jure* population size by asking for the names of those who stayed at the house sometimes and rarely. The total *de jure* population according to my census was 5,031. This figure likely reflects various sorts of reluctance to fully pursue these lists on the part of informants and interviewers (including myself); the national figure probably reflects an enthusiasm in the other direction (see Chapter 9).

residents the deceased heads of households buried within compounds, emphasising the importance of the house founders and a sense of their continued presence there (see Chapter 6).

This point helps to explain the discrepancy between the 1991 national census results and the figures from my own 1991 census. According to the national (essentially *de jure*) census results, the town's population (11,392) is about three times that of my *de facto* census figure (3,574; see Table 3.1).[2] This *de facto* figure would increase considerably during the Christmas season when many people come back to Ìtàpá for various festivities, family meetings and weddings. Thus, depending on how people are counted and when a census is taken, the numbers included in a town's population may vary considerably (see Chapter 9). The following discussion is based on *de facto* population figures from my 1991 town census.

A schematic profile of the town's population reveals a particular configuration, showing large numbers of children and smaller numbers of adults, with adult women in the age groups from thirty-five to fifty-four approximately doubling the number of men of comparable age (see Figure 3.1). This configuration of a broad base of young people whose numbers are relatively evenly divided in terms of gender, with a pyramid topped by a few old people is a common pattern in many African countries (Olúsànyà 1988: 88). This population pyramid also reflects a particular configuration of household structure, child dependency and migration. Specifically, many adult men live and work outside the town while many older adult women with children remain there. This pattern of out-migration nonetheless co-exists with the persisting ideal that prosperous sons (and daughters) of Ìtàpá should build houses in their home town. This has led to a situation where there is a relatively large percentage of houses with *de facto* women heads (see Table 3.2; see Cohen and Odhiambo 1989), later repopulated by older

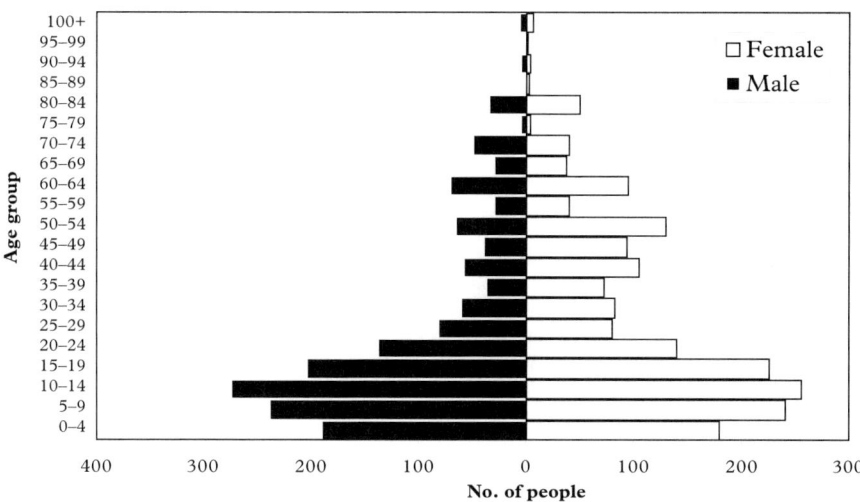

Figure 3.1 Population pyramid for Ìtàpá-Èkìtì, 1991

retired men returning to the town. However, not all women household heads are heads by default. Some prosperous women – often traders and teachers – have built houses themselves, reflecting a certain income-based gender equality (Barber 1991; Renne 1993d).[3]

WORKING AND RESIDING IN THE TOWN

While wealth can override gender hierarchies, a gender division of labour nonetheless exists in the town. Generally, men farm and women trade. In 1992, 23 per cent of the men described themselves exclusively as farmers while another 18 per cent practised various trades – carpenters, electricians, mechanics and businessmen – in combination with farming (see Table 3.3a). Thirty-seven per cent of women described themselves as traders, with an additional 13 per cent working as seamstresses or hairdressers. Only 3 per cent described themselves as farmers (see Table 3.3b), all of whom were over thirty-five years of age. Two occupations, however, were practised by both men and women, namely teaching and schooling. Five per cent of men and 3 per cent of women in the town were teachers, while 21 per cent of men and 32 per cent of women described themselves as students. The survey conducted in 1997 (among women only) indicated a similar configuration of women's work: 39 per cent were traders, 15 per cent were seamstresses or hairdressers, and 6 per cent were farmers (see Table 3.3c). While the latter figure suggests that women in Ìtàpá-Èkìtì have not taken up farming to the extent that women elsewhere in Yorubaland have (Guyer 1997), several women were not interviewed at the time of the

Table 3.2 Household composition: per cent distribution of households by sex of head of household, household size, and presence of foster children, Ìtàpá-Èkìtì, 1991

Number of household members always present (Total, n=402)	Household head Male % (n)	Household head Female % (n)	NA[b] % (n)	NDHS, SW-1990[a] Male	NDHS, SW-1990[a] Female
1	2.0 (8)	0.5 (2)	0.5 (2)		
2	1.2 (5)	2.0 (8)	1.0 (4)		
3	2.2 (9)	2.7 (11)	0.5 (2)		
4	3.5 (14)	2.5 (10)	–		
5	5.0 (20)	1.7 (7)	0.5 (2)		
6	7.2 (29)	3.0 (12)	0.25 (1)		
7	5.5 (22)	3.0 (12)	0.5 (2)		
8	6.7 (27)	–	0.5 (2)		
9	9.0 (36)	1.7 (7)	–		
10–19	28.3 (114)	3.2 (13)	0.25 (1)		
20–29	2.2 (9)	1.7 (7)	–		
30+	1.0 (4)	–	–		
Percentage head by sex	73.9 (297)	22.1 (89)	4.0 (16)	81.2	18.8
De jure heads	64.2 (258)	6.7 (27)	–		
De facto heads	9.7 (39)	15.4 (62)	–		
Mean size of all households: 8.9				4.9	
With in-foster children (n=183)	31.8 (128)	12.9 (52) 45.5[c]	0.7 (3)		8.6

a Data from 1990 (Nigerian Demographic and Health Survey 1992: 12) for south-western Nigeria.
b NA=Not applicable. These houses are occupied by tenants.
c Percentage of all houses with in-foster children; disparity of total of fostering percentages by household is due to rounding.

second survey as they were away harvesting highland rice, a relatively new occupation for Èkìtì Yoruba women (I. O. Orùbuloyè, personal correspondence). Teaching, one of the mainstays of white-collar work in Ìtàpá, was practised by slightly more women in 1997 (5 per cent) although the number of women students declined substantially to 17 per cent.[4] It is women teachers and successful traders who, through their economic acuity and leadership qualities, have sufficient resources and followers to start houses of their own (see endnote 3). Yet, one woman trader who had built her own house in Ìtàpá actually moved to Adó-Èkìtì for business reasons: 'I have come here just to make progress. Adó-Èkìtì is bigger than my town and I strongly believe that trading activities can be more effective here … In fact what I make here daily I can't make in a week at Ìtàpá' (OI-2, Adó-Èkìtì, 1991). The possibility of becoming a self-made 'big woman' has been a real one because of the flexibility of the town's social and political organisations, discussed in Chapter 2.

Almost 75 per cent (n=297) of the 402 houses in the census *are* headed by *baálé*, literally 'the father of the house' (see Table 3.2). These men's

Table 3.3a Characteristics of Survey Men, Ìtàpá-Èkìtì, 1992

Age group	Marital status				Educational level[a]						Occupations[b]												
	Un-married		Married		NE		Prim		Sec		Post		Student		Farmer		Carpenter		Apprentice		Teacher		Driver	
	%		%		%		%		%		%		%		%		%		%		%		%	
20–24 (n=110)	91.8 (101)		8.2 (9)		–		7.3 (8)		82.7 (91)		10.0 (11)		89.1 (57)		4.3 (3)		42.9 (9)		72.2 (13)		–		15.4 (2)	
25–29 (n=66)	60.6 (40)		39.4 (26)		3.0 (2)		15.2 (10)		71.2 (47)		16.1 (5)		10.9 (7)		14.3 (10)		28.6 (6)		22.2 (4)		26.7 (4)		15.4 (2)	
30–34 (n=31)	25.8 (8)		74.2 (23)		3.2 (1)		22.6 (7)		58.1 (18)		16.1 (5)		–		17.1 (12)		4.8 (1)		5.6 (1)		13.3 (2)		16.7 (3)	
35–39 (n=20)	15.0 (3)		85.0 (17)		–		30.0 (6)		50.0 (10)		20.0 (4)		–		7.2 (5)		9.5 (2)		–		20.0 (3)		–	
40–44 (n=33)	3.0 (1)		97.0 (32)		9.1 (3)		33.3 (11)		42.4 (14)		15.2 (5)		–		18.6 (13)		9.5 (2)		–		33.3 (5)		16.7 (3)	
45–49 (n=18)	–		100 (18)		–		55.6 (10)		27.8 (5)		16.6 (3)		–		11.4 (8)		–		–		6.7 (1)		16.7 (3)	
50–54 (n=24)	–		100 (24)		20.8 (5)		62.5 (15)		4.2 (1)		12.5 (3)		–		27.1 (19)		4.8 (1)		–		–		–	
Total (n=302)	50.7 (153)		49.3 (149)		3.6 (11)		22.2 (67)		61.6 (186)		12.6 (38)		21.2 (64)		23.2 (70)		7.0 (21)		6.0 (18)		5.0 (15)		4.3 (13)	

Age group	Electrician %	Business %	Mechanic %	Misc %
20–24	33.3 (4)	16.8 (2)	45.4 (5)	22.7 (15)
25–29	50.0 (6)	50.0 (6)	27.3 (3)	27.3 (18)
30–34	16.7 (2)	8.3 (1)	18.2 (2)	10.6 (7)
35–39	–	8.3 (1)	9.1 (1)	12.1 (8)
40–44	–	8.3 (1)	–	13.6 (9)
45–49	–	–	–	9.0 (6)
50–54	–	8.3 (1)	–	4.5 (3)
Total	4.0 (12)	4.0 (12)	3.6 (11)	21.9 (66)

a NE= no education; Prim=Primary; Sec=Secondary; post=post-secondary education.
b Many men combine farmwork with these occupations. Miscellaneous occupations include bricklayers (8), printers (6), tailors (6), office workers (5), painters (4), petrol attendants (4), cobblers (4), unemployed (4), welders (3), pastor (2), medical workers (2), herbalists (2), data missing (2), and one (1) of each of the following: vulcaniser, surveyor, roadman, ricemill operator, refrigerator repair, Quranic teacher, police, palmwine tapster, lumber contractor, graduate-NYSC, blacksmith, barber and chemist.

Table 3.3b Characteristics of survey women, Ìtapá-Èkìtì, 1992

Age group	Marital status		Educational level				Occupations[a]							
	Unmarried %	Married %	NE[b] %	Primary %	Secondary %	Post-secondary %	Student %	Trader %	Seamstress %	Hair-dresser %	Appren-tice %	Farmer %	Teacher %	Misc[c] %
15–19 (n=110)	97.3 (107)	2.7 (3)	–	12.7 (14)	87.2 (96)	–	74.5 (82)	6.4 (7)	4.5 (5)	2.7 (3)	6.4 (7)	–	0.9 (1)	4.5 (5)
20–24 (n=60)	46.7 (28)	53.3 (32)	–	25.0 (15)	71.7 (43)	3.3 (2)	15.0 (9)	36.7 (22)	16.7 (10)	13.3 (8)	1.7 (1)	–	–	16.7 (10)
25–29 (n=33)	18.2 (6)	81.8 (27)	6.0 (2)	15.2 (5)	69.0 (23)	9.1 (3)	6.1 (2)	48.4 (16)	15.1 (5)	6.1 (2)	6.1 (2)	–	6.1 (2)	12.1 (4)
30–34 (n=16)	–	100.0 (16)	25.0 (4)	50.0 (8)	18.8 (3)	6.2 (1)	–	81.4 (13)	–	6.2 (1)	–	–	6.2 (1)	6.2 (1)
35–39 (n=27)	–	100 (27)	29.6 (8)	55.6 (15)	7.4 (2)	7.4 (2)	3.7 (1)	63 (17)	11.1 (3)	–	–	7.4 (2)	7.4 (2)	7.4 (2)
40–44 (n=21)	–	100 (21)	28.6 (6)	47.6 (10)	14.3 (3)	9.5 (2)	–	61.9 (13)	4.8 (1)	–	–	23.8 (5)	9.5 (2)	–
45–49 (n=27)	–	100 (27)	63 (17)	22.2 (6)	14.8 (4)	–	–	81.5 (22)	3.7 (1)	–	–	11.1 (3)	–	3.7 (1)
Total (n=294)	48 (141)	52 (153)	12.6 (37)	24.8 (73)	59.2 (174)	3.4 (10)	32 (94)	37.4 (110)	8.5 (25)	4.8 (14)	3.4 (10)	3.4 (10)	2.7 (8)	7.8 (23)

a Some women combine farmwork with these occupations.
b No education.
c Miscellaneous includes weavers, unemployed, hotel workers, a soda maker, postmistress, printer, unidentified worker and housewife.

Table 3.3c Characteristics of survey women, Ìtàpá-Èkìtì, 1997

Age group	Marital status				Educational level					Occupations[a]							
	Un-married %	Married %	NE[b] %	Primary %	Secondary %	Post-secondary %	Student %	Trader %	Seamstress %	Hair-dresser %	Appren-tice %	Farmer %	Teacher %	Misc[c] %
15–19 (n=33)	85 (28)	15 (5)	–	9 (3)	91 (30)	–	67 (22)	–	9 (3)	6 (2)	–	–	–	18 (6)
20–24 (n=67)	54.0 (36)	46.0 (31)	–	13.0 (9)	73.0 (49)	13.0 (9)	43.0 (29)	13.0 (9)	12.0 (8)	12.0 (8)	–	–	2.0 (1)	18.0 (12)
25–29 (n=45)	11.0 (5)	89.0 (40)	–	7.0 (3)	89.0 (40)	4.0 (2)	2.0 (1)	49.0 (22)	16.0 (7)	9.0 (4)	–	4.0 (2)	2.0 (1)	18.0 (8)
30–34 (n=37)	–	100.0 (37)	3.0 (1)	11.0 (4)	86.0 (32)	–	–	62.0 (23)	3.0 (1)	11.0 (4)	–	5.0 (2)	–	19.0 (7)
35–39 (n=24)	–	100 (24)	4 (1)	21 (5)	63 (15)	13 (3)	–	50 (12)	–	4 (1)	–	8 (2)	21 (5)	17 (4)
40–44 (n=48)	–	100 (48)	25 (12)	48 (23)	21 (10)	6 (3)	–	50 (24)	10 (5)	2 (1)	–	17 (8)	8 (4)	13 (6)
45–49 (n=15)	–	100 (15)	33 (5)	40 (6)	13 (2)	13 (2)	–	53 (8)	–	7 (1)	–	7 (1)	7 (1)	27 (4)
50–54 (n=30)	–	100 (30)	67 (20)	23 (7)	10 (3)	–	–	77 (23)	–	–	–	7 (2)	7 (2)	10 (3)
55+ (n=6)	–	100 (6)	83 (5)	17 (1)	–	–	–	67 (4)	–	–	–	–	–	33 (2)
Total (n=305)	23 (69)	77 (236)	14 (44)	20 (61)	59 (181)	6 (19)	17 (52)	41 (125)	8 (24)	7 (21)	–	6 (17)	5 (14)	17 (52)

a Some women combine farmwork with these occupations.
b No education.
c Miscellaneous includes weavers, unemployed, hotel workers, a soda maker, postmistress, printer, unidentified worker and housewife.

50 ANTHROPOLOGICAL AND DEMOGRAPHIC CONCERNS

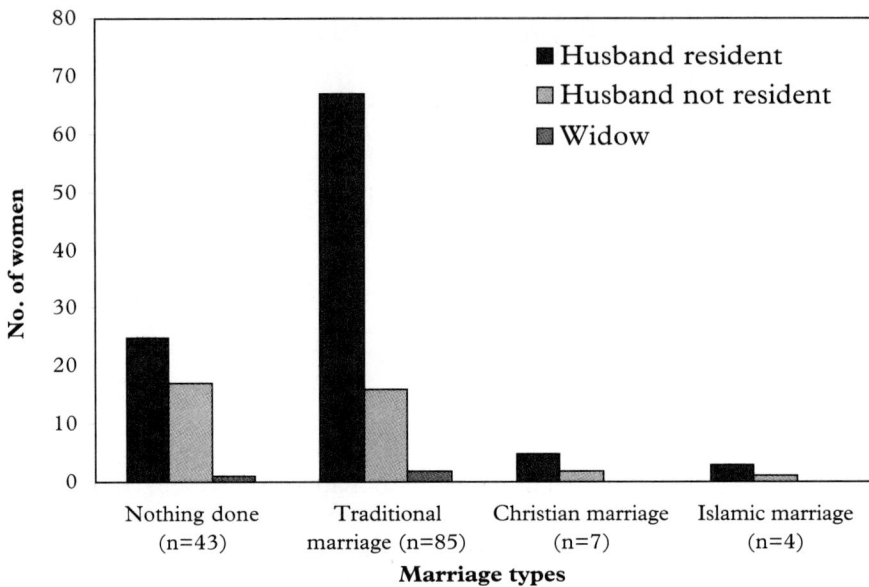

Figure 3.2a Marriage types and husbands' residences, women aged 15–39 (n=139), Ìtàpá-Èkìtì, 1997

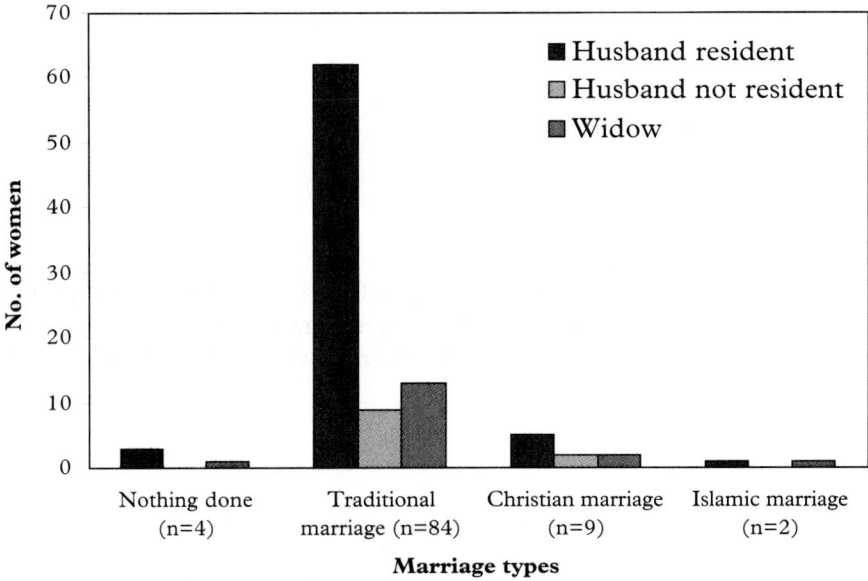

Figure 3.2b Marriage types and husbands' residences, women aged 40–65 (n=99), Ìtàpá-Èkìtì, 1997

houses also constitute the largest households in the town. Thus, with the exception of 'big women' house owners (n=27) and the more commonplace *de facto* women heads (n=62), households generally conform to the prevailing patrilineal ideology that men head lineages and households, and that descent, including access to family property, titles, and names, is claimed through men. Most married women live in their husbands' houses or compounds rather than those they have built themselves. Indeed, moving to one's husband's house constitutes a defining aspect of marriage. In the past, the physical act of moving was part of the ritual performance of arranged marriage, carried out amid dancing and singing, and culminating in the virginal bride stepping on a piece of calabash as she crossed the threshold of her husband's family compound (Ògúntúyì 1979).[5]

More recently, when marriage is no longer arranged and is often more informally contracted (see Chapter 4), moving to one's husband's house (as well as bearing a child) may be, for many young men and women, the preliminary step in establishing a long-term marital arrangement (see Figures 3.2a and 3.2b). For example, of the 139 women aged fifteen to thirty-nine who reported that they were married in the 1997 survey, only 61 per cent had performed some aspect of traditional marriage, even if this only meant an 'introduction' between the families. Thirty-one per cent of the women in this age group had made no introduction, agreement (between family members) or bridewealth payment. Only 8 per cent had had a formal Christian or Islamic ceremony.

CHILDREN AS FOLLOWERS

Marriage, defined by patrilocal residence if not by other formalities, is yet another aspect of a particular way of attracting and acquiring followers, in this case, wives and their offspring. That there is a certain tension in 'keeping' them has been discussed in the literature on Yoruba marriage and social organisation (Eades 1980; Mann 1986; Olúsànyà 1970) since Yoruba women retain rights within their own patrilineages. After a colonial court system was established in the 1920s with procedures for divorce, it presented another obstacle in the keeping of wives (Lloyd 1968a; Renne 1992), yet for some it provided an opportunity for attracting more wives.

In Ìtàpá, around one in ten of the married women interviewed in 1992 and one in twenty of those interviewed in 1997 had been divorced once in their lives. Younger married women (under thirty years; see Figure 3.3) are less likely to be divorced, in part, because their marriage arrangements are often still somewhat fluid. Bridewealth may not have been paid and marriage rituals are unlikely to have been performed and as a result more formal divorce proceeding, such as going to court, or informal ones, such as simply returning bridewealth, are not necessary. Furthermore, young women's children would also be young, giving men less incentive to initiate

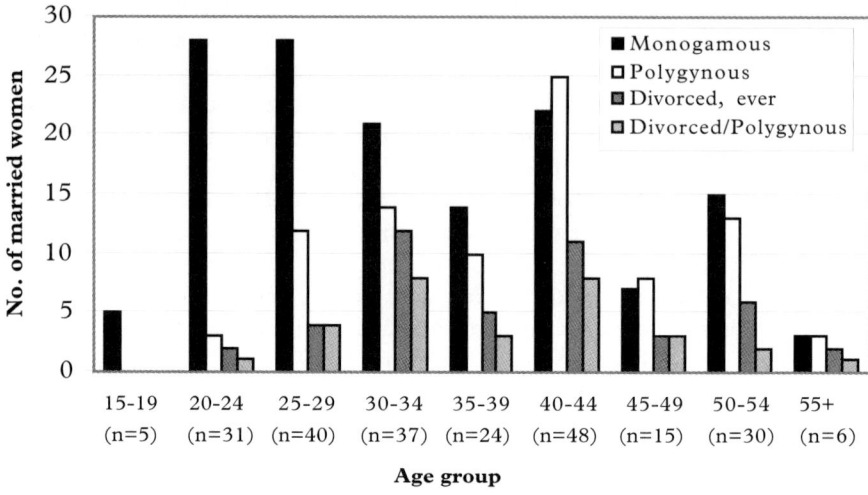

Figure 3.3 Divorce and marriage patterns, Ìtàpá-Èkìtì, 1997

a formal divorce to ensure child custody. It was the slightly older women, in their thirties, who were more likely to be divorced. These divorced women were more often in polygynous marriages compared with their non-divorced counterparts (see Figure 3.3). Thus divorce and polygyny provides certain men with another avenue for attracting a larger following of wives although these women's children from prior marriages are not generally included in this group. These children are jurally bound to their fathers (and their patrilineage) who, in the case of divorce, may insist on and win legal custody (Bascom 1984). Yet even in these gender-based child custody decisions, resources and affective ties may override official ideology and mothers may successfully keep their children with them. Children may also later choose to reside with their mothers (or as adults, have their mothers reside with them).

Women's and men's distinctive claims to and needs for children give rise to similarities and differences in women's and men's strategies for having the number of children they ideally want (see Appendix III on contraception use by Ìtàpá women and men). For example, one man, a twenty-nine-year-old (in 1991) farmer with three children, explained his own fertility strategy in discussions with his wife:[6]

> I have not been discussing it with her but her lukewarm attitude toward having more children clearly shows that she doesn't want many children. At times if she is invited for sex she will feel reluctant

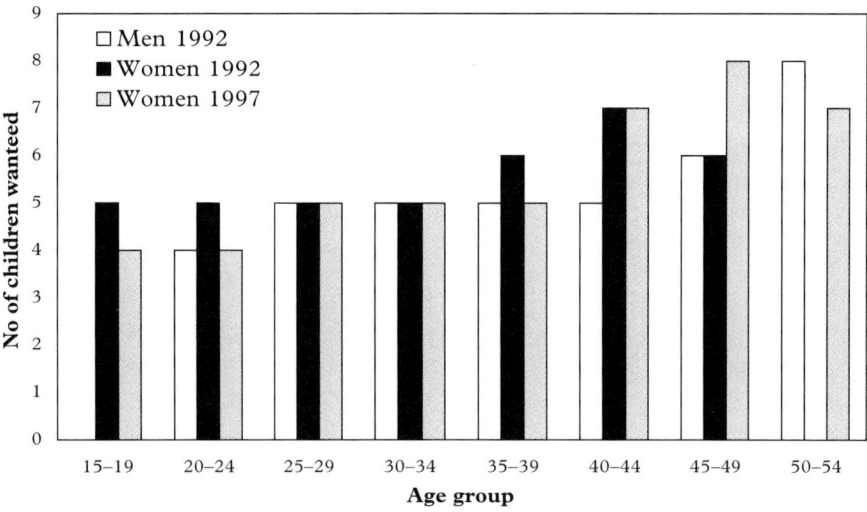

Figure 3.4 Median ideal number of children wanted, by sex and age group, Ìtàpá-Èkìtì, 1997

> saying, 'Please I want to rest.' She is afraid of having many children. [But] since I am the husband I know what I can do to persuade her to have five children. I will continually tell her stories about the evils of having few children. And if at four children, she says she is OK, I will take it ... I know at four children she won't allow any further pregnancy.
> (LIM- JM13/10-66, Ìtàpá-Èkìtì, 1991)

Despite their differences, which are generally minor (Bánkọlé 1995; Renne 1993d), both women and men want children. However, there are generational differences that affect these preferences. Older women and men wanted similar large numbers (or 'whatever God gives') whereas younger men and women wanted four or five children (see Figure 3.4). These differences may reflect, in part, the impact of educational expenses that have increased significantly since the mid-1980s. For older men and women, education was only for a few; more children meant more hands to help on farms. Presently men are expected to pay for all their children to attend school. This fact perhaps explains their desire for slightly fewer children (four rather than five) than their young women counterparts, suggested by the comments of one schoolteacher:

> As I've said, I've got three children. So after having the second child, I discussed with my wife that we should not have more than four children. Her reaction then was that we should have as many as possible.

But I made her to realise the economic implications of having so many children, although being a trader she thought that she could take care of many children. But as things are going now she has even discovered herself that having very many children may not be to her advantage and she has actually come to agree with me about having four. Now, if we could have another one, that would be enough. Even when we had the last one, she was discussing with me, if at all we [are] to enjoy ourselves, we may have to go to see a doctor for a private discussion about family planning so that there won't be unnecessary conception at the time we may not need it. The situation of things in the country has actually enlightened her to believe that having very few children could be of advantage.

(LIM-AC13/8-19, Ìtàpá-Èkìtì, 1991)

His point about 'very few children could be of advantage' suggests a reinterpretation of the social ideals of raising up children well, from having many uneducated children-followers to having just a few who are well trained. Indeed by 1997, the number of children that young women (aged fifteen to nineteen) said that they wanted had also declined to four.

CALCULATING FERTILITY IN ÌTÀPÁ

The total fertility rate calculated on the basis of two women's surveys (1992, 1997) also declined over this period, suggesting that women and men not only said that they wanted to have fewer children but were also acting on what they had said (see Tables 3.4a and 3.4b).[7] One interesting aspect of this decline relates to the education of women, and is suggested by the discontinuity in average parity figures between women in their thirties and forties. Survey information suggests that women in the thirty-four to thirty-nine year age group were three times as likely to have had some secondary education as women in the forty to forty-four year age group (see Table 3.4a). While a direct causal connection between secondary education and lower fertility cannot be made from this data, these figures support arguments that educated women tend to have different expectations of what constitutes ideal child-rearing practices as compared with their non-educated counterparts (see Chapter 7). These expectations for their children would also coincide with those of their educated and economically obligated husbands and even with the children themselves.[8]

Another aspect of this shift in thinking about the benefits of raising many children is that younger women and men are less likely than their elders to raise foster children. This situation partly reflects the fact that they would not have the wherewithal or experience to raise foster children and would be less likely to ask for or be given such charges. However, as will be discussed in Chapter 5, some younger educated people have reassessed the practice of child-fostering for social as well as economic reasons. Much as the ideal of

Table 3.4a Total fertility rate (TFR), Ìtàpá-Èkìtì, 1992

Age group	No. of women	CEB[a]	Average parity	Births	ASFR[b]
15–19	110	4	0.036	3	0.027
20–24	60	40	0.667	16	0.267
25–29	33	66	2.000	14	0.424
30–34	16	67	4.187	2	0.125
35–39	27	141	5.222	5	0.185
40–44	21	133	6.330	3	0.143
45–49	27	167	6.185	2	0.074

Total 5 x 1.245
TFR = 6.23
= 6.2

[a] CEB = Children ever born
[b] ASFR = Age-specific fertility rate

Table 3.4b Total fertility rate (TFR), Ìtàpá-Èkìtì, 1997[a]

Age groups	No. of women	CEB	Average parity[b]	Births[c]	ASFR
15–19	33	6	0.1818	2	0.061
20–24 [1 dk/96 birth]	67	40	0.5970	16.564	0.247
25–29	45	98	2.1777	13	0.289
30–34 [1 dk/96 birth]	37	142	3.8378	8.564	0.232
35–39 [1 dk/96 birth]	24	104	4.333	4.564	0.190
40–44 [1 dk/96 birth]	48	317	6.6041	1.564	0.033
45–49	15	105	7.000	0	0.000

Total 5 x 1.052
TFR = 5.26
= 5.3

[a] Calculations were based on births twelve months prior to conducting the survey (that is, July 1996–June 1997).
[b] Note also the jump between 35–39 and 40–44 year-olds in average parity figures which corresponds with inverse proportions of education levels of the two groups:
Women ages 35–39 (n=24) had 25% NE (no education) & primary, 75% secondary & post-secondary education; women ages 40–44 (n=48) had 73% NE and primary, 27% secondary & post-secondary education.
[c] There were seventeen births in the first half of 1996, and twenty-two births in the second half, with a total of thirty-nine birth plus four for which the month is not known. Adjustment for unknown month dates=22/39 total births=0.564. This 0.564 was added to the age-group births for which each were missing.

having many children is being reassessed in terms of a moral parenting that focuses on doing more for fewer children, child-fostering – either raising another person's child or giving out one's own – is considered by some to be a problematic practice that should be avoided. Nonetheless, the in-fostering of children has more than doubled over the period from 1992 to 1997. Thirty-three per cent of married women aged thirty years and older surveyed in 1997 were fostering children compared with 12 per cent in 1992. These women, particularly older women whose own children have left home, rely on the labour and companionship of these children. The fact that they often provide childcare for children whose parents have died or who are unable to care for them (sometimes referred to as 'crisis fostering' (Bledsoe and Isiugo-Abanihe 1989; Goody 1982, 1984)) suggests why the changing interpretations of fostering made by some young people are not carried out in practice. This contradiction in ideals and practice is partly related to local economic conditions which produce uncertainty about employment, income, and even longevity, as one man explained:

> I don't want to have more than four children ... My reason for choosing that number is that the problem of this nation is weighing [on us] more and more every day, one might think the situation will change for the better and it may not ... And look, death can come at any time, I don't want to have many children because death can come at anytime, I don't want to leave my children to suffer, the children may be too young when death will come.
> (MRI-95: IC2/8-7, Ìtàpá-Èkìtì, 1995)

In such cases, having people who provide support, in case there is a need to out-foster children who cannot be cared for, is critical regardless of the ideological preferences of younger men and women.

INFANT AND CHILD MORTALITY

The vital importance of having people – as social, economic, and emotional support – contributes to fears surrounding the uncertainty of child survival. Perceptions that children may die also contribute to women's assessment of how many children they should bear. Infant mortality, while lower than the national rate, is still relatively high in the town.[9] Nine of 188 infants born in the five years prior to the July 1997 survey died before reaching their first birthday, reflected proportionately as forty-eight deaths per 1,000 live births. These figures are considerably lower than infant deaths of children born during the five-year period prior to the 1992 survey, when nine out of 142 infants born died before reaching their first birthday (proportionately sixty-three deaths per 1,000 live births). It is difficult to draw conclusions from these small survey samples of child mortality that also reflect the idiosyncracies of data collection.[10] Yet these unadjusted figures for infant mortality

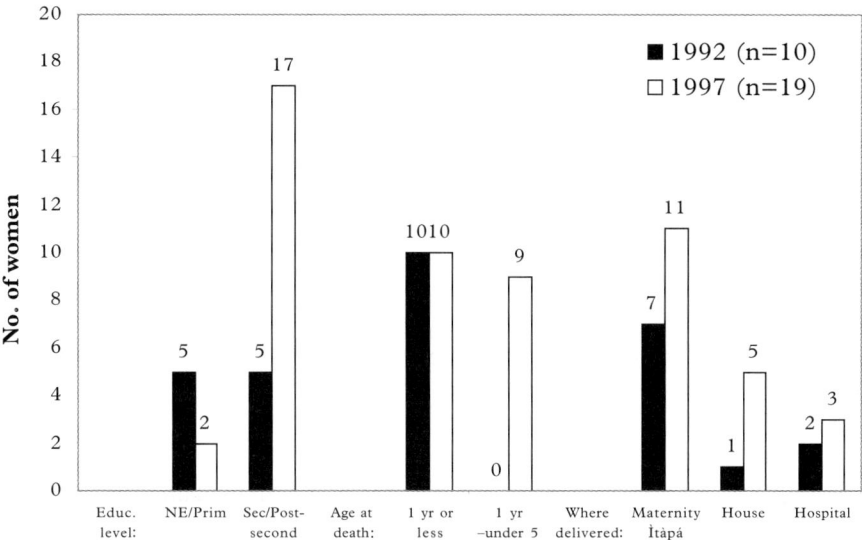

Figure 3.5 Women's experience of infant/child mortality, 1992, 1997

(before their first birthday) nonetheless suggest that, despite higher levels of education and the presence of a local maternity clinic, the expectation that an infant may not live to its first birthday is not unwarranted (Adétúnjí 1995).

Another way of considering the fear of infant and child death is to look at these numbers from the perspective of mothers, many of whom have experienced the death of a child. Of the 235 mothers interviewed in the 1997 survey, 104 had lost at least one child under the age of five.[11] While a much larger proportion of women aged thirty-five and older had experienced child death (approximately 70 per cent) compared with women aged fifteen to thirty-four (approximately 20 per cent), these figures are partly a reflection of their increased number of births. Yet even for the younger group of women, it means that one in five have experienced a child's death. The uncertainty surrounding child survival supports women's and men's efforts to have at least four children, regardless of their educational background.

The characteristics of the nineteen women who had given birth in the five years prior to the 1997 survey and had lost children aged five and under may be seen in Figure 3.5. The majority (n=17) had secondary and post-secondary education and delivered their children at maternity centres or hospitals. The idea that women with more education would experience less infant and child mortality would seem intuitively correct since such women would have more knowledge of modern healthcare and experience of access to modern maternity and primary healthcare clinics, but this does not seem to be the case here. Rather, declining public health services, uncertain local transportation and reduced economic wherewithal to seek private care when needed seem to be offsetting the health benefits of education. This trend was also noted in the Nigerian Demographic and Health Survey (Nigeria, Federal Office of Statistics 1992: 78):

> The small decline [in under-five mortality] is largely attributable to a drop in the neonatal rate from fifty-two to forty-two deaths per thousand live births; mortality between one and fifty-nine months of age has shown no improvement over the period. The latter finding may reflect the offsetting effects of improved health services on the one hand, and the deteriorating economic position of the average Nigerian household, on the other.

Another aspect of child and maternal health, namely *where* women give birth to children, also seems to have been affected by 'the deteriorating economic position of the average Nigerian household' and the everyday uncertainties of Nigerian life in the 1990s.[12]

WHERE WOMEN DELIVER

Improved child survival and attendance at maternity centres and hospitals are also associated with maternal education. For example, in the 1990 Nigerian Demographic and Health Survey, a connection was found between women's education levels and where they delivered their children: 'The proportion of births delivered in a health facility increases steadily from 16 per cent of births to mothers with no education to 82 per cent of births to mothers with completed secondary or higher education' (Nigeria, Federal Office of Statistics 1992: 90). However, the findings from the Ìtàpá surveys suggest that this 'expected pattern' of higher levels of women's education and the utilisation of modern health services is contradicted by recent practices relating to childbirth in Ìtàpá. Of the sixty-eight women aged fifteen to twenty-nine interviewed in the 1997 survey who gave birth in the five-year period prior to this survey (total number of children=98; see Figure 3.6a), twenty delivered twenty-two children at home. Of these twenty women, three had primary school education, eleven had some secondary education, and four had completed secondary school or had postgraduate education.[13] Of the forty-eight women who delivered only in the Ìtàpá Maternity Centre or in private hospitals and clinics who were in the same age range (fifteen to twenty-nine), four had primary education, thirty-three had some secondary education, and eleven had completed secondary school or had postgraduate education. Thus in terms of education, the characteristics of these two groups are proportionately similar.

When these women were asked why they delivered at home, their answers varied. Some attributed it to the late hour ('it was midnight'), some said it

DEMOGRAPHIC DIMENSIONS OF ÌTÀPÁ-ÈKÌTÌ 59

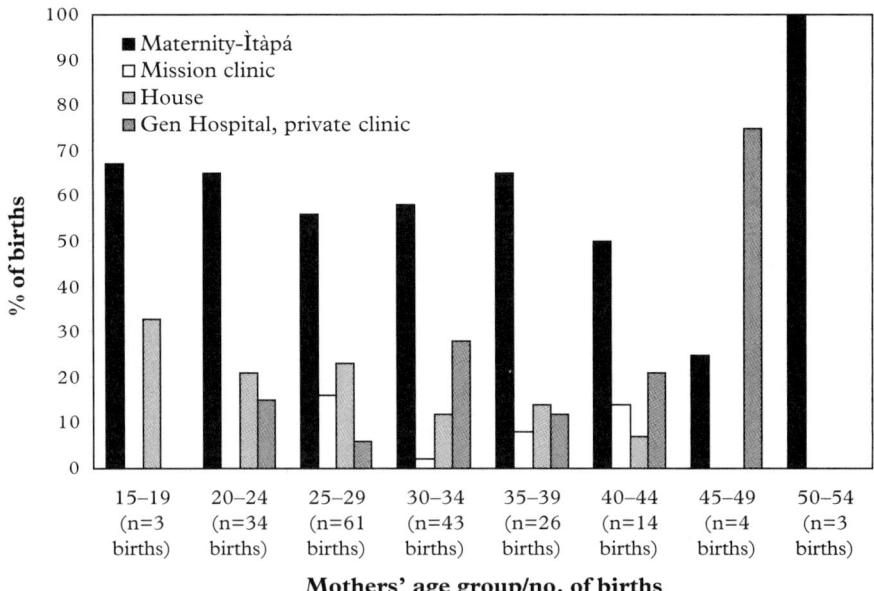

Figure 3.6a Children born, July 1992–June 1997, where delivered, by age of mother

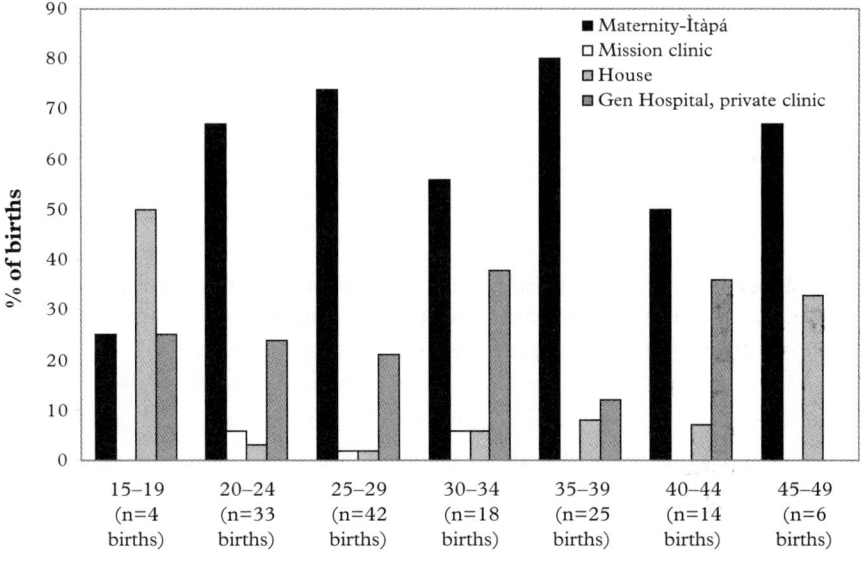

Figure 3.6b Children born, January 1987–December 1991, where delivered, by age of mother

was unexpected, some said there was no transport or there were strikes, some said that a native doctor had assisted them at home, and some said that they did not like their treatment by hospital staff. None said it was for financial reasons, although this might have been a shameful thing that women would not want to admit. Indeed, the *sotto voce* comment of one small boy to his mother during a survey interview suggests that hospitals rather than houses are considered to be the more proper birthplace. When this woman was being questioned about the children she had borne and where they had been delivered, her son whispered, 'Tell them I was born in the hospital.' Furthermore, when women were asked why many young women were giving birth at home, several mentioned the problem of money:

> Ah, in Ìtàpá today, I myself and my friends we give birth in the maternity but some women prefer to give birth at home because they could not meet the [financial] demands of the hospital personnel ... They don't have money to purchase what they use during and after delivery, even the olive oil, many couldn't provide it.
> (CBI98-YB, Ìtàpá-Èkìtì, 1998)

When women were asked to describe the events surrounding the delivery of their children at home, the contingency of events, such as the lack of public transport owing to fuel scarcity or national strikes or the lack of people in the house to help, affected where they delivered. Thus it appears that the deteriorating infrastructure as much as their own personal economic situations and preferences was affecting their actions, as several women who had delivered at home described:

> During my time, I gave birth at home because the hospital people were on strike, the nurses were on strike, that was 1993 [after the annulment of the presidential election on June 12]. No one was in the hospital.
> (CBI98-TD, Ìtàpá-Èkìtì, 1998)

> My labour started at about four in the morning. There were no vehicles on the road then. I had my booking at Ìlúpéjú Clinic but there was no way to get there.
> (CBI98-AO, Ìtàpá-Èkìtì, 1998)

Although a majority of women (71 per cent) in Ìtàpá gave birth in clinics or hospitals in the five years before 1997, 29% of the women who gave birth during this period did so at home. It is not likely that these home deliveries represent a reaction against the medicalisation of childbirth (Davis-Floyd and Sargent 1997), although they do reflect some resentment towards treatment by hospital staff (see Barber 1987) and fear of staff incompetence.[14] Yet their actions may reflect certain personal characteristics of these women that would make them more likely to deliver at home rather than in a

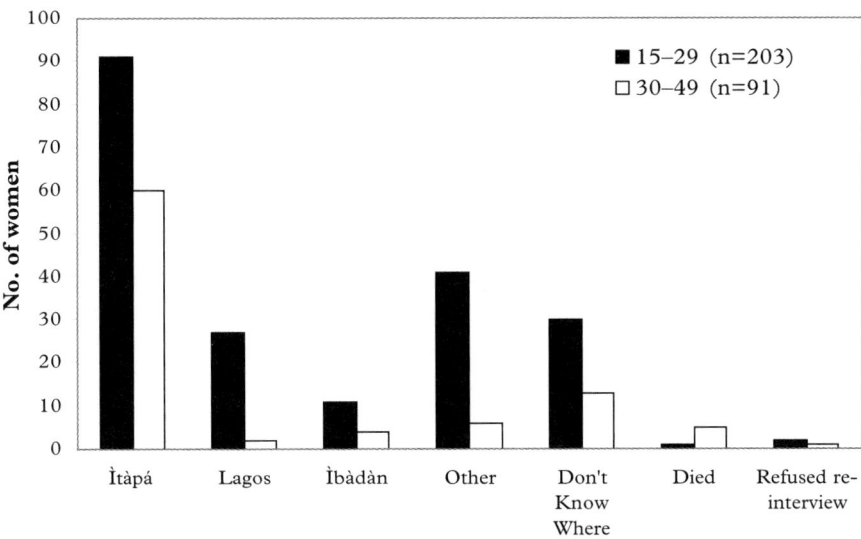

Figure 3.7 Women (n=294) from 1992 Ìtàpá survey in 1997

clinic.[15] For example, in the period between the two surveys, many younger women migrated out of the town, a fact that was discovered when we attempted to reinterview women from the 1992 survey. Of the 170 women (aged fifteen to twenty-nine) interviewed in the 1992 survey whose whereabouts could be located and who could be reinterviewed in 1997, 46 per cent (n=79) had migrated to cities and towns elsewhere in Nigeria; 54 per cent of Ìtàpá women (n=91) in the same age group had stayed (see Figure 3.7).[16] Those remaining are perhaps less adventurous and less financially able and might also tend to deliver at home. But if level of education is used as a surrogate for financial ability and ambition, then in terms of education there was little difference between those women (aged fifteen to twenty-nine) interviewed in the 1992 survey who migrated out and those who stayed in Ìtàpá. Those who moved to major cities such as Lagos or Ìbàdàn to look for work might be more likely to deliver in a clinic or hospital because of more facilities and more income-generating options.[17] Nonetheless their educational backgrounds do not distinguish them from women who stayed in the town and delivered at home.

Even for women remaining in Ìtàpá, there are at least three clinics and hospitals in Ìtàpá itself where they could deliver. Except in cases of unexpected deliveries 'at midnight', a lack of facilities in the town would not appear to explain the increase in home childbirth. Rather it would appear that an accumulation of contingent events related to the current political economy – lack of transportation, labour starting in the middle of the night, no one in the house to help and national strikes, as well as lack of economic wherewithal – has affected their actions.

It should be noted that some women have stayed at home to give birth all along. In the 1992 survey, nine women interviewed said that they had delivered at home at least once in the period from January 1987 to December 1991 (see Figure 3.6b). However, of these women who had delivered at home, only three were under the age of thirty. In the 1997 survey, twenty-seven had delivered at home at least once in the period from July 1992 to June 1997, whereas twenty of these women were under the age of thirty (see Figure 3.6a). This increase in childbirth at home by young women who have some secondary school education represents a disjunction with a sense of ọlàjú, 'enlightenment' and 'enlightened' behaviour associated with education (Peel 1978). Indeed, of the fourteen (out of twenty) women aged fifteen to twenty-nine who delivered at home in the past five years reinterviewed in 1998, ten of them had *themselves* been delivered at a clinic or hospital. In order to get a sense of the disjuncture with a certain expected trajectory that the present-day pattern of home deliveries represents, the historical context of Ìtàpá women's attendance at clinics is given.

CHILDBEARING DURING THE COLONIAL PERIOD IN ÌTÀPÁ

Prior to the building of mission and government maternity hospitals and clinics during the colonial period, women gave birth in their houses, attended by local midwives (*agbẹ̀bí*) and, in cases of difficult deliveries, by traditional healers (*babaláwo*). Colonial and mission health services were not initially available in Ìtàpá; residents had to travel to neighbouring towns for treatment and medicines. For example, in 1932 a Wesley Mission dispensary was established in Ìkọlé-Èkìtì (about 12km to the east of Ìtàpá) along with a Native Administration dispensary, set up at Ìlúpéjú-Èkìtì (about 2km to the west) during the same period: 'There is a Methodist Missionary Dispensary at Ìkọlé supervised by the Nursing Sister living at Ifaki under the doctor at the Wesley Guild Hospital at Ilesha. The Doctor also supervises the Native Administration Dispensary at Egosi [Ìlúpéjú]' (Matthews 1941, NNAI). By 1953, the dispensary at Ìkọlé had expanded into a fully-fledged maternity clinic referred to in a Ministry of Health document as the Methodist Maternity Centre, Ìkọlé (Ministry of Health, Ondo State 1953, NNAI).

The centre at Ìkọlé gained popularity among Ìtàpá women who travelled a considerable distance to deliver there, particularly from the early 1950s to the mid-1960s. Not only was it the major centre for child delivery in the area at that time, but its reputation also benefited from the presence of the British nursing sister, Miss Louise Trott, locally known as Yèyé Tọ́rọ́. Several older women mentioned going to Ìkọlé to deliver children at the centre under the supervision of Yèyé Tọ́rọ́. Her reputation for saving

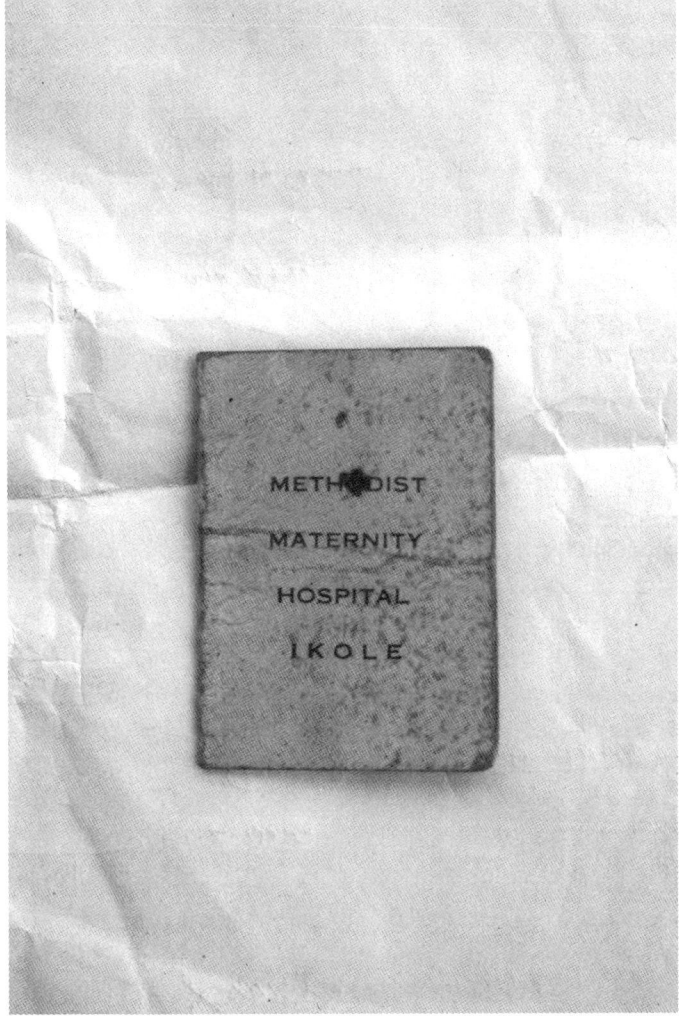

Figure 3.8 Card used for attending Methodist Maternity Hospital, Ìkọ̀lé Èkìtì, Ìtàpá Èkìtì, July 1998. (photograph by the author)

children's lives encouraged women to seek out her care and also to accede to her distinctive childbirth measures (see Figure 3.8). According to several older Ìtàpá women who delivered under Yèyé Tọ́rọ́'s guidance, it was worth the effort (some walked) required to get there:

> Yèyé Tọ́rọ́ was both a midwife and a doctor and nurses were many then in the Methodist Maternity Clinic, more than they have today.

Figure 3.9 The Ìtàpá Maternity Centre was built in 1976 and is now called the Oye Local Goverment Health Centre, Ìtàpá Èkìtì, July 1997. (photograph by the author)

For example, if you wanted to give birth to a baby in her hospital, she would ask nurses to stay around you. If there was a small problem, Yèyé Tọ́rọ́ would be called by ringing a bell and quickly she would come. As soon as the bell is rung, she knew that there must be something wrong and quickly she would come. *During Yèyé Tọ́rọ́'s time everyone liked to deliver in Ìkọ̀lé, it was a thing of glory and pride to deliver in Ìkọ̀lé.*

(YT-5, Ìtàpá-Èkìtì, July 1998; my italics)

Louise Trott left Ìkọ̀lé in around 1965 and English replacements were sent who stayed for three-year assignments. In 1975, the government took over the Centre from the Wesley Mission. According to an English midwife working there in the early 1990s, the Centre never regained its earlier popularity (S. Wray, Ìkọ̀lé-Èkìtì, April 1992).

The decline in attendance at Ìkọ̀lé may also be attributed to the development of local maternity centres in towns and villages from which women seeking Yèyé Tọ́rọ́'s assistance had come. In Ìtàpá, the building of a maternity centre began in 1963 under the auspices of the Ìtàpá Progressive Union. The centre was built, in part, to address the problems of infant and maternal mortality and of pregnant women needing to travel to neighbouring towns (Ìkọ̀lé, Ìrè, and Ìlúpéjú) for hospital deliveries, and in part as an indication of the town's social development and progress (cf. Sargent 1989).

A LOCAL DEVELOPMENT PROJECT: THE ÌTÀPÁ MATERNITY CENTRE

The building of the Ìtàpá Maternity Centre (see Figure 3.9), now known as the Oye Local Government Health Centre, Ìtàpá-Èkìtì, exemplifies local development efforts that both improve women's ability to safely bear children and serve as a conduit for innovations such as antenatal health care and contraceptive use that have consequences for fertility. According to Ìtàpá Progressive Union documents, building the maternity centre (*ilé alábiyamọ*) begun in 1963 represented a considerable organisational effort by many people. At the time of its opening in 1969, the Ìtàpá Maternity Centre was under the jurisdiction of the Ekiti North District Government. Successive local governments have paid for trained personnel to staff the centre although local people also contributed their time and efforts (see Chapter 10). When the Centre opened, many Ìtàpá women began to come there to deliver. From the 1997 survey responses based on the birth histories of 235 Ìtàpá women alone, 160 women have delivered 477 children there since its inception.

In the 1970s and first half of the 1980s, the registration and delivery fee was ₦20 while drugs were provided free of charge. After 1983, the delivery fee was raised to ₦50. However, the Centre has experienced budget cuts as federal support for social services has declined in recent years (Popoola 1993). These cuts have led to higher childbirth costs owing to increased user-fees and payments for medication (Owa et al. 1992). Presently, while the local government pays the salaries of centre personnel, women delivering at the clinic pay for childbirth expenses, which include ₦450 for delivery fees[18] and approximately ₦550 for associated items.[19] The combined expense, around ₦1,000, is considerable (for example, the monthly salary of a typist comes to approximately ₦1,300.) While many Ìtàpá women continue to deliver their children at the Centre, the high cost of child delivery along with recent discontent with some personnel appointed by the local government officials, has deterred women from delivering there.[20] Other studies from south-western Nigeria suggest that a decrease in clinic and hospital deliveries (Guyer 1997: 189) and an increase in home deliveries is occurring elsewhere in the region. Onwudiegwu's (1993) study of the effects of the depressed Nigerian economy on the use of maternal health services found a similar pattern, based on hospital records at Ọbáfẹ́mi Awólọ́wọ̀ University Teaching Hospital in Ilé-Ifẹ̀ to the south-west:

> A noticeable drop in the utilisation of maternal health services was evident. Pregnant women could no longer afford the cost of maternity

services in secondary and tertiary health institutions. There was a decline in the patronage of antenatal clinics. Hospital admissions decreased as well as hospital deliveries. In contrast to the low patronage of hospital services, both maternal and perinatal morbidity and mortality were observed to be on the increase.

(1993: 311; see also Ekwempu et al. 1990)

Data from the Ìtàpá Maternity Centre suggests a similar trend for primary health institutions. That more than half of the women who delivered at home from July 1992 to June 1997 were under thirty years old and had some secondary education signals a change in expected patterns of behaviour in this community associated with ideas about *idàgbàsókè*, or development.

Attendance at schools and at maternity clinics is viewed as an important aspect of development. Education is important, in part, because it prepares individuals for interactions with a type of medical healthcare system, of which maternity clinics are part. Childbirth in clinics is important because many believe that it reduces the risk of infant and maternal mortality.[21] Through the building of schools and a maternity centre, people in Ìtàpá have sought to 'raise up' their children and town. In particular, the attendance of educated expectant mothers at the Ìtàpá Maternity Centre was viewed as a way of keeping their children from leaving, that is, from dying. In this sense, efforts to reduce infant and child mortality represent another strategy for increasing the town's population by attracting and keeping people and hence 'raising it up' or developing it. That they have been successful in doing this to some extent is evidenced in infant mortality rates that are about half that of the national average. Nonetheless, the fact that one in five young women have experienced the loss of a child (under five years of age) suggests that despite their best efforts, uncertainties associated with the larger political economy are impeding their progress.

CONCLUSION

The comings and goings of people, particularly children, is a vital concern of Ìtàpá women and men. Whereas, in the past, young children who died were frequently spoken of as 'going back' (that is, as *àbíkú* 'born to die' children; see Renne 2002: 555), more recently parents have been successful in keeping their children from going in this sense, a situation attributed to attendance at clinics and hospitals, increased immunisation programmes, and improved sanitation in the town, all of which have led to improvements in children's chances of survival. Nonetheless, the uncertainties of life in Nigeria in the 1990s, reflected in sporadically available kerosene and transport, in national strikes and in epidemics, reinforce fears of the uncertainties of infant and child death. If the repeated departures associated with *àbíkú* ('born to die') children have declined, some infants continue to die before their first birthday. The loss of these children contributes to a sense that children can leave at any time, as one man, in explaining why he hoped to have five children, said, 'I am thinking in terms of unexpected death. Nigeria is complex now with evils daily. Anything can happen, I will risk having five children rather than risk just two' (LIM-PC30/8-53, Ìtàpá-Èkìtì, 1991). Having more – rather than fewer – children, as this man suggests, is likely to remain yet another strategy for managing the uncertainties of life during a period of deteriorating infrastructure, uncertain economics and unpredictable political leadership.

Like that man, most women and men in Ìtàpá hope to have four or five children. The total fertility rate of 5.3, based on 1997 survey data, suggests that many have succeeded in this goal. Through the births of these children and despite the deaths of some, the town is growing.[22] The in-fostering of young children by older women also adds to this youthful population, which a population pyramid of the town makes graphically clear. The coming of children to the town, through births and in-fostering, somewhat compensates for the uncertainties associated with their leaving through infant and child mortality and for the out-migration of young adults.

A further examination of the demographic dimensions of the town also suggests that a certain re-evaluation of the benefits of unlimited fertility is underway in Ìtàpá. Over 90 per cent of young women (aged fifteen to nineteen) in 1997 had some secondary education and they want the same for their children. They marry spouses of their choice and have discussions about their child-bearing preferences. That both women and men would like to have fewer children is evidenced in a decline in the total fertility rate of the town from an expected lifetime birth-rate of 6.2 children per woman in 1992 to 5.3 children by 1997. These younger people would not want to out-foster their children and many prefer not to in-foster others. Rather, they would like children whom they themselves can care for well, in terms of education, health, housing, food and clothing. Whereas the ideal that one must have followers – in this case, children – is strongly supported by both women and men, there is a shift in thinking about quantities of children in favour of their qualities, particularly those associated with education. Several people cited the proverb *Ọmọ tó jáfáfá kan sọsọ, ó yá ju igba irúnbí ọmọ* ('One outstanding child is better than 200 useless children'). These re-evaluations of fertility and the proper development of a child are related to shifting assessments of social relationships, reflected in changes in thinking about constituting a marriage, about blood ties and family obligations, and about relations with the dead. These are discussed in the following three chapters.

PART II

BODIES, PERSONS AND SOCIAL RELATIONS

4

WOMEN'S BODIES, VIRGINITY AND MARRIAGE

For this reason a man will leave his father and mother and be joined to his wife, and the two will become one flesh.

Ephesians 5: 25, 31

Changing social practices, particularly the demise of arranged marriage, have contributed to changes in premarital sexuality in much of southwestern Nigeria (Guyer 1994; Mann 1986; Olúsànyà 1970). In the early part of the century, young women's activities were closely watched, virginity was prescribed and their marriages arranged. Once sexually mature (when they had begun to menstruate), they would be brought to their husband's house where they would have intercourse for the first time with their husbands and their status as virgins would be confirmed. Ideally, all young women who moved to their husband's houses were virgins. However, the importance of virginity (*ibálé*) rested as much on ideas about fertility (Boddy 1989: 55) as on women's chastity being a point of pride for men (Olúsànyà 1967: 15; Fadipę 1970: 66; Caldwell et al. 1991). Many believed that if a woman met her husband as a virgin, she would immediately become pregnant, as one older woman explained: 'It was traditionally believed that any woman who was a virgin will have to get pregnant the first month. The belief was that she had not spoiled herself before moving to her husband's house' (LVI-7, Ìtàpá-Èkìtì, 1992). Two related ideas supported this claim: women who were virgins had not 'spoiled' (*ibàjẹ́*) themselves (that is, their fertility) through socially unsanctioned sexual liaisons, and fecundity was related to one's social and moral behaviour. Thus, young women had an interest in remaining virgins as they were not only socially rewarded for this behaviour by their families and by their husbands, but also because they believed that they would be biologically rewarded, by immediate pregnancy.

With the introduction of a colonial court system and procedures for divorce (through repayment of bridewealth) in the first part of the twentieth century as well as other changes in the political economy of colonial Nigeria, the system of arranged marriages was undermined (Lloyd 1968a; Caldwell et al. 1991; Renne 1992: 222). A different method of establishing marital relations emerged, with important consequences for premarital sexuality and fertility. Eventually what developed was a pattern whereby young women moved to their husband's houses after developing sexual relations with their future husbands, often after becoming pregnant. In some cases, the pending child came to be what cemented these relationships rather than bridewealth or other preliminary marital exchanges. While these exchanges might be carried out at a later date, this shift had consequences for virginity. Instead of being thought of as enhancing her fertility through socially correct behaviour, a virgin came to be perceived by many as socially backward (*óluukoo* or *òtu*) – because virginity was associated with arranged marriage – and as anti-social (*sùègbè*), because young women's attendance at social events and subsequent sexual forays were one way of finding a husband. Recently, some have even come to associate virginity with certain diseases and conditions identified with infertility, such as gonorrhoea (*àtọ̀sí*), epilepsy (*wárápá*) and amenorrhoea. Thus, changes in marital arrangements have led to a reversal of the moral evaluation of virginity by many women from something good to something bad, a reversal that may be expressed in terms of health and fertility. In order to understand the process whereby the perception of virginity, marriage and fertility have changed over the past seventy-five years, this chapter considers the comments made by ninety-five women between the ages of fifteen and eighty living in Ìtàpá-Èkìtì in 1992.

Older townswomen, for whom virginity was critically important, had well defined ideas about what physiologically constituted virginity and its loss. Yet some of the younger women, for whom virginity is no longer important and is even potentially problematic, did not know what evidenced virginity at all. This reassessment of what constitutes virginity underscores the interpretive nature of such readings of the body which, grounded in a particular social and historical context, 'must be regarded as a narrative of culture in anatomical disguise' (Laqueur 1990: 236). For these Èkìtì Yoruba women, the shift in the perception of the *ibálé*-hymen – from something whose presence was preserved and celebrated at marriage to an old-fashioned tradition which should be quickly dispensed with – relates to changing ideas about what constitutes 'enlightened' behaviour and enhances fertility, which in turn reflects shifts in the basis of authority and knowledge in Èkìtì society in colonial and post-independence Nigeria.

THE MEANINGS OF VIRGINITY

What women living in Ìtàpá-Èkìtì meant by the term virginity, of which the meaning was influenced by local knowledge of the body as well as by social and political concerns, cannot be assumed. Virginity was referred to generally by the term *ibálé*, which also more specifically refers to a part of the body.[1] One traditional healer (*onísègùn*) described its bodily manifestation as looking like a red 'plastic-film wrapping' covering the vagina (*òbò* or *ojú ara*), something like an 'internal security system'.[2] This vaginal covering was also described by an older woman as being:

> Something like blood, very thick and immediately the man was able to penetrate, the thing will just break and that shows the girl has been dis-virgined ... It was called *ibálé* and at the same time *ayèré*. It was the thing that stained the white cloth and shows that one has been dis-virgined.
>
> (LVI-1, Ìtàpá-Èkìtì, 1992)

Another, younger, woman compared it to the breaking of a palm kernel:

> It was usually difficult to be able to penetrate the first time. For about three hours the man will still be trying because it will be very hard. And it was painful that day. It will just be as if someone was trying to crack a palm kernel. If the woman was still a virgin, immediately the man was able to penetrate, blood will just stain the white cloth that has been spread on the bed. That shows that she has not known a man before.
>
> (LVI-4, Ìtàpá-Èkìtì, 1992)

Several other women mentioned this hardness of the *ibálé*: 'The place was hard and thick and when the man was able to penetrate, the place will soften, then blood will come out' (SVI-14, Ìtàpá-Èkìtì, 1992).

These descriptions are, to the best of my understanding, what physiologically constitutes the 'hymen' for Èkìtì women. The western perception of virginity as a particular bodily state defined by the presence of a particular bit of anatomy, the membranous hymen which when pierced results in bleeding, is similar in some ways to the Èkìtì perception of virginity, but is not the same. For example, no woman mentioned the use of manual examinations to ascertain whether the *ibálé*-membrane was intact. Rather, for them, the membrane – the reddish plastic-like covering which is hard and then softens after penetration – and the resulting blood were conflated. If the *ibálé*-membrane is present, there must be blood, as explained by one older woman:

> Q: Do you know of any example when a girl insisted that she was a virgin but she didn't bleed?
> A: There was nothing like that because it was compulsory in the past that when dis-virgined, you must see blood. If blood was not seen, it means that one has been dis-virgined before.
>
> (LVI-10, Ìtàpá-Èkìtì, 1992)

As if to emphasise this point, there is no linguistic distinction made in Yoruba between the hymen, hymeneal blood and virginity. The word *ibálé* refers to all of them – to the membranous thing (*ibálé*) that is pierced or penetrated (*jà*), to the blood-like thing (*ibálé* or *ayèré*), thick and dark, that stains the white cloth which confirms a woman's virginity, also referred to as *ibálé*.

CONTROLLING VIRGINITY

The importance of virginity was related to ideas about fertility and about the control of young women's bodies. By restricting the movements of young women within and outside houses, parents protected the integrity of the *ibálé*, much as the *ibálé* itself, that 'internal security system', protected their future fertility from being 'spoiled' or 'broken'.[3] The power of fathers to exert such control, and the consequences when this power was undermined during the period of British colonial rule, is evidenced in related shifts in imagery of the house and the female body. As Turner (1984: 2) has observed, there are 'parallels between the idea of government of the body and the regime of a given society'.

In Èkìtì society, a father's authority over members of his house-compound – his wives and their children – was reinforced by an ideology of patrilineal descent (discussed in Chapter 2). This ideology was represented in everyday ways by the power of the *baálé* (literally, 'father of the house') over the passage of people though a central front door (*ojú ilé*), both controlling and protecting inhabitants on 'the inside' from 'the outside'. Thus, a prospective suitor soliciting an arranged marriage would be 'screened' by a young woman's father; the girl herself would be hidden in the house, as one woman explained, 'In the past if a girl is given to a man and the man comes to greet her in the house, the girl will be hidden. If the girl was seeing him off, she will turn her back to him.'

Once arrangements had been made between this man and the prospective bride's father, annual payments of yams (*iṣu ọbutan*) and labour (*ọ̀wẹ̀* or *ẹ̀bẹ̀sẹ́*) were given to the father. This process culminated in the payment of bridewealth, *idána*, which was timed to take place after the appearance of the menarche. The veiled bride would then be taken through the doorway of her father's house, outside, to her husband's house where her entry was marked in various ritual ways. Later in the evening, she was uncovered both literally and figuratively by her husband, after which the bloodied *aṣọ ibálé* cloth was publicly displayed. The cloth would then be taken to the bride's parents, marking the successful conclusion of their control. She was thereafter 'covered' by members of her husband's household who awaited her first child which was expected to arrive shortly.

OLDER WOMEN'S EXPERIENCES

This sequence of events was described in interviews of thirty-eight older women (aged thirty-five to eighty), twenty-one of whom had experienced arranged marriages, who were asked an extended set of open ended questions about their experiences and perceptions of virginity (see Table 4.1, and Appendix I). Of these thirty-eight women, 82 per cent (n=31) were virgins when they moved to their husbands' houses; this was in contrast to the fifty-seven younger women (aged fifteen to thirty-four) who were also

Table 4.1 Early sexual experience of Ìtàpá-Èkìtì women, aged 35–70+[a]

Age group	Arranged marriage		Virgin when married[b]		Ever divorced		Pregnant when married		Virginity increases fertility		Virginity causes disease	
	Yes	No	Yes	No	Yes	No	Yes	No	Yes	No	Yes[c]	No
35–39 (n=4)	–	100 (4)	–	100 (4)	–	d (2)	d (2)	d (1)	d (1)	–	25 (1)	75 (3)
40–49 (n=8)	12 (1)	88 (7)	63 (5)	37 (3)	12 (1)	88 (7)	67 (2)	33 (1)	50 (4)	50 (4)	12 (1)	88 (7)
50–59 (n=7)	71 (5)	29 (2)	100 (7)	–	29 (2)	71 (5)	–	–	86 (6)	14 (1)	–	100 (7)
60–69 (n=13)	92 (12)	8 (1)	100 (13)	–	23 (3)	77 (10)	–	–	77 (10)	23 (3)	–	100 (13)
70+ (n=6)	67 (4)	33 (2)	100 (6)	–	33 (2)	67 (4)	–	–	100 (6)	–	–	100 (6)
Total (n=38)	58 (22)	42 (16)	82 (31)	18 (7)	d (8)	d (28)	d (3)	d (2)	d (28)	d (8)	d (2)	d (36)

a Figures appear as percentages with numbers in parentheses.
b Virgin when moving to husband's house; if no, pregnant column indicates whether woman was pregnant before she moved.
c In both cases, the disease mentioned was *warapa* (epilepsy).
d Data missing.

interviewed, of whom only 28 per cent (n=16) were (or said they would be) virgins when they moved (see Table 4.2). According to older women, coming to one's husband's house as a virgin was a thing of pride. Of these thirty-one virgin older women, twenty-five were also given something as a 'virginity payment' – often a specially prepared meal of roasted yam with red oil (*ègèyè òwúrò*), cloth or money. The proverb *Eni bá ti bá ibálé dé'lé okọ a jẹ ègèyè òwúrò sùgbón ẹni tí kò bá ti bá dé'lé okọ kò ní rí ègèyè òwúrò jẹ*, 'Anyone who comes to her husband's house a virgin will eat roasted yam but anyone who does not will not eat it', refers to the special dish given to reward a young woman's socially correct behavior. Yet while no women over fifty years who was interviewed said she had not been a virgin at marriage, there must have been some instances of this since several pejorative terms were used to describe such women, for example, *oníjẹ̀kújẹ* ('someone who eats around'), *aláìpé* ('something is missing'), *àìkàrágbá* ('broken calabash'), *àlòkù* ('something used'), *àjọdí ikòkò* ('broken pot'), *alágbèrè* ('owner of low morals'; prostitute) and *onísẹkúsẹ* ('corrupted'). Older women said that no husband would disclaim a non-virgin wife, but that the social ostracism that went with being found 'a broken calabash' would undermine a wife's position within the marriage in the future.

Associated with these ideas of something being missing, used or broken was the idea that such women could have difficulty getting pregnant. Indeed,

Table 4.2 Early sexual experience of Ekiti women, aged 15–35, 1992[a]

Age group	Marital status		Virgin at marriage		Virginity		Disease from virginity		
	S	M	Y	N	Good	Bad	Y	N	DK[b]
15–19[c] (n=7)	100 (7)	–	57 (4)	43 (3)	29 (2)	71 (5)	29 (2)	71 (5)	–
20–24[c] (n=21)	91 (19)	9 (2)	14 (4)	86 (17)	33 (7)	67 (14)	47 (10)	33 (7)	19 (4)
25–29 (n=23)	39 (9)	61 (14)	26 (6)	74 (17)	22 (5)	78 (18)	39 (9)	44 (10)	17 (4)
30–34 (n=6)	–	100 (6)	50 (3)	50 (3)	50 (3)	50 (3)	17 (1)	83 (5)	–
Total (n=57)	61 (35)	39 (22)	28 (16)	72 (41)	30 (17)	70 (40)	39 (22)	47 (27)	14 (8)

a Figures appear as percentages with numbers in parentheses.
b DK: did not know.
c For age groups 15–19 and 20–24, these figures represent their present states, virgins or non-virgins, and not necessarily whether they will be virgins when they marry.

a woman who did not get pregnant during the first month of marriage could be accused of having 'spoiled' herself through prior sexual relations: 'If a girl did not get pregnant on time or in the first month ..., the man will be saying that she has mis-used herself before coming to his house and that is why she has not become pregnant' (LVI-2, Ìtàpá-Èkitì, 1992). This thinking about the need for protection from things 'from outside' is also reflected in ideas about bodies and pregnancy.

Protected thresholds and imminent fertility

The idea of the protected threshold-doorway of a house, referred to as the *ojú ilé* (literally 'eye of the house') is linguistically related to the vaginal threshold, the *ojú ara* ('eye of the body') with its covering, the *ibálé*, protecting the passageway between the inside (*inú*, womb) and the outside (*aiyé*, world).[4] A house's front doorway represents the opening between inner domestic and outer public space, just as the vaginal opening distinguishes between inner and outer domains. The Yoruba phrase for womb, *ilé omo* ('house or room of the child'), further reinforces this comparison between the house and the female body, both of which may be perceived as structures which protect those within from outside dangers.

This representation of protection and vulnerability associated with covered thresholds and with the inside and outside of houses and bodies corresponded with the authority of fathers to regulate the passage between these two spaces. Their authority to control these movements was reinforced not only by their status as heads of households, but also through their ritual knowledge used to control the passage of bodies between spiritual domains, for example at funerals and at childbirth.⁵ However, with the incorporation of Èkìtì region within the boundaries of Lagos Protectorate of colonial Nigeria, agreed upon in 1893, the power of the father-*baálé* was undermined, initially by the institution of a colonial court system and later by the introduction of schools.

These changes in the bases of authority and knowledge were not immediately or uniformly felt throughout Èkìtì. It was only after the formation of the Northeastern District (consisting of Ìjèṣà and Èkìtì regions) in 1899, that the consequences of the British presence became tangible. For example, a sense of the presence of colonial officials (described from the British point of view) is evidenced in the comments of the 'Travelling Commissioner' for the District, Major Reeve Tucker, who toured Èkìtì in 1899:

> I have called in all the tributary villages to the capitals of the several Ekiti Kingdoms and have placed the Bales [*sic*; village heads and local quarter heads]⁶ securely under their Kings. The Bales who were endeavouring to make themselves independent, a lingering remnant of their old wars and disputes, I have effectively placed under their proper kings. At each capital I held a palaver and explained the Government policy to them.
>
> (de la Mothe 1921, NNAI)

The reality of British control was made more evident with the establishment of a separate Ekiti Division in 1913 (de la Mothe 1921) and the building of an administrative centre in Adó-Èkìtì in 1914 (Ògúntúyì 1979). Despite the fact that British colonial officials instituted a form of governance known as 'indirect rule' whereby traditional chiefs administered everyday local affairs, there was no doubt where the political buck stopped. British officers retained control of more important political decisions, underscoring the fact that a fundamental shift in the basis of authority had occurred in colonial Nigeria (Àjàyí 2000; Beidelman 1971; Chanock 1985).

Attending 'customary' court

One particular innovation served as the catalyst for the demise of arranged marriage, namely the introduction of procedures for divorce in colonial courts introduced by the British. On 1 March 1920, Èkìtì ọbas (kings) meeting at Adó-Èkìtì agreed to support the British initiative for the establishment of a system of Native Authority courts which included rules for divorce (Ògúntúyì 1979: 130; cf. Caldwell et al. 1991; Renne 1992). As a result of this agreement, young women were able to extricate themselves from arranged marriages (Lloyd 1968a) by repaying bridewealth (or a comparable sum for brideservice) to the original suitor who had made such payments. By doing so, young Èkìtì women and men were able to select spouses of their choice. During the 1930s and 1940s, many took advantage of this opportunity, as described by women from Ìtàpá-Èkìtì (see Table 4.1). However, other aspects of the marriage process remained the same during this period, at least in this rural north-eastern Èkìtì town. Once bridewealth had been returned to the 'first husband' and permission to marry had been granted by her father, the traditional marriage ritual proceeded as if an arranged marriage was being performed. Young women maintained both the practice of going to their husbands' houses as virgins and the idea that virginity assured fertility. Thus, in the case of one sixty-year-old woman, she divorced her arranged marriage husband before actually moving to his house and was then able to move to her chosen husband's house a virgin:

> My father arranged the marriage between myself and my [first] husband ... But when I grew up to go to his house, I told my father that I cannot marry the man again, that I have seen the man who I love and would like to marry. So I divorced the man in Native Authority Court ... we went to court and [my husband] paid back the dowry to the first man. He paid £15 and since then we have been living together as husband and wife.
> Q: Did your father become angry for leaving the man he chose for you?
> A: Nobody became angry because of that since if you did not love him, you could reject him and marry the one you loved.
> (LVI-10, Ìtàpá-Èkìtì, 1992)

This incident took place in the early 1950s. Marrying for love rather than by arrangement expanded these women's social options although their sexuality remained circumscribed in part because of the belief that virginity enhanced one's fertility. As this woman remarked, 'it was the *ibálé* [virginity] that made me get pregnant immediately and I also believe that it was the work of God'.

This pattern of choosing one's husband but remaining a virgin persisted during the 1960s. However, by the early 1970s sexual intercourse before marriage had become commonplace, as may be seen from the interviews of fifty-seven younger Ìtàpá-Èkìtì women (see Table 4.2). In 1992, women between forty and forty-five years of age experienced this shift most dramatically – five were virgins at marriage and three were not – compared with the women aged fifty years and older, all of whom said they had been virgins (see Table 4.1). Furthermore, of the three non-virgin women of the younger group, two were pregnant when they moved to their husbands' houses. Such behaviour would have been considered scandalous in their mothers' time.

CHANGING PERCEPTIONS OF SEXUALITY AND FERTILITY

One of the problems of arranged marriage and the prohibition of premarital sexuality had been the possibility that a woman or man would be infertile. When asked whether nowadays it was good or bad to be a virgin when coming to one's husband's house, one woman answered: 'Virginity is not good. Because in the past that we are talking about, we still have some people who used to marry an impotent man or a woman who does not have "nature" [i.e. frigid or infertile]' (LVI-9, Ìtàpá-Èkìtì, 1992). Consequently some came to see premarital sexual relations as a necessary part in the process of selecting a spouse. Furthermore, despite the prevalence of an ideology that women immediately became pregnant when virgins, some people began to question this belief:

> We have some people who will be a virgin and when they got to their husband's house they will not get pregnant until they visit a diviner while we have those who were not virgins and immediately they moved to their husband's house, they got pregnant. It all depends on destiny. So I do not believe that being a non-virgin means that one will have a problem getting pregnant.
>
> (LVI-11, Ìtàpá-Èkìtì, 1992)

Rather than trust in one's own or a future wife's virginity to ensure fertility, the uncertainties of fertility and of choosing and keeping a wife (or husband) could be solved by getting pregnant. In the 1950s young women did not readily go to their future husbands' houses. However, by the end of the next decade they did, particularly as opportunities for meetings between adolescents of the opposite sex increased with the advent of universal primary education in the Western (Yoruba speaking) Region of Nigeria in 1955. Many parents took advantage of this programme, sending their daughters as well as their sons to local primary schools. These parents began to realise that education enhanced their daughters' chances of marrying well (since educated men preferred wives who could comport themselves in an 'enlightened' fashion) and increased their ability to acquire white-collar employment.[7] However, school attendance not only meant that they were exposed to new ideas and fashions in school, to 'enlightenment' or 'civilisation', but also that young women's physical movements were un-monitored, as the comment of one older woman illustrates:

> Civilisation has come and things have changed. Is it children who are fifteen years old who have become pregnant and go to their husbands' houses without taking anything from him [i.e. bridewealth] who will be virgins? All this was caused by the school because they were exposed to immoral acts. And they will say they are going to school, they will just branch to their boyfriend's house which no one could do

80 BODIES, PERSONS AND SOCIAL RELATIONS

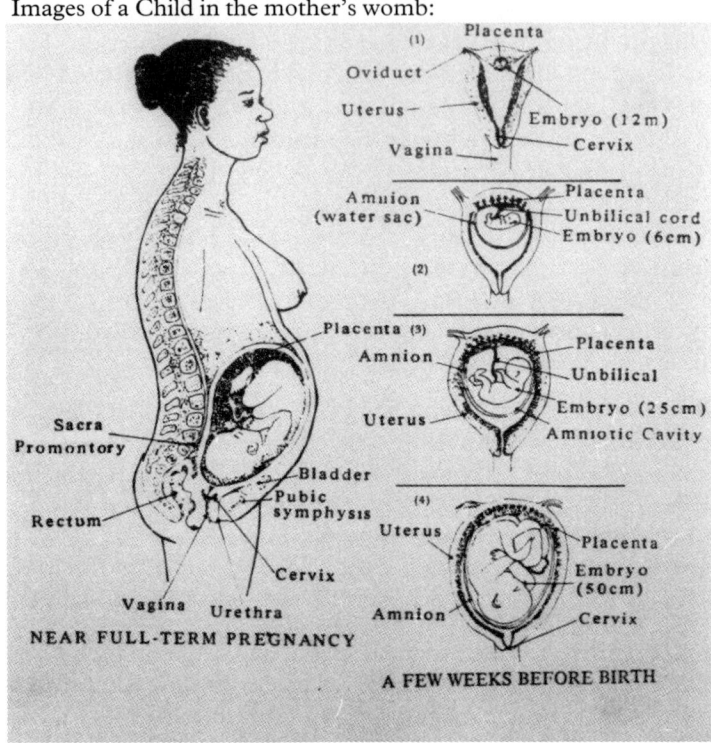

Figure 4.1 Illustration of ovulation cycle, from health textbook. (Usua & Dada 1978: 129)

in the past. So because of this, virginity is uncommon today.
(LVI-10, Ìtàpá-Èkìtì, 1992)

Not surprisingly, of the thirty-eight older women interviewed, over half (58 per cent) mentioned schooling and civilisation as major factors in the decline of virginity among young women. Others attributed increased premarital sexuality to a more open attitude toward sexuality in general, including exposure to television and videos as well as more relaxed sexual behaviour at home:

> It is what the parents were doing in their presence that they want to be copying like [the man] having fun with the mother in the presence of the children. In the past days, it was never done in the day. It was normally done at night when nobody will see them. But things have changed today. Some children will be playing among themselves and will be telling each other that this is what their mother and father did

yesterday, that they are going to practise it. All these things hinder virginity.

(LVI-4, Ìtàpá-Èkìtì, 1992)

Like their educated male counterparts, young women who attended school were likely to disparage certain practices associated with a parochial past, preferring modern, 'enlightened' behaviour instead. Hiding in the house, away from the eyes of men, came to be considered as 'antisocial' behaviour (*sùègbè*). Thus, when young men pressed girlfriends and fiancées for premarital sexual relations, young women may have been inclined to concur not only for emotional reasons but in order to appear 'enlightened', rather than traditionally chaste. These changes in premarital sexual behaviour reflected a new set of values related to individual choice of spouses. Furthermore, exposure to new concepts such as Western models of reproductive biology (see Figure 4.1) taught in school undermined the idea that virginity could enhance fertility.

Premarital sexuality and antisocial, unhealthy virgins

Of the twenty-three young women born between 1962 and 1966, 74 per cent said (in 1992) that they had not or would not come to their husbands' houses as virgins (see Table 4.2). Furthermore, 78 per cent of these women evaluated being a virgin as a 'bad' thing that could cause problems for young women in several ways. It is difficult to know how young girls felt about pressure from boyfriends or to what extent they themselves encouraged premarital sex. Some were clearly uncomfortable about their acquiescence, as was one woman who had become pregnant before moving to her husband's house:

> It was not my father who arranged the marriage for me. I was moving with a man and when I wanted to travel, the man used a trick to invite me to his house so that he can test whether I was still a virgin. He had prepared a white cloth which he used. When I got to his house, we had fun and I was dis-virgined. Immediately that month I got pregnant but I was still living in my father's house. My father called the man to come and take me. So he brought things for *idána* and that was how I got married to my husband.

(LVI-13, Ìtàpá-Èkìtì, 1992)

While this woman said that she had been 'tricked' into going to her fiancé's house, others explained their behaviour differently, saying that they had not been 'reborn' Christians at the time or that they feared losing their boyfriends' affection. Yet others saw it as an opportunity for increased 'enjoyment' and sociability. Furthermore, for some, the continued presence of the *ibálé* reflected not only antisocial behaviour but also the possibility of a hidden disease, which would actually lead to infertility. One of the most

Table 4.3 Diseases associated with virginity, Ìtàpá-Èkìtì, 1992

Disease	Symptoms	Times mentioned
Àgàn (barrenness)	Cannot get pregnant; no children	2
Aisan ìdílé (inherited disease)	Types of madness; feeble-minded	1
Akíríboto (no vagina)	Runs from men; frigid	4
Àtọ̀sí (gonorrhea)	Genital ulceration; white pus; painful urination	5
Somuroro (breast ailment)	Red, shiny, swollen breasts	1
Wárápá (epilepsy)	Convulsions	3
Dindinrin (imbecile)	Madness, unusual behaviour; mute	2

frequently mentioned conditions described to me was *akíríboto*, 'no vagina', which led young women to run away from men (see Table 4.3).⁸ Several women also mentioned that a woman who remained a virgin might be difficult to penetrate and therefore undesirable:

> It is not easy for a woman [who is still a virgin] to get pregnant because it will be difficult for the husband to dis-virgin her. It is said that as one grows older the *ibálé* will be getting harder [to penetrate].
> (SVI-17, Ìtàpá-Èkìtì, 1992)

Some women even described young men as being afraid of having intercourse with a virgin wife:

> It is not common nowadays and people will be saying that such a woman is not social and as a result the husband will fear that something is wrong with the woman and he may send her out.
> (SVI-22, Ìtàpá-Èkìtì, 1992)

However, young women mentioned other diseases related to infertility more generally:

> There are diseases [associated with virginity]. Because when I was still a virgin one man told me that as old as I am that I'm still a virgin, that if he knew my mother he would tell her that she should take me to a diviner.
> (SVI-26, Ìtàpá-Èkìtì, 1992)

A similar situation developed with regard to menstruation, also perceived as a necessary precursor to fertility. Women distinguished the blood of *ibálé* from that of menstruation (*nǹkan oṣùurẹ̀*; Abraham 1958: 492), the former only coming out once while the latter appeared monthly, but in the past a young girl who failed to menstruate before first intercourse was believed to risk infertility by 'spoiling herself'. Such thinking – that premenstrual intercourse would cause menstrual disorder and a delay in pregnancy – discouraged young unmarried women from engaging in premarital sex that could mar their virgin status and marriage prospects. By following the socially approved sequence of virginity, menstruation and marital intercourse, bodily disorder – amenorrhoea and delayed fertility – could be avoided.

Presently, young women believe that they risk infertility if their menstruation is delayed and they do nothing to ameliorate the situation. Delayed menarche, now defined as not beginning menstruation by approximately fifteen to twenty years of age (Renne 2001a), can, like virginity, be viewed as a sign of possible infertility which nonetheless has several remedies, including premarital sexual intercourse. Several women mentioned intercourse as a way to stimulate menarche, based on the idea that intercourse 'forces' out menstrual blood, as one woman explained:

> Medicine can be done to bring it [menstruation] out. But losing one's virginity can make it begin ... It depends on the body system of every body. Some people may have a strong body and they may not be able to see their menses on time.
> (LVIa-27, Ìtàpá-Èkìtì,1992)

Additionally, traditional medicine may also be taken to stimulate the onset of menstruation for young women:

> Things can be done if a girl does not see her menses. Her parents will take her to a *babaláwo*, and *ikó odidẹ* [red parrot feather (Apter 1992: 113–114; Buckley 1985: 228] with ... *osun* [red camwood] will be mixed together with some other things and the girl will have to see her menses after she has used it.
> (LVIa-30, Ìtàpá-Èkìtì, 1992)

Like young women who do nothing to counter amenorrhoea, young woman who balk at the social norm of coming to their husbands' house as non-virgins risk being considered infertile. The recentness of these shifts in thinking is evidenced by the remarks of one seventy-year-old woman:

> Q: In the past, were any diseases associated with women who were virgins?
> A: There were no diseases associated with them. It is nowadays that people will be saying that she is having a disease.
> Q: What kind of disease?
> A: It is you children of today who know that! I do not know.
> (LVI-35, Ìtàpá-Èkìtì, 1992)

What appears to have happened in this Èkìtì town, and probably in other parts of south-western Nigeria as well, is that changing social arrangements have led to a moral reassessment of premarital sexuality which is reflected in ideas about fertility and disease.

OTHER VIEWS AND PARADIGMS

Not all young women subscribe to this view of virginity as 'bad'. Instead they have chosen to maintain their virgin status as a private matter between themselves and their husbands:

> Q: Since you were a virgin when you were married, did people think that you were having a disease?
> A: I don't know what people were saying because not everyone knew I was a virgin at that time.
> Q: Was your virginity announced then?
> A: It was not announced because nowadays things have changed. It is only the husband who will know and that is all.
> (SVI-17, Ìtàpá-Èkìtì, 1992)

Some young women have also redefined what being a virgin at marriage means. Rather than refer to the specific day one moved to one's husband's house, a woman who meets her fiancé a virgin, has intercourse with him alone, and subsequently marries him may refer to herself as a virgin at marriage. For example, one twenty-three-year-old woman remarked, 'Yes, I was a virgin when I got married last year because it was the man who dis-virgined me whom I married' (SVI-6, Ìtàpá-Èkìtì, 1992).

While it was more common for young women to mention disease in association with virginity, some, such as this unmarried secondary school student, held other opinions that indicate the presence of alternate paradigms:

> You know there are so many diseases that one can contract from men. So as to not be affected with all these diseases, I will wait until I get married. Because once a girl is dis-virgined, she will think that she is free and can meet many men and can contract disease.
> (SVI-57, Ìtàpá-Èkìtì, 1992)

For this young woman, disease is associated with a *non-virgin* state – not a virgin one – which implicitly may threaten one's fertility, not demonstrate it. For another woman, the prospect of abortion associated with the loss of virginity was a more explicit threat to fertility:

> Some of our girls today that were dis-virgined before they moved to their husband's house may, because of that, [become pregnant and] spoil themselves by doing abortion. And this may result in their not being able to get pregnant when they want to because she has wasted some of the children she was supposed to have.
> (SVI-42, Ìtàpá-Èkìtì, 1992)

These alternate assessments – that one's virginity is a private matter, that one can maintain one's virginity by marrying one's first and only boyfriend, and that non-virgin status may lead to disease and infertility – suggest that just as ideas about virginity have changed in the last seventy years, these ideas are themselves subject to re-evaluation. What stands out in all these shifting interpretations of virginity is the importance of fertility. Despite the many changes in Èkìtì society, certain ideas continue which, if not held by the majority, are nonetheless maintained by some. For example, the idea of 'spoiling oneself' persists, even while it has multiple and sometimes contradictory meanings: some associating it with keeping one's virginity, others with the loss of virginity, and most with frequent recourse to abortion.[9] Several women voiced a continued belief in the relationship between virginity and pregnancy:

> A non-virgin girl may have difficulties in getting pregnant because it was believed that she had spoiled herself. Because I still have some of my age mates who were not virgins when they got married that up till this present moment, they are unable to get pregnant. And at times, I used to think that perhaps they have spoiled and mis-used themselves that made them not to be able to get pregnant immediately.
> (LVI-21, Ìtàpá-Èkìtì, 1992)

Some parents and others in positions of authority have sought to counter the negative imagery of virginity as unhealthy, antisocial and unmodern by different images related to Christian associations with sexuality and to beliefs about discipline and disease. For example, in one manual on sexual education and marital guidance, a professor at the University of Lagos writes:

> Virginity is no longer given the high premium, which it deserves. Some youngsters sometimes say that only 'novice' and girls who are not sociable will remain virgins on their wedding day. This is a misplaced moral value. The best way for a woman to enhance her prestige and honor in marriage is to remain a virgin to the time of her marriage.
> (Ọlayinka 1987: 64)

He also suggests that a man who is impatient for sex and flirts with other women increases 'the possibility of your catching a venereal disease' (Ọlayinka 1987: 65), countering the idea of unhealthy virginity.

While it is unclear how widely these alternative interpretations of virginity are presently being accepted by younger women and men, they represent some of the ways in which definitions of virginity may be reinterpreted in the future. A few younger townswomen did mention Christianity in explaining their positive attitudes toward virginity:

> It is good because the woman will not be put to shame when married and also the man will like her very well ... I will not be a virgin because I have been dis-virgined and it was a mistake – I was not a born-again Christian then.
> (SVI-30, Ìtàpá-Èkìtì, 1992)

> Q: Are any diseases associated with being a virgin?
> A: People may not think that there is any disease. It may be that the girl is a good Christian and maybe the girl is self-disciplined.
>
> (SVI-28, Ìtàpá-Èkìtì, 1992)

Thus, when one sixteen-year-old woman was asked whether she would be a virgin when she married, she replied, 'I will be a virgin when married because I have made a vow with my God.'

Consequences for fertility

As these reinterpretations of virginity, marriage, fertility, menstruation and disease make clear, changes in the moral evaluations of pre-marital sexuality can be rapid and dramatic, as one sixty-year-old woman, who witnessed these changes within her lifetime, observed:

> It should be good [to move to one's husband's house as a virgin] but things have changed. What you children today are taking to be a thing of joy [pre-marital sexual intercourse] was not so in the past. And things that were good in the past [virginity] are now no longer good today because everything has changed.
>
> (LVI-22, Ìtàpá-Èkìtì, 1992)

The shift in ideas about premarital sexuality and in the perception of virginity in relation to fertility reflects changes in inter-generational relations of authority – between sons, daughters and their parents – in part associated with Western education. The belief that virginity led to immediate pregnancy was related to a particular type of society in which marriages were arranged, in which daughters were 'protected' in their fathers' houses until marriage, in which brideservice and bridewealth were presented to the bride's father, and in which ritual knowledge was controlled mainly by male elders. During the colonial period, this system of arranged marriage declined, and pre-marital sexual behaviour and bases of knowledge changed as men and women, seeing themselves as Western-educated and 'enlightened', sought other means of establishing marital relations. The belief in fertile virgins was undermined by this complex of events and by the obvious fact of fertile non-virginal ones. Indeed, during the 1970s, getting pregnant before marriage became one of the primary ways of establishing one's fertility. To be considered socially correct, modern and fertile, one should be educated and should not be a virgin. These changes associated with acquiring a spouse and in redefining to some extent what marriage means have had implications for fertility in other ways as well. For example, in arranged marriage a husband and wife might become fond of each other after spending years together and bearing children but the idea that they should love one another was not a critical factor in their relationship. What was important was the successful conception, bearing and raising of children,

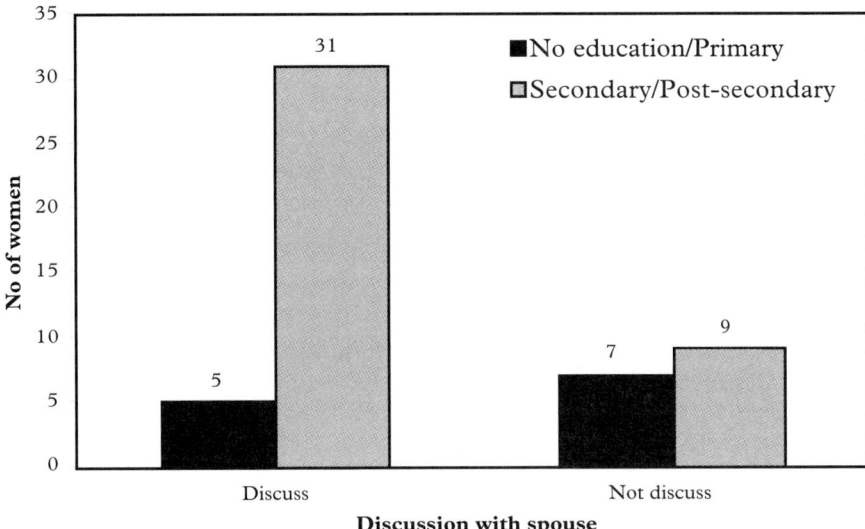

Figure 4.2 Educational levels of women who discuss childbearing with spouses

a goal that was taken for granted. Talking with one's spouse about having children would have been uncommon since it was an unspoken assumption that immediately after marriage a woman would become pregnant. Ideally, she would continue to get pregnant repeatedly, after the requisite three-year gestation and nursing period were completed each time, until her first child married (Orùbuloyè 1981a). Furthermore, speaking about the specific number of children wanted would be even more unusual, since such an outcome was ultimately 'up to God' (cf. Oyèmádé and Ògúnmúyiwá 1981: 110) and not within human control.[10]

The process that affected this way of thinking began with young women and men going with their chosen spouses to a Native Authority court to divorce arranged-marriage husbands in order 'to marry the one you loved', as one woman cited earlier explained. The idea of marrying for love contributed to an intimate communication lacking in arranged marriage. Later, as young women began attending primary schools, this sense of agency in selecting a spouse, along with the ideal of love relationships, supported spousal discussions of, among other things, their childbearing aspirations. It was not that their preferences were all that different from other members of Èkìtì society or that there were considerable differences between spouses on this score (Bánkọlé 1995). In 1992, Ìtàpá women and men both said they wanted at least four children (see Chapter 3; Renne 1993d). In interviews conducted in the previous year, 61 per cent of women and 81 per cent of men said that they discussed their childbearing aspirations with spouses or future spouses.[11] These discussions between husbands and wives about childbearing represent a major departure from earlier practices.

In Èkìtì, widespread attendance of women at school since the mid-1950s appears to have had an effect on the discussion of family size. For women, the relationship between education and those saying they discussed family size was statistically significant (see Figure 4.2).[12] This connection between love, education and joint discussions about childbearing was made explicit by one eighteen-year-old woman secondary student:

> Q: Have you discussed the number of children you want to have with your boyfriend?
> A: Yes, we discussed it and resolved to have four children.
> Q: Who decides the number of children, husband or wife?
> A: Any one of them especially where there is love.
> Q: What of where there is no love?
> A: The husband will pronounce and have the final say in this case.
> (LIW-OC20/8-44, Ìtàpá-Èkìtì, 1991)

What appears to be emerging is a form of marital relationship, also expressed in new ways of thinking about virginity and fertility, based on an ideal of love between husband and wife (Hollos and Larsen 1997). If there is love and trust, a husband and wife can make joint decisions about family size (Caldwell 1980: 244). This woman's remarks also suggest that family size is now considered within the realm of conscious choice, a prerequisite to thinking about limiting fertility, according to Coale (1973: 65). For the townspeople of Ìtàpá-Èkìtì, this consciousness of choice is associated with literacy (cf. Caldwell 1976: 11) since, 'Illiterates don't dictate to God, they believe in whatever God gives,' as one man put it. Thus, education in the Yoruba context would appear to be a preliminary and necessary step in specifying the number of children wanted.

It is not simply the ability to quantify these choices that is enhanced by education. Schooling also contributes to the sense of being 'enlightened', of having ọlàjú, in both women and men and justifies their ability to make their own decisions – about virginity, about pre-marital sexuality, about marriage and about childbearing.[13] For these reassessments of virginity and fertility, of menstruation and marriage, represent arguments over a new set of values relating to individual choice of spouses and childbearing. However, they also reflect inter-generational contests over the moral grounds that legitimate such behaviour, particularly when younger townswomen and men attempt to circumvent parental pressures to have more children. One aspect of these contests – the reassessment of the practice of child-fostering – will be examined in the following chapter.

5

CHILD-FOSTERING, BLOOD TIES AND PARENTHOOD

Àgbàbọ́ kò d'ọmọ ẹni
To raise a child doesn't make a child one's own.

Yoruba proverb

Blood is a juice with curious properties.

Goethe, *Faust*, Part I

Train children in the right way, and when old, they will not stray.

Proverbs 22, 6

If the reinterpretation of virginity was part of the process by which new ways for finding a spouse and for ensuring fertility were being devised, then rethinking the benefits and disadvantages of child-fostering is part of a process of redefining the boundaries of kinship ('blood') ties and what constitutes proper parenthood. Child-fostering – *gbàgbàbọ́ ọmọ*, 'raising another's children as one's own' – is a common practice in many West African societies.[1] In Ìtàpá, young children (previously weaned) might temporarily go to live with a relative or close family friend, either within the town itself or outside it. In return for feeding, clothing, housing and sometimes schooling and other training, foster children did farm and domestic work (Renne 1993c). Many townspeople have experienced fostering, either as children fostered by relatives and family friends or as foster parents, and have various views on the practice. For some, the relationship is viewed as mutually beneficial as children acquire discipline working for foster parents who benefit from their labour:

> It is good to foster out children, this is because a child who lives outside of his or her immediate family will learn a series of wisdoms, because if he's living with the mother, what he or she would learn there is different from what they would learn under another person. I have my child who is about eleven years old now with her father's senior sister at Temidire in Ìkọ̀lé-Èkìtì ... This woman had an accident and she couldn't do anything unless she had a helper. Then I decided to give out my daughter to her and I believe that my child will learn more and receive more training under this woman.
>
> (HPF-F5, Ìtàpá-Èkìtì, 1993)

Others also see it as beneficial for birth parents, particularly if there are economic or family crises (such as death or illness) which make it difficult to raise one's children, as was the case for one boy in Ìtàpá: 'His father has died and his wife – my husband's junior sister – has many children so my husband asked to take one of the children,' as one woman explained (FoI-94b, Ìtàpá-Èkìtì, 1991). Other people emphasised its benefits for the foster child in terms of education and character-building:

> What I think about fostering is that if one's child is raised by an educated person, the child will have a good experience and the child may enter into any higher institution through the educated person. For example, my brother spent ten years with Mr and Mrs D. at Ìlúpéjú and then went to the University at Ìlọrin.
> (FoI-19b, Ìtàpá-Èkìtì, 1991)

> I have lived with a person before and my experience then and now is that there is no work that is too much for me to do, I am not afraid of any job. My brother and his wife gave me all sorts of work to do, thinking that they're maltreating me, but today it has been my gain and a loss to his children, because up to date, many of them are lazy.
> (MRI-IA29/8-50, Ìtàpá-Èkìtì, 1995)

For others, mainly younger townspeople, fostering is regarded as exploitative and as detrimental to the educational and moral development of a child. According to their interpretation of fostering, some of the very benefits – that children will get advantageous schooling and character-moulding discipline – are turned on their head, as one man explained from his own experience:

> I can't foster out my children, I have stayed with a person before, a brother, so I have experienced the ills surrounding fostering. During that period, there was never a time that my brother couldn't send me on an errand. It could be 12 o'clock at night and I have no right to challenge him. And the way he would beat me, nobody can beat his child like that.
> (MRI-OA/FE31/8-57, Ìtàpá-Èkìtì, 1995)

Furthermore, older people, particularly indulgent grandmothers (Bledsoe and Isiugo-Abanihe 1989), were seen as spoiling their charges, rather than disciplining them:

> The only person who has requested to foster my child is very old and I can't give my child to an old person. My child once lived with that person and during that period, they spared the rod and spoiled the child. This is very obvious in the life of that child up until this moment.
> (HPF-M17, Ìtàpá-Èkìtì, 1993)

For these people, the biological or 'real' parents are the best parents for a child because the child's care and character will be shaped directly by them:

> In my own case, as long as I am still alive, my child can't live under anyone because there is no amount spent, or care given, I will still condemn it, [saying] that I would have done better. And at the same time, I should be able to predict the character of my child ... For example, I am fostering a child (he is with me now), he came to me while in Primary 2 [second grade]. Frankly speaking, he does not resemble his other brothers and sisters who come from the same parents with him. He takes everything after me ... in talking, walking, he doesn't resemble the father and mother.
> (MRI-CS16/8-27, Ìtàpá-Èkìtì, 1995)

By construing parenthood in this way – that the biological parents are the best parents – the boundaries delineating closeness of kin and consequently lineage obligations are also being redefined, for example:

> Recently a close brother was telling me he wanted me to take care of his child which I reluctantly rejected, not because I could not meet the demand, but because I wanted a child from *the same blood relations*. I would want a child from a *closer* family.
> (MRI-GC30/8-56, Ìtàpá-Èkìtì, 1995)

Several people mentioned the importance of 'the same blood relations' in fostering children as insurance against an unfortunate placement. Yet despite people's misgivings about child-fostering, it continues to be seen by many as a moral act, as 'a way of helping others who are in need of help', as one man put it. In cases of death, illness, divorce or economic hardship, some townspeople continue to raise foster children as their own, even if they do so reluctantly:

> The only thing or the major thing that can make me foster is that if the child loses either of the parents and solicits for my help, I used to have compassion for such people.
> (MRI-GC30/8-56, Ìtàpá-Èkìtì, 1995)

> Yes, I can foster if such a child is from a poor home, if the parents find it difficult to raise the child themselves. But I personally don't cherish raising any of my children elsewhere or raising other's children under me.
> (MRI-C81/8-5, Ìtàpá-Èkìtì, 1995)

These contrary visions of child-fostering – as something one should avoid but that one has a moral obligation to do – have implications for fertility and population in Ìtàpá. On the one hand, child-fostering has supported high fertility in the town, with children providing labour for the elderly, for infertile women and for more well-to-do households. Also, by providing a safety valve for those with many children who do not have the wherewithal to raise them, child-fostering redistributes the costs (and benefits) of bearing children among the wider extended family, rather than simply among the immediate biological parents (Bledsoe 1990a; Caldwell 1977a). On the other hand, child-fostering may be seen as encouraging irresponsible childbearing among those who cannot afford to raise their children 'properly'. Those who dislike the practice advocate limiting fertility so that people need not resort to out-fostering their children.[2] While they may agree to in-foster other people's children, they prefer to restrict this, as the man cited above explained, to 'very close blood relations'. This struggle for control over children, their labour and the meanings attributed to child-fostering suggests several things. First, some people will have smaller families themselves not only to avoid out-fostering but also because they are attempting to reduce their kinship obligations, limiting them to their immediate families. Secondly, this attempt to reduce obligations may be part of a process of nuclear family formation associated with lower fertility (Caldwell 1977b). Thirdly, this process encourages parents and children to think that out-fostering is a form of deprivation that should be avoided whenever possible.

Yet as one man remarked, 'One never knows what the future will bring'. If some younger townspeople ideally prefer not to foster children, limiting both their childbearing and the extent of the kin for whom they feel responsible to attain this ideal, the contingencies of living in Nigeria in the 1990s have supported certain practical strategies in this regard. As Goody (1990: 123) has noted:

> It is this continuing interdependence [on kith and kin], although less strong than before, that ... in the short term at least reinforce the intersection and the mutual dependencies. In this sense extended ties of kinship (what some mean by the vague phrase 'extended families') are critical aspects of contemporary Africa ... they are essential to situations in which the community can neither supply nor afford other forms of welfare.

Child-fostering also serves as a source of 'social capital' (Astone et al. 1999), in the sense that the social relationships forged from fostering can provide useful resources, for out- and in-fostering parents as well as for foster children. This is particularly true during times of family crisis, as when a birth parent dies and a foster parent provides for the child. But fostering can also be used to extend a network of social relationships, which may provide future assistance.[3] As will be seen, child-fostering continues in Ìtàpá-Èkìtì, despite some young people's disapproval, because of the practical needs for child labour by some and for childcare by others.

Table 5.1a Relationship of in-foster children to foster parents, Ìtàpá-Èkìtì, 1991

Foster parent's:	Female %					Male %				
	0–4	5–9	10–14	15–19	Total	0–4	5–9	10–14	15–19	Total
Son's child (no.)	38 (3)	39 (9)	23 (8)	23 (3)	30 (23)	42 (5)	38 (6)	42 (5)	11 (1)	35 (17)
Daughter's child	50 (4)	39 (9)	29 (10)	31 (4)	35 (27)	58 (7)	44 (7)	8 (1)	34 (3)	37 (18)
Junior/senior brother's child	12 (1)	9 (2)	15 (5)	23 (3)	14 (11)	–	–	17 (2)	22 (2)	8 (4)
Junior/senior sister's child	–	13 (3)	21 (7)	23 (3)	17 (13)	–	6 (1)	17 (2)	22 (2)	10 (5)
Junior sister or brother	–	–	3 (1)	–	1 (1)	–	–	8 (1)	–	2 (1)
Other kin	–	–	6 (2)	–	2 (2)	–	12 (2)	8 (1)	11 (1)	8 (4)
Friend's child	–	–	3 (1)	–	1 (1)	–	–	–	–	–
TOTALS % (no.)	100 (8)	100 (23)	100 (34)	100 (13)	100 (78)	100 (12)	100 (16)	100 (12)	100 (9)	100 (49)

Table 5.1b Relationship of out-foster children to foster parents, Ìtàpá-Èkìtì, 1991

Foster parent's:	Female (n=26)				Male (n=13)			
	5–9	10–14	15–19	Total	5–9	10–14	15–19	Total
Son's child (no.)	20 (1)	–	10 (1)	8 (2)	50 (1)	–	–	8 (1)
Daughter's child	–	9 (1)	–	4 (1)	–	–	–	–
Junior/senior brother's child	60 (3)	36 (4)	20 (2)	34 (9)	–	33 (1)	38 (3)	30 (4)
Junior/senior sister's child	20 (1)	19 (2)	40 (4)	27 (7)	–	–	12 (1)	8 (1)
Junior sister	–	36 (4)	10 (1)	19 (5)	–	–	–	–
Junior brother	–	–	–	–	50 (1)	67 (2)	50 (4)	54 (7)
Other kin	–	–	10 (1)	4 (1)	–	–	–	–
Friend's child	–	–	10 (1)	4 (1)	–	–	–	–
TOTALS % (no.)	100 (5)	100 (11)	100 (10)	100 (26)	100 (2)	100 (2)	100 (8)	100 (13)

Table 5.2 Foster parents' experience of being fostered, Ìtàpá-Èkìtì, 1991

Age group	20–39	40–59	60–79	80+	Total
Women (n=106) *Fostered to:*					
Grandmother	11 (2)	16 (6)	11 (4)	–	11 (12)
Father's senior/junior brother/sister	16 (3)	13 (5)	6 (2)	23 (3)	12 (13)
Mother's senior/junior brother/sister	26 (5)	6 (2)	11 (4)	15 (2)	12 (13)
Senior sister or brother	5 (1)	2 (1)	14 (5)	8 (1)	8 (8)
Mother's co-wife	11 (2)	2 (1)	–	–	3 (3)
Don't know relation	5 (1)	–	3 (1)	8 (1)	3 (3)
Total fostered	74[a] (14)	41 (16)	45 (16)	54 (7)	50 (46)
Not fostered out	26 (5)	59 (23)	55 (19)	46 (6)	50 (53)
Don't know	–	2 (1)	–	–	1 (1)
TOTALS % (no.)	100 (19)	100 (39)	100 (35)	100 (13)	100 (106)
Men (n=9) *Fostered to:*					
Father's senior/junior brother/sister	100[b] (1)	50 (1)	—	—	22 (2)
Mother's senior/junior brother/sister	—	—	25 (1)	—	11 (1)
Friend of father	—	—	25 (1)	—	11 (1)
Don't know relation	—	—	—	50 (1)	11 (1)
Total fostered	100 (1)	50 (1)	50 (2)	50 (1)	55 (5)
Not fostered out	—	50 (1)	50 (2)	50 (1)	45 (4)
TOTALS % (no.)	100 (1)	100 (2)	100 (4)	100 (2)	100 (9)

a These relatively high figures may reflect the introduction of free primary education in the Western Region in 1955.
b These numbers are too small to draw conclusions.

This chapter examines the changing socio-economic context in which this process of contested reassessments of child-fostering in Ìtàpá-Èkìtì is taking place. It consists of three sections. The first section looks at child-fostering as it is practised in this Èkìtì town, focusing on who is fostering children and the reasons for their being fostered. The second section considers young townspeople's belief that child-fostering is detrimental to children's development, as exemplified by the extended story of one man's experiences as a foster child. The issues raised by this account, particularly the accuracy of his claim that foster children are overworked, are then evaluated using time-study data of foster and non-foster children's activities. The final section concludes the chapter with some remarks concerning recent patterns of child-fostering – based on comparisons of 1992 and 1997 survey data and on interviews from 1991, 1993 and 1995 – and the demographic implications of changing interpretations of child-fostering, child labour, kinship obligations and moral parenthood in this Èkìtì Yoruba town.

CHILD-FOSTERING IN ÌTÀPÁ-ÈKÌTÌ

The term, ọmọ àgbàbọ́, foster child (Abraham 1962: 232), literally refers to 'taking' (gba) a child (ọmọ) to 'feed' (bọ́), the latter verb referring to a critical element of this relationship. However, foster parents have other responsibilities to their charges including clothing, providing shelter and medicine, and sometimes paying school fees. In Ìtàpá, a child may be considered to be fostered if these responsibilities are met by someone other than the immediate biological mother or father regardless of whether they are present in the town or even in the same household.[4] Of 1,835 children being raised in Ìtàpá, 19.2 per cent (n=353) were being raised by foster parents, according to my 1991 household census. An additional eighty-seven children, of whom one or more parents resided in Ìtàpá, were being raised outside the town.[5]

In order to obtain a better understanding of the dynamics of child-fostering practices in Ìtàpá, 115 foster parents, selected from the initial household census, were interviewed in 1991 about their relationships to the foster children they were raising. Their responses, as suggested above by comments about family distance and blood ties, indicated a preference for close kinship relationships between foster children and parents (see Table 5.1a; see also Hammer and Sutton 1988: 291). In-fostering parents were most often grandparents, raising children for their own sons and daughters (67 per cent). Only one child (1 per cent) was in-fostered by a person who was not kin-related. Children being fostered outside Ìtàpá (n=39) were also being raised by foster parents who were close kin, although the pattern of kin relations was somewhat different from those of children raised in the town (see Table 5.1b). The experiences of these foster parents suggest that

Table 5.3a Reason for child being in-fostered, Ìtàpá-Èkìtì, 1991[a]

Reason	Female (n=78)					Male (n=49)				
	0–4	5–9	10–14	15–19	Total	0–4	5–9	10–14	15–19	Total
Birth parent: Schooling	13 (1)	17 (4)	–	–	6 (5)	25 (3)	19 (3)	–	–	12 (6)
Died	13 (1)	13 (3)	9 (3)	31 (4)	14 (11)	8 (1)	–	17 (2)	56 (5)	16 (8)
Divorced	25 (2)	26 (6)	6 (2)	23 (3)	17 (13)	8 (1)	13 (2)	25 (3)	–	12 (6)
Travelled	12 (1)	9 (2)	3 (1)	–	5 (4)	–	–	8 (1)	–	2 (1)
Many children, no money	25 (2)	4 (1)	6 (2)	8 (1)	8 (6)	8 (1)	6 (1)	8 (1)	–	6 (3)
Total % (no.)	88 (7)	70 (16)	24 (8)	62 (8)	50 (39)	50 (6)	38 (6)	58 (7)	56 (5)	49 (24)
Foster parent: Needs help	13 (1)	13 (3)	53 (18)	15 (2)	31 (24)	33 (4)	25 (4)	42 (5)	22 (2)	31 (15)
Barren	–	–	6 (2)	–	3 (2)	–	6 (1)	–	–	2 (1)
Total % (no.)	13 (1)	13 (3)	59 (20)	15 (2)	33 (26)	33 (4)	31 (5)	42 (5)	22 (2)	33 (16)
Foster child: School, discipline	–	4 (1)	6 (2)	23 (3)	8 (6)	17 (2)	31 (5)	–	–	14 (7)
Requests	–	13 (3)	12 (4)	–	9 (7)	–	–	–	22 (2)	4 (2)
Total % (no.)	–	17 (4)	18 (6)	23 (3)	17 (13)	17 (2)	31 (5)	–	22 (2)	18 (9)
TOTAL % (no.)	101 (8)	100 (23)	101 (34)	100 (13)	100 (78)	100 (12)	100 (16)	100 (12)	100 (9)	100 (49)

[a] Total percentages may not add up to 100 due to rounding.

this pattern was common in the past in this rural Èkìtì Yoruba town, although more children were fostered to other family members rather than to their grandmothers (see Table 5.2).

Reasons for child-fostering

According to the 1991 Ìtàpá foster survey data, 31 per cent (n=24) of in-fostered girls were raised by their grandmothers to help these older women (see Table 5.3a). Another 31 per cent (n=24) of girls were in-fostered because their parents were divorced or had died, a form of fostering sometimes referred to as 'crisis fostering' (Goody 1982). In-fostering of boys showed a similar pattern (see Table 5.3a). The figures indicate that fostering because of parental need for childcare is the most common reason

Table 5.3b Reason for child being out-fostered, Ìtàpá-Èkìtì, 1991[a]

Reason	Female (n=26)				Male (n=13)			
	5–9	10–14	15–19	Total	5–9	10–14	15–19	Total
Birth parent: Died	–	–	10 (1)	4 (1)	50 (1)	–	13 (1)	15 (2)
Divorced	20 (1)	–	–	4 (1)	–	–	–	–
Has many children	20 (1)	36 (4)	10 (1)	23 (6)	–	–	13 (1)	8 (1)
Total % (no.)	40 (2)	36 (4)	20 (2)	31 (8)	50 (1)	–	25 (2)	23 (3)
Foster parent: needs help	20 (1)	27 (3)	30 (3)	27 (7)	50 (1)	33 (1)	–	15 (2)
Total % (no.)	20 (1)	27 (3)	30 (3)	27 (7)	50 (1)	33 (1)	–	15 (2)
Foster child: School, discipline	40 (2)	27 (3)	50 (5)	39 (10)	–	–	38 (3)	23 (3)
Requests to live w/ foster parent	–	9 (1)	–	4 (1)	–	67 (2)	25 (2)	31 (4)
Total % (no.)	40 (2)	36 (4)	50 (5)	42 (11)	–	67 (2)	63 (5)	54 (7)
Don't know reason	–	–	–	–	–	–	13 (1)	8 (1)
TOTAL % (no.)	100 (5)	99 (11)	100 (10)	100 (26)	100 (2)	100 (3)	101 (8)	100 (13)

[a] Total percentages may not add up to 100 due to rounding.

for in-fostering in Ìtàpá. Help for older relatives was given as the second most common reason. This demand for in-fostered children was seen in the 33 per cent requested for child-fostering by foster parents and in the childcare requested by birth parents for 50 per cent of these children, reflecting the two primary reasons for child-fostering within the town: birth parents' need for childcare and older foster parents' need for child labour.

Out-fostering showed a somewhat different pattern with education given as a principle reason for fostering girls (39 per cent) and boys (23 per cent) (see Table 5.3b). In addition, a large proportion of boys (31 per cent) opted to move into an out-foster relationship, reflecting both their desire to see the world and to acquire further education or job opportunities. Foster-parents outside Ìtàpá were almost three times as likely (59 per cent) to ask to raise out-fostered children (who were often their younger brothers or sisters) compared with 18 per cent of birth parents who asked that children be taken. This pattern suggests that senior siblings are continuing to help junior ones in their education.[6]

Education is viewed as a crucial element in child training and social mobility (Orùbuloyè 1981b). An important rationale for out-fostering one's children is to place children with people who will best be able to raise, train and sponsor them. Children, as well as parents, rest their hopes for a successful future on their access to educational opportunities, sometimes made available through the sponsorship of foster parents. However, some parents now feel that the advantages of close parent-child ties no longer need be sacrificed for educational advantages, since most younger townspeople have been to school, with many attending secondary school in the town. Barring death or divorce, there is no one, they say, who will raise their children better than they can themselves. Furthermore, some people were disappointed in their educational expectations as recounted in their own experiences as foster children.

A CHILD-FOSTERING EXPERIENCE

The following story illustrates important aspects of child-fostering: struggles over scarce labour, fierce competition for positions in higher educational institutions and the ambiguities of kin obligations, among others. In 1991, the speaker, Báyò (a pseudonym), was thirty years old, had a secondary school certificate and worked as a farmer. He had two children and wanted to have three more.

> In my own opinion, I have vowed in life not to give out my children to anyone. This is one reason why I want that specific number [five]. I don't demand any help from anybody before I can bring my children up. When one fosters out *Ibi tí ojú ènìyàn kò tó, ojú Ọlọ́run nìkan ló tó* (One may not be able to see [one's child's condition], only God sees everything). I can still recall the time when my grandfather died, one of my senior brothers came home. I was happy to see him and then I immediately decided to follow him and stay with him in his station. I was happy because it would be my first outing to a distant place. On getting to our destination (near Òṣogbo) I was asked to go back from Primary 5 to Primary 1, while my classmates at home who were no better than myself, have gone far in secondary school. I started to look at them as being outstanding [the lucky ones]. I was made to harvest pepper every day, not school. I attended school twice a week and even in the examination period I was compelled to harvest pepper. What surprised me most was when one of my brother's children broke a plate without my knowing it. His father came saying his child couldn't do that, that I must have broken it. He beat the hell out of me and asked me to do 'jump frog' [leap like a frog] for about three hours. When it got to the extent of having no energy in me again, I was rushed to the hospital. The next day, when I told them I would die, they decided to take me home. I have suffered much because I was fostered out.

In this wise, I have made up my mind not to foster my children out to anybody. I can help foster any child but myself, I will not give out my children to anybody.

In sum, fostering is bad. This is because if you fostered your child out to someone who has not had any issue, they may not know the value of the child. But if the person has children, you may give a child to them believing that whatever evil they do to the child, their children will share from it in the future, the God of Vengeance will do likewise to their children.

(FS5/8-8, Ìtàpá-Èkìtì, 1991)

Two elements stand out in that man's account of his fostering experience. First, rather than go to school regularly, he was made to harvest pepper everyday. Secondly, there was his shock at being falsely accused and severely punished by his brother. As a result of his experience, he vowed that he would not foster out any of his children. However, there are also elements in this rendition which suggest that competing claims are at stake here, claims which are part of ongoing process in a struggle for control over people, things and meanings. Báyò chose to follow his senior brother after the death of his grandfather, having certain expectations of rights and responsibilities of close blood kin, that such people should help, not exploit, one's relations. He was hoping to continue his schooling under the sponsorship of his brother. Yet the introduction of universal primary education and increasing cash-crop production have led to labour shortages in some rural areas so that immediate family is often one's best source of farm labour (Peel 1983: 120). Whereas Báyò saw living with his senior brother outside Ìtàpá as an opportunity to improve his future chances through schooling, his brother saw him primarily as a source of labour. Furthermore, the dilemma faced by many parents in the early colonial period over whether it was more advantageous to send a child to the farm or to school has been resolved in favour of education. The resulting large numbers of students vying for access to secondary and post-secondary institutions has led to fierce competition for these positions. Beyond the question of labour, the senior brother's lack of interest in promoting his junior brother's education may have been in the interest of favouring his own children's chances (see Bledsoe 1990b: 76).

Beyond the economic and social issues of agricultural labour, kinship obligations and educational expectations, the meaning of fostering is being recast here in an interesting way. Unlike in the past, when fostering was considered to be good because it provided older or infertile women with foster children and taught such children discipline, here fostering is considered bad in such cases because people 'might not know the value of the child', that is, they might mistreat the child. Furthermore, the idea commonly expressed by older townswomen that 'in the future, they will be rewarded for the care they gave their foster children', is, in this case, turned on its head. Rather than reward, the offspring of foster parents will be visited with divine retribution for the bad care given to foster siblings by their parents. The meaning of fostering as something good – helping others who in turn help you – has become something different. Fostering, in this interview, is perceived as bad by Báyọ̀ and his decision not to foster his children out is the morally correct one.

FOSTERING AND CHILD LABOUR

The position taken by Báyọ̀ against fostering out his own children and the moral justification of his decision based on his mistreatment were expressed in different ways by others. While their reasons were also related to the rights and obligations of blood kin, unlike Báyọ̀ who emphasised his attenuated schooling and unjust beating, many described their mistreatment in terms of food. Not only was food often insufficient but in its separate preparation and serving, food served as a symbol for the internal distinction between foster and non-foster children within a household (see Bledsoe 1990a). These distinctions reflected in food are not inconsequential, as Medick and Sabean (1984: 14) have observed, 'Rights and obligations surrounding the sharing of food are often direct translations of rights in other spheres or symbolize such rights.' For example, one man described being given *gàrí* (dried cassava meal) by his foster father:

> He gave me a measure that should sustain us until the evening and what I used to do then was that I would put water on it, so that by the time I wanted to take it in the evening, it would have swollen or multiplied. [When he saw this,] he beat me like a goat, the remnants of food from his children was supposed to be my own portion.
> (MRI-FC28/8-47, Ìtàpá-Èkìtì, 1995)

In another example, a twenty-seven-year-old woman related her own experience in terms of an awareness of a hierarchy of social relations reflected in food as well as in the indignity of washing another person's dirty underwear:

> The person you give your child to will not take proper care of the child. I can give an example of when I was learning some handwork and I was living with my uncle. Can you imagine that I used to wash his wife's underpants? Then she used to give me very small amounts of food with only a small fish head. I used to be given the same measure of food as that of her smallest child, her last-born, but she would give *her* the better part of the fish.
> (LIW-TG3/8-4, Ìtàpá-Èkìtì, 1991)

As a result of their personal experience, many believe that foster children are underfed, overworked, and that their access to education and hence

Table 5.4a Comparison of time spent on school, work and leisure by pairs of fostered and non-fostered children, Ìtàpá-Èkìtì, 1991

Activity	Of 33 pairs[a] of foster/non-foster children, foster children spent:					
	Less time		More time		Equal time	
	%	(no.)	%	(no.)	%	(n)
At school	52	(17)	24	(8)	24	(8)
At work[b]	21	(7)	73	(24)	6	(2)
At leisure[c]	67	(22)	21	(7)	12	(4)

a Includes 26 foster children paired with 33 non-fostered children, some of whom reside in the same house.
b $x=11.88$, $p<0.001$, Yates corrected.
c $x=6.06$, $p<0.05$, Yates corrected.

future success is hindered (Renne 1993c, 1995c). Indeed the findings of a time-study conducted in Ìtàpá in 1991 (see Appendix I) support this claim. At the household level, the activities – ranging from fetching water, sleeping, attending school and going to farm – of thirty-three pairs of foster children and non-foster children, matched according to age and preferably sex, were compared. When analysed by pairs, the number of foster children who had less schooling than their non-fostered counterparts was almost the same as the number who had the same or more schooling (see Table 5.4a). However, foster children spent significantly more time working than the non-fostered children of the pairs and significantly less time on personal and leisure activities.

At the aggregate level, foster children (n=31) and non-foster (n=71) children, regardless of house affiliation, were grouped according to age and sex (see Table 5.4b). Based on time percentages (of leisure, work and school), fostered and non-fostered children were compared according to amount of time spent schooling (30 per cent or more of the time) or working (40 per cent or more of the time). There was no significant difference in the amount of time spent schooling by either fostered or non-fostered children, either when taken as a group or when compared according to age and sex. However, as in the paired analysis, there was a significant difference between fostered and non-fostered children in the time spent working. Sixty-nine per cent of all fostered boys worked 40 per cent or more of the time compared with 33 per cent of non-fostered boys. Fostered girls also showed a significant difference in the amount of time working, except for girls in the 15–19 age group, perhaps because these girls were more likely to be engaged in domestic work and marketing. Fostered and non-fostered girls spent similar amounts of time attending school.

While data from a one-month time-study is not conclusive evidence, the results suggest that, at least for boys, the general belief that foster children

Table 5.4b Comparison of time spent working by fostered and non-fostered children, Ìtàpá-Èkìtì, 1991

Sex/Age group	Foster (n=31) Works 40% of time or more			Non-foster (n=71) Works 40% of time or more		
	Y	N	Total	Y	N	Total
	% (no.)			% (no.)		
Male						
5–9	44 (4)	56 (5)	100 (9)	21 (3)	79 (11)	100 (14)
10–14	100 (5)	–	100 (5)	31 (4)	69 (9)	100 (13)
15–19	100 (2)	–	100 (2)	35 (6)	65 (11)	100 (17)
Data missing – age	–	–	–	100 (2)	–	100 (2)
TOTAL % (no.)	69 (11)	31 (5)	100 (16)	33 (15)	67 (31)	100 (46)
Female						
5–9	60 (3)	40 (2)	100 (5)	25 (2)	75 (6)	100 (8)
10–14	86 (6)	14 (1)	100 (7)	42 (5)	58 (7)	100 (12)
15–19	100 (2)	–	100 (2)	80 (4)	20 (1)	100 (5)
Data missing – age	100 (1)	–	100 (1)	–	–	–
TOTAL % (no.)	80 (12)	20 (3)	100 (15)	44 (11)	56 (14)	100 (25)

are subjected to more work than their non-fostered counterparts is borne out. The issue of access to schooling is more complicated. There was no significant difference between foster and non-foster children in the amount of time spent on schooling but this does not mean that there are not differences, as one Ìtàpá woman explained:

> One woman I know in Lagos, she gave her child to her mother to bring up. Whenever the child wakes up each morning, she has to scrub the floor and do a lot of domestic work before she allows her to go to school. So she always goes late to school and the school she goes to is not very good. But that woman's children do less work and go to a better school.
>
> (LIW-CK7/8-11, Ìtàpá-Èkìtì, 1991)

The amount of work a child performs prior to going to school and the differences in educational standards of schools attended are questions unanswered in this time-study approach. Thus people's perceptions that foster children work more and go to school less may be borne out by more finely-tuned studies. On the one hand, this belief supports some people's decision not to out-foster. On the other, the data makes clear the extent to which children, both fostered and non-fostered alike, continue to be a major source of domestic labour in this rural Èkìtì Yoruba town despite school attendance, making the possibility of in-fostering children still an attractive option for some adults.

Fostering to blood relations

While some people cite inadequate, poorly prepared food and overwork as the primary reasons for their disapproval of child-fostering, others feel that this mistreatment can be overcome by biological closeness, expressed in terms of blood:

> If my child is with my mother, I will have no course to fear, she will know that her own blood has the child and she will care for the child as she will care for me. But if a child is given out to another person outside one's immediate home or family, it may be dangerous.
>
> (LIM-JB13/10-67, Ìtàpá-Èkìtì, 1991)

Several people who saw advantages in child-fostering said that they would only foster their children to close blood relations. The idea that one should limit fostering to blood relations was evident from 1991 fostering data on the relationships of foster parents to children (see Table 5.1a and 5.1b). What appears to be changing is that some people are taking these kinship restrictions even further, stressing the importance of biological parents to the exclusion of all other blood relations. Again, these concerns are also expressed in terms of food, although in a different way: 'I have lived with someone before. When I was with him, he only cared for my stomach, whereas my parents would care for me *in all spheres*' (LIM-IC14/8-21, Ìtàpá-Èkìtì, 1991). Despite the fact that food may be sufficient, a child's needs may be unfilled in 'other spheres'. In other words, anyone can feed a child, as the proverb beginning this chapter suggests, but no one can care for a child like the child's own parents.

It has been suggested that young people developed these ideas about child-fostering and parenthood from reading materials in school, from the media and from church teachings (Caldwell 1977a: 101–3). Indeed, some townspeople seemed to make the association that education affected parents' preference not to out-foster their children, as did this sixty-five-year-old grandmother who was raising her son's four-year-old daughter, Bólá: 'Educated people's children are not fostered nowadays. Even this one [Bólá] will go soon. One has to take care of them very well so that they will be advantageous to their parents in the future.' Yet even while younger, educated people may insist that they will not out-foster their own children, some are willing to in-foster the children of others. They support their position, in part, by saying that they know, as educated people, how to raise children best.

Who is the Best Parent?

In Ìtàpá, ideas about who can best rear and discipline a child are being contested and redefined. Previously, discipline was considered a primary reason for out-fostering children. Now some younger people justify their refusal to out-foster their own children by saying that foster parents may either be too harsh with their charges (as exemplified in Báyọ̀'s story) or too lax (as exemplified by grandmothers who spoil them). Grandmothers were also criticised for not being the best parents because of their lack of education. For example, grandmothers might not know about modern methods of personal hygiene (see Chapter 7):

> Ah, well you know these old people the care they give to children – we young people we don't like that ... For example, as a parent when you wake up early in the morning, you must make sure you cater for your children, starting from taking care of their teeth and other things, but these old people they just give them food, their food is the only essential something for the children.
> (LIW-LIC14/8-28, Ìtàpá-Èkìtì, 1991)

Thus, present ideas about being a 'good parent' not only include providing sufficient food, clothing, schooling and emotional support, but also stress the importance of knowing about modern conventions of health and diet. Biological parents are also said to be able to strike the best balance in terms of discipline and affection in child-rearing. As one secondary school girl remarked, 'A real parent will care better for the child.' In other words, the 'real' parent is the best parent.

If what constitutes being a good parent is being reconsidered, children are also perceived as changing, requiring higher standards of care. Foster children may be perceived as causing family problems, exacerbating family tensions with their accusations of maltreatment:

> It creates an unpleasant situation between father and mother or among the family group ... If there is a drastic reduction in food compared with what her or his immediate parents give at home, such a child may write and complain of insufficient food, whereas the same quantity was given to him or her as will be given to one's own child.
> (LIM-EC27/9-61, Ìtàpá-Èkìtì, 1991)

Unlike children in the past who were fostered to maintain family connections and to strengthen their own (or their parents') social network, foster children are now perceived as possibly jeopardising these ties. Paradoxically, in order to maintain the tradition of good extended family relations, it may be better for children to be raised by their biological parents.

As a result of potential problems, a few people said that rather than in-foster a child, they would send money for the child to be raised by the child's parents elsewhere, as one man explained:

> Raising or fostering a child is good and at the same time, it is bad. When you feel that you want to help a child, it is better to help them while they stay with the immediate parents. [You can] spend whatever you feel like for them there, they will show more appreciation than when you keep them under your roof. Our people are so difficult, when you foster a child they think that the child is being enslaved under you, they won't think about what you do for the child.
> (MRI-CS16/8-27, Ìtàpá-Èkìtì, 1995)

Although this practice was not commonly mentioned, the substitution of cash for kinship relations is one way of maintaining family obligations without the difficulties of raising a foster child in one's home. The idea of a shrinking circle of blood relations that one can trust represents an attempt to reduce one's financial and moral responsibilities to a broad group of extended kin. Thus, attitudes about what constitutes being a 'good parent' and the need for securing the best possible education for one's children not only reflect changing ideas about child-fostering and parent-child relations but also indicate an appreciation of the economic constraints of child-rearing, both of one's own children and fostered ones. Nonetheless, many of the people who say they will not out-foster their own children because fostering is 'bad' say they would in-foster another's person's child because it is 'good'. Most people acknowledge that fostering provides some sort of insurance for children left in precarious situations as a result of death or other family crises, and in this context fostering is considered a moral thing to do. Furthermore, fostering a family member's child and sponsoring it in school provides certain immediate (house help) and future benefits (possibly social connections), making it an economically sensible thing to do as well. This apparent contradiction in attitudes toward in- and out-fostering was explained by people in several ways. Some said that they, unlike other foster parents, would be 'good parents' because they are educated or because they would raise a foster child just as they raise their own. Others said that it was their duty to help family members in need. For them, their position is actually morally consistent in that they, as the best parents, are raising their children themselves and, as good family members, are raising the children of extended kin who are in need. This position also coincides with the continued need for child labour and the economic difficulties of living in contemporary Nigeria.

CHILD-FOSTERING, KIN CONNECTIONS AND FERTILITY

Ìtàpá women and men are saying contradictory things about child-fostering, depending on their age, their sex, their education and their socioeconomic status. Some younger people condemn foster parents for starving foster children but when food is sufficient, they may say that food is not the only thing children need. They may cite their own experiences of mistreatment as foster children and then criticise contemporary children who run away from their foster homes as hypersensitive. Older people may criticise the young, saying that ọ̀làjú (civilisation, education) has spoiled them, discouraging them from continuing time-tried practices such as fostering. They may say that they are selfishly concerned with their immediate family and not with the welfare of other kin. These contradictory statements and contesting voices, rather than being overlooked, should be considered as part of a strategy for dealing with the uncertainties of life in present-day Nigeria.

From what young Ìtàpá people are saying, it would appear that child fostering is on the decline.[7] Yet people are hedging their bets. This is evident from a comparison of the responses of women in 1992 and 1997 to the survey questions 'Do you have other children [foster] you have *not* given birth to eighteen years or less living with you?' and 'Do you have any sons or daughters you have given birth to who are alive but do *not* live with you?' Rather than seeing an overall decrease in child-fostering, women's responses in 1997 indicate an increase in in-fostering among women aged thirty-five to forty-four, although it has decreased for women aged twenty to twenty-nine (see Figures 5.1a and 5.1b). Differences in out-fostering are not so clear-cut (see Figures 5.1c and 5.1d), with slightly more women aged thirty to thirty four (38 per cent) out-fostering in 1997 compared with 1992 (33 per cent) but with more women out-fostering in the thirty-five to thirty-nine age group in 1992, although neither of these differences are significant. This continued child-fostering in and out of Ìtàpá-Èkìtì exists because of uncertainty, in terms of family crisis such as death or divorce and in terms of the economics of strikes by unpaid teachers and of food and petrol shortages, as one man explained:

> There is nothing bad in fostering because man proposes, God disposes, and nobody knows what the future holds. Because if you help, if you just render help to one of your brothers or sisters, it may develop in the future, he or she may help you, ... even if you have a vehicle to help you, he or she can help your children.
>
> (LIM-SC27/7-1, Ìtàpá-Èkìtì, 1991)

Exactly how this uncertainty will impinge on future child-fostering patterns is unclear.[8] Yet despite the distinctions made between the care given by foster and biological parents, and between the literate and the illiterate, even educated people who say they will not out-foster their own children realise

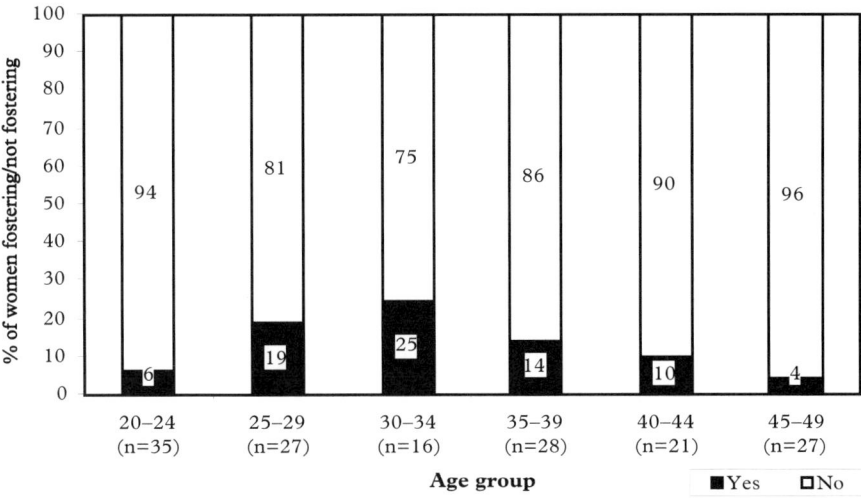

Figure 5.1a In-fostering by age of foster mother, Ìtàpá-Èkìtì, 1992

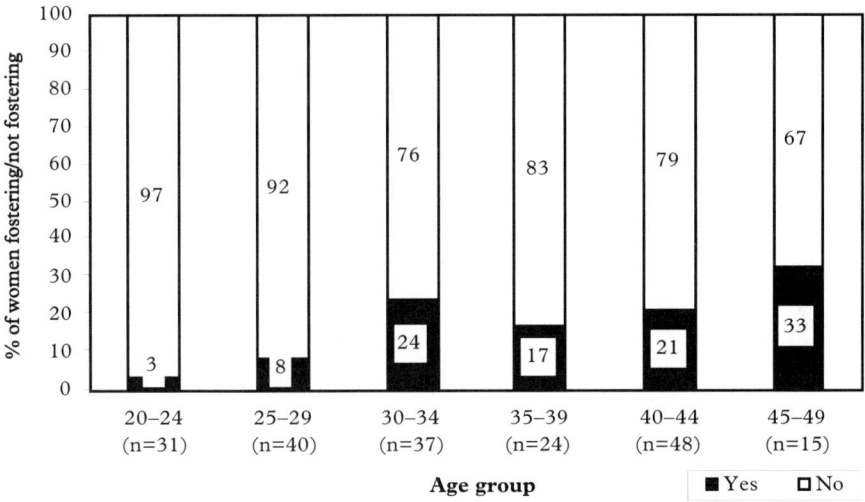

Figure 5.1b In-fostering by age of foster mother, Ìtàpá-Èkìtì, 1997

that fostering can be helpful in cases of death, divorce and economic hardship and may be beneficial in the long term. Because of these contingencies, some are reconsidering their views of fostering, with many people saying that fostering has both good and bad aspects.

For example, Báyọ̀, the man who recounted his experience as a foster child in 1991 had revised his assessment of this practice when re-interviewed in 1995:

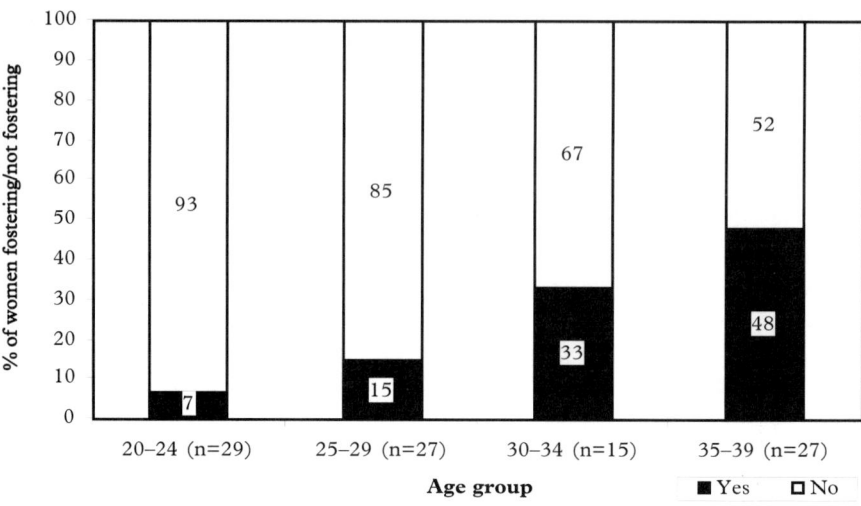

Figure 5.1c Out-fostering by age of foster mother, Ìtàpá-Èkìtì, 1992

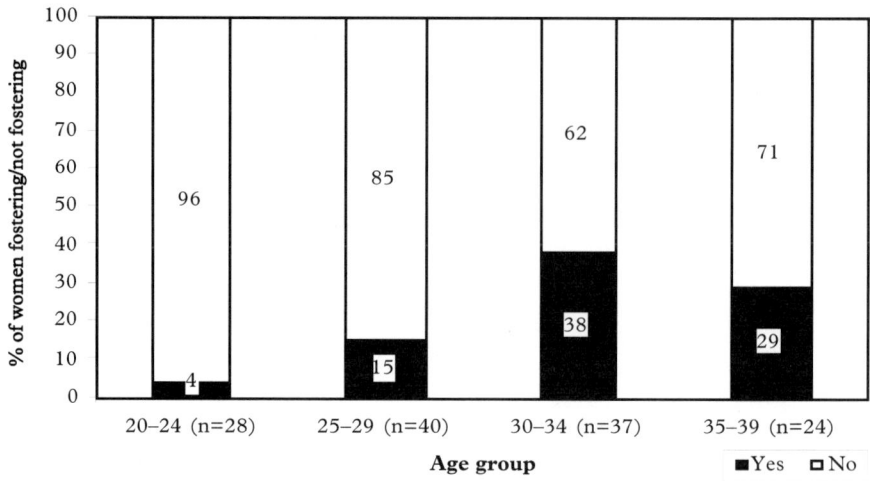

Figure 5.1d Out-fostering by age of foster mother, Ìtàpá-Èkìtì, 1997

To me personally, it is good to foster and it is not good. Why? It is good in that no matter the nature of the child, he or she's still a helper in the house, he will render some assistance in the home. And at times, there could be impromptu journeys, the foster child could at least stay with the little children at home.

I can raise for others, but I can't give any of my children to anyone,

> I pray that I don't have any problem, I can't allow anyone to raise any of my children for me. I have lived with my brother, *there was not any problem in the course of my stay with him.* The type of hardship I faced then was an attempt to put me through, although I saw it then as servitude but I have grown to see it as part of the training I had to receive.
> (MRI95-FS5/8-8, Ìtàpá-Èkìtì, 1995; my emphasis)

In this interview, he has re-evaluated his treatment as a foster child, suggesting that what he interpreted as harsh treatment was actually necessary discipline. Rather than categorically condemning fostering, he now sees it – as an adult possibly needing household help – as a potentially useful practice. On the other hand, he has not changed his position about out-fostering his children and says, 'I pray that I don't have any problem' that would necessitate his doing so. When comparing the number of children he said that he wanted in 1991 and 1995, he hoped for the same number: five. Of the forty (of the original sixty-six) men reinterviewed in 1995, 37.5 per cent said they wanted the same number, 42.5 per cent said they wanted fewer or the same, and 12.5 per cent said they wanted more.[9] The economic situation is clearly part of the reason for these responses:[10]

> Well, with the mercy of God, if He could provide me with five children, I will be alright. I have decided that number because of the economic situation in the country. Although the economic situation is bad, I should be able to oversee five children.
> (MRI-PC6/8-9, Ìtàpá-Èkìtì, 1995)

However, some people's preferences not to out-foster their children has contributed to this decision, as Báyò's earlier comments suggest. As he put it in 1991, 'I have vowed in life not to give out my children to anyone. This is one reason why I want that specific number [5]. I don't demand any help from anybody before I can bring my children up.' Others echoed this sentiment: 'This is one of the reasons why I said I want just four children. I don't need to give any of them out. I should be able to finance their needs' (LIM-FC28/8-47, Ìtàpá-Èkìtì, 1991).

Along with the adverse moral connotations that some associate with out-fostering, there is an element of shame in out-fostering children that also supports the idea of having fewer children whom one can raise oneself:

> The meaning of asking someone to foster for you is an indication that you're not capable of raising your children. It means you cannot fulfil your obligations as a parent, that is why you're asking someone else to help you out, it is a way of asking for money, for economic assistance. It equally indicates that you can't train the child or discipline him or her.
> (MRI-AC16/8-28, Ìtàpá-Èkìtì, 1995)

This man's re-evaluation of the moral dimensions of parenthood is expressed in revised ideas about parental competence as well as economic capacity.

CONCLUSION

Caldwell (1977a: 91) has argued that extended family involvement in child-rearing, including child-fostering, supports high levels of fertility by spreading the economic burdens of raising children. This raises the question of what effects, if any, decreased out-fostering, based on the perception that out-fostering children (except in cases of crisis) is a sign of bad parenting, would have on fertility levels. From people's comments, it would seem that this ideal – limiting one's family size to the number of children one can care for oneself – is supporting, although perhaps not causing, lower fertility. Yet in practice, people cannot always avoid death and illness nor can they afford to limit their investment in others – as the survey figures on fostering suggest – particularly when they may need help from these people in the future. Their attempts to reduce their obligations to a wide group of others while at the same time maintaining as broad a social safety net as possible is driving these redefinitions of child-fostering, blood ties and parenthood in seemingly contradictory but strategic ways. Similar reconsiderations regarding obligations with another set of kin – the dead – are discussed in the following chapter.

6

BURIAL, REBIRTH AND RELATIONS WITH THE DEAD

Ọmọ kò ní àyọ̀lé, ẹni ọmọ sin ló bímọ
There is no joy in having children, until the child buries the one who gave birth.

Yoruba proverb

Even I myself knew already that deads could not live with alives, because I had watched all their doings and they did not correspond with ours at all.

Amos Tutuọla, *Palm-Wine Drinkard*

When the Ọbalókè (the King of Oròkè) died at the age of sixty-four on 27 January 1992, his death set in motion a series of actions done to mark his position as a traditional chief in the town. Immediately, a family emissary was sent with a goat for the Ẹlẹ́kọ̀lé (the King of Ìkọ̀lé, a large town to the east of Ìtàpá) who sent a goat in return to acknowledge that he had been notified.[1] Upon this emissary's return, family members told the Ìràfà – the seven highest town chiefs and the Ọwátàpá – of the death, after which the quarter heads within Oròkè Quarter were contacted. Then the chiefs and their juniors (the 'little chiefs') from all the quarters in Ìtàpá, as well as their wives and children, came to the house of the deceased Ọbalókè. His body had been dressed in regal finery including a beaded crown that made reference to his chiefly status and he was seated in a chair in his parlour as if he were still living (see Figure 6.1). Around 11 o'clock that evening, men from the three Oròkè sub-quarters (Ẹbí Ọmọba, Dẹ̀mí and Ọ̀wà) carried the body in a coffin – purchased in Ìkọ̀lé for ₦1,000 and lined with almost thirty pieces of white guinea brocade cloth (white cotton damask) contributed by or on behalf of every living child (cf. Johnson 1921) – to the grave site, where the coffin was secretly buried. Seven days later the family organised a night funeral party to commemorate the Ọbalókè's passing (cf. Barber 1991).

When a high chief such as the Ọbalókè dies, his (or her) burial reflects the belief that the activities performed on their death should be in 'energies proportionate to the social status of the deceased' (Hertz 1960: 77). The burial of the Ọbalókè was performed in a way that reflected his social standing in the community, although since the title of Ọbalókè is not one of the highest-ranking chiefs in Ìtàpá, he was buried by family members.[2]

Figure 6.1 Funeral observances for the late Ọbalókè (seated in the middle), Ìtàpá-Èkìtì, February 1992. (photograph by Féyiṣayọ̀ Àjàyí)

Immense amounts of time and money are often lavished on the dead, whether or not they are chiefs. Other members of the community are also buried in ways that reflect their social status and success in life or, as some townspeople say, the success and standing of their children. Indeed, it is critically important for family members to commemorate their dead through an elaborate funeral which includes invitations, programmes, a fancy coffin, enormous quantities of food for guests (preferably including the meat from several cows), hired musicians, and possibly hotel accommodation and obituary announcements (either by radio or newspapers) (Láwuyì 1991). The expenses incurred in the burial of wealthier townspeople have escalated as paved roads, motor vehicles and mortuaries allow family member to preserve the body in order to prepare for a funeral some weeks after the death. As will be discussed, expensive funerals are performed not only because they honour the memory of the deceased but also because they reflect on the viability of the entire family (Arhin 1994). Not performing an adequate funeral reflects badly on family members, particularly the deceased's children, who may be ostracised by their fellow townspeople (Ogbuagu 1991), as one older man explained, 'If we who are alive do not perform the ceremony, other people who have done such ceremony in honour of their parent will be looking at us as a disgrace to the deceased father or mother' (FI-2, Ìtàpá-Èkìtì, 1991).

In addition, a well-performed funeral is also perceived as a sort of repayment for the debt children have incurred to their parents:

> When a child is good, such a child will realise that someone was behind his or her success. You can also look at it this way: can one be born today and tomorrow bathe oneself? Can one eat by oneself? Somebody has been caring for the baby, right from the pregnancy up to its maturity. When such a person dies, should the deceased be neglected and not accorded proper funeral rites? How we care for the deceased in performing funeral ceremonies is similar to how we care for the new born baby when born.
> (FI-23, Ìtàpá-Èkìtì, 1991)

It also indirectly expresses people's desire to be buried in a similar fashion themselves. For these reasons, having many children who can come together to perform a funeral commensurate with their means is vitally important for both women and men (Levine 1982), as one man explained:

> It is important to have many children, for example, when my father died, we had a fine funeral because we were many. We killed about twelve cows and thousands of people were invited. No matter how great a person is, he can't invite as many people and I don't think he can be bold enough to kill twelve cows so that everybody will be looking forward to eating and drinking from him. Whereas in a family of fifteen children, each has his or her group for entertainment.
> (FI-25, Ìtàpá-Èkìtì, 1991)

Certain aspects of present-day burials reflect changes in burial practices and beliefs about the dead as town residents have converted to Christianity or Islam, acquired Western education, migrated to large urban centres, and have access to new forms of wealth that have implications for this need for many children, as another man noted:

> Nowadays, only one child can even do more than that because of introduction of education, unlike in the olden days, only one person cannot do that. Nowadays it is possible that someone has only two children. They may do something more tangible than someone who has ten children now, because the two children may be wealthy, and well-educated. But in the olden days, it wasn't like that, if you have many children, they will all be engaged, in the same farming with their parents, so it is only what the individual has, that will be the limit of their possessions or wealth.
> (FI-1, Ìtàpá-Èkìtì, 1991)

For those *ọmọ Ìtàpá*, 'children of Ìtàpá', who die while living outside the town, who have children with salaries and incomes independent of the rural economy, elaborate burials may be organised for them by only three or four children who coordinate wake-keeping parties beginning in the city of residence and ending with burial in Ìtàpá.

Along with these changes in burial and funeral practices have come changes in the underlying religious beliefs. For example, the Ọbalókè (whose burial is described above) had a Standard VI education and was a local government judge as well as a member of the Methodist Church. While he clearly supported the local political order of ranked chiefs in Ìtàpá and was buried accordingly, some of the ideas that underwrite chiefly authority, particularly those associated with the worship of indigenous deities, were not relevant for him, as will be seen.

These changing religious beliefs are also evident in new ways of thinking about the burial of other categories of people aside from chiefs and kings. Some Christians, for example, are now buried in church cemeteries (*ilé isìnkú*), thus defining themselves principally as members of the Church, rather than as family members who are buried in their houses.[3] Similarly, Muslims distinguish themselves from traditional religious practices by being buried immediately in special burial grounds near their mosque or at a distance from their houses. These alternative ways of thinking about what constitutes a proper burial, why they are important, and their effect on subsequent relations with the dead are related to changing social relations among the living. As in the demise of arranged marriage, a reduction in senior house-heads' performance of certain rituals associated with the dead has contributed to a lessening of their control over junior family members, including elders' insistence on the need to have many children for a proper burial.

In this chapter, I examine this process whereby burial practices and beliefs about the dead are being redefined, focusing on the implications of these redefinitions for thinking about rebirth and kin relations as well as for fertility. In the first section, burial practices associated with particular categories of people and the ways that they have changed are discussed. In the second section, I consider what people say about relations between the living and the dead that reflect changing religious beliefs as well as conflicting ideas about ritual practice. Despite these changes and conflicts, it is important to note certain continuities in burial procedures. By coming back to 'sleep' in one's house, as a Yoruba proverb puts it, townspeople maintain a sense of groundedness in a particular place, physically represented by the continuity of names and by family claims to property and political office. In the final section, the continued importance of being buried in one's hometown – for reasons that are both interested and emotional – is considered in the light of people's sense that they need children, although not necessarily as many as they needed in the past.

TYPES OF BURIALS AND SOCIAL CATEGORIES IN ÌTÀPÁ-ÈKÌTÌ
House burials

For the ordinary townsperson who dies at 'a ripe old age', the most common form of burial in Ìtàpá-Èkìtì continues to be house burial. Of the 283 occupied houses surveyed in Ìtàpá-Èkìtì in 1992, 58 per cent had visible graves.[4] Bodies are generally buried under the floor of a room in a house (Ògúntúyì 1979: 34) or under the front stoop of the house (see Figure 6.2; Bender 1972: 236):

> If it is an old person, a room may be dug inside his house, it just has to be under the roof of his or her house. After the burial, the portion may be cemented over and decorated ... There are some who die in the prime of life, this group is not normally buried inside the house, it is usually outside but not under the roof.[5]
>
> (FI-20, Ìtàpá-Èkìtì, 1991)

Depending on a person's status, wealth and religion, the body will be buried almost immediately in a coffin (*opósín*), if a Christian, or in a white shroud, if a Muslim.[6] The bodies of the more well-to-do Christians may be kept in a mortuary as family members notify relations and friends and make preparations for the funeral, which may take place several weeks later. A similar

Figure 6.2 House with grave (*orórì*) on front stoop and fish decoration above the doorway, Rẹ́mọ, Ìtàpá-Èkìtì, December 1992. (photograph by the author)

distinction, reflecting the wealth of the deceased and his or her descendants, was also evident in the past, as one elderly man explained:

> Those who were not rich were buried by wrapping them with mats. Their graves were not large, and after the corpse was wrapped with a mat, then the bark of a big tree would be removed to cover further the deceased person so when the body was lowered into the grave, the soil would not spoil the white cloth used to cover it.
>
> There were wood carvers who carved coffins with *ìrókò* wood for wealthy people. Having cut down the *ìrókò* tree, the wood carvers would cut deep into the wood with small axes, just the size of the person who would be using it and some were carved with various designs to decorate them and to make them attractive. It was not necessary that one would die before his coffin would be made. They used to be made during the lifetime of such wealthy people and some would live another fifteen years [after making the coffin] before they died. Then, some elderly ones would relax inside the coffin and would behave as if they would look when they died while their children and wives and people around would be singing their *oríkì* [praise verses]. They would tell him that some time he would sleep in that room [coffin] never to wake again and they would be greeting him and rejoicing with him.
>
> (RI-1, Ìtàpá-Èkìtì, 1998; see also Johnson 1921: 137–9; Ògúntúyì 1979: 34)

This description of elderly people relaxing in their coffins within the house, being greeted by members of their family, captures the sense of community consisting of the living and the dead that such burials were performed to convey. The burial of bodies in graves inside or next to houses emphasised a particular connection made between house, body and spirit, noted by one man who said, 'Our body is just a house, and the spirit owns the house. When the spirit departs, the body will die ...' (FI-13, Ìtàpá-Èkìtì, 1991). For some, burial in the family house also means that the children of the house may readily make offerings to the grave of the deceased. The spirit of the deceased may then continue to interact with its offspring in response, as one Ìtàpá man described it:

> This deceased person is somewhere [close by] looking at us, and if the person is either our father or mother, we believe that, if we perform the ceremony very well, he or she has the hope of paying us back in good measure ...
>
> (FI-2, Ìtàpá-Èkìtì, 1991)

The burial of bodies next to or within the family house represents both the continuity of particular families (literally, houses in a dynastic sense; see

Figure 6.3 St. James African Church graveyard, Ìtàpá-Èkìtì, July 1997. (photograph by the author)

Chapter 8), and for some, the traditional religious ideas about the cyclical nature of existence in which the spirits of the deceased are reborn in the newborn bodies of family members (Ògúntúyì 1979: 29). House burials, then, relate to earlier traditional religious beliefs about reincarnation and the ability to communicate with deceased kin, as one woman explained:

> As for me I can't die and be buried beyond my house. Some people die and are buried in the cemetery (it's a foreign thing because it's a foreign religion [Christianity]); there are also cases of those who were alive but who were eventually buried in the bush.
> But for those buried at home, they are the ones that actually appreciate the ceremonies performed for them. Until about the fifth week, the dead will still abide with the living place where it died. For those whose death is being celebrated, they stand by the side, observing all that is happening.
>
> (FI-23, Ìtàpá-Èkìtì, 1991)

Many Christians also prefer house burial rather than cemetery interment (see Figure 6.3), despite the association of house burial with traditional religious practice. This is partly because their houses are prestigious monuments to their achievement in life where they would like to continue to reside:

> Burying people in the bush? It is not good. How can you suffer yourself to just have a building and in the end you will not be buried in that house? In our case here, many people try to have a building because of the Last Day; people would want to be buried in their own building ... In Lagos and Ìbàdàn, strangers that are poor are buried in the cemetery ground but rich ones are taken home to their town.
> (DI97-15, Ìtàpá-Èkìtì, 1997)

The preference for house burial is also, in part, related to the unprotected, bushy nature of cemeteries: 'People see cemeteries as jungle and bushes, they have the idea that people who died miserable deaths are buried in the bush. So since one's parents didn't die miserably, they have to be buried in the house' (DI97-13, Àkúrẹ́, 1997). Yet being 'buried in the bush' – in the uncleared, forested areas on the outskirts of the town – does not necessarily indicate a dishonourable death but may instead mark the distinctive political or spiritual status of the deceased.

Burial in the bush

Two categories of people are buried in the bush. One category consists of people who are identified as having spirit-world connections, such as Ifá diviner-herbalists (babaláwo), hunters (ọdẹ) and Ṣàngó priests (Onísàngó; priests of the God of Lightning). This group also includes the Ọwátàpá (king) and high-ranking chiefs in the town, including the Ọbalókè whose burial is described above. These individuals' particular powers are marked by their distinctive forms of burials. For example, when an Ọwátàpá dies:

> Kings don't have a burial ground, they are buried in an unknown place. But after doing all sacrifices, and on the seventh day, or the third day, depending on the place, they will tell the public about his death. But they would have cleared everything, no one will see his corpse, it is after then that the public will be told that Ọbá ti wàjà, 'the king is dead'. After telling the public, all the branches of the trees in the palace and market will be cut, then after this, all the elders of the town, as well as the Ẹlẹ́gbẹ́ and Ọmọ Ogún, will be running up and down the town three times. Whatever animal is seen on the street will be killed, goats, sheep and any other animal will be killed and they will all be gathered before the elders of the town. The elders will receive their share, the Ẹlẹ́gbẹ́ will receive theirs, the Ọmọ Ogún will also receive theirs – that is the indication that they are doing the Ọba's funeral. There are special people [who bury the Ọwátàpá]. They are not the chiefs, they are special groups of people in the town who are responsible for it and the sacrifice ... So we don't know, how they usually do it, even we the high chiefs in the town must not witness it, we can't see them.
> (FI-12, Ìtàpá-Èkìtì, 1991)

Other high-ranking titled chiefs would also be buried in the bush by Ifá priest-diviners with each particular title determining precisely what is done:

> When someone dies, if he is an important chief in the town, all the chiefs in the surrounding area will come there after being informed of the death by the deceased's family. They will say that 'the father's body is hot'. After saying this, the chiefs would have known that the man is dead. They will carry along leafy branches while going to inform the other chiefs. For example when the late chief Ọbaàró died, I, as a chief in his area, they came to give me ₦10 to inform me of his death and likewise to some other chiefs in our street, saying that the body of the man is 'hot'. So whenever we are given something like that, we will all gather and go to his house to do some sacrifices and for the sacrifices we will receive some things from the children of the deceased. In some cases we will receive animals, money, wine, foods, and after these things have been given to us, we usually do one thing, that *A ń ságùn*, 'running around the streets' that belong to us. [It is] all the town if it is the Ọba or any chief that is for the general town (Olómọdétàpá), it will be done throughout the town.
> But for those chiefs like myself who are quarter heads, we will do it as from Ìláròo to Ẹgẹ̀tún. Some set of chiefs called *Ẹlẹ́gbẹ́* will run round three times, and they will run round after each time they will have received something from the family of the deceased. After doing all these things, all the high chiefs and the elders would sit down in the deceased house and would report to us that they have finished. Whatever things has been given to us, the chiefs would be gathered and some will be given to the *Ẹlẹ́gbẹ́* and to the *Ọmọ Ogún* [young soldiers] who only took part in the running but who are not chiefs ... And then the high chiefs will take ours.
> (FI-12, Ìtàpá-Èkìtì, 1991)

When others, such as an *oníṣàngó* (Ṣàngó priest) dies, 'the burial will be performed by [other] *oníṣàngó* [in order to] maintain the peaceful atmosphere in the town and to rid it of infectious diseases ...' (FI-25, Ìtàpá-Èkìtì, 1991; cf. Barber 1991: 123–7). Similarly, special rituals and burial in the bush (*igbó awo*) are performed by the surviving members of the hunters *Ẹgbẹ́ Ọdẹ* and *babaláwo* diviner-herbalist groups. All of these people are buried in the bush to protect the town from their extraordinary, spiritual power rather than because they had died inauspiciously.

The other category of bush burials consists of people who have died 'bad deaths' (Ajiṣafẹ 1924). Depending on the type of death, these individuals might be buried in several different ways. For example, children who died as infants and who are identified as *àbíkú* (or 'born to die' children) are likely to have their bodies buried in the bush, outside the settled area of the village (Ògúntúyì 1979: 35).[7] Those who suffered death from drowning and by falling from trees are buried next to a stream or under the tree they fell from. Two other types of people – hunchbacks and women who died in labour – are routinely left in the bush by *babaláwo* using special methods. The former are put into clay pots and buried to prevent 'a serious outbreak of disease', as one woman chief put it (FI-4, Ìtàpá-Èkìtì, 1991), whereas the bodies of women who died in labour are tied to an *irokò* tree in the bush, along with their belongings, in the hope that their spirits will not return to perpetuate this misfortune.

CHANGES IN BURIAL PRACTICES

The burials of these categories of people whose conditions of death are considered to be dangerous in some way (see Hertz 1960: 85) and are buried in the bush (as opposed to the town) distinctively illustrate changes in 'traditional' burial beliefs and practices. Some of these changes are associated with religious conversion while others are attributed to 'modern developments' such as schools and hospitals. For example, instances in which women who have died in labour are tied to a tree in the bush are now extremely rare, as two people explained:

> In the case of a pregnant woman, in the past such people are buried in the bush, together with all their belongings but today not many women died with pregnancy. Civilisation has overcome that, whenever a woman in this situation is at the point of death, the child will have to be removed.
>
> (FI-22, Ìtàpá-Èkìtì, 1991)

> If a pregnant woman is about to deliver and tends to have some complications, such a woman will be rushed to the hospital and even when taken to the hospital, even if the woman eventually dies, she will be operated on immediately in order to bring the baby out from her womb. Therefore such a woman can be buried normally at home, this will not be a problem case anymore [the way it was before] due to the absence of the ability of removing the child from the dead mother's womb – the way modern medicine does it.
>
> (FI-9, Ìtàpá-Èkìtì, 1991)

Similarly, the bodies of children who die young are no longer buried in the bush as a result of the decline in infant mortality:

> In the past, cases of *àbíkú* were usually buried in the forest just because they are still young children. Young children when they die are not usually buried within the living quarters. But nowadays the *àbíkú* case is not so usual. Due to the emergence of medical doctors, childcare

has been improved and therefore death among children has been very infrequent, making the occurrence of *àbíkú* rare now.

(FI-17, Ìtàpá-Èkìtì, 1991)

In these cases, changing practices are attributed to medical doctors and hospitals – to 'civilisation', whereas in others, Christianity is the factor that explains these changes:

> In the case of somebody falling off a tree in the past, if it were a palm tree that he fell from, such a tree would be cut down and the deceased buried at the base of such a tree with the feathers of a parrot being placed at this grave, so that such a thing would not reoccur. If it were that a tree (or branch) accidentally fell on one, such a tree would be cursed by the herbalist and cut down and the deceased buried at its base. But nowadays with Christianity taking over the past ways of life, such is not usually done anymore. Instead, sacrifices are performed at the spot of death and the deceased is then brought home in order to bury such a person at home. Such sacrifices are performed in order to prevent future reoccurrences.
>
> (FI-20, Ìtàpá-Èkìtì, 1991)

Some, but not all, practices that are specifically associated with traditional religious worship, such as the placement of parrot feathers (*ikó odídẹ*; Apter 1992: 113–14) used in the Yẹmọja festival, would be avoided by many Christians and Muslims.

Changes in burial processes also suggest that a certain diminution in the powers and importance of traditional chiefs has taken place (see Apter 1992: 166–9). For example, one man described the ways in which chiefs had been honoured at past funerals but which are no longer being done:

> In the past, if someone had died in the last year, during the one's year's remembrance, the people in the town would be informed that the family wanted to do the funeral of that deceased father if he was a chief in the town. All the different categories of chiefs in the town would come together and they would arrange seating in small groups. Mats would be spread. Those male chiefs would sit separately and each would be dropping some amounts [of money], saying that they were doing the funeral of a particular person. They would mention the name and amounts donated by individuals to everyone there.
>
> Now it is different. If one's father died all these things are not done any longer; the different categories of chiefs are no more invited. The family will only go and buy cows and invite many people and they will be eating and dancing ...
>
> (FI-8, Ìtàpá-Èkìtì, 1991)

This past respect for the chiefs and the king was also reflected in specific distributions of meat given to the Ọwátàpá (King of Ìtàpá) during funeral observances. These special attentions paid to the seating and feeding of the king and chiefs has diminished in favour of a more general distribution of meat among funeral guests in recent years. These changing practices suggest the erosion of the political and economic powers of town elders – househeads, chiefs and the king – as well as the impact of Christianity on traditional practices during the colonial and postcolonial periods.[8]

Conversion to Christianity and Islam

During the twentieth century, the majority of Èkìtì residents converted either to Christianity or to Islam (see Chapter 1), and this affected some of the ways in which bodies were buried. Some have emphasised similarities with burial in the past, with one older man, the Alameku (the head diviner-herbalist in the town) saying, 'It is almost the same but the only difference is that in the past, people didn't kill cows but goats' (FI-20, Ìtàpá-Èkìtì, 1991). Others have stressed differences in beliefs about the afterlife and in specific burial practices, as did another older man, a member of the Christ Apostolic Church:

> The reason for the funeral ceremony in the olden days is not the same with that of nowadays, in fact, that of the olden days is no more used [relevant]. Because nowadays we are doing it for the sake of Jesus Christ, since we were in the darkness in the olden days and what we were even doing then was not clear to us. But when we now know Jesus ... we now believe that, yes, it is those that died in the Lord (*Olúwa*) are those who will meet God. And when we now see the introduction of Christianity, after someone has been baptised, we arrange a funeral ceremony in honour of such person. The Christians will be responsible for every one of the needed rites in [the] ceremony to be performed ... for the Christians, be it thanksgiving service, the burial, and many things from the Bible [that] will be read in the presence of that dead body, then the baptismal certificate (*ìwé ìsàmì*) of the person will be enclosed along with the dead body inside the casket (*opósín*).
>
> (FI-1, Ìtàpá-Èkìtì, 1991)

What is particularly interesting in this man's explanation is the way that ideological differences in explaining life after death are symbolically expressed in what is buried with the deceased. For Christians, the deceased will be buried with his or her baptismal certificate in a coffin filled with many fine cloths. In a Muslim burial, 'the Muslim corpse must not use more than six cloths to cover the corpse' (FI-14), as one man noted, emphasising the immateriality of life on earth. For past practitioners of traditional religion in Ìtàpá, food and other items needed for a journey would be supplied:

Figure 6.4 Women from the royal family bringing water for cleansing the palace shrine during the annual *Ìtàlè* festivities, Ìtàpá-Èkìtì, February 1992. (photograph by the author)

> Nowadays, it is known that there is no benefit as such to the deceased but in the past, our people had the belief that the reason for having a funeral ceremony is that whatever we used in performing such will be conveyed to heaven where the deceased would use it him or herself. For instance, when a grave is dug, in the past, and the corpse is to be buried, a dish of pounded yam, complete with meat and stew, will be prepared and when the corpse is buried, such a dish will be placed beside it within the grave with the belief that it would have something to eat when moving to the land of the dead. But Christianity has made us to realise that all this is vanity and nonsense. All the things performed during a funeral ceremony tend to have no effect on the one being buried apart from the fact that it enables people to celebrate a feast together and also to show that the deceased possessed children who are reputable and successful in life.[9]
>
> (FI-17, Ìtàpá-Èkìtì, 1991)

This man's comment that things performed during the burial 'have no effect on the one being buried' points to an important shift in beliefs about the spirit of the deceased and relations between the living and the dead. According to some traditional religious practitioners, the deceased's spirit can be contacted by the living through sacrifice (ẹbọ). This communication may be accomplished through a special ceremony or during the Ìtàlè festival, one of the three major traditional rituals officiated by the Ọwátàpá, held annually in Ìtàpá (see Figure 6.4).[10]

CELEBRATING *ÌTÀLÈ* AND COMMUNICATING WITH THE DEAD

The celebration of *Ìtàlè*, as described by one chief, is a time when animals are killed (*wọn se sa*) by each house-head to feed the spirits of deceased family members who are said to be present in the town at this time:[11]

> The belief is that ... those who died have something that they can do for us still living. That is the reason that yearly they celebrate one festival in this town called *Ìtàlè*. If someone is a male he will be told to kill ram for the sacrifice and the father of that person will come and eat out of that meat. But if someone fails to kill ram, we are told that his father, when he comes will not get anything to eat, but will be going about to eat other people's meat. This is because at this time all of us will be killing ram during the festival so that our own father will not be going up and down to beg for meat somewhere else from those who are not his children.
>
> (FI-2, Ìtàpá-Èkìtì, 1991)

For some, this is also a time to make requests of the deceased who are believed to intercede for their children:

> There is one festival in Ìtàpá here when everybody will be asked to kill a goat or ram to appease the dead and to ask them, to inquire for their wants ... I have seen a case where as a result of this ritual, a woman gave birth to a new baby. I have equally seen a case where a family was full of social unrest, today they will cry, tomorrow they will cry, but when a prophetess advised them to appease their dead father and mother, surprisingly when this was done, there has never been anything of that sort again.
>
> (FI-22, Ìtàpá-Èkìtì, 1991)

In times of crisis, the appeasement (*ètùtù*) of dead parents may also be performed, as one man explained:[12]

> I know of a case of a person who when the parents were alive, he did not bear children at all. He had tried all possible ways but all came to failure .... He was instructed to sacrifice to his parents [after they died], with a ram to be given to the father. After this was done, within a year, that he should ask for good children after sacrificing that ram ... A person who had gone to *babaláwo*, *Aládurà* and even medical doctors and still the problem prevailed, when he now offered the sacrifice to his father, he was then answered and gave birth to a boy. Definitely his

father has not left him and since he knows of all the suffering that he had gone through and he knows that definitely his child will give birth to children who will witness his fruitful end. So that's how he became a father of children.

(FI-11, Ìtàpá-Èkitì, 1991)

For some townspeople, the need to appease their parents may be suggested by a herbalist-diviner or through an Aládurà prophet or prophetess. The idea of making an offering may also come to people in dreams, one of the principal means that they mentioned for communication between the living and the dead:[13]

> You [may], for example, see your father in a dream – who informs you to go and do a particular thing ... But [not] to discuss with him physically, it is not possible. They do see us but we cannot see them and we can [only] see them in dreams ..., [when] you may be told after prayer to go and offer something to your father.
> (FI-5, Ìtàpá-Èkitì, 1991)

However, others were uncertain about whether the living and dead could communicate or whether the spirit of the deceased was present at the time of its funeral. One man gave an example to explain his doubt:

> That area [of funerals], I really don't understand myself. Because, one day, an old man instructed his children to slaughter a cow. The man had built a house and had just finished roofing it. He then told his children to take the cow to the part of the house that would be his living quarters. He then laid down a white cloth and even wore a fine dress, declaring that he wanted to perform a joyous ceremony. The cow was slaughtered and all of its blood was retrieved and poured over the place where he intended to sleep [be buried]. After making sure that all the blood was collected and used as intended, he then brought all the children together and asked them whether any of the cow's blood actually reached him. They answered by saying that none had reached him. He then said that when he died, none of the blood of the animals killed during his funeral will reach him either. Therefore, they should try by all means to care for him now when he is still alive. This made me to believe that the corpse gains nothing although there may be certain things being thought by the old people when they die.
> (FI-10, Ìtàpá-Èkitì, 1991)

Furthermore, some were outright sceptical about the possibility of this communication, as was one man who stated, 'I don't believe that there is any relationship between the living and the dead. Some say that they talk with their dead fathers in their dreams. Well, I don't believe in that. He who dies is dead, he is gone!'

BELIEFS ABOUT RELATIONS BETWEEN THE LIVING AND THE DEAD

It is impossible to say what the extent of the range of beliefs about relations between the living and the dead was in the past. Presently, with several different religious ideologies being observed in the town, there is no single interpretation of this subject. In an extended interview in 1991, the late Ọbalókè thoughtfully expressed his views, which reflect his background as an older, educated Christian man who was also a local government judge and a traditional chief in the town. His comments are instructive for they indicate the complex ways that people are assessing and reassessing their beliefs about the dead and their implications for social relations among the living.

While the Ọbalókè did not rule out the possibility that spirits of the deceased could be present, he thought that communication with them was less frequent than commonly claimed. For example, he considered the *Ìtàlè* festival less in terms of a return of ancestral spirits and more as a memorial day:

> My own opinion about sacrificing to the dead as it is usually done in the *Ìtàlè* festival is that it is a form of remembrance of the dead ones, of their works when alive, and to show that all their deeds were not in vain. For our ancestors, in the past we believed that they came to the realm of the living once a year and whenever they came, we have to prepare food and drinks for them so that they would not journey back in hunger. We also had the belief that how much we gave them is how much they would also give back to us. It is part of the basis of performing *Ìtàlè*, for them to know that we haven't forgotten them and also to recognise them as those who can protect us from any danger.
>
> [ER: Do you believe that in cases where a barren woman is instructed to sacrifice some things on her father's grave ... that she will be able to bear children?]
>
> Such things happen. I believe there are such cases that are genuine but most of the cases that occur nowadays, they are fake, not genuine. Even without using anything but by using the truth on one's lips to say something, a thing will come to pass.
>
> (FI-17, Ìtàpá-Èkìtì, 1991)

Yet despite his views of a more limited interaction between the spirits of the dead and living at burial and commemorative rituals such as *Ìtàlè*, the late chief's ideas about spiritual rebirth reflect traditional religious beliefs about reincarnation:

> My belief is that when one dies, there is a particular destination to which the spirit goes because we hear that those that have died are

those that are being reborn. That's why life cannot come to an end. Those that are going are still coming back. Examples like the case of àbíkú testify to the fact that those who die come back again. Because if it is not so, the one who died and had his finger cut and when another child is born he has a stump of a finger – this implies that definitely, the one that left is the one that has come back. But for those that die out of old age, I know that there is a particular destination for their spirits and they still come back to the living realm, being reborn (cf. Morton-Williams 1960: 35).

The Ọbalókè also gave the example that when a woman dies and a wife for the family gives birth to a baby girl soon after, the child will be named Yétúndé (literally 'Mother has newly arrived') because of the rebirth of the deceased woman's spirit. And 'if the case is with a male, such a child is named Bàbátúndé, meaning that the father that has gone [died] has come back.' His views about rebirth contrast with his more hesitant remarks about resurrection:

Well, according to what we have learnt of Christianity, it is stated as a fact that resurrection exists but I myself, as an individual, there is a limit to my belief in such a concept. Because since the world has started, some millions of years ago, we have not witnessed any case of resurrection occurring before, apart from Christ's case which we have heard. We haven't witnessed any before or after this case. So, that's why my answer tends to be restricted a bit, whether it is [possible] or not.

These remarks suggest that he found Christian teachings in this regard to be less persuasive than traditional explanations. Indeed, his comments would seem to support Hefner's (1993: 23) observation that conversion has both ideological and political dimensions that intersect in particular ways in certain historical settings.[14]

In responding to questions about burial and relations with the dead, some people expressed total rejection of past practice, as did one Muslim man when he insisted that children come to a childless couple from God, not from praying to their parents. Others, such as practitioners of traditional religion, maintain past beliefs such as the idea that the spirit of the deceased is present for five weeks after its demise and is present at the time of burial. Still others support nuanced reinterpretations of these past practices and beliefs, for example, casting communication with dead relations as prayer rather than as sacrifice to the dead, and referring to the naming of children as Bàbátúndé and Yétúndé as honorifics for the dead rather than as instances of ancestral rebirth. These shifts in interpretation suggest that for many, the idea of continued relations with the dead are too important to abandon (McCall 1995) because of the continued salience for relations among the living. Three principal areas in which connections between dead and the living continue to be made include naming practices, burial in the family house and the need to have children.

CONTINUITY, CHANGE AND KIN RELATIONS

When asked about the importance of naming (see Olúsànyà 1989b: 82), one man explained this in terms of family continuity:

> It is from the beginning, all families have names.[15] Although they may build several houses – about 30 to 100 houses, the family will be bearing a single name. But on the seventh day after birth, a child will be given [its own] name. Now all these Davids and Gabriels are from the Bible and didn't exist before. But on that naming day, the child's hair will be cut, and the child will be washed and given that family name.
>
> (FI-8, Ìtàpá-Èkìtì, 1991)

The linking of individuals, past and present, through names is also materialised through the use of *oríkì orílè* (Barber 1991: 13), a form of oral poetry associated with particular quarters in the town. These poems include references to extraordinary historical events, to family deities and to the natural landscape of family land (see chapter 2). These connections of family, names and place are further emphasised through two forms of burial: the burial of infants' hair cut at the naming ceremony on family land, and the burial of bodies in family houses, with the deceased person's name and date of demise written on a concrete grave cover.

Another way of linking the dead and the living through names, aside from the names Bàbátúndé and Yétúndé (or Ìyábò), is to perform a ritual known as *ìdíléde* (FI-19, Ìlúpéjú-Èkìtì, 1991). Newborn infants are taken to a diviner who ascertains the particular ancestor reborn in the new child and consequently the child's future preferences and habits, as described by one African Church official:

> I have not done it before but many people believe it and many people have been going to find out such things. In some place, they are told that the child came to follow a particular person, some will say the type of religion the child should follow, the food he or she should be eating, or that they must not walk at a particular time. They usually go somewhere to ask some people who are specialists in this. But personally, I don't believe it.
>
> (FI-13, Ìtàpá-Èkìtì, 1991)

As was the case with this man, unless one is a practitioner of traditional religion, people are disinclined to perform this ritual, preferring Muslim or Christian naming ceremonies instead.[16]

Regardless of religious affiliation, the importance of having children to maintain the family name is critical, as one woman chief indicated. 'The way a name may not die is if one has children. But if one is childless, after about fifteen years, it will be forgotten and the name will die' (FI-15, Ìtàpá-Èkìtì, 1991). Furthermore, by bearing children, people not only maintain the family name but also maintain their claims to family houses, land and titles, in part by their physical presence (see Chapter 8), as the following proverb suggests: *Ẹni t'ó jó kòkó, kò run gún; ẹni t'ó jólé, kò run gún; ṣùgbọ́n ẹni tí a bí tí kò túra ẹ̀ bí, ó run gún* (Anyone who sets a cocoa plantation on fire, doesn't destroy inheritance; anyone who sets a house on fire, doesn't destroy inheritance; but anyone who is born and fails to give birth him/herself destroys inheritance) (FI-8, Ìtàpá-Èkìtì, 1991).

While coming home to Ìtàpá to be buried, as explained above, is considered to be both more prestigious and morally appropriate than being buried as a stranger in Ìbàdàn or Lagos, there are other reasons for being buried in one's house, as a grave serves as a form of mark of ownership. Not surprisingly, 68 per cent of the ninety-four *ọmọ Ìtàpá* living in Adó-Èkìtì, Àkúrẹ́, and Lagos interviewed in 1992 said that they preferred to be buried in their houses in Ìtàpá. Furthermore, the extensive preparation needed for a home-town burial brings family members together (Àjàyí 1993) and strengthens urban and rural ties (Adépọ̀jù 1974).[17]

Having children is critical then, not only for the continuation of family names and houses, but also for the successful realisation of these home-town burials, with each child contributing his or her share, as one man described:

> For example, my father died in 1978 ... when we were in Ìbàdàn. Immediately he died, a meeting of his children was ... convened together and we started discussing the funeral programmes for the deceased's burial, with each tendering various suggestions on the issues brought up. We then agreed on certain plans of action with the elder persons amongst us allocating the various roles present in the programme to each individual. Those who will be responsible for meat, drinks, food etc. [were assigned] even down to the youngest child. Everything was arranged and implemented to the last point and it was generally successful. When the corpse was carried home, it was first laid in the house; then it was laid in state [in a coffin] for all to see the deceased for the last time; this was done for two hours. After this, the corpse was buried with a Christian funeral service performed for him.
> (FI-18, Ìtàpá-Èkìtì, 1991)

It is interesting to note that particular aspects of this funeral – the preservation of the body in the mortuary, transporting the body from Ìbàdàn in an ambulance, the Christian funeral service, the use of a programme and coffin – are considered to be examples of progress and necessary improvements over prior practices. Other changes, such as burial in cemeteries or the use of wills or death certificates, are not.[18] This selectivity suggests that ideas about progress in Ìtàpá are locally constituted, and continue to include having many 'good' children who can perform a 'spectacular' funeral.

Nonetheless, these three continuities – naming, house burial and funeral performance by children of the deceased – have been affected by certain aspects of what is locally construed as development. For example, while improved transportation allows ọmọ Ìtàpá to return home for family funerals and Christmas-related events, this has not increased the participation by those living outside in festivals associated with traditional religious practice such as Ìtàlè. Thus, while family members may feel an emotional and/or spiritual connection with their dead parents, it is mainly those who permanently reside in Ìtàpá who regularly observe these connections through rituals presided over by male house-heads, quarter chiefs, and other knowledgeable elders. The reduction in young people residing in the town and the decline in the number of followers of such rituals suggests that the authority of traditional chiefs, religious leaders and house-heads over young people – based on their ritual knowledge – has been undermined by urban migration.

Furthermore, conversion to Christianity and Islam has affected some people's belief in the rebirth of ancestral spirits. Unlike the late Ọbalókè, many Christians and Muslims believe in an afterlife where the departed spirit resides 'by the side of God', or 'in Heaven above', rather than coming back to earth reborn as a new child. For them, naming a child for or praying to a deceased parent is done simply to honour their memory rather than to mark ancestral rebirth or to communicate directly with the dead.

Finally, some people stated that having many children is no longer necessary for performing an impressive funeral since a reduced number of children who are educated, wealthy and responsible (that is, 'good') children may be able to perform an equally imposing one. Indeed, the costs of education (described in Chapter 1) preclude the ability to raise many such children, lending further support to this reassessment. Thus while arranging an appropriate funeral for a parent and having sufficient children to do so continues to be important, what constitutes a sufficiency has changed, particularly if the children are 'good', as one man observed:

> Only one child can do it, in fact, it is possible for a single person to do what twenty people will do. The reason for having many children in the olden days is that 'whosoever is buried by children, he is the one that has children'. In the olden days there could be someone having five children, and all of them died in his presence. (May God not let us bury our own child.) That is why they used to have many children in the olden days since we didn't know which one would be left to bury us. But good children are the best, not the number as [the proverb says], 'more children, more poverty' … If the children are many and

are well-to-do, they will organise a fitting funeral ceremony in honour of their father or mother, but if they are poor, they won't do anything.
(FI-3, Ìtàpá-Èkìtì, 1991)

These shifts in thinking about the number of children needed to perform 'a fitting funeral ceremony', about the importance of children's performing annual sacrifices for their deceased parents, and the ritual need to identity ancestors reborn in newborn children suggest a certain attenuation in relations between the ancestors and descendants, including beliefs about the formers' intervention in the latters' fertility. These reassessments about relations with the dead and the related reduction in the performance of sacrifices for dead parents in cases of infertility has undermined the authority of senior elders, lending legitimacy to some younger people's preference not to have as many children as their parents and grandparents had in the past. Nonetheless, no one suggested the possibility of not having any children. Bearing children, who perform funerals and maintain a wide range of family ties, continues to be a defining element in what constitutes a moral person.

CONCLUSION

When one older man was asked about the effects that the dead have on their living descendants, he answered with uncertainty but honesty, 'This is a very hard question because what you cannot see with your two eyes, you cannot easily affirm it' (FI-13, Ìtàpá-Èkìtì, 1991). Despite this lack of eye-witnessed evidence (or perhaps because of it), women and men in Ìtàpá hold a range of ideas about what constitutes proper burial and relations between the living and the dead. For some, these ideas – supported by changing religious beliefs, improved transportation, Western education, urban living and new sources of wealth – have altered the dependency of the young on rituals associated with death controlled by their elders. This chapter and the previous two have examined various aspects of these changing ideas about relations between juniors and elders – evidenced in thinking about virginity, about child-fostering and about ancestral relations – all of which have implications for the population of the town. In Chapter 4, young people's redefinition of virginity and the decline in arranged marriage have altered the control of seniors over their juniors' marriages and timing of childbearing. In Chapter 5, the reconsideration of child-fostering represents some younger people's attempts to limit the demands and obligations to a broad group of extended kin, specifically in terms of raising a child. In this chapter, reinterpretations of burials and relations with the dead by some people reinforce the questioning of town elders' authority in general and over childbearing in particular, legitimating the possibility of having fewer, 'good' children. Yet despite these changes in belief and practice, the enduring importance of having people – children, followers, supporters

– continues to support relatively high levels of fertility (described in Chapter 3). The following three chapters examine some of the reasons associated with practices and policies of the Nigerian State that make having many people, particularly children, a vital necessity for the residents of this rural Èkìtì town.

PART III

POPULATION, DEVELOPMENT AND THE STATE

7

PERSONAL HYGIENE, PUBLIC SANITATION AND WESTERN EDUCATION

> Cleanliness of the home, cleanliness of the body,
> Cleanliness of our food, cleanliness of our surroundings,
> Cleanliness can conquer all diseases.
> Yoruba children's song, cited in Adéwùyá, *Family Living*

> It was the children who usually first spotted the khaki pith helmet framed against the sky, followed shortly by a youngish face which was set in a conscious, official duty sternness. It pronounced every household guilty until proved innocent. Next followed a disproportionately long neck which, everyone remarked, must have been his main qualification for the job of Sanitary Inspector. It enabled his face to peer round tight corners, pry underneath beds, into cupboards and reach between rafters and negotiate awkward shelves ...
> Ṣóyinká, *Iṣárà*

In Ìtàpá-Èkìtì, sanitary inspectors known as *wolé wolé* (literally, 'look house, look house') began to make their appearance probably in the late 1930s.[1] Like the pith-helmeted, long-necked inspector described by Wọlé Ṣóyinká, these men – often young and with some education – worked for the colonial Native Authority.[2] They inspired fear, disdain and sometimes respect among the townspeople, depending on the situation and individuals involved, as one man explained:

> During the period of Sanitary Inspector Òṣiré from Ìjèṣà-Iṣu-Èkìtì, things were going on in an orderly way at Ìtàpá because he would first send a message to the Kabiyesi [the King] telling him of the exact date he would come for a visitation. And Kabiyesi in turn would send out a message through the town crier that the sanitary inspector would be coming for inspection on Friday of that week, for example, so people would be fully prepared to receive him warmly. But when Inspector Adébáyọ̀ from Ìkọ̀lé came, things were turned upside down because this man would enter into our town without any notice. He caused confusion in the town and even people who had planned to go to the farm that day would find it difficult to go. If this man caught anybody in a dirty environment, he would fine such a person [£2] and would

ask him to report to court on a particular day and if you didn't want to appear in court, the person in question would pay the sanitary inspector. (SI-3, Ìtàpá-Èkìtì, 2000)

These inspections, associated with *igbàlódé* ('civilisation' and a contemporary state of affairs), were both invasive and instructive. Indeed, the introduction of public sanitary measures was one of the principal ways that townspeople learned new ideas about public sanitation. For example, the well-liked Inspector Òṣiré,[3] rather than fining people found guilty of violations, 'would assemble them at the palace and would lecture them; the people of the town learned from him' (SI-5, Ìtàpá-Èkìtì, 2000). These sanitary inspectors were also responsible for inspecting the grounds and facilities of government schools, the principal place where people learned new ways of thinking about public health and the related topic, personal hygiene. Primary school students were taught about care for their bodies and clothing, about food preparation and about cleaning their environment. They were also regularly inspected by their teachers to ensure that they met these standards. In a similar but less regular way, their teachers were also inspected – regarding their presentation, class lessons and school environment – by officials of the Ministries of Health and of Education who occasionally visited the town (Burke 1996: 38). Thus, both students and teachers shared experiences and particular forms of knowledge about new ways of cleaning their teeth, bathing and eating food acquired through Western education that led themselves to distinguish themselves from other townspeople without this education, including at times their own parents and grandparents.

This chapter discusses changes in the everyday perception and practice of hygiene. It begins by examining the ways in which one aspect of Western education, primary school health classes, have affected parent–child relations and, indirectly, people's thinking about fertility and family size. It then considers the contradictory position of the Nigerian state, both during the colonial and post-colonial eras, which promoted and continues to promote health practices without providing the infrastructure that would make these practices realistically possible. The first section looks at the institutionalisation of healthcare during the colonial period and the subsequent changes in the practice of everyday 'disciplines of the body' practised in Ìtàpá that occurred with the teaching of health classes in primary school. The second section examines how healthcare practices learned in school are reflected in what is considered 'good' childcare and in the differing views of parents and children. Finally, it considers how the state's failure to provide the infrastructural support for community public health intersects with these changing practices associated with cleanliness and childcare as well as with thinking about family size.

IMPARTING CLEANLINESS PRACTICES

Cleanliness is next to Godliness
Ìmọ́tótó ni Ìwàbí-Ọlọ́run
    Cited in Obogbaimhe, *Primary Health Education*

The institutionalisation of hygiene practices which took place during the colonial period in southern Nigeria (from approximately 1900 to 1960) included establishing a Medical and Health Department (Brown 1992), starting training schools for sanitary inspectors (Ekiti Div 1/1, File no. 857; Ekiti Div 1/1, File no. 995; Ondo Prof 1/1, File no. 612; Ondo Prof 1/3, File no. D.21), writing public health ordinances (for example, CSO 26/2, File no. 15683, vol. I, 1925; CSO 26/2, File no. 30314) and teaching domestic science (Denzer 1992) and health classes (Millman 1930; IBMINED 1/2, File no. CIW 432; IBMINED 1/2, File no. 3427A) in schools. The personal and public hygiene practices imparted through these measures had political, economic and moral implications as well as health benefits (Turner 1984). For British colonial officials' concern with the control of bodies – through personal hygiene and environmental ordinances – reflected a larger interest in political order (Comaroff and Comaroff 1992) and in the control of labour associated with economic interests (Packard 1997):

> To record epidemics, attack uncontrolled disease and improve health was to exercise an indirect effect on the size of the population ... It was the requirements of contemporary states which were emerging, requirements which treat the population as an anonymous force, whose potential is primarily to be measured in terms of its labour power.
>   (Vigarello 1988: 142)

These policies had moral implications as well. Whereas some colonial officials and missionaries genuinely hoped to contribute to better health conditions in south-western Nigeria, the reduction of diseases associated with hygienic practices also enhanced the morally benevolent image that colonial and mission officials sought to convey (Hunt 1999; Vaughan 1991). This dual concern with altruistic health interventions and with the political control of bodies, considered to be a critical aspect of development, may be seen in colonial documents from the 1930s:

> The extension of health work and the development of a 'health conscience' by instruction and demonstration, especially in the densely populated Native Administration areas, is considered to be one of the most important fields of development to which the activities of the Health Service should be directed.
>   (Medical and Health Department, Session Paper no. 23, 1932)

This governmental concern with the internalisation of a 'health conscience' and with the ordering of bodies for the good of national development has continued into the post-colonial era, as evidenced in the following excerpt from the book *Health is Wealth:*

> No wonder people say 'health is wealth', and also that the health of the people is the health of the nation. This is why we hear on the radio and television that 'Health is wealth, hygiene promotes health, dump your refuse at authorised sites' – 'A healthy Nation is a wealthy Nation; help keep Nigeria clean'.
>
> (Okeem and Okeem 1987: 8–9)

Recent state health initiatives associated with development include the Primary Health Care Programme, the Space Your Children campaign (see Chapter 1), and the EPI Immunisation programme.

Personal hygiene in this context reflects an emphasis on the view of the body as 'the site of personal strategies of health' (Turner 1984: 172), where individuals have a moral responsibility to control their bodies and environment through sanitary practices for the sake of national development.[4] The process whereby values associated with particular bodily practices were internalised relates more generally to a perception of development colloquially referred to as 'enlightenment', *ọlàjú*, literally 'opening up one's eyes' to ideas and things from outside, which was also reflected in the building of schools, hospitals and roads.[5] Yet *ọlàjú* may also be expressed in terms of changing values and practices learned in primary school health classes. Indeed, it is through such everyday practices such as brushing teeth and cleaning one's nails, along with more grandiose projects such as the building of bridges, that this 'enlightenment' associated with *idàgbàsókè*, development – in contrast to those associated with a 'backward, unenlightened' past – has concretely been experienced.[6]

THE PRACTICE OF CLEANLINESS, PAST AND PRESENT, IN ÌTÀPÁ-ÈKÌTÌ

By concentrating on health and hygiene taught in primary schools, I do not mean to suggest that indigenous ideas relating to cleanliness and health did not exist.[7] They surely did, as one older man describing the ostracism of people who were deemed to be dirty (*ọbùn*), makes clear:

> … No one would like to associate or eat with a dirty person. If it is a woman who was a food vender, no one would buy from her, no matter how beautiful the woman might be, she would be condemned – that she was a dirty woman. Anyone who could not bathe adequately or dress well was called *ọbùn* in the past. Anyone who could not take adequate care of the nose, nails, plaiting of the hair regularly, were all called *ọbùn* … There were many who were not beautiful but were very clean (*èèwọ̀*) and people did admire them in the past.
>
> (SI-10, Ìtàpá-Èkìtì, 2000)

Furthermore, older villagers described various practices – from bathing in local streams to cutting hair with iron knives – which indicate a concern with personal cleanliness, appearance and health. For example, in the past:

> One could assess the cleanliness of people through their legs. It is through the leg that we know who is prospering in the world (*Ẹsẹ̀ la fi rímọ ẹni aiyé yẹ́*). In the past whenever we bathed ourselves we would use palm oil to rub ourselves ... Some people would use *adun* (palm kernel oil) ... and to make our bodies disease-free, we would add medicine to the oil before rubbing it on our bodies.
> (HPF-A5, Ìtàpá-Èkìtì, 1993)

Yet some of these practices have changed along with associated concepts of cleanliness. Thus, Vaseline is now used rather than palm kernel oil (which has a strong odour) and people bathe with Lux soap rather than with locally produced black soap (*ọṣẹ dúdú*; cf. Burke 1996).

When younger people were asked to compare the care they received as children with the care that they presently give their own children, some (but not all) emphasised the differences rather than similarities in hygienic practices:

> My mother, she wouldn't care whether you bathed or brushed your teeth – at times I would only wash my legs. Then the nature of food – at times I would be given cold food [in the morning].
> (HPF-M1, Ìtàpá-Èkìtì, 1993)

> In the past my mother would find ashes or broken bottles or plates, she would grind them and then wash my teeth with it, using cotton wool. They saw this as their Maclean [a brand of toothpaste] but now when civilisation is common, even when the *pákò* stick is used, we will still wash again with Maclean.
> (HPF-M16, Ìtàpá-Èkìtì, 1993)

> During my childhood experience, my parents would only see me covered with just any type of dress, not minding whether it was dirty or tattered – although if tattered, my mother would put two or three dresses together so that the torn areas would be covered.
> (HPF-F20, Ìtàpá-Èkìtì, 1993)

These interviews reveal as much about the dearth of material resources, in particular, and the availability of healthcare products and clothing in the market, as they do about differences in health practices. Presently, a range of processed soaps are available for washing rather than materials from local plants (for example, the akee apple tree (*Blighia sapida*)), and an abundance of mass-manufactured (new and secondhand) clothes are sold, allowing children to wear a variety of clothing, rather than one or two handwoven cloths. Thus cleanliness (ìmọ́tótó) is not only associated with progress because it was acquired through Western education but also because it depends on the improved material and economic conditions which allow people to practise it. While not everyone learned about hygiene in primary school (some learned from watching others and from clinic posters), the practice of 'modern' forms of hygiene is enhanced by school attendance in two ways. First, students are specifically taught about cleanliness in primary school health classes (Brackett and Wrong 1930). Secondly, education is viewed as critical for obtaining employment in the modern sector, which in turn allows individuals to earn an income sufficient to practise up-to-date hygienic techniques.

HEALTH INSTRUCTION IN PRIMARY SCHOOL

Ọkàn pípé wà nínú ara líle
A sound mind in a sound body.
Cited in Akure Health Week Programme, 1950[8]

People remembered learning about personal hygiene, particularly in primary school. They have vivid memories about what they were taught – food preparation, teeth brushing and nail care – and why these practices were encouraged, for example:

> We were taught how to take care of our fingernails. Anyone who refused to cut and clean their nails, our teacher would beat the person on the back of their hand and especially fingers. We cut our nails every Sunday and were inspected in school every Monday. I was told that we cut them so that the insects (kòkòrò) could not enter our bodies.
> (HPF-F19, Ìtàpá-Èkìtì, 1993)

Moral values associated with cleanliness (goodness) and dirtiness (badness) were also instilled along with these particular bodily techniques of hygiene. These ideas were reinforced through inspection (see Figure 7.1) and corporal punishment as well as through the praise of neat students and the shaming of dirty ones, as this woman's comments suggest:

> There was a particular time in the week when all pupils would be inspected ... Those students who appeared neat would be invited out and made an example of how we should dress ourselves. At other times, those who failed to dress properly or who were dirty would be called out only to be put to shame. We would be told not to behave like such students but like the good ones ... Health defectors were caned and could be bathed publicly, using stinging plants with sand to 'wash' their bodies.
> (HPF-F3, Ìtàpá-Èkìtì, 1993)

These ideas were also emphasised in primary school health texts and posters with images of good and bad health behaviour, for example, in drawings of

Figure 7.1 Primary school health textbook depicting children showing hands to teacher during class inspection. (from E. A. Obogbaimhe, *Primary Health Education 6*, Ibadan: African Universities Press, 1983, p. 41)

the proper use of pit latrines and fingernail length.[9] Although a few people mentioned seeing health films with titles such 'Home Care' and 'Care of the Body' shown in cities such as Àkúrẹ́ and Lagos respectively, they were more likely to remember and describe posters and calendars used in school:

> There were pictures, not real films, in the school then – it looked like a calendar, usually placed in the headmaster's office. Some had inscriptions on how to take care of oneself. No film of any sort had ever been shown to us in school.
> (HPF-F3, Ìtàpá-Èkìtì, 1993)

> I haven't seen any film but I have seen pictures about health – it was drawn on the calendar whereby a child was passing faeces and another one was eating and how a fly flew from the faeces and dropped on the food the other boy was eating and how this boy developed cholera (*onígbámẹ́jì*, literally 'the owner of two calabashes'.
> (HPF-F14, Ìtàpá-Èkìtì, 1993)

Some of these posters were provided by the colonial government, with money provided by the Colonial Development Fund.[10] However, the health propaganda films (see Morton-Williams no date; Okediji and Ogionwo 1973; Vaughan 1991) described in extensive correspondence in archival documents had no direct impact on students schooling in Ìtàpá.[11]

Despite the relative dearth of materials both at school and at home, people remembered what they learned in primary school health classes with considerable detail and with a certain pride:

> I learned in school that each time, everyday of my life, that I got out of bed, that first of all I must wash my face ... and to remove everything from my eyes; then I learned to sweep every morning both inside and outside [the house] and to put the refuse in the bush.
> You see, those teachers teaching us then, as soon as we got to school early in the morning, they would check our fingernails and they would ask us to show our teeth. Because if the remains of yesterday's food were on our teeth, they would cane the person. One person would be ordered to get sticks (*pákò*) from the nearby bush and they would be given to the person to use to wash their teeth ... .
> I learned that each time [after using the toilet, one] must wash it with Izal or Dettol, that was how we washed the school toilet then – in my own place we used to go to the bush, so toilet habits that I learned could only be practised in school. I also used to go to the stream and bathe, since we had no bathroom.
> And I used to wash my school uniform then, I did this every weekend ... the nature of school uniforms differed then from what we use today, those ones gave room for dirtiness, the only problem was the invasion of lice, both on our body, head and cloth. It was a common thing to scratch our bodies and heads because of lice. You would see many children then smelling of Gamalin [insecticide] in the school.
> (HPF-M10, Ìtàpá-Èkìtì, 1993)

While most students did not have access to pit-latrines and many could not afford to buy the toothbrushes or toothpaste described in classes and school textbooks, these practices and images of educated, 'modern' behaviour raised expectations of what life should be, and this included 'good' and hygienic childcare. These changing expectations have had an effect on parent-child relations.

CLEANLINESS, CHILDCARE AND FAMILY SIZE

> You must always behave well anywhere you are. When you need something like books, pens, rulers, or uniform, you should not cry. You should feel free, if you have been a good child, to tell Mummy and Daddy to provide them for you.
> Obogbaimhe, *Primary Health Education, 4*

As the health text excerpt suggests, children who have attend health classes in primary school have come to expect certain things ('books, pens, rulers, or uniform') from their parents ('tell Mummy and Daddy to provide them for you') that place limits on parents' ability to care for many children.[12]

These demands are contrasted with the past, when children were said to be satisfied simply with food and a few clothes. For example, when asked about the Federal Government's 'Four is enough' programme (which recommended women have no more than four children), one man cited children's increased demands and the expenses of childcare as the reasons for his support:

> In the past when our grandfathers gave birth to many children, they had their reasons and one of the reasons was the belief that they would help in farmwork. Children's demands now surpass the past when a child can wear a dress for four years without a change, no demand for shoes. But today a parent has to do all that. A parent spends on his or her children throughout their lifetime, our government is doing nothing to assist parents so the idea of having four children to me is good.
> (DI97-4, Ìtàpá-Èkìtì, 1997)

The cleanliness practices taught in primary schools in Ìtàpá have led to heightened expectations of what constitutes proper childcare. 'Good parents' train their children to bathe daily, wash their clothes weekly and provide their children with the accoutrements of 'modern' hygiene: toothbrushes, toothpaste, Lux soap and a variety of clean clothes. These expectations are upheld by educated parents as well as by their children, as the following examples suggest:

> When I was a child, care of teeth was not always there. Many times I would eat without washing my teeth. For one week or more it would remain so. But now if I mistakenly give out food to my children when they have not brushed their teeth, they would reject the food.
> (HPF-M11, Ìtàpá-Èkìtì, 1993)

> My children complain that soda soap eats up their hands whenever they wash plates with it, whereas it was the soap I used throughout my childhood experience. I never knew then that it eats your hands or makes your hands wrinkled.
> (HPF-F2, Ìtàpá-Èkìtì, 1993)

> When I was born, I ate concoctions throughout, my parents would just go into the bush and get whatever roots and leaves and other things together. They would cook them for me to eat and bathe in. But now our children today can't take such foods.
> (HPF-F3, Ìtàpá-Èkìtì, 1993)

> In the past, one could spread a rag on the ground and ask children to sleep on it at night. But no one could do that to children of today. A cover cloth could be given to four children but not today. In fact things

aren't easy now, things are just too hard for people.

(CI95-4, Ìtàpá-Èkìtì, 1994)

Their children, who allegedly would turn up their noses at food taken before brushing their teeth, to soda soap, to herbal 'concoctions', and to single cover cloth, exhibit some of the qualities of the 'rotten' children described by Caldwell (1977b). He argues that this behaviour is a factor in explaining why parents decide to have fewer children, a point to which I will return later.

Along with this implicit criticism by children of their parents' behaviour, some of these same parents receive very explicit complaints from their own parents who disapprove of their healthcare innovations:

> Even now my parents are complaining, why should I be cleaning only four teeth [of an infant], that I should allow everything to grow before washing.
>
> (HPF-F14, Ìtàpá-Èkìtì, 1993)

> I wash my child's head with soap nearly every two days, but my mother complained that this should [only] be once a week or every two weeks.
>
> (HPF-M8, Ìtàpá-Èkìtì, 1993)

> I bathe my children everyday, just like my parents did for me but unlike my mother I use soap and sponge every time, which my mother condemns.
>
> (HPF-F9, Ìtàpá-Èkìtì, 1993)

This elderly parental disapproval seems to stem from the belief that they know best and that scarce resources should not be wasted on excessive bathing and the frivolous use of soap. Their different views on healthcare were also evident in how children were treated when sick, as one middle-aged father explained:

> My parents took care of my hygiene when I grew up ... they did well because I do exactly what I learned from them for my children but [with some exceptions]. I see that each time any of my children are sick I make sure that I seek medical assistance but in the case of my parents, the sickness must have been very serious before attempting to take me or my brothers to the hospital.
>
> (HPF-M13, Ìtàpá-Èkìtì, 1993)

This attitude about going to the hospital, taught in primary school texts (Obogbaimhe 1981: 7), suggests another aspect of the connection between education and family size. Improved healthcare learned in school contributes to lower infant mortality (Cleland and Wilson 1987: 22) and lessens the need to have many children in order to ensure the survival of some.

These expectations of hygienic childcare appear to be held generally by younger educated adults, some of whom say that they want to limit their family size to the number of children they can adequately care for. Yet they may not only face inter-generational disagreement over what constitutes proper childcare; they may also be hampered by contradictory state policies that undermine their ability to provide this care.

KEEPING CLEAN IN A CONTRADICTORY STATE

While the colonial and post-colonial state has been responsible for imparting much of this new knowledge about hygiene in government-assisted primary schools and through community sanitary inspections, it has failed to provide the sort of infrastructural support that would have made the application of this new knowledge tenable, creating a certain contradictory situation. In order to follow the health tenets learned in schools promoted by the government, local citizens need to carry out these measures themselves. Aside from the state's failure to implement an adequate system of water and sewage, it has contributed to other impediments, political and economic, to local public sanitation as well.

For example, the sanitary inspection of towns and schools was used as a source of political control, not only by British colonial officers but also by Native Authority officials operating under the system of 'indirect rule'. For example, in 1935, the King of Ìkọ̀lé signed a public health ordinance ostensibly designed to be 'in the interest of my people [that] Rules should be made for the improvement of sanitation throughout my district', including the authorisation of sanitary inspection:

> (8) It shall be lawful for District or Village Heads or Government and Native Administration Sanitary Staff or Native Administration Dressers with the authority of the District or Village Head to enter any premises at any time from 6 am to 6 pm for the purpose of examining as to the existence of any of the above nuisances. If any District Head or Village Head, responsible member of the Sanitary Staff or Native Administration Dresser is satisfied of the existence of any nuisance, a notice shall be served, called an abatement notice, on the person by whose act or neglect the nuisance arises, calling on that person to abate such nuisance within a certain period.
>
> (9) Failure to carry out any abatement order shall result in the person being dealt with by the Native Court. The maximum fine for any of the offences against rules 1–7 above shall be one pound. Any person who hinders or obstructs any District Head or Village Head, Sanitary Official or Native Administration Dresser in the execution of his duty shall be liable to such fine as the Court may order with a maximum of five pounds.

(10) These rules shall be in force from the date of His Excellency's approval and shall apply to the town and all villages throughout my District.

(Elékọ̀lé 1935, NNAI)

Two important aspects of these rules include the delineation of fines and their application to 'all the villages throughout my District'. The scepticism of the Ekiti Division District Officer on the value of formulating such rules somewhat missed the point:

I submit these rules without much enthusiasm. It is most improbable that in the larger districts any attempt will be made to enforce the rules in the sub-villages. Perhaps, however this does not matter. Further, I am doubtful as to whether any really methodical attempt will be made to enforce the rules even in the parent towns, in the absence of Sanitary Inspectors, who are definitely not wanted by the chiefs or people. There is, I suppose no harm in having the rules available for enforcement in case the impulse towards cleanliness should at any time come upon any town.

(Swayne 1935, NNAI)

Such rules furthered the control of the Ẹlẹ́kọ̀lé over towns such as Ìtàpá (which had long fought this control; see Chapter 2) that were under his jurisdiction, even if these inspections were only intermittent.[13] Furthermore, the possibility of imposing fines – an almost foregone conclusion if visits were unannounced as was the case with Sanitary Inspector Adébáyọ̀ mentioned earlier – made these potential visits even more remuneratively attractive.

Similarly, government officials in charge of sanitary inspection failed to check the more egregious behaviour of their inspectors. In Ìtàpá, for example, some of the same unprincipled state sanitary inspectors who visited houses also visited schools, as described by one man:

There were times when sanitary inspectors visited our school. There was one man called Adébáyọ̀ Wolé Wolé who would come and inspect parts of our body and school surroundings. [But] they concentrated more on the teachers and school environment, more than on the students and they would visit the toilet.

(HPF-M11, Ìtàpá-Èkitì, 1993)

This particular focus on teachers, rather than students, suggests that these inspections may have been seen as a source of income by some of these inspectors. This extortion could sometimes be personal and vindictive, as was described by one man:

The way these sanitary inspectors behaved in the past was very primitive. For instance, there were different political parties in the past: the Action Group, the NCNC, among others. If you and the sanitary inspectors did not belong to the same political party, they could count it as an offence ... and they will punish you ... They were a very wicked set of people.

(SI-1, Ìtàpá-Èkìtì, 2000)

However, people in Ìtàpá were not entirely defenceless in these situations. One woman described her efforts at applying what she had learned in school [probably in the early 1960s]:

About our environment, I learned that bushes around should be cut regularly and to sweep and hoe but my Daddy then would engage us in cleaning our environment only when there was word that the sanitary inspectors were coming.

(HPF-F18, Ìtàpá-Èkìtì, 1993)

By following public health rules outlined by the state only when forced to do so, some townspeople showed their contempt for these interventions. Somewhat later, in the 1980s in conjunction with the War Against Indiscipline (a government programme), a local sanitation committee (with one member from each of the town's eight quarters) was established to indirectly control these government sanitary inspectors:[14]

The reason why we introduced the local committee on sanitation was to prevent our people from falling into the traps of these wicked sanitary inspectors. These [committee] people would go around the town before the visit of the government sanitary inspectors and by so doing, every corner of the town would be made clean. And the question of fines would not arise because many times, the local committee and the sanitary inspectors would go around the town together for a thorough inspection.

(SI-1, Ìtàpá-Èkìtì, 2000)

Townspeople themselves were also able to lessen the impact of government attempts to implement particular public health programmes, such as the requirement to build latrines in every compound, by using various subterfuges.[15] For example:

In the past, latrine [ṣálángá] construction was introduced by the sanitary inspectors. People would dig the ground and cover it with planks and soil, with a small hole on the top. We [actually] made use of the bushes and the back of the house as a toilet but [made a latrine] for the sanitary inspector to see, for an adage says, 'seeing is believing'. When they came, we constructed one for temporary use because they used to collapse frequently after construction.

(SI-4, Ìtàpá-Èkìtì, 2000)

More recent attempts by the government to force townspeople to build latrines have failed, not so much because some townspeople are opposed to building them but because many cannot afford to do so:

> It is good to have a latrine in the house but I don't see it as development. The cost of digging a latrine is too much, a poor man can't easily make one. Anyone wanting to have a latrine now will have at least 3,000 naira.
>
> (DI97-38, Ìtàpá-Èkìtì, 1997)

Yet some older people are opposed to latrines, saying that they cannot imagine having such filthy things within their houses, as this older man, a farmer, explained:

> I don't see anything good for a person to defecate in the house where he's living. In the past no other person wanted another man to see his or her excreta, even if by accident a person excreted at the back of the house, by cockcrow (early in the morning), he or she would have to wrap it to be thrown into the bush. At the time one was excreting in the past, women normally used their wrappers to cover themselves and men used to pull their *agbádá* down so that people would not see their private parts. People in the past counted it an abomination for one to glance at another person while excreting. Anyone who did what the modern people are doing today, in the past could be seen as *ọbùn*, filthy, dirty person; and people would not like to eat with such a person; and they wouldn't allow such a filthy person to touch their belongings. How could one be living in a house, excreting and urinating in it?
>
> (SI-10, Ìtàpá-Èkìtì, 2000)

However, many younger people view them as a form of progress that will benefit the town, as did this retired schoolmistress:

> It is bad to defecate just anywhere so I decided to have a latrine and everyone in the quarter makes use of it. Not many educated people can excrete just anywhere so they need a place to hide to defecate ... To have a latrine is good, but not many people have accepted this and I don't know one reason. But to me, it would be a good thing if the people of about every three houses could have a latrine and this is going to be part of development.
>
> (DI97-3, Ìtàpá-Èkìtì, 1997)

But it is not the government that will build the latrines for every third house, as suggested. Rather, it will be the townspeople themselves who have been responsible for most of the public sanitation improvements in Ìtàpá. Aside from the locally constituted sanitation committee, townspeople have also

Figure 7.2 Incinerator near main market, Ìtàpá-Èkìtì, July 2000. (photograph by the author)

built a small incinerator near the main market (see Figure 7.2) and a wall around one of the main sources of water in the town, Ọṣun Stream (see Figure 7.3). It is through people and their labours that these self-help developments (Adédèjì and Otite 1997), as well as building latrines, clearing streams and sweeping houseplots have been accomplished. It is primarily through their own efforts that people in Ìtàpá have been able to live up to the hygiene expectations raised in primary school health classes.

150 POPULATION, DEVELOPMENT AND THE STATE

INFRASTRUCTURAL SUPPORT AND THE STATE

While students have learned the lessons taught in health classes in government-sponsored primary and secondary schools in south-western Nigeria, the actual execution of this learning is often not possible, as one man explained:

> About the care of our toilet and bathroom, I learned how to wash it everyday. This was only possible at school because a toilet was present

Figure 7.3 Young man fetching water from Ọṣun Stream, Ìtàpá-Èkìtì, July 1997. (photograph by the author)

but I could not put this [learning] into practice at home because our bathroom to this moment is not washable, it is just a room made of palm leaves. And taking care of the toilet at home is equally impossible because we use the bush (and at times possibly an area around the house (ààtàn, refuse heap), to pass excreta. I believe we were taught this to make us free from infectious diseases that can possibly be gotten from toilets and bathrooms.

(HPF-M16, Ìtàpá-Èkìtì, 1993)

This man's point that learning to wash non-washable bathrooms (and for many rural residents, non-existent toilets) is impossible 'to this moment' underscores the impracticality of such teachings without these facilities. The colonial and post-colonial state promoted health plans, yet neither was able to implement infrastructural support for these changes. As one Nigerian medical doctor (Lucas 1980: 241) observed:

The authorities failed to adopt and execute bold master plans. Buried in the archives are innumerable recommendations for dealing with urban sanitation but relatively few of these were implemented. For example, a special report on the plague epidemic strongly recommended the installation of a central sewage system into Lagos. That was in 1926 – and there were subsequent studies and reports – but at Independence, central sewerage had not been installed in Lagos (nor has it still in 1978).

Likewise, in Ìtàpá, despite health class instruction, sewage (with some exceptions) continues to be disposed of in the bushy areas surrounding the town and water is primarily obtained from streams and by collecting rainwater. There was until recently only one well (next to the Ọwátàpá's palace) and while for a few years piped water flowed in the town, it has since stopped. This situation has affected how hygiene is practised in the town, even when children were learning in school that:

We should wash our hands after the use of the toilet. [But] this was not practised then because there was not water around the school premises to do that ... but in the advanced classes (Primary 5 and 6), we were made to buy bowls that were placed in front of the classes so that we could wash our hands when dirty.

(HPF-M11, Ìtàpá-Èkìtì, 1993)

Some new concepts of cleanliness learned in primary school, such as keeping one's nails short and dirt-free, can be applied within the infrastructural capacities of rural communities such as Ìtàpá-Èkìtì. Others, particularly those aspects of personal hygiene and public sanitation requiring quantities of water, specifically, toilets, bathrooms and the washing of clothing and food utensils, are only accomplished through manual labour, such as fetching water from streams, which is largely provided by children.[16] In other words, if people aspire toward fulfilling the standards of cleanliness learned in state-sponsored schools and enforced (to some extent) by the state, they may need to have more rather than fewer children who can contribute their labour to make this possible.

This need for labour in the practice of personal hygiene and public sanitation as learned in primary school is further complicated by the deteriorating economic and political situation in contemporary Nigeria. The implementation of the Structural Adjustment Programme (SAP) and the subsequent currency devaluation (in 1986) have undermined townspeople's ability to purchase basic commodities such as food, kerosene and clothing, aside from hygiene-related products.[17] Some children work on family farms or sell produce as a subsistence economic strategy. Despite the fact that many younger parents (and their children) have incorporated the idea that personal and public hygiene practices are crucial elements of good childcare – supporting shifts in thinking about what constitutes proper care and how many children can be properly cared for – economic uncertainty and infrastructural disarray in Nigeria today underscore the need for having people, particularly in rural areas.

CONCLUSION

In this chapter, I have shown how changing personal hygiene and public sanitation practices over the last eighty years have contributed new ways of thinking about family size in Ìtàpá. The practices, mainly learned in primary schools, represent some of the small, intimate ways that people have experienced cultural changes, which have had an effect on their thinking about 'proper' childcare and about having fewer children.[18]

These changes concerning hygiene learned in schools may predispose parents to have fewer children for several reasons. This knowledge gives educated parents moral authority to make these changes, in that they know how to practise 'good' childcare and thus can raise fewer, but 'better' children, thus countering the demands sometimes made by elderly relatives – those 'veritable props of childbearing' (Olúsànyà 1989b: 76) – for many children. Their education also provides them with the sorts of jobs and economic wherewithal to practice 'good' childcare: to dress their children neatly, to bathe them regularly, to clean their teeth and to pay for healthcare (for example, medication and hospitalisation) that may improve the chances of their children surviving.

However, these shifts in what is considered proper childcare and hygiene by educated parents in Ìtàpá have not changed the idea that one needs children to perpetuate the family (Olúsànyà 1989b), nor that having many children can be a source of pride and status. But it is no longer the case that simply having many children is what is important. Rather, having children who are 'properly' cared for – with 'good' healthcare, hygiene and education – is what is respected. Yet meeting these new standards of 'good' childcare is becoming increasingly difficult, both in terms of expenses and the efforts involved. Taking sick children to the hospital entails considerable labour, for example, bathing and dressing them as well as organising transportation. Thus expectations of what constitutes 'good' childcare include an escalation of the efforts required to raise each child properly, which are reinforced by the expectations of children themselves that these needs will be met. These children's expectations may appear to coincide with the idea of 'rotten' children, described by Caldwell (1977b) as children who demand much in terms of expenses but who fail to make good returns on their parents' investment, hence leading parents to have smaller families. However, this idea fails to capture the underlying substance of these changes. Rather, it is the details entailed in the redefinition of 'good' childcare and hygiene – such as going to hospitals but also the daily bathing 'with a sponge and soap', the cleaning of fingernails and the ironing of frequently washed clothing – that have contributed to a sense of the possibility of 'a new order of things' (Hocart 1987: 37).

In these ways, health classes taught in primary schools and public sanitation ordinances have affected the thinking of women and men in Ìtàpá, supporting the argument that health interventions have been a powerful means of social control by the colonial and post-colonial state. Yet these new ways of thinking about childcare also coincide with local understanding of progress, as something acquired from outside (Peel 1978), with power abiding with those who have access and control over these new things. While district officers, local government officials, sanitary inspectors and other representatives of the state are in positions of power by virtue of this control, various townspeople themselves, mainly through education, have been able to acquire access and control over hygiene knowledge which has given them a certain power within their own community. While some people disagree with some hygiene innovations, exemplified by elderly parents' criticism of their sons' and daughters' childcare practices and reflecting their dislike of certain generational shifts in power, many view these new practices as an improvement over earlier ones. Several older people, for example, mentioned the former problem of lice, which more frequent washing of clothing and bathing with medicated soap has alleviated. Furthermore, hygiene innovations that are unacceptable to many people in Ìtàpá, such as indoor latrines, have been resisted, reflecting the belief that some 'traditional' practices represent something of fundamental value, which should be maintained.

In other words, while the introduction of hygienic practices during the colonial period represented an often condescending imposition of European knowledge for interested purposes, men and women in Ìtàpá have used this knowledge selectively to promote their own interests as well (see van Beusekom 2002: xxi). For them, having children and raising them up to be moral adults who will in turn raise children who will do likewise is vitally important. If new childcare techniques relating to personal hygiene and public sanitation will help them to do this, many people will practise them. They may do so even if it means having fewer children, despite the fact that the lack of state infrastructural support encourages them to do otherwise.

8

HOUSES, DESCENDANTS AND LAND TENURE

Àjò ò lè dùn kónílé ó má re lé
No matter the 'sweetness' of the place, people will depart to their homes later.

Yoruba proverb

I beg you not to regard money as the essence of life. If you do, it will only lead you onto a false path where, sooner or later, you will be alone. Money gives no security. On the contrary, it destroys all that is human in us.

S. Ousmane, *The Money Order*

Prior to the early 1900s, houses in Ìtàpá consisted of mud-block rectangular structures with doors consisting of mats (*awèrè*) made from woven palm fronds and roofs thatched with particular types of leaves such as *gbòdògì* (*Sarcophrynium* species; Abraham 1962: 246) and *ewé ìrà* (*Bridelia* spp.; Abraham 1962: 313). The danger from fire and the discomfort associated with these thatched roofs have viscerally contributed to townspeople's sense of progress. In the past, during the rainy season, 'People had to climb up on the roof to cover the leaking spots with broken pots so that people could sleep well and at times, we would climb up on the house two or three times a night to remove the filled-up pots' (DI97-18, Ìtàpá-Èkìtì, 1997). Presently, all the houses in the town are roofed with iron sheets. This improvement in roofing was initiated by men who walked to urban centres such as Ìbàdàn, Ifè, Ilésà, Ìlorin, and Òṣogbo to work planting yams and cocoa trees in the early part of the twentieth century (see Chapter 1). They used their earnings on their return to Ìtàpá to build houses roofed with iron sheeting, as the descendants of one such man explained:

> ... The late Pa Olúwájànà traveled to Warri where he worked for many years. On his return to Ìtàpá in 1903, he decided that he must have a building of his own and in the process he used all his earnings to purchase iron sheets, nails and wood planks. Since there were no sawmills then to get planks, they had to improvise by making use of a manual system of sawing felled trees. This system of sawing was as follows: a person would be standing in a grave-like pit dug underneath

Figure 8.1 Built around 1920 by Daniel Dada, one of the first houses with an iron roof in Ìtàpá-Èkìtì. Ìtàpá-Èkìtì, August 1997. (photograph by the author)

the log and another person would stand on top of the log. They would then draw the saw up and down to cut the planks. The people Pa Olúwájànà used to cut planks for his house were paid 9d. [nine pence] per day. The problem with this system was that the sliced timbers used to have rough faces, with irregular shapes and variable sizes ... the timber used for roofing the Olúwájànà house were sawed for up to two weeks before enough planks could be collected The iron sheet during Pa Olúwájànà's time cost about £1 1s. 0d. [one pound and one shilling] per bundle and nails were 6s. [six shillings] a bag; he used about eight bundles of iron sheets to roof his house. The labor for roofing was a communal affair based on the efforts of friends so his labor cost was just to provide food to feed the laborers.

(cited in Owóèyè 1999: 26)

The considerable effort that went into building and roofing such a house is testament to the determination of these men and importance of such structures in Ìtàpá-Èkìtì. According to Owóèyè (1999: 26):

While most people interviewed mentioned the use of communal labor to roof these early houses, the fact remains that not many of them could have had enough money to buy enough sheets at one time. So they had to buy bundles of iron sheets in increments; they would buy a little as they could afford it. They would then hire people to carry these bundles of iron sheets by head down to Ìtàpá. They would take bush paths either from Iléṣà, Òṣogbo, etc. as there was no road or vehicles then. Carriers of these bundles were paid two shillings after they successfully carried the sheets to Ìtàpá. A bundle was to be shared by two people when it arrived in Ìtàpá.

Early migrants, such as Akúrúyẹjó, Chief Onígẹmọ and Olọmọditapa Daramọla who came back to build new houses with iron roofs in Ìtàpá (see Figure 8.1), are widely remembered by older residents and are viewed as pioneers of development in the town. Somewhat later, when iron sheets became more easily available in the post-war years, many townspeople followed their lead. Indeed, having a house roofed with iron sheets came to be a sign of being an 'enlightened and modern' person, as one man explained:

> Many children used to build houses for their parents to live in it ... A child who is not developed who lived in a leaf-roofed house, if he wanted to build a house, he would build a house roofed with leaves. An educated, modern person would build a modern house with iron sheeting. It is as a result of civilisation (òlàjú) and development (idàgbàsókè) that leads a child to come home to remove the old type of roofing from his father's house and to replace it with iron sheets.
> (DI97-36, Ìtàpá-Èkìtì, 1997)

Aside from being a measure of an individual's status and a monument to their success in life, houses also represent a family's political vitality and economic commitment to a community (Berry 1985: 78). They also serve as a safety net for family members when urban affairs go awry (Eades 1980: 63), and convey a sense of social and geographical identity. Ṣóyinká (1988, 1989) captures this sense of social identity associated with houses in his portrayal of the intimate comforts (see Figure 8.2) of early childhood at his father's family home, connecting the past, people and place in Isara:

> But the walls have retained their voices. Familiar voices break on the air, voices from the other side of the rafters. Isara was second home – Essay's natal home. All the grandparents were Father and Mother – and somehow we said these as if with capital letters. There the rafters were smoky, bare of the usual ceiling mat. There were objects in corners of the roof, wrapped in leaves, in leather ... Isara was another kind of home, several steps into the past. Age hung about every corner, the patina of ancestry glossed all objects, all human faces ...
> (Ṣóyinká 1988: 66)

However, there are persuasive economic as well as cultural and personal reasons why people want children to maintain houses. In rural Ekiti State, where written titles to land rarely exist, houses serve to 'stake one's claim' to

Figure 8.2 Detail of interior of Mr M. O. Fálọdún's house, with shelf and assorted objects. Walls are often used for recording important dates and club contributions, as well as for hanging family portraits, Rẹ́mọ Qtr., Ìtàpá-Èkitì, 1992. (photograph by the author)

land in small towns. They are thus critical in securing land tenure rights where government policies, such the Nigerian Land Use Decree of 1978, discourage the sale of rural land.[1] The building and maintenance of houses, and hence continued claims to plots of land in Ìtàpá, are thus preserved through one's descendants.

This chapter examines both cultural and economic aspects of family houses, rural land tenure and fertility in Ìtàpá-Èkìtì in relation to the broader political economy of the contemporary Nigerian State. Specifically, it considers how changes in rural houseplot transactions, traditional practices associated with houses, and household composition at the local level, together with federal land tenure policies, have affected townspeople's sense of a need for people in general and for children in particular.[2] In the first section, the social and cultural significance of houses and of house ownership in Ìtàpá-Èkìtì is discussed, focusing on the religious implications of houses and household graves.[3] In the second section, changes in houseplot transactions are examined. Houseplots within the town consist predominantly of family-owned land although more recently cash may be given for 'ownership' of choice, non-family houseplots. This change in the transfer of houseplots relates to a process of land commoditisation: from personal and family-based, oral and undocumented land transactions to impersonal and cash-based, written and surveyed transfers.

In the third section, the relationship between types of houseplot transfers and household composition is considered to see what, if any, relationship exists between cash-based land transfers, changes in traditional house-related practices and household composition. Specifically, two questions are addressed. Do houses associated with family houseplot land transfers have different household configurations compared with those using cash in land transfers? If so, what do these differences imply about the continuing importance of family houses and consequently for the importance of having many children to maintain these claims? This section is followed by a discussion of current federal land tenure policies and their effect on the trend towards the sale of rural houseplot land. I argue that the ambiguities of the Land Use Act counter the economic security associated with the regularisation of houseplot ownership, specifically the use of written documentary evidence, and implicitly counter limiting family size. Thus, present land tenure policy may actually support the need for children in order to maintain land claims in the town, thus undermining the federal *National Policy on Population for Development, Unity, Progress and Self-Reliance* introduced by the Federal Government in 1988 (Federal Republic of Nigeria 1988; see also Olúsànyà 1989a).

Finally, the relationship of house and land ownership to fertility is discussed. In Èkìtì, changing land tenure practices reveal a situation in which ideals of kinship, continuity of the family house and high fertility exist within a cash economy in which the circle of kin to whom one is obligated is narrowing in some ways (see Chapter 5), and where status may be reflected as much in expensive things as in many people.[4] While people in this rural Èkìtì town continue to build family houses and bear children to perpetuate a father's name as they have in the past, such 'traditions' are hardly unchanging practices but rather are constantly being remade (Hobsbawm and Ranger 1983), reflecting the economic and political contingencies of contemporary Nigeria. This chapter suggests some of the ways that people from Ìtàpá-Èkìtì are simultaneously conveying an ideal of traditional continuity and hence a form of political legitimacy, while constituting very different arrangements regarding family houses and land tenure in practice, which support shifts in social relations that may contribute to smaller family size.

HOUSES AND PEOPLE

Orí ibá mọ ibùsùn ibá tún ibẹ̀ ṣe
If one knew where one would be buried, one would take good care of the place.

Yoruba proverb

The word for house in the Èkìtì dialect is *ulé* (*ilé*, Ọ̀yọ́ Yoruba). *Ulé* may also be translated as 'compound', referring to the physical structure of the building itself. As has been discussed in Chapters 2 and 6, traditional Èkìtì Yoruba houses consisted of square or rectangular structures with a central corridor, surrounded by individual rooms each with their own doors and locks, which open into this general space. A cooking area for the occupants of these rooms, which may include an entire family constellation or a single individual (either a family member or tenant), was usually located behind the house. Presently, houses in the town range from mud-block, iron-roofed structures with four rooms branching off a single corridor to large two-storey houses, with a large parlour, twelve or more rooms and boys' quarters, with some having indoor kitchens and plumbing. The mean number of people living in each house in 1991 was 8.9 people.[5]

The word *ulé* (house) also suggests a core group of people who claim membership by virtue of patrilineal descent from a common ancestor as well as other residents within the compound who may or may not be related to this core group. As Barber (1991: 154–5) explains:

> *Ile* [houses] are physical entities, places where people live together ... But the word *ile* means not just a building, but the people within it ... Fellow members of one's *ile* are duty bound to support with their presence any celebration or ceremony that one holds: marriage, child-naming, housewarming or religious festivals. They are one's 'people', and without a solid background of people one is socially non-existent.

Several men expressed this fear of social non-existence and their need for children, particularly sons, in terms of the empty house:

> My problem is so transparent in that I am the only son for my parent. As a result of this, I want some boys so that our house foundation can

be laid on a rocky land. We can have more men in our house because no matter how rich these female children may be, they will tilt their wealth more to their husbands' houses than to their father's house. I don't want our house to become desolate.
(LIM-IC9/8-16, Ìtàpá-Èkìtì, 1991)

Implicit in the image of the abandoned, desolate house is the idea of the individual in society without social support and identity.

The social ideal of a house headed by a man and his subsequent male descendants, as well as a preference for virilocal residence after marriage, is reinforced by practices that symbolically represent patrilineal continuity, such as the burial of the dead. As has been discussed in Chapter 6, where and how one is buried has social, cultural and political implications. In Ìtàpá, houses themselves often serve as a sort of family monument, where the family names may be inscribed above the doorway and the bodies of the deceased owner, his wives and their male children are often buried near the house. Graves are covered with a cement slab with the occupant's name and date of burial written on top. This material evidence – the house and graves – of family members reflects traditional religious beliefs, for example, that the spirits of ancestors, whose bodies were interred in or next to houses, might potentially intervene for the well-being of family members or might be reborn in a future child (Eades 1980: 122).

At present, however, rituals concerned with ancestors and their spirits are less commonly practised by many townspeople who have converted to Christianity and Islam. Many townspeople's concern with building and maintaining a family house has more to do with descendants, in particular males, who will inherit and (it is hoped) live in the house, perpetuate its founder's name by their presence and, importantly, help to maintain or extend family claims to land.[6] The continuing practice of burying family members under the floor of rooms and in front of houses (Chapter 6) emphasises the importance of bodily association of subsequent generations with particular plots of land, serving as material evidence of people's right to build and reside there. While some may prefer burial in church cemeteries to dissociate themselves from so-called 'pagan practices', home burial is both emotionally, politically and economically important for many who continue this practice.

HOUSEPLOT TRANSFERS IN ÌTÀPÁ

Houses in Ìtàpá-Èkìtì have been most frequently built on land acquired through family land division rather than on land acquired with cash. Only 13 per cent (n=43) of the 333 houseplot transactions from approximately 1910 to 1989 documented in 1992 include cash payments for land, whereas 49 per cent (n=162) of these transactions consist of the division of family land (see Table 8.1).

Table 8.1 Houseplot Land Transfers and Household Characteristics

Household characteristics	Type of houseplot transaction[a]					
	Cash		Family		Not family	
	%	(no.)	%	(no.)	%	(no.)
House-head						
Male	65	(22)	66	(86)	68	(80)
Male *de facto*	9	(3)	10	(13)	9	(11)
Female	–		5	(7)	10	(12)
Female *de facto*	24	(8)	15	(20)	10	(12)
Not applicable[b]	3	(1)	4	(5)	3	(3)
Extended family[c]						
Yes	58	(19)	58	(73)	54	(62)
No	42	(14)	42	(53)	46	(53)
Not applicable[d]	3	(1)	4	(5)	3	(3)
Tenants present						
No	59	(20)	89	(116)	81	(96)
Yes	41	(14)	11	(15)	19	(22)
1–5	57	(8)	87	(13)	82	(18)
6–10	36	(5)	13	(2)	9	(2)
11+	7	(1)	–		9	(2)
TOTAL	12	(34)	46	(131)	42	(118)

a Includes data for occupied households only (n=283), out of 333 houseplot transfers recorded.
b No house-head as only tenants in residence.
c Extended family relationships refer to adults in same or older generation as house-head.
d Percentages may not add up to 100 due to rounding.

This prevalence of family land transactions is explained, in part, because houseplot transfers for cash are a relatively recent occurrence. Seventy-five per cent of these cash transactions have taken place within the last twenty years (see Figure 8.3). These land sales take place between unrelated townspeople, with the buyer acquiring a plot, often from former farmland owned by members of another kin group. Much of this land is located on the edge of the developed parts of the town, particularly around the main road. The use of cash in these transactions implies both an impersonality and a finiteness of ownership that make it morally inappropriate in land agreements between family members. Different sorts of transactions take place between family members, depending on their particular relationship.

For land transactions among patrilineal family members, nothing in cash or kind is given although occasionally gifts of kola nuts are made for prayers. To acquire a houseplot, a man may ask his father for land:

> My father gave the land to me around 1961 having known that then I was mature enough to have a building and because my job of bicycle

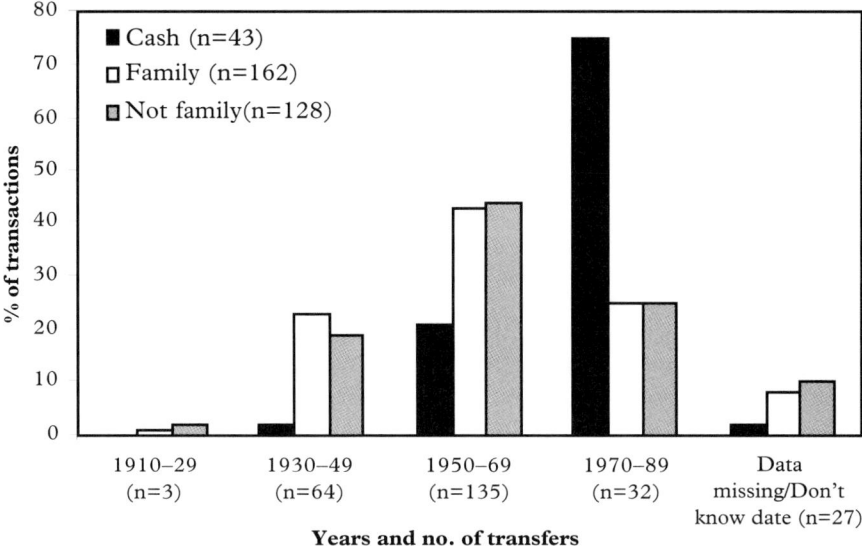

Figure 8.3 Transaction types by date of land transfer

repairing was then so lucrative. He delayed it until that period when my senior brothers were also ready to have their own house. The transaction took place between myself, other senior brothers and our father, the then Ọdọ̀fin [a high-ranking chief, also a quarter head].

(LTS-99, Ìtàpá-Èkìtì, 1992)

A man may also acquire a plot through a general division of family land among family members after the death of a previous occupant. Family land is owned jointly by a patrilineage although a family member's tenure of a particular houseplot continues as long as a house is erected and is maintained. Houseplots with abandoned, collapsed houses which are not immediately rebuilt revert back to the patrilineage:

I obtained land from my father in 1970 but immediately after my father's house was demolished in 1983, *without wasting a minute*, I decided to build the house so that my wife, myself and my children can stay in it.

(LTS-88, Ìtàpá-Èkìtì, 1992; my emphasis)

In general, houses recently built in Ìtàpá belong to a particular individual, rather than a descent group, to be inherited jointly by his or her children: 'Our house it is a family house, May God provide houses for our children, this is a family house. No one out of the children can claim to possess it.' While no one child can inherit his or her father's house to the exclusion of other children or need necessarily reside in the house, they may nonetheless accrue certain benefits from its ownership, as described by one man:

> If it is a house, [the children] can renovate the house and then be using it for rental if the house could not be shared among many wives, perhaps due to its small size. Then the money earned by the rental can be used to carry out some projects by the family.
> (FI-5, Ìtàpá-Èkìtì, 1991)

Tenure of a family plot on which a house is built, however, refers to use rights only. The land itself, technically speaking, continues to belong to the patrilineal descent group although as long as the house is maintained, the owner and his or her children can claim use rights to the land in perpetuity.

In Ìtàpá, another common form of houseplot transaction is through appeal to members of another patrilineal group to allow non-family members use of a houseplot. Thirty-eight per cent (n=128) of houseplot transactions in the town are of this type, 20 per cent (n=20) of which were transacted through women (that is, non-patrilineal), either through matrilateral (n=23) or affinal (n=2) kinship connections. While these transactions do not involve cash, they may involve considerable expense as certain items must be given to the owners to confirm the transaction. The approximate expense for commonly given items such as a bag of salt, a bottle of Schnapps, a goat, a bundle of iron sheeting (for roofing) and a quantity of kola nuts would at present come to around ₦400 ($20 in 1992).[7] These material things would be given along with 'a lot of prostrations' as one man put it, referring to the sometimes extended negotiations which precede the transfer of non-family plots. Further, additional 'gifts' must be given in the event that non-family residents decide to build a new house, a situation described by one man:

> The land was initially acquired by my mother in 1945. She hails from this quarter and built her house here. No payment was made initially but when the new structure was to be made [in 1987] I gave them a carton of beer to offer a prayer. When I was about to build the new structure, I only told about two people that I was about to rebuild my mother's house. Even before then, some people had come to me and advised me to make use of the plot immediately.
> (LTS-84, Ìtàpá-Èkìtì, 1992)

This man's comments underscore the importance of houses in 'staking a claim' for houseplot land. As in the case of houseplots acquired through family connections, non-family land would revert to the original family owners to be redistributed in the event that the extant house collapsed or was demolished.

Even in cases of family land, a viable structure can be critical. For houses not only mark a land claim but may quite literally establish the boundaries of a plot in the case of contested claims and increased demand:

> There weren't any boundary marks as Daddy was still hoping to have a bigger building then. So he didn't mark any particular area for himself. But when demand was on the increase, most of the land that would have been acquired by Daddy was given to other people. So the very area occupied by the building remains our area of dominion.
> (LTS-101, Ìtàpá-Èkìtì, 1992)

This man's remark captures the negotiability of land boundaries as well as the sense that flexible boundaries have potential benefits and disadvantages.

GOOD FENCES MAKE GOOD NEIGHBOURS

The ideal of common descent, reflected in generous sharing and in trust of kin, is represented in the non-remunerative partitioning of land, which carries over into ideas about boundaries of houseplot land. Peter Lloyd, writing on Yoruba land tenure in the early 1960s, observed that boundaries, often marked by natural features of the landscape or by planting particular types of bushes or trees (see Figure 8.4), were flexible, reflecting a family's numbers and political position:

Figure 8.4 House plot boundary with ọ̀dàn tree, Rẹ́mọ, Ìtàpá-Èkìtì, June 1999. (photograph by the author)

Table 8.2 Houseplot boundaries by land transaction types

Type of Boundary	Cash %[a] (no.)	Family % (no.)	Not family % (no.)
Trees			
Lapa lapa, etc.[b]	2 (1)	15 (25)	10 (13)
Pòrògún[c]	–	7 (11)	10 (13)
Other (kola, etc.)	5 (2)	9 (15)	16 (21)
Total	7 (3)	31 (51)	36 (47)
Non-traditional markers			
Pillars	30 (13)	7 (12)	8 (10)
Walled	28 (12)	1 (2)	3 (4)
Pegged	5 (2)	3 (5)	3 (4)
Total	63 (27)	11 (19)	14 (18)
Roads, paths, etc.	9 (4)	12 (20)	9 (11)
Stones	–	1 (2)	3 (4)
Four holes at corners	–	–	3 (4)
Bottles, ashes	2 (1)	1 (1)	2 (2)
Neighbouring houses	5 (2)	4 (6)	5 (6)
House to boundary	2 (1)	–	1 (1)
Swept area	–	1 (1)	3 (4)
Nothing	5 (2)	28 (45)	17 (22)
Data missing	7 (3)	11 (17)	7 (9)
Surveyed			
Yes	60 (26)	19 (31)	10 (13)
No	33 (14)	74 (120)	83 (106)
Data missing	7 (3)	7 (11)	7 (9)
TOTAL (no.)	(43)	(162)	(128)

a   Percentage of transaction group type.
b   *Lapa lapa* trees (*Jatropha curca*) as well as *àjẹ̀kòbàlé* (literally, 'witches do not land on it' (*Croton amabilis*), *alabose* and *ọ̀dàn* (*idí ọ̀dàn: Ficus thornigiri*) trees were commonly mentioned.
c   *Pòrògún* trees (*Dracaena fragrans*) are 'often planted in fetish groves' (Abraham 1962: 551). See also Abraham 1962: 622 for use of *porogun* in rituals associated with the thunder deity, Shango.

> The members of one group grow in number so that their land is insufficient for their needs, while a neighbouring group perhaps decreases in numbers and has vacant land. Two solutions are possible: either the boundary is moved, by peaceful or violent means, or some of the members of the group with insufficient land join the group with land to spare. Boundary moving by peaceful arbitration seems to have been rare; more frequently it seems to have happened that the members of one group 'trespassed' on to the land of the other, staying for so long that they could claim the land as being that of their own descent group.
>
> (Lloyd 1962: 87)

To avoid these 'trespassing' tactics, what appears to be happening in this rural Èkìtì town is that people are getting land surveyed (which includes erecting survey pillars at the four corners) and building walls (see Table 8.2), particularly in cash houseplot transfers. One man expressed his fears about his neighbour's intentions as follows: 'Real boundaries are yet to be marked but pillars will be used and lasting plants will be planted as the owner of the plot at the back is likely to start a dispute' (LTS-200, Ìtàpá-Èkìtì, 1992).

The reification of houseplot boundaries represents a shift away from the expectations of shared land ownership among kin. Yet the ideal of kin sharing resources and helping one another without the use of impersonal money continues to be expressed in people's statements about houseplot sales, patrifilial obligations regarding houses, and property boundaries:

> There are no boundary marks since this land belongs to family.
> (LTS-31, Ìtàpá-Èkìtì, 1991)

> It is not ideal to be counting the amount you spend in repairing your father's home.
> (OI-7, Lagos, 1991)

However, despite the continuing practice of houseplot transactions without the exchange of cash or kind, there is the sense, as one man put it, that 'Now everything is cash'. Indeed, I was told by another man in 1992 that the town chiefs had decided to ban the use of cash in the purchase of houseplots. Cash was seen as discouraging outsiders from building houses, because of the additional expense, and thus inhibiting the growth of the town.[8] Eight years later, however, several plots of land acquired along the main road and elsewhere where land is in demand included cash transactions.[9]

Household composition and types of house plot transactions

Owó ló máa ń bojú ọrẹ́ jẹ́
Money is what spoils friendship

Yoruba proverb

The shift in boundary marking types is associated with a particular type of houseplot transaction: those made with cash. Houseplots transacted with cash are more frequently surveyed than non-cash family or non-family land houseplots (see Table 8.2). These changes suggest a tendency toward the commoditisation of houseplots and houses, undermining the idea of the family house built on a shared, unbounded space.

This use of cash in houseplot transfers is also significantly related to the presence of tenants in a house.[10] Forty-one per cent of cash-transacted houseplots have one or more tenants present, compared with only 11 per cent of family houseplots (see Table 8.1). The idea of someone paying rent

Table 8.3 Family type and household composition, by houseplot transaction type[a]

Transaction/ family type[b]	No. of households w/o tenant				Mean no. in house	No. of households with tenant				Mean no. in house
	M	M[c]	F	F[c]		M	M[c]	F	F[c]	
Cash (n=33)										
Nuclear (n=8)	5	–	–	–	5.0	3	–	–	–	13.0
Matrifocal (n=13)	–	1	–	3	5.5	2	–	–	7	9.1
Traditional (n=12)	10	–	–	–	10.7	2	–	–	–	19.0
Total	15	1	–	3		7	–	–	7	
Family (n=126)										
Nuclear (n=19)	18	–	–	–	6.4	1	–	–	–	14.0
Matrifocal (n=43)	9	4	8	19	6.9	3	–	–	–	6.7
Traditional (n=64)	50	7	–	–	15.9	5	2	–	–	13.9
Total	77	11	8	19		9	2	–	–	
Not family (n=115)										
Nuclear (n=15)	13	1	–	–	5.8	1	–	–	–	12.0
Matrifocal (n=46)	10	5	10	6	6.6	4	2	3	6	7.6
Traditional (n=53)	47	4	–	–	12.1	3	–	–	–	7.6
Total	70	10	10	6		8	2	3	6	
TOTAL (all)	162	22	18	28		24	4	3	13	

a Occupied houses only, not including houses with tenants only.
b Family types: Nuclear: male-headed with wife and children; Matrifocal: female-headed or male-headed household with non-conventional configuration (wife not present, few or no extended family members, and usually only two generations); and Traditional: male-headed with one or more wives present, children, extended family members, adult son with wife, children or daughter with children (usually three or more generations).
c De facto-househead.

to reside in a house is very different from the traditional practice of strangers being absorbed within family houses, initially in fictive kinship relationships which may later be forgotten or ignored (cf. Elias 1951: 108). These changes suggest that while a house may continue to represent the continuity of a family and its name, it may also be viewed as an investment, as a source of rental income, which in urban areas may be quite substantial.[11] Even in Ìtàpá-Èkìtì, where amounts paid for room rental are low (from approximately ₦10 to ₦50 a month in 1992), residence on the basis of cash rather than kinship or clientage in houses, represents a change in this rural southwestern Nigeria town (although already existing in many urban areas). A person may build a family house in his or her home town for the sake of prestige (Trager 1998) but need not reside there nor have many children to populate the house. Such a house would not only bolster local social and political status (see Berry 1993: 161) but also might generate rental income, although this might not be the primary reason for building it. Furthermore, as discussed earlier in the section on land tenure, a claim to a houseplot by building a house might later become valuable in its own right, depending on its location.

Tenants are not only more common in houses built on cash-transacted plots, they are also more common in houses with *de facto* women heads. Thirty-three per cent of *de facto* female-headed houses have resident tenants while only 15 per cent of male-headed houses do (see Table 8.3). Furthermore, while men were identified as the owners (or builders) of these *de facto*-headed houses, it was generally not their wives but their mothers, sisters, or daughters who acted as house-heads. These houses were built with the intention of possible future, but not present, residence by an owner and his family who often reside in large urban centres such as Àkúrẹ́, Ìbàdàn or Lagos (Adépọ̀jù 1974; Berry 1985). Thus, while the traditional ideal of building a family house in one's home town based on one's kinship connections is maintained, very different arrangements – for example, cash for land, tenant residents and survey pillars – are being instituted at the same time. This process of commoditisation of land transactions and house ownership may have implications for fertility, which is discussed in the following section.

LAND OWNERSHIP AND FERTILITY

This examination of family houses and houseplot tenure relates to arguments about land-holding and fertility discussed in the demographic literature (Cain 1985, 1986; Stokes and Schutjer 1984; Stokes et al. 1986). In the 'land-security' hypothesis proposed by Stokes and Schutjer (1984: 204), land ownership substitutes for the security of having many children, providing a source of prospective income and hence security in old age. This hypothesis should apply with some qualifications, even though this study considers houseplot ownership and tenancy in the rural town of Ìtàpá-Èkìtì, rather than the ownership of agricultural land and farm income. For example, the ownership and working of farmland have somewhat different labour requirements than renting and maintaining a house. Nonetheless, as Barnes (1986: 68) observed for one of the growth areas of urban Lagos during the 1970s:

> Ownership of property was itself an important urban occupation ... Real estate was an investment from which all or part of an income could be derived. It also represented a form of savings, a security against unforeseen financial problems, and a pension against retirement.

Even in rural towns such as Ìtàpá-Èkìtì where the demand for housing is less, potential house rental income could affect people's sense of needing many children for future economic security. In Ìtàpá, 1992, the median number of children wanted by younger survey women and men, aged twenty to twenty-four, was five children, compared with the total fertility rate of the town which was 6.2, as was discussed in Chapter 3. These figures reflect several factors, including the belief that raising fewer children well and within one's means is better than raising many poorly, as one young, unmarried woman explained:

> The reason [I want five children] is just to take care of them. Assuming I have a small [amount of] money to take care of them. If I have five children I can take care of them ... I want three boys and two girls. Those three boys will be the owners of that house so it won't be [empty]. If it is girls they will just go to their husbands' house ... You know those boys we will be living together in that house, even if they have wives, they will be living with us in the house.
> (LIW-CN1/8-1, Ìtàpá-Èkìtì, 1991)

Her remarks suggest that the importance of the family house and name described by Olúsànyà (1989b) may persist, even when individuals want fewer children than their parents did. House ownership and potential house rental income may contribute to a sense of future security that lessens the need to have many children for old-age support. However, houses appear to be viewed as an alternative security investment by those who already plan to limit the size of their families, not as a substitute for having children. They are particularly not a substitute for sons who continue to be perceived as crucial for maintaining both the physical structure of the house and houseplot land claims (Lloyd 1962: 87). As Cain (1985: 6) has argued, 'children may be regarded as a security asset that complements, rather than substitutes for, land.' The workings of one government programme relating to land tenure suggest why this complementary strategy of houses and children might be a sensible one.

THE 1978 LAND USE ACT

Ọmọ tí a kò kọ́ ni yóò wó ilé tí a kọ́
The child who is not well trained may grow up to destroy the house that was built.

Yoruba proverb

One might expect that cash-transacted houseplots which are often surveyed and frequently bounded by permanent boundary pillars or walls would be recorded in written documents, either privately held or lodged with local government officials. However, these transactions are rarely documented. Indeed, there are good reasons why people do not put these transaction in writing, which relate to the Government's land tenure policy known as the 1978 Land Use Act.

In 1975, the federal government set up an Anti-Inflation Task Force in which the issue of formulating a uniform land reform policy was raised. While the government did not initially accept this body's recommendation that all land be nationalised and subsequent transactions regulated by the state (the essence of the Land Use Act), it appointed a Land Use Panel to consider the issue further. The minority report, which advocated nationalisation of all land, was accepted by the government in 1978.

The reasoning behind the implementation of the decree was: (1) to 'rationalise customary tenure so as to make it more secure, uniform, and available as security for raising capital' (Francis 1984: 13), and (2) to undermine the authority of groups with vested interests in continuing 'customary' land tenure in favour of more socially just forms of land distribution and ownership. The latter goal had some credence as 'immemorial customs' have been altered in the colonial period to suit the needs of those (both British and African) with political power (cf. Chanock 1985, 1991; Colson 1960; and Moore 1991). Yet the actual administration of this decree may result in what is simply a variation of this theme, in a post-colonial context. Government bureaucrats replace colonial officials and traditional chiefs as those with the political power to legally expropriate land, undermining the rights in land of the very people the Act was ostensibly composed to benefit.

According to the Act, all rural and urban land is held in trust by the state, with state Governors having authority over urban land and local government 'Land Allocation Advisory Committees' controlling rural land. Their authority covers all post-1978 land transfer decisions. Rural land, while inherited on the basis of customary rights and held according to 'customary' land tenure practices, is claimed on the basis of occupancy, which replaces all previous forms of title. Documents certifying rights of occupancy can be issued by local governments to interested parties. However, there are certain contradictions. For example, the transfer and subdivision of rural land is prohibited by the Act in section 36, sub-section (5) (Francis 1984: 9). Furthermore, the sale of rural land is illegal, according to the Act, unless approved by the local government committee.

Ironically, the implementation of the 1978 Land Use Act may have slowed the regularisation of rural land transfer. For example, in Oyo State where documents of conveyance are made by solicitors, deeds will be backdated to the period prior to 1978 (cf. Myers 1990: 244n). Elsewhere in Yorubaland, 'The conditions of dubious legality created by the Act in fact led to a rise in the price of land' (Francis 1984: 15). As Chanock (1991: 77) has observed regarding African land tenure during the colonial period, 'The circumstances which created the assertion of the illegitimacy of sale weakened the potential for individual use to harden into a recognition of ownership.'[12]

It should not be surprising, then, that the residents of Ìtàpá-Èkìtì have chosen to ignore this Act altogether. Land transactions involving cash are not documented and to avoid complications and extra payments, these transactions are not reported to local government officials for certification.[13] Land transfers and houseplot subdivision for inheritance are also not reported, both being treated as customary land practices. Finally, disputes over land are generally settled by theỌwátàpá and his council of chiefs, rather than in local Customary Courts. One man who was also a judge in the Local Government Court described this process:

> There are cases when such is done although not in the court, but on the home-level. When this occurs, the affected parties are consulted and then we find out from them the reasons for the disagreements. After leaving all sides of the story, we will then appoint some people from the elders who settle these issues to go and check the property in question, whether farmland or other things. After this is done and we have received the report of such inspection, if the early division was correct, we will confirm it as genuine. But if it were otherwise, we would then select some people to go back and re-divide it for them.
> (FI-17, Ìtàpá-Èkìtì, 1991)

Thus, rather than relying on the contradictory practices set forth in the Land Use Act, people view their security in rural land ownership as resting on local assertions of customary tenure and on the political and economic clout to support these claims. The material presence of house and people – preferably one's children who are well-trained (that is, educated), as the proverb suggests – who will know how to look after one's interests are vital to the maintenance of these claims.

CONCLUSION

Houseplot transactions in Ìtàpá-Èkìtì reflect two countervailing tendencies in contemporary Nigeria. On the one hand, there is a tendency towards the regularisation of land transfers, reflected in cash transactions and land surveys, and towards the narrowing circle of kin obligations, reflected in greater tenant occupation of houses on cash-transacted plots and walled boundaries. Houseplot ownership substantiated by cash and surveyed boundaries, as well as the number of tenants residing in houses in the town, suggests changes in practices associated with the perpetuation of family houses and names, which may support fertility decline. Indeed, in his essay on continued high fertility in sub-Saharan Africa, P. O. Olúsànyà emphasises the importance of lineage, family name and house in perpetuating people's desire for children. He argues that the perceived need to preserve the continuity of the Yoruba patrilineal descent group through time is 'the crux of the problem of persistently high fertility' (Olúsànyà 1989b: 88). Further, he considers this Yoruba preoccupation – which includes both the building and maintenance of family houses in one's hometown, occupied by one's offspring – to be obsolete, particularly for educated, urban migrants:

> The idea of a child being the 'pillar' of the ancestral home and the perpetuator of the family name (a cultural hangover from the time the lineage was localised and depended for its survival on members' procreative activities) has become irrelevant ... The extent of change in this vital intermediate variable will more clearly indicate the imminence or otherwise in a decline in fertility.
> (Olúsànyà 1989b: 92–3)

While the ideal of perpetuating the family home and name has not diminished in Ìtàpá-Èkìtì, the practices of land transfer and household composition associated with this ideal have changed considerably, supporting a preference among some to have fewer children.

On the other hand, federal land tenure policy confounds this tendency towards the regularisation of land transfer and, possibly, fertility decline. By instituting a contradictory and unworkable land transfer scheme, the government may incidentally be contributing to a sense of needing children to maintain one's land and property holdings. Thus, despite the Nigerian government's recent measures to encourage smaller families (for example, the 'Four is enough' policy aired in 1988 (Olúsànyà 1989a)), contradictory rural land tenure policies as laid out in the Land Use Act encourage ambiguity rather than land security (Berry 1993: 336) and hence, implicitly work against these population programmes. Moreover, the unworkable government policy regarding land undermines its credibility as people tend to ignore or be suspicious of government pronouncements more generally (see Chapter 9).

While the Nigerian Land Use Act was established, in part, to promote equitable rural distribution and the regularisation of both rural and urban land tenure through state control, it appears to have worked out rather differently on the ground, tending to favour the claims of those with political connections (Francis 1984). Thus, the Nigerian material is a poignant reminder that while Thomas (1991) has argued that state-sponsored economic reform and fertility levels should go together, this may not always be the case. Fertility may decline despite the absence of effective land reform and the regularisation of land ownership. Conversely, land reform may generate uncertainty as it actually works in practice, reinforcing people's perception that they need many children.

Finally, it is probably useless to argue whether cultural factors – the belief in the importance of continuing the family name and ancestral home – or economic factors – the value of children in maintaining the family house and claims to houseplots – take precedence in explaining fertility in this Èkìtì Yoruba town. As Olúsànyà (1989b: 91) has noted: 'To Africans both are of course, inseparable ... Children are good not only because they perpetuate the family name but also because of their role within the family and larger group.' For people living in Ìtàpá, ideas about the reproduction of family houses and names, like land tenure and children, are intimately linked, which underscores the difficulties of analysing the relationship between houses, land tenure and fertility in any event. Furthermore, the fact that house owners and their families may not be residing in the house they own in town but rather live in large cities elsewhere accentuates the limitations of research which neither extends beyond the immediate home community (Berry 1985: 18) nor investigates the nature and extent of urban-rural ties and their implications for fertility.[14]

Nonetheless, people's practices and perceptions associated with land do appear to be changing, as evidenced by houseplot sales and household composition in Ìtàpá-Èkìtì. For many younger, Western-educated men and women in the town, ancestral practices have little salience in their lives even while they may continue to couch land tenure practices in terms of tradition. It remains unclear whether increased houseplot sales represent a shift to individual ownership of rural houseplots (Berry 1993: 121) which may later be resold by the person's children, or whether the land and house themselves will become ancestral property owned by future descendants. It should be clear, however, from the foregoing discussion that the direction which the building of family houses in one's home town and rural houseplot transfers has taken is neither obsolete nor irrelevant. These actions, as well as those relating to family size, reflect the sociocultural and economic realities of contemporary Nigerian society. The importance of numbers of descendants – of individuals, of families, of towns and of regions – is examined in the next chapter.

9

COUNTING BODIES: CENSUSES, VITAL REGISTRATION AND THE CREATION OF EKITI STATE

> Register the dead and help the government plan for the living.
> National Population Commission poster, Ọyẹ́-Èkìtì

> Unfortunately, many population figures are published without a clear indication as to how they were arrived at.
> R. Kuczynski, *Colonial Population*

> 'What – a purchase deed to dead souls?'
> 'Oh no! ... We will write down that they are alive, just as they are actually entered in the census ...'
> Gogol, *Dead Souls*

Women and men in Ìtàpá have devised their own ways of keeping track of children born and of their ages, as one woman explained:

> In the past, there was a registration of births in Ìtàpá, [it was] called *òwìwí*. Chief Káyọ̀dé from Ẹgẹ̀tún who died recently made sure that every child born in the town in the past was registered by him. This was done until the time that he died and he was the one who helped most illiterate people to know the date of birth of their child. They would just go to him and ask for the dates when their children were born, he did this for all of the people in the town.
> (DI97-3, Ìtàpá-Èkìtì, 1997)

Chief Káyọ̀dé used a string of beads, called *òwìwí*, to keep track of these births.[1] Each child that was born would be noted with a bead added to a string so the entire number and ages of offspring of a father were recorded. There were other ways to record the ages of their children as well. One system, known as *a ti marki*, consists of making marks on the parlour door lintels (Frontispiece), with one mark being made each year for each child residing there. Alternately, the literal writing of children's birth dates on house walls was another form of record-keeping (see Figure 9.1). However, many older townspeople do not know their precise numerical ages (see Figures App. 1.1 and App. 1.2). Rather, they are aware of their age in social terms, for example by their position in relation to elder and junior siblings, whether they have borne children (and grandchildren), what social clubs

Figure 9.1 House interior with birth dates written on wall in chalk. The first entry reads *Ojo ti iyawo ọga Jimoh bimọ Tunde ni 17/7/94* ('The date that househead Jimoh's wife gave birth to Tunde was 17/7/94'), Oroke Qtr., Ìtàpá-Èkìtì, July 1997. (photograph by the author)

they belong to and their political status in the town. Yet as more people have acquired secondary education and are sending their children to school (which requires a birth certificate), they are increasingly aware of their own birth dates and have registered their children's births.

The idea of keeping track of people in terms of numbers, with written documentation, is not an unacceptable idea in Ìtàpá as examples of earlier (*òwìwí*) and later (birth certificates) record-keeping show. However, the documentation of numbers of people, either through census-taking or the registrations of vital events, has not been unequivocally accepted in the town. Many people have accepted some forms of counting bodies, such as the decadal census, and several people cited this as an example of townspeople's having learned the importance of being counted:

> Education and civilisation have taught us to value the census, we now realise that we should know the population of our people. People now realise that it is on the basis of population that government would provide social amenities and that allocation is based on population. There was ignorance in the past but ... not now.
> (CI95-2, Ìtàpá-Èkìtì, 1994)

Yet other forms of counting bodies, such as the registration of deaths, continue to be perceived as an unnecessary government intrusion and are generally ignored, as one man explained:

> No death has ... been registered. If the government needs information about those things, they need to go about to collect the information. It is an abomination ... to go to the government telling them the death of an aged father or mother.
> (CI95-10, Ìtàpá-Èkìtì, 1994)

Understanding why one type of body count and not another would be viewed as appropriate or within the legitimate purview of the state clarifies the ways that Ìtàpá residents have responded to attempts by the Nigerian state to reinforce its authority, through its efforts to 'count and classify their populations, [and] to gradually replace religious institutions as the registrar of the life-cycle facts, of birth, marriage, and death' (Cohn and Dirks 1988: 224). By considering Ìtàpá people's responses to 'social technologies' (Cohn and Dirks 1988: 225) such as the national census and vital registration, the culturally negotiated process by which these technologies have been accepted or rejected may more clearly be seen. The representatives of the state may use the counting of bodies as a way of objectifying its citizenry (Cohn 1987),[2] conditioning them to think of themselves in terms of categories, for example, Èkìtì, Yoruba, and so on (Kertzer and Arel 2002). Nonetheless, there are some ways, however small, that women and men in Ìtàpá have acted in terms of their own views of these procedures and of government development and population policies more generally.

This chapter documents the historical background of the state's efforts at collecting numerical information about men, women and children in Ìtàpá. It also examines how residents of this small rural town in Ekiti State have experienced and responded to these exercises, and how their thinking about counting bodies has selectively changed, in part, in response to local developments and to efforts to establish Ekiti State. The first section documents census-taking in the Èkìtì area by the colonial government, and state attempts to implement a system of vital registration. The second section discusses townspeople's responses to these efforts and their reassessment of birth registration and census-taking as aspects of development, focusing on their experience of the 1991 census exercise. The impact of this census on the subsequent formation of Ekiti State in 1996 is then considered from the perspective of Ìtàpá residents. In the concluding section, the contradictions arising from state officials' efforts both to promote the counting of bodies and population-related programmes designed to encourage smaller family size are examined. While many townspeople see government prescriptions to have no more than four children as reasonable advice under the current economic conditions, they also appreciate the importance of a growing population in supporting the town's bid for political recognition and development assistance, suggesting that people's responses to population-related programmes cannot be understood outside their larger political and social context.

THE HISTORICAL BACKGROUND

According to the Èkìtì historian, Monsignor A. Ògúntúyì, census-taking in Èkìtì was introduced in the early part of this century by British colonial officials:

> The Ekitis were counted by the District Officers in 1919. It was not a complete census because only taxable male adults were counted. An entry of Fr Wouters diary showed that the head tax of six shillings (60k) per head was introduced on 11th January 1919 in Ekiti. In the following year, 1920, they were taxed six shillings per head (flat rate). All the elders, (males) in every compound were bound to pay unless they were reasonably excused. Defaulters were punished if caught.
>
> (Ògúntúyì 1979: 125)

It was through this initial association of the counting of heads with the application of a head tax that various strategies regarding census-taking in Èkìtì developed (Aluko 1965). One common strategy to avoid being counted, and hence being taxed, was to head for the bush until the census-taking exercise was completed, which was described by one older Èkìtì man:

> In the past, in the colonial period, what prompted the white people then was to know people that are of ages to pay tax. In those days, a house with a househead and we would be asked to pay one shilling. Every house paid one shilling. They conducted the census and went away and after their arrival, there was the introduction of payment of taxes ...
>
> Census in the colonial period was easier and peaceful but the attendant problem of tax collection hardened the situation. This was because many people ran out of town every time. When they couldn't get money, the 6s. [six shillings] to pay this tax, they ran and [some] died in the bush ...
>
> (CI95-4, Ìtàpá-Èkìtì, 1994)

Another way of undercutting the legitimacy (and hence effectiveness) of census-taking was employed by some Anglican pastors in Èkìtì who attributed the six-month influenza epidemic (locally referred to as *lùkúlùkú*, 'strike and kill', which began in October 1918) to the first census, which was conducted early the following year: 'According to Chief Ajayi, the Odofin of Isaba-Ikole, some Anglican pastors, recalling the incident of David's census, thought that God was not pleased with the taking of the census of the people (Psm 24: 10–15)' (Ògúntúyì 1979: 123).

The attitude toward census-taking, that it was an exercise conducted to extract wealth (in the form of taxes or labour or children) from the local population, continued in later censuses held in 1931 and in 1952, as was surmised by J. R. V. A. Bromage, the Ekiti Division District Officer:

> The work of the [1952] census was tackled with enthusiasm generally throughout the division. It is, in fact, feared that in places the enthusiasm may have been excessive and that inter-town rivalry and a hope of better claims on development funds may have led to exaggerated figures being put forward. *It was, however, noticed that in at least one place the 1931 census was associated with an increase in taxation,[3] and led to suspicion of Government intentions.* Memories in Ekiti are long.
>
> (Bromage, 1952, p. 4, NNAI; my emphasis)

Even as late as the 1962/1963 censuses in Ìtàpá, townspeople hoped to reduce their taxes and other obligations to a minimum through absconding to the bush or failing to mention all their children.

There was a similar attitude toward vital registration. Most older Ìtàpá residents ignored early attempts by the colonial government to get them to register the births or deaths of family members. Nor was there much enthusiasm for pursuing a vital registration programme on the part of colonial officials owing to a lack of personnel, as the following exchange regarding the 'Duties of [a] Travelling Medical Officer' suggests. On 8 April 1925, the Director of Medical and Sanitary Service, D. Alexander, wrote:

> Registration of Births and Deaths: the institution of such registration forms a very important step towards the practical working of any public health scheme ... It would be of great value if such a machinery of registration was set agoing prior to the appointment of the Medical Officers of Health to each Province. ['by whom?' written in pencil in the margin]. For any such statistics to be of practical value the figures have to cover definite period ...

In response, J. Davidson, Lt Governor, Southern Province, wrote on 4 June 1925:

> The Registration of Births and Deaths presents great difficulties. The indigenous African strongly objects to such registration and it is doubt-

ful to what useful extent one officer travelling two or three Provinces could effectively carry on any system. Of course if it is intended to pass this difficult section of the M.O.H.'s work on to the District Officer or a Native Administration something might be done, but not for many years to come will the information be in any degree reliable.

(Alexander 1925)

Even when a Registration of Births and Deaths Adoptive Bye-laws Order was formulated thirty years later in 1956 for implementation by regional local government councils (Ekiti Division 1/1, File no. 1042B, 1953–7), the procedures outlined in these measures were neither taken up nor enforced in the Ìtàpá area, at least initially.[4]

More recently, however, while the use of death certificates has never been widely accepted (as was discussed in Chapter 6), women began to receive birth certificates for their children after giving birth in government (and church) hospitals and clinics, and this was seen by some as a improvement over past practices:

> In the past, individuals kept records of dates when their children were born, within the shortest time, they would misplace these records and they would later be linking the dates of birth of their children with interesting festivals in the town ... or they can say a person was born during the *Itila* [Hitler] war or during the time government was tarring our road. This has brought a lot of inaccuracies in dating the time children were born. I believe birth certificates are important and I have birth certificates for my children [as] my wife gave birth to my children in the hospital.
>
> (DI97-30, Ìtàpá-Èkìtì, 1997)

Nonetheless, for women delivering at home or in the houses of local herbalists, birth registration continued to be viewed by many as an unnecessary expense.

RE-ASSESSING STATE BODY COUNTS
Vital Registration

It was when children began regularly attending primary school in the mid-1950s that people began to register the births of their children in order to obtain the requisite birth certificates needed for school registration, which was perceived 'as a means of achieving something ..., rather than being an end in itself, which discourses of statistical importance imply' (Jewkes and Wood 1998: 1054). Several people noted the value of registering the birth of children for this or other reasons:

> This [birth registration] is part of development, it is one of the prerequisites for admission to higher institutions, the birth certificate

has to be attached to the admission form. Even individuals need birth certificates to secure a job. Any parent who refuses to register his or her child, the child will face the problem when he is older. They will have to go through a long process through affidavits, spending more than they would have spent.

(DI97-25, Ìtàpá-Èkìtì, 1997)

Apart from school registration, a birth certificate is also necessary for overseas travel, as one woman mentioned:

I registered the birth of my children and this is part of development. I registered them so that in the future time, they may wish to travel out, these certificates will be useful to them. In that, wise people will know the truth about their births, where and when they were born.

(DI97-15, Ìtàpá-Èkìtì, 1997)

In contrast, there was almost universal disapproval of death registration because people could see no reason for doing this:

Do you think it is possible for a person to give birth to a child and the child can die while the father lives? Do you think it will be appropriate for the unhappy person to go the government asking for a death certificate? For example, I married a woman and she died, do you now want me to board a vehicle to the government and go and register her death? Will the loss of my wife give me joy? Will the certificate give me joy? I don't see this as a part of development. One attempts to forget about the dead person, [but] they would be recalled each time the death certificate is seen. Each time the death certificate is seen, it brings sadness to the home. I lost a child and a wife and they are asking me to get their death certificates – what for? Can someone develop in the grave? Not at all! This is not part of development.

(DI97-36, Ìtàpá-Èkìtì, 1997)

Townspeople's views of vital registration reflected their assessment of the exercise being of some demonstrable advantage to them. Their changing participation in national censuses reflects their reassessment of the value of census results for the development of their town and the Èkìtì area more generally. This reassessment may most clearly be seen by considering their behaviour during the last four national censuses.

National Census exercises

According to a government report on the 1952 Nigerian census, 'The [1952] Census was the first comprehensive enumeration ever made of the people of the Western Region' (Chambers 1956: iii). Considerable preparation went into conducting this census including the training of enumerators, the printing of census forms and posters, and public education. For example,

District Officer Bromage, Ekiti Division, sent out letters on 30 Oct 1952 to all *baále̩* of the towns and villages in È̩kìtì in order to convince them of the need to encourage their subjects' participation:

> My Good Friend:
> During November Supervisors and Enumerators will be visiting all towns and villages in È̩kìtì to prepare for the coming census [8 October 1952] and to explain to you and your people what it is all about. You have probably seen papers and posters already.
> 2. The object of the Census is not to obtain information about *individual* people; but to obtain figures concerning *groups* of people. We are not interested in the fact that Buraimo Ojo is thirty years of age. We are interested in the fact that in Ikole District there are so many children under the age of fifteen. Giving this information cannot harm any man and it will be of the utmost benefit in the development of Schools, Medical Services, etc.
> 3. I hope therefore that you and your people will do your best to co-operate with the supervisors and enumerators. The supervisor carries with him a yellow badge the enumerators a pink badge. You will find the names of the supervisor and enumerators for your area written below.
> Your Good Friend, JRB, D.O., Ekiti Division
> (Ekiti Div 1/1, File no. 918/F/129)

Despite this message, many people in Ìtàpá did not cooperate with the enumerators and subsequent information suggests that there was some undercount in the 1952 census (Aluko 1965; Duru 1968). After independence in 1960, another nationwide census was conducted in 1962, although the results were ruled invalid and another census was taken in 1963 (Ekanem 1972; Eke 1966; Yesufu 1968). There was a substantial overcount in both the 1962 and 1963 censuses (Udo 1968), although this was probably not the case in Ìtàpá. For example, the 1963 census results showed the town with a population that was relatively low (5,730), as compared with neighbouring È̩kìtì towns such as Ayégbajú-È̩kìtì (6,303) that many Ìtàpá residents considered to be smaller than their own. One man voiced his surprise at this shocking outcome:

> What baffles me there are stories about small villages that are claiming to be more populated than Ìtàpá, how they came about this I don't know. Ayégbajú, for example, nearly doubled in the 1963 census. It is very surprising and what could have caused that, I can't tell.
> (CI95-4, Ìtàpá-È̩kìtì, 1994)

With the publication of the results of the 1963 census, it became clear to some that the relatively small population of the town was detrimental to

Ìtàpá's access to government funds. If, as one woman (a retired schoolmistress) explained, townspeople were unresponsive in the past, it was because of their lack of understanding of development planning:

> [The census] is part of development as it would help to know the number of people in a particular place. In the 1963 census, some people were hiding their children so that the census-takers might not know they had many children, some people who had ten children then would say they had four. This was because people didn't know why government was taking the census. They did not know that it is the number of people in a town that would help government to decide what to do.
>
> (DI97-3, Ìtàpá-Èkìtì, 1997)

Not surprisingly, many people took pains to make sure that the town's population was well represented during the 1973 census and the 1991 census exercises. Although the results of the 1973 census were ultimately rejected for political reasons in 1975 (Adépòjù 1981; Ẹbigbọla 1981: 43), townspeople went to great lengths to get their population counted in 1991.[5]

The 1991 National Census

People in the town learned about the upcoming census exercise in several ways: through local quarter meetings, radio spots, and the announcements of the town crier. For example, according to one older woman trader:

> It was in the meeting, our quarter meeting, that the news reached me that there would be a head count. In fact many people started to wonder the need for a census when the one in 1973 or 1983 failed. The first thing I heard again was the public announcement on the media, telling us why we should have ourselves counted.
>
> (CI95-8, Ìtàpá-Èkìtì, 1994)

There were three primary actions taken in preparation for the official census in November 1991 (aside from the preliminary exercise that took place earlier in the year). The first was the urging by community leaders that all ọmọ ilú, 'sons and daughters of the town', should be at home during the census exercise so that they could be counted:

> The preparations I made were that I made sure that my people got the information accurately, that we should all register our names so that we might not be backward again in the distribution of social amenities. I started to mention to them small towns around us here claiming to be greater in population. That they should see it as important; though some people still flaunted the advice saying, there's nothing to benefit from census, some went to their farms.
>
> (CI95-20, Ìtàpá-Èkìtì, 1995)

Secondly, preparations were undertaken to see that the enumerator–visitors were properly accommodated, as one woman chief described:

> There were a lot of preparations made, for example, a person like myself, a chief in the town, we planned on how to host the census officials in terms of what they would eat and drink and how to portion out the preparations. Another thing was that since we have been made to know the value of head counts, I had to send to my people to come home, that they shouldn't allow themselves to be counted in favour of another town.
>
> (CI95-10, Ìtàpá-Èkìtì, 1994)

Thirdly, some house-heads made lists of household members to hand to enumerators who came:

> Not any preparation was made as such, but we made sure to list the people whom we wanted to be censused were written down, expecting the census-takers to come. As soon as they arrived we handed this list to them to write in the census register.
>
> (CI95-23, Ìtàpá-Èkìtì, 1995)

By making these preliminary preparations, people of the town hoped to ensure that 'all hands would be on deck' and counted during the upcoming exercises.

When the enumerators began their work on 27 November 1991, they received a friendly welcome. Some were local people, from the town itself or neighbouring towns; others were strangers. In general, they received good marks from townspeople: 'Generally, the behaviour was good because most of the questions they asked were normal and straightforward, they asked of names and age of the individual. We both behaved well' (CI95-1, Ìtàpá-Èkìtì, 1994).

The enumerators collected census data in several ways. Some people gave them the names of those people present in the house at the time of their visit, while others gave the enumerators lists of residents. Of the twenty-five individuals interviewed in 1995 about the 1991 census, nine (36 per cent) said that family members had travelled home to participate in the census.

The exercise continued for two more days without incident, with a final enumeration of 11,392 individuals recorded for Ìtàpá (Department of Population Activities 1997: 31). These provisionally released figures represented a large increase in the town's population and were hailed as a important victory for the town:[6]

> I heard about the 1991 census. I heard that people would be counted and that every individual should reschedule his or her journey so that the effects of the restrictions might not be felt and that everyone should be indoors so that everyone should be counted. In fact, the

1991 census is good ... I overheard that our population is now higher than the 1963 count, when Ayégbajú and villages around us were greater than Ìtàpá.

(CI95-13, Ìtàpá-Èkìtì, 1995)

However, while townspeople were clearly pleased with these results, the immediate consequences of these figures for the town were more opaque.

When asked in 1995 to assess the results of the 1991 census, people's replies reflected both an understanding of the rationale behind census-taking and a certain doubt as to whether they would see any practical results from the exercise:

> I know for sure that census takes place to bring progress to the town. Government can use the result to decide on what to do for any community. It is left for the government if government wishes, it can be cancelled or upheld. Government has the upper power to do whatever it feels, we can only side talk. What government wishes, it does. No manner of persuasion can make the government change its attitude. Whatever our government does, we need to abide by it. What I think that is making the government to cancel it is that this present government isn't stable, it is not the right one. It is the political situation in Nigeria that is causing this.
>
> (CI95-21, Ìtàpá-Èkìtì, 1995)

> The 1991 census was peaceful and has raised the morale of everybody because of the general increase in the population. The idea was that the population of a place determines what would be done to compensate the place in terms of schools and other social infrastructure. But at the moment, not much has come to our hearing about the intention of our Government. Oddly enough, the story in circulation now is that the census result should be cancelled.
>
> (CI95-7, Ìtàpá-Èkìtì, 1994)

Some people were more than sceptical:

> The benefits? The result I haven't heard, it was a mere child's play. Babangida has set the programme just to share the wealth of our nation with other people. The only benefit I found in it was that many of the unemployed were engaged and took a certain amount for the three days. *It was a fabulous pay!*
>
> I don't think I can benefit from it. If our government upholds it and if it is cancelled, it is the same. The government might be willing to cancel it because the present government and the last one, as I gathered didn't like each other. He [Abacha] may be doing that to tarnish the ex-president's reputation.
>
> (CI95-13, Ìtàpá-Èkìtì, 1995)

> A blessing was in the 1991 census, for example, those who did the job of census-takers were given money, they could use the money to do reasonable things, that is one advantage. Those of us who were counted, apart from disturbing us, I don't think there's any gain. Since 1991 to date, the government hasn't done anything new in my town, the government is just wasting money by conducting a census.
> (CI95-15, Ìtàpá-Èkìtì, 1995)

In their comments, townspeople are referring to the earlier, cancelled censuses held in 1962, 1963 and 1973. They are also making indirect references to the political events that transpired between the time of the 1991 census and 1995 when they were interviewed. During this interval, the 12 June 1993 presidential election was conducted and results indicated that Moshood Abíọ́lá was the victor although former President Babangida annulled the election results 'before the final vote could be counted' (Maier 2000: 70). After nationwide strikes all summer, Babangida resigned in August 1993 and Ernest Shonekan was named to head an Interim National Government. Less than three months later, on 17 November 1993, General Sani Abacha forced Shonekan to resign and took over the government. The comment about the 'present government isn't stable, it is not the right one' reflects these events, as do the comments that General Abacha annulled the census results to embarrass his rival, the ousted President Babangida, and to preclude an immediate election and return to civilian rule. Their disappointment that 'the government hasn't done anything new in my town' as a result of the census, was heightened by Babangida's failure to name any new states in 1992.[7] However, this disappointment was ameliorated by the creation of Ekiti State on 1 October 1996.

THE CREATION OF EKITI STATE

> *Kete Èkìtì ni mo kí pátá kú oríre, kete Èkìtì ni mo kí pátá, nti bímọ rere.*
> I greet all Èkìtì people for the gift, I greet all Èkìtì people for the new child.
> Chief Elémùré and his New Dimensions, *Èkìtì Kete*

For the residents of Ìtàpá-Èkìtì, the creation of Ekiti State was momentous event:

> I am very happy about the state and pray for the state each day. I listen to Ekiti State Radio and I enjoy it unlike in Ondo State, where for a week, we may not get them on the air. At times, we would be listening to it and the station would just go off the air. No language on Ekiti Radio that is strange to us now. In fact, we are just starting, I know everyone will benefit from the new state. I have not 'eaten' anything but I am sure that something good will come my way. My children can

look for work and get it. I have people who can assist in securing jobs in Ekiti State.

(DI97-17, Ìtàpá-Èkìtì, 1997)

Like this woman, many in Ìtàpá felt that people living in the Èkìtì area – essentially the northern half of the former Ondo State – had previously been ignored as funds given to the state were used to develop areas surrounding the former state capital at Àkúrẹ́:

> Anyone who visited Àkúrẹ́ would accept the fact that it is good that the capital is close to the people. Àkúrẹ́ became highly populated with fine structures; bushes were turned into big buildings. This is one of the reasons why we people in Èkìtì were agitating that we have a state capital near us, we would want Adó-Èkìtì developed like Àkúrẹ́ and Ìbàdàn.
>
> (DI97-22, Ìtàpá-Èkìtì, 1997)

Consequently, considerable efforts went into lobbying for a new state, described in addresses made at the Adó-Èkìtì Stadium by Èkìtì leaders to celebrate the new state on 1 October 1996 (Àjàyí and Arowosoge 1996; Olowoporoku 1996; Social Progress Party 1996). Preparations began in 1980 when a memorandum calling for the creation of Èkìtì State was signed by many Èkìtì politicians and commissioners in the Ondo State government. However, leadership disagreements hampered the unity of this effort and it was only in 1987 that a group of Èkìtì Ọbas, traditional chiefs and political leaders took the initiative, drafting another memorandum that called for the creation of Ekiti State. Despite these efforts, they were unable to get Èkìtì included in the new groups of states created in 1991 by President Babangida. Nonetheless, the Ọbas decided to continue their monthly meetings and lobbying and in 1993 the Èkìtì Forum was formed:[8]

> The forum was used to sensitise and spread awareness to Èkìtì people that confrontation with the Federal Government had not paid us well in the past that rather Èkìtì areas had become the ghettos of Ondo State. It was therefore resolved that Èkìtì must start to act independently and take its destiny in its own hand rather than imitating the rest of the Yoruba[9] who are more relatively developed. A new baptism of political orientation started to germinate in the minds of Èkìtì leaders.
>
> (Àjàyí and Arowosoge 1996: 11)

The address goes on to describe numerous trips to Abuja and meetings with presidential staff members in August 1994, culminating in a meeting two weeks later with General Abacha:

> This was the first time in the history of Ekiti that a cross section of Ekiti Obas and Leaders would meet the Head of State of this country

to table the problems of the Ekiti area ... When Ekiti Obas and leaders narrated their story and their mission, the Head of State embraced us, felt happy and promised to assist us to have Ekiti State once it was a very genuine case.

(Àjàyí and Arowosoge 1996: 16)

One of the arguments made by Èkìtì political leaders to support their position were the results of the 1991 census, as the Èwí (king) of Adó-Èkìtì made clear in an interview made in 1992:

> We shall not rest on our oars. President Babangida has said that military rule is outdated, so any injustice that can bring problems in the Third Republic should be removed now. One ... such injustice is the refusal to create Ekiti State. We are 1.6 million by the controversial 1992 [sic; 1991] census. We want necessary infrastructure to be brought like what obtains in other areas that are not as populous as Èkìtì land.

(Ọmọtọsọ 1992: 16)

Two years after the 1994 Abuja meetings, Ekiti State was created.[10] The joy felt throughout Èkìtì at this turn of events was expressed by the popular Èkìtì band leader, Chief Dr Elémùré Ògúnyẹ́mì, in the song *Èkìtì Kete* ('Èkìtì Together'; see Figure 9.2):

A ti rí nǹkan tí a nwá ò	We have got our request!
Èkìtì Kete	All Èkìtì people ...
Èkìtì l'ọmọdé l'ágbà	Èkìtì people, young and old
A ti ríbi ṣe èyíí sí ò	We have got a place to get the state! ...
Ẹ jẹ́ ká ni ìfẹ́ ara wa	Let us all love ourselves
Kí a sì wá papọ̀ ṣọ̀kan	And let us all be one.

When asked to assess how they had benefited personally from the creation of Ekiti State, some Ìtàpá residents mentioned specific improvements such as better radio broadcasts, increased work opportunities and easier access to state officials at the various ministries now located in the state capital at Adó-Èkìtì. Others, noting the return of Èkìtì people from many parts of Nigeria attracted by employment opportunities in the state, were optimistic for the future:

> At least within the short period of creation of Ekiti State, there were some people who we haven't seen for ten years, who are now living in Ìtàpá. They are back to their father's land. And we have those who are equally close to the town and many are now taking active roles in development of the town. Employment services can in future get to us here.

(DI97-15, Ìtàpá-Èkìtì, 1997)

Figure 9.2 Ekiti Kete ('Èkìtì Together') bumper sticker made shortly after the naming of Ekiti State in October 1996.

Others were hopeful but were also reserving judgment, such as one elderly woman who was not particularly impressed with what she had seen so far, saying, 'If Ìtàpá is developing in the state, I will like that – but nothing has come to Ìtàpá since [Ekiti State was created]' (DI97-16, Ìtàpá-Èkìtì, 1997).

Some people mentioned different types of state-sponsored projects that they hoped would be sited in the town, such as a factory, a teachers' college and government offices. These local projects would in turn attract more people to live in the town, which, with a growing population, would develop further. Indeed, with the creation of Ekiti State and the increase in the 1991 census figures for the town, people were confident about the prospects of a new local government being named with Ìtàpá as its headquarters (see Chapters 2 and 10):

> There are many advantages that Ìtàpá can gain from the new state, for example, people are now agitating for a new local government with Ìtàpá as the centre. I pray that we don't have any enemy who will go against us. Ìtàpá is at the centre and eventually Ìtàpá will become the headquarters of the proposed local government council.
> (DI97-23, Ìtàpá-Èkìtì, 1997)

At the very least, townspeople hoped for an increase in the number of wards granted to Ìtàpá and surrounding towns that would increase its voice in the current local government:

> We are expecting something good from it [the 1991 census], the result hasn't been publicised. The government will compensate the town, I'm sure. Ìlúpéjú with two wards can't be greater [in population] than Ìtàpá, Òmù, Osín, and Ìjèlú with only one ward. We have heard from people that Ìtàpá may be divided into one and a half wards. We will now be able to produce our own counselor [*sic*] rather than combining [sharing] a counselor with Osín, Ìjèlú, and Òmù people.
> (DI97-14, Ìtàpá-Èkìtì, 1997)

The possibility of political benefits and government grants, linked with the increased population demonstrated by the 1991 census by this middle-aged Ìtàpá man, was further related to another government initiative, the 'Four is enough' policy:

> If we had decided to stop procreation some years ago, we would not be as populous as we are today. The population of Ìtàpá in the past was so low because our people ran away during the head count of 1963 and up to date, the result is still affecting Ìtàpá. What we ought to be given would be given to other towns. Look at our population in the 1991 census report, with about 12,000 people. This is because the government policy of four children was not introduced then. But with the present census results, I know we will be pleased by our government.
> (DI97-14, Ìtàpá-Èkìtì, 1997)

The policy to which he is referring, 'Four children is enough', was introduced in 1988 during the Babangida regime. While promoted (but not enforced) by various government organisations including the Ministry of Health and the National Population Commission, this policy reflects a certain contradiction in government programmes concerning population. As this man's comments suggest, if the townspeople had been following the prescribed policy before the 1991 census, their population would not have increased to the extent that it did, making possible the political and economic developments sought from government. These contradictions are evident from townspeople's responses to recommendations sponsored by the Ekiti State Department of Population Activities, which has sought to promote this policy.

THE DEPARTMENT OF POPULATION ACTIVITIES, EKITI STATE

The Department of Population Activities was established in October 1996, by the Military Administrator, Lt. Col. M. I. Bawa, as outlined in the 1989 National Population Commission Decree (Iro 1987: 142).[11] According to a version of this decree published by the Federal Ministry of Health and

Social Services, the Decree included the provisions for establishing local 'Offices of Planning and Coordination for Population Programmes' (Ekiti State no date: 23). The Department's functions include maintaining connections between federal, state and local government agencies on matters concerning population, in making contacts with non-governmental organisations, and in sponsoring special events for educating local people about the census, vital registration and other population issues.[12]

In Ekiti State, the Department has sponsored several special events, including a seminar on vital registration for traditional rulers held in July 1997 and annual World Population Day programmes, both held in Adó-Èkìtì. As part of the 1997 programme, department officials sponsored an essay competition on the topic 'The new generation, their reproductive health and rights', and published a poster that was distributed throughout the state, entitled 'Contribute your quota at Family Level to Guarantee a Self-Sustaining and Progressive Nigeria'. This poster listed several recommendations including, 'Avoid giving birth to more than four children', and 'Space children for about three years', referring to the earlier 'Four is enough' and 'Space your children' programmes.

In Ìtàpá, the reception of these two recommendations ranged from condemnation to enthusiastic acceptance. People who accepted the 'Four is enough' policy saw it as being sensible in a time when it was difficult to find the necessary means to raise many children:

> To me the government would have made it two children and not four. For example, in Èkìtì here it is accepted by all that a child must have education and to send a child to school takes much from the parents. What people really depended on in the past was that people had to farm seriously and they actually realised much from this. But now when old people go to farm and [there is] no assistance from anybody, the father will cut himself, clear the ground himself. So they find it difficult to produce what will sustain the family. If they therefore decide to produce children in large numbers, they definitely have to die earlier. So if the children are few, they might be able to give the maximum and the best because of what education takes now is so immeasurable.
>
> (DI97-9, Ìtàpá-Èkìtì, 1997)

Others argue that the government, which has done nothing to help them to rear their children, has no grounds for making such recommendations:

> Ah, what actually happens is that government is just using its mouth anyhow. It is an abuse of power, not many people will accept this policy. No government is feeding me and my children. It is part of civilisation (*òlàjú*) to do this. What really [is] happening is that people should have fewer children so that they can care for them. That people should live

a better life by giving birth to fewer children isn't a policy that should come from the government. Every reliable person should know that things aren't good now and aren't easy. The little we have in hand would be enough if the number of children is reduced to the barest minimum. There should not be any policy as regards the number of children. Anyone can stop after two children and some can stop after six children. God should allow individuals to go according to their resources. The policy has no meaning to people but anyone who deems it good can cherish and accept the policy. But not everybody can accept it. Our government thinks that it is the only way our battered economy can be revamped.

Having many children is in itself development, reduction in the number is not part of development. The Nigerian economy is not buoyant, it does not encourage having many children and this has been the best weapon to stop people from having countless numbers of children. The policy has no meaning to people, it is a toothless dog. Without the policy – but with the present economic situation – procreation may be reduced.

(DI97-43, Ìtàpá-Èkìtì,1997)

While these two positions on the role of government in deciding family size differ greatly, both the male schoolteacher and the woman trader quoted above agree that having smaller families is necessary in order to adequately care for children, including providing them with education. The teacher emphasises this point by saying that people should only have two children, the trader by recommending that 'the number of children [should be] reduced to the barest minimum'. However, they sharply disagree about the government's 'Four is enough' proposal, reflecting their views of the role of the state in population matters and on the connection between population and development. For the woman trader, it is civilisation (*ọ̀làjú*), not the federal government, that has led people to have smaller families. Because people have *ọ̀làjú* (are 'civilised'), they must have fewer children in order to educate them well. Yet while having smaller families may be considered to be a result of *ọ̀làjú*, it is not part of development (*idàgbàsókè*). Rather, it is a stop-gap measure by 'Our government [that] thinks that it is the only way our battered economy can be revamped'. It is not an improvement – socially or economically – in people's lives or community. In contrast, the male teacher views the policy of 'Four is enough' as both *ọ̀làjú* and *idàgbàsókè*, since limiting family size will lead to better-educated citizens who can best bring development to the town. These different positions also reflect these two people's distinctive backgrounds, with the government worker–teacher supporting the policy and the self-employed trader rejecting it, as one man, a chief and retired teacher, explained:

The suggestion of the government on having four children is a nice idea, this is because if one could have four children and is able to bring them up, it is going to be well for such a family ... What happens is that not everyone can abide by this policy, only government officials can take it, business people [traders] and farmers can't accept that policy, since it is not the government that will sponsor the children.

(DI97-4, Ìtàpá-Èkitì, 1997)

His observation that non-government workers 'can't accept that policy, since it is not the government that will sponsor the children' refers to the point made earlier, that people will participate in government programmes when they can see some concrete benefits for themselves, their families and their town. The retired schoolteacher, who has a pension and who would have had various subsidies as a government employee when working, can support the role of the government in population policy as the government helped him to raise his own children. The woman trader received no such benefits from the government, 'No government is feeding me and my children,' and hence she does not see that the government has a legitimate voice in these matters. Furthermore, the declining economy and deteriorating infrastructure, attributed by some to fiscal mismanagement by their political leaders,[13] has undermined the government's credibility in encouraging people to participate in its population-related development initiatives. As one man put it, 'Why should Abacha have ten children and [he is] asking me to have four?' (DI97-27, Ìtàpá-Èkitì, 1997).

The politics of numbers

What stands out in townspeople's responses to government attempts to count them – either through census-taking or in limiting the number of their children – is whether they see that these exercises will have some positive effect on their lives. Not surprisingly, their scepticism about the federal government's ability to change their lives for the better, with the possible exception of the creation of Ekiti State, has affected their response to government initiatives. For example, the repeated cancellation of census results is undermining people's willingness to participate in future censuses, as one older farmer explained:

> I pray that my God forgives us – I don't see anything good in the census. I can't expect any reasonable thing out of it. I know why our government is intending to cancel it, they know that census used to precede election, [and] since they wouldn't want an election to hold now,[14] the only way would be to cancel the census. Let the government cancel it, believe me, no one would go out for any invitation in the future time.
>
> (CI95-20, Ìtàpá-Èkitì, 1995)

This effect was noted by the Ekiti State Director of the National Population Commission regarding their efforts to encourage vital registration:

> A general apathy of our people to registration affects our monthly returns. Our people see the exercise as one of those technocratic imposition[s] rather than [as] something of mutual benefit. This is a spill-over of our people's general lack of interest towards most government operations.
>
> (Ọlanipẹkun 1997: 4)

This 'lack of interest toward most government operations' has had two somewhat contradictory effects on population programmes. On the one hand, it has undermined participation in programmes supported by the National Population Commission's offspring, the Department of Population Activities, which include efforts to end early marriage and support for the 'Four is enough' and 'Space your children' campaigns, and it has reinforced people's sense of the irrelevance of the state in matters of life and death. On the other hand, people's disenchantment with 'macro-economic decline and perceived state failure' (Kawonise 1997: 108) reinforces the idea that having many people can be a way of legitimating claims for new local governments, wards and states, as was the case with Ekiti State. In the federal government's failure to distribute available development funds equitably, it has undermined the credibility of the national population policy that its leaders have introduced:

> When our government was attempting to formulate a policy, it used to be fine and straight. They would make people know the possible benefits. The idea was that villages where there were no roads, roads would be constructed there. Water would be supplied, postal agencies would be built, and people believed that when their population is large, they would have the right to demand anything from the government. Up to this moment, nothing good has shown up from the government, apart from those things that were there a long time ago. Before 1991, we have voted for local government chairmen, they would come and make fake promises and go.
>
> (CI-15, Ìtàpá-Èkìtì, 1995)

In other words, people are questioning government pronouncements about population when its political leaders do not seem to have their interests at heart.

CONCLUSION

The former premier of the Western Region, the late Ọbáfẹ́mi Awólọ́wọ̀, observed regarding the difficulties of conducting a national census that 'egalitarianism would have been crystallised among our people' (cited in

Adépòjù 1981: 34) if everyone's lot had improved, thus undermining the linkage of population increase and development funding in people's minds.[15] Furthermore, with the equitable distribution of concrete improvements throughout Nigeria – including good roads, clinics and schools, electricity and pipe-borne water – the incessant hankering for new states and local government headquarters might have been dispelled.

Under the present difficult circumstances in Ìtàpá-Èkìtì, and Nigeria generally, this is not likely to happen. Nor is it likely that people will participate in government population programmes, unless they can see some concrete benefits for themselves in doing so. In Ìtàpá, people see a benefit in having somewhat smaller families, registering the births of their children and participating in national censuses. While these actions display a certain autonomy vis à vis the state on the part of rural townspeople who decide whether or not to be counted, they nonetheless have had little or no say, until recently, in how their government is spending federal development funds, as one man observed:

> Whatever the government deems fit, they can do it. If they like they can put things straight and if they like they can bend or break it; government may start a programme, later they may decide not to do it again.
> (CI95-11, Ìtàpá-Èkìtì, 1995)

Indeed, Ìtàpá women and men have had few means for holding their national and state leaders accountable. At best, they could demonstrate displeasure with their government by not participating in its programmes. Despite their happiness with the creation of Ekiti State and the various development initiatives that its leaders have undertaken since 1996 (including repair of the main road through Ìtàpá; see Chapter 10), the contradictory policies of the federal government have undermined townspeople's willingness to view the various forms of population counts advocated by their government as development (*idàgbàsókè*) for themselves or for their community, as one man explained:

> Ah, what they said initially was that the population of the place would allow our government to decide what our government would do for us. To me, I see things as topsy-turvy, things have not been straightened by the government. It was my belief that the government wanted to assist us through the result of the census but the reverse has been the case. Instead of solving our problem, it is adding more; our government only makes pronouncements but [they are] never fulfilled.
> (CI95-4, Ìtàpá-Èkìtì, 1994)

In Ìtàpá (and elsewhere in Nigeria), people will actively participate in government programmes when they see that their government is 'solving

[the] problem', rather than 'adding more'. Furthermore, the needed changes must occur at the federal level, according to one older farmer:

> What happens to the head happens to other parts of the body. This is the situation [in Nigeria]. It is what is happening that is retarding development of the federal government that is retarding the development of every home and every individual.
>
> (DI97-10, Ìtàpá-Èkìtì, 1997)

The following chapter examines some of the problems retarding development in Ìtàpá and relates them to what is happening 'to the head'.

10

CONCLUSION: LOCAL DEVELOPMENT, POLITICS AND TWO FUNERALS

The road was endless. One road lead to a thousand others, which in turn fed into paths, which fed into dirt tracks, which became streets, which ended in avenues and cul-de-sacs. All around, a new world was being erected amidst the old.

Ben Okri, *The Famished Road*

How can porson give something to government? When we have paid tax finish, then they begin to ask for dash again. Na good government so?

K. Saro-Wiwa, *Sozaboy*

INTRODUCTION: THE ROAD TO PROGRESS

In May 2000, the fourth phase of work began on the Ìtàpá–Ìkọ̀lé road. This work, paid for by the newly-installed civilian state government 'in apparent response to the general clamour for improved road network in Ekiti State' (Ajetunmọbi 2000: 1), represents the principal form of federally-sponsored development in many rural Èkitì towns and villages. Indeed, the first two phases of roadwork were conducted by the colonial government, and the third – when it was actually paved – by the newly-independent federal government, and most recently, by the Ekiti State government.[1] Previously, local men (and some women) participated in road construction without payment as part of community work (*àárò*) but they were paid for their efforts during the last two phases of roadwork. Their labour has been considerable, particularly in the earlier phases when heavy construction equipment was not available. Nonetheless, this work was considered worthwhile and as one older man exclaimed, 'Ah, we have to thank God for everything, the advantages of the road were many!'

Having access to a good road is one among several changes for the better that townspeople have experienced over the last seventy-five years. As has been noted in earlier chapters, they have also benefited from the presence of schools, hospitals and clinics, a community bank, town hall, post office and, more recently, a sawmill (see Figure 10.1), which were constructed largely through their own efforts although often with some government assistance. One of the individuals in the town who was singularly responsible for

Figure 10.1 Sawmill newly opened in Rẹ́mọ, Ìtàpá-Èkìtì, July 2000. (photograph by the author)

initiating these projects and acquiring government assistance was the late Chief S. A. Dada.[2] His history is instructive, not only as it exemplifies the circumstances that motivated local development during the last century in many parts of south-western Nigeria, but also because of his role in attempts to settle the townwide dispute that is impeding present-day progress.

THE FATHER OF DEVELOPMENT IN ÌTÀPÁ

The career of Chief Dada in some ways parallels that of other successful Yoruba men who were educated in the colonial school system and who converted to Christianity, yet who also maintained a strong sense of their people's cultural heritage and history.[3] For example, while attending Government Teacher Training College, Ìbàdàn in 1946, he challenged the expatriate principal's frequent statements about 'the civilising benefits of colonialism', citing quotations from Azikiwe published in the *West African Pilot* (Dada 2000: 19). He was also an outspoken and active leader in the African Church (Dada no date) and was the first president of the Ìtàpá Progressive Union (IPU). What made his career unique among Ìtàpá citizens was his generosity in providing funds for educating many of his fellow townspeople, much in the way that responsible senior brothers within families would support the education of their juniors, in a process referred to as a 'sibling chain of assistance' (Caldwell 1977a: 20). This patronage was not entirely disinterested since, as he told one of his colleagues, 'the more we are able to increase their number [of educated], the easier for us to help the people,' that is, they would be political allies, seeing things from their perspective.

Chief Dada was also instrumental in promoting IPU projects and soliciting government funds through his letter-writing efforts. In one letter written in 1960 to the District Officer at Adó-Èkìtì, he requested support for several projects, including a post office, maternity clinic and secondary school.[4] These projects were subsequently carried out, not by the colonial government but by members of the IPU and town residents. When sufficient funds were unavailable locally, as was the case with Ìtàpá-Osín Secondary School built in 1975, Chief Dada provided his own contributions so that such projects could get government approval:

> I got the government requirements, they said they wanted ₦40,000 as deposit. So we launched a deposit, fund-raising – we got ₦23,000. Well, I added my own ₦17,000, to make ₦40,000 and got this deposit to the government, that is why the government approved the grammar school ... And again before the school reached five years I was able to get a building grant of ₦30,000 from the government with which we built the science laboratory.
> (Interview: S. A. Dada, Ìbàdàn, 1997)

Nonetheless Dada faced considerable resistance, both from family members who considered themselves to be the rightful beneficiaries of his financial success and from local townspeople whose political fortunes were bound up in the earlier system of traditional chieftaincy. While these people welcomed the benefits of development projects sponsored by him, some came to view him as a meddling outsider whose often outspoken criticisms contradicted their own decisions. After a particularly rancorous debate over the naming of a new Ọwátàpá in 1986 (Dada supported the losing candidate), he vowed that he would not live in the town again but rather remained in his residence known as 'Ìtàpá House' in downtown Ìbàdàn. Yet he continued to maintain contact with various townspeople who sought his advice and assistance. He also continued to express his views on various political actions taken by Ìtàpá residents. This continued concern and indirect involvement became more direct when a long-standing dispute between the two main sections of the town escalated in recent years.

THE DISPUTE: CENTRIFUGAL AND CENTRIPETAL TENDENCIES

The twin tendencies of centripetry and centrifugality have been historically critical factors in the development and population growth of the town of Ìtàpá-Èkìtì. People dispersing for economic or security reasons as well as people being attracted back to the town because of familial obligations and opportunities characterise the town's history over the last 150 years. Indeed, the basis of the present-day dispute has its roots in the nineteenth-century warfare that led to the dispersal of much of the town's population.

As described in Chapter 2, there are eight quarters in the town. Four of these quarters are grouped together as Ẹgẹ̀tún and are considered to be descendants of one of the three principal settlers, Ọbaàró, the blacksmith. The other four, known collectively as Rẹ́mọ, are considered to be the descendants of Ẹlẹ́mọ, the hunter. While not geographically contiguous, three of the four quarters grouped as Rẹ́mọ are located at the eastern half of the town, while three of the Ẹgẹ̀tún quarters are located in the western half. According to Chief Dada during his testimony before the Council of Ọbas in September 1999, the Ẹgẹ̀tún people were more severely affected by nineteenth-century warfare because of their proximity to the road leading north to Bida and Ìlọrin, compared with Rẹ́mọ to the east:

> The problem is shortage of personnel in Egetun, which started in the nineteenth century (around 1845). Ìtàpá was one of the towns raided by Etsu Nupe. Many residents of Egetun were carried away and that section of the town was depopulated ... Since that time Egetun has not caught up with Remo in the number of Chiefs.
> (Dada, Address to the Council of Ọbas, Ọyẹ LGA, Ọyẹ-Èkìtì, 30 September 1999)

During the last century there have been intermittent tensions – largely reflecting the uneven division of power among titled chiefs associated with the two sections[5] – when centripetal forces advocating division of the town alternated with centrifugal forces advocating unity. Since both sides are expected to contribute equally to town collections and projects, this has led to a situation that might be described as 'taxation without equal representation'. In the early 1950s, the effects of this imbalance were evident in a customary court case over a delinquent loan filed by a chief from Ẹgẹ̀tún against a man from Rẹ́mọ. The Ọwátàpá who headed the court, along with his council of chiefs who were mainly from Rẹ́mọ, voted to have the plaintiff, an Ẹgẹ̀tún chief, removed from the council of chiefs to punish him for pursuing the debt. During this period, there were fears that the town would split, as evidenced in a letter from the Olomodakomo of Akòró (a quarter in Ìtàpá) to the Ekiti District Officer:[6]

> Sir, We are putting this matter before the D.O. for kind consideration and approval. The matter between the Owatapa of Itapa and Chief Obaisa are of his chiefs to be settled favourably among them, we do not want the matter or the quarrelling to go further. *We do not want the matter to divide the town of Itapa into two separate halves.*
> We are very grateful.
> Yours obediently, Olomodakomo of Akoro

The aggrieved plaintiff, Chief Ọbaísà, took the matter to the Acting District Officer, William Simpson, who ruled in his favour.[7] As a result of the apparent unequal representation of the two sides on the council of chiefs that contributed to this dispute, the council was restructured so that both were equally represented. Subsequently, relative peace prevailed until the mid-1990s.

DISUNITY AND UN-DEVELOPMENT

The deteriorating relations between the two sections of the town and their effect on local development was summarised in the welcome address made at the twelfth annual Ìtàpá Day Celebration in 1999 (see Figure 10.2). Twelve years earlier, the speaker noted, it would have been easy to muster support to rebuild the Ọba's palace and the community, though diverse in its interests, was united around this plan. However, such a project would be impossible at present, he said, not because of financial constraints but because of disputes and disunity. The speaker continued:

> Today all these things have been dragged into [the] mud ... There is already the transmission downstream to the grassroots of the negative aspects of what is happening in the town such that our sons and daughters fear coming home to do anything ... We have built a pyramid of problems for ourselves in the community.
> (A. Àjàyí, 2 October 1999, Ìtàpá-Èkìtì)

The sense that the town's political leadership had failed to promote community development because of their own self-interest was also voiced by several townspeople, including one older woman:

> When Ọwátàpá Òjó [the previous king] was on the throne, it wasn't the same thing as with the present government in Ìtàpá ... If a case was taken to him, no matter your strength and richness, he would treat everyone accordingly. He gave equal recognition to all people; he would not take bribes and he tempered justice with mercy. I pray that God will help us erase this nonsense that is ravaging the town.
> (DI97-16, Ìtàpá-Èkìtì, 1997)

The sense that justice went to the highest bidder, along with suspicions that money levied for local development projects were not used for these purposes has had a direct effect on fundraising efforts.[8] One sign of trouble in the town occurred during the 1998 Ìtàpá Day celebrations when Ìtàpá residents accused the organisers (members of the Ìtàpá Progressive Union) of misuse of funds raised during the event. How, exactly, were monies supposedly for development of the town being spent? Chief Dada expressed a similar sentiment in an interview conducted the previous year:

Figure 10.2 Programme cover for an earlier Ìtàpá Day, 1996. This Ninth Annual Ìtàpá Day on 5 October 1996 was entitled 'Coming Together for Development'.

>
> All the Ìtàpá Day[s] they are doing is just to provide the ọba with stipend. You see, it is a way of making the chiefs get money, to say they spend it for sacrifices for the progress of the town which some of us don't believe in. Ask them how that money is spent, they won't be able to account for it. They will say they have spent it. How? Nobody should ask.
>
> (S. A. Dada, Ìbàdàn, August 1997)

As a result of these criticisms, the Ìtàpá Progressive Union board was disbanded and an interim board appointed in its place. Yet this interim board could not solve the town's problems, partly because of the continued imbalance in representation on the king's council and partly because of the actions of certain town chiefs who were seen as playing one side off against the other. There was talk, as in the 1950s, that the town would divide into two.

In May 1999, leaders from the Ẹgẹ̀tún community sent a memorandum to the Chairman and Council of Ọbas, Ọyẹ Local Government, to ask for a re-structuring of the chieftaincy positions in Ìtàpá. Leaders from the Rẹ́mọ community responded with their own memorandum a month later, arguing that such a restructuring would go against 'their rights and heritage'. The intransigence of the two sides and the danger it posed to the unity of the town convinced Chief Dada to address the Chairman and the Council of Ọbas, Ọyẹ Local Government, in late September 1999. According to him, 'The two memoranda are a jumble of facts and fiction. None is correct. They are all propaganda about their respective positions' (Dada 1999: 6). At the meeting, he discussed the memoranda in some detail after which he made some suggestions for solving the problems of the town. His recommendations included a rejection of both the Rẹ́mọ and Ẹgẹ̀tún memoranda, a restructuring of the hierarchy of chiefs to promote equal representation, and the resumption of peace in the town (Dada 1999b: 7).

While Chief Dada was highly respected by many in the community, his advice and admonitions did not stop Ẹgẹ̀tún residents from essentially boycotting the 1999 Ìtàpá Day celebrations that took place the next month. In November, Chief Dada called another prominent son of Ìtàpá, the lawyer A. O. Àkànle, to arrange a meeting to be held in December 1999 to discuss a resolution to the Ẹgẹ̀tún–Rẹ́mọ dispute (A. O. Àkànle, interview, July 2000, Adó-Èkìtì). Unfortunately Chief Dada was unable to witness a resolution of the dispute as he died on 1 December 1999 at the age of seventy-three. It was his funeral that temporarily re-united the town.

'THE END OF AN ERA'

The funeral for Chief Dada took place in Ìtàpá-Èkìtì on 16–19 February 2000. Visitors came from all over Nigeria, reflecting Dada's prominent roles in the African Church and educational communities in Nigeria. As part of the ceremony, his most recent book, an autobiography (Dada 2000), was launched and the town hall was named in his honour (see Figure 10.3).

In one funeral speech, Prince David Makajuọla Ajaja referred to Chief Dada's death as 'the end of an era' – an era of optimism reflected in development philanthropy[9] and national pride. Yet he also used his speech as an opportunity to exhort the funeral attendees to settle the dispute in the town:

> The death of Chief S. A. Dada should represent in all respect the end of imbibing the wrong notion that Ìtàpá is an embattled and

Figure 10.3 Town hall named in honour of the late Chief Samuel Ayọ̀ọlá Dada on December 1999. Ìtàpá-Èkìtì, July 2000. (photograph by the author)

beleaguered enclave where we live amidst mutual suspicion and hostility replacing brotherhood and cooperation. As a matter of fact, we are tired of these avoidable protracted wrangling and squabbles. Imagine we have no good township roads, no potable water, no regular supply of electricity, no industries and no functional health centres. Apart from the monumental achievements of our pioneering leaders in Ìtàpá land, no other leaders of note have done anything tangible to move Ìtàpá forward progressively.[10] Instead, they will prefer to precipitate issues that will divide rather than unite us.

(Ajaja 2000: 10–11)

For as Chief Dada himself explained in 1997, the town of Ìtàpá cannot develop without political consensus among the two parts:

> Ah, they must be united, which is far from them now. The leadership is very important, see, well, when the leader, the Bible says everyone must be a leader of the church, but to govern his own house. So the leadership is faulty ... Without the leadership being corrected we can hardly benefit because there is some of us who have kept away from that town.

As in other towns in south-western Nigeria, this support from 'sons and daughters of the soil' living outside is a critical resource for local development of the town (Trager 1998, 2001). Not only are these people being 'kept away from the town', for fear of getting embroiled in its conflicts, but those who can, having acquired some education or outside connections, leave. The problems facing the town are problems of politics and political leadership.

In some ways, the crisis of political leadership in Ìtàpá is related to the faulty national leadership of former military regimes, particularly the late General Sani Abacha (Maier 2000) and General Ibrahim Babangida (Apter 1999), whose greed and duplicity has been exposed in the Nigerian press (Ọlọ́runfẹ́wa 2000) and ridiculed in the popular media.[11] Through the use of contracts and access to foreign currency, favourable currency exchange rates, and funds from international lending institutions such as the International Monetary Fund, these two political leaders were able to remain in power from 1985 to 1998 (see Appendix II). The end of the military regime and the election of a civilian president in 1999 augured the possibility that the nation's situation might take a turn for the better. This may take some time, however, considering that the country's infrastructure (providing light and water, as well as refining petroleum) was essentially gutted during the two prior military regimes, and that debt repayments for loans made by the personnel of international monetary organisations exceeded $30 (US) billion (Onishi 2000b: 18). Since 35 per cent of the country's annual foreign exchange earnings go to service this debt, the current government's ability to pay for infrastructural repairs and social services is considerably hampered. In any event, the nation's present-day problems are not primarily the result of a burgeoning population impeding economic and social development.

POPULATION AND DEVELOPMENT

Malthus published *An Essay on Population* (1914) in 1798, arguing that population growth would soon outstrip food production leading to starvation, poverty, and misery. Only 'positive' (for example, death [*sic*]) and 'preventative checks' (for example, delayed marriage) could ameliorate this situation. This dire view of population growth was later challenged by economists such as Boserup (1965, 1990) who argued that technological changes could improve food production, supporting a larger population.[12] In contrast, social theorists such as Marx (1867) argued that it was the development of a capitalist labour system with its inequitable distribution of wealth that led to the poverty of large numbers of people, rather than this situation resulting from overpopulation, as Malthus claimed. What is less well-known is that contemporaries of Malthus, such as the Marquis de Condorcet (1795), offered interpretations of the relationship between population growth and progress that distinctly differed from those proposed by Malthus. While Condorcet believed, like Malthus, that population growth could strain available resources, he also believed, unlike Malthus, that humans could formulate solutions – through technology, conservation and education – to these problems (Condorcet 1970 [1795]: 221).

More recently, the economist Amartya Sen (1994; 1999) has made a similar point, arguing that poor economic production (associated with an underdeveloped infrastructure, illiteracy and discrimination against women) and political disruption are what are causing poverty and suffering, rather than population growth per se. When solutions to these economic and political problems are found – through economic growth, infrastructural improvements and better education and healthcare – population growth will decline, not vice versa. In discussing the current problems in sub-Saharan Africa, he notes:

> A lower population growth rate could have reduced the magnitude of the fall in per capita GNP, but the main roots of Africa's economic decline lie elsewhere. The complex political factors underlying the troubles of Africa include, among other things, the subversion of democracy and the rise of combative military rulers, often encouraged by the cold war ... The explanation of sub-Saharan Africa's problems has to be sought in these political troubles, which affect economic stability, agricultural and industrial incentives, public health arrangements, and social services – even family planning and population policy ... To dissociate the task of population control from the politics and economics of Africa would be a great mistake and would seriously mislead public policy.
>
> (Sen 1994: 65–6)

Sen's position is akin to the earlier thinking of demographers who saw structural, economic and social changes as critical for the population reduction. Prior to the late 1940s, demographers and policymakers assumed that population would only decline after social structural and economic changes, reflected in a certain level of development (that is, a literate populace, hospitals and infrastructural improvements such as roads, water and light), had been established (Hodgson 1983: 10). Sen has coined the term 'collaborative' to refer to this way of thinking about how population growth might be reduced.

By the early 1950s, however, many US demographers and politicians had begun to reassess this position. Population growth, formerly perceived as a variable dependent on socioeconomic and systemic factors, was recast as an independent variable which had important implications for development (Hodgson 1983: 12). According to this reasoning, limiting population growth by 'investing in a family planning programme was an especially efficient way of increasing aggregate income per capita' compared with investments in infrastructural development. 'Such a superbly efficient line of investment has an obvious appeal to international aid agencies' (Demeny

1988: 457), who might be said to be practising a form of development 'on the cheap'.[13]

Sen has referred to this approach and other more drastic interventions focused specifically on controlling births as the 'override' approach to population growth reduction. It is not difficult to see how this approach echoes the earlier pessimism of Malthus about human capacity for positive change and the need for human behaviour to be 'overridden' by compulsion: by death, poverty or government decrees. In contrast, the 'collaborative' approach echoes the earlier views of Condorcet, who believed in human capacity for 'collaborative' change 'through reasoned decisions and actions [that] have tended ... to find the solution of the population problem in economic and social development' (Sen 1994: 64).

The residents of the town of Ìtàpá-Èkìtì, to the extent that they view population growth as a 'problem' for development, would decidedly come down on the side of 'collaborative' change. Even if they are not doing a particularly good job of collaborating at the present moment, no one actually believes that the town will divide in two and there is a sense that the educated young people of the town can reverse the town's fortunes.[14]

POPULATION AND PROGRESS IN A YORUBA TOWN

The idea that population growth hampers development and that its reduction will set the stage for development 'take-off' contradicts how Ìtàpá men and women conceptualise the town's progress: *idàgbàsókè*, likened to the process of raising a child. Indeed, as has been seen in the previous chapters, development – much of it locally sponsored – has occurred in the town, initiated by a group of educated men in the 1950s. More recently, the total fertility rate has dropped to some extent as parents are reassessing the benefits of child-fostering, the costs of education and the limits of familial obligations. However, two factors have complicated this process. First is the idea that a growing population is an important part of what is defined as progress or development of a town. People realise, however, that the population of the town can increase by becoming an economic and political centre (rather than simply by an increasing birth rate), hence their tireless efforts at making the town a local government headquarters. Secondly, and more importantly, is the fact that the uncertainties associated with government policies and actions have made it imperative that extended, large families continue, in order to maintain claims in land, government positions and other privileges. Thus, this perception of progress as *idàgbàsókè* is not simply a case of 'cultural lag', wherein ideas about having many children as a form of wealth and prestige persist when other forms of wealth and prestige have made such thinking obsolete. Rather, in a political economy that continues to be based on patron–client relations and with deteriorating infrastructural supports and maternal and child healthcare services, having many children makes sense in facing the uncertainties of everyday life. Surely, at least one child will survive and do well, bringing the rest of the family (and even the town) along with them. This is not to say that people are not reassessing what constitutes having 'many' children. They have done this, as Chapter 3 has shown. One of the paradoxes of progress in this town is that while the total fertility rate is declining, earlier development projects in the town are deteriorating and present progress is stagnating. What has been largely ignored is the role of politics in explaining this process.

CONCLUSION

This book is about how 'people' (population) and 'progress' (local development) are perceived by the residents of a small, rural town in south-western Nigeria and how their thinking is changing. Based on research conducted over a period of nine years, the findings of this case study suggest that collaborative local development projects have contributed to an actual improvement in their lives and a modest decline in fertility rates in the town. However, this local development has taken place in the face of considerable political and economic uncertainty. Local disputes have exacerbated this situation, discouraging Ìtàpá descendants living outside the town from participating in and contributing to projects there. Furthermore, federal programmes and politics have undermined some of the changes relating to population and development in the town.

Despite the fact that the federal political picture has changed dramatically during the period during which research for this book was being conducted, the economic picture has not.[15] For example, the federal government's facilities for generating electricity have deteriorated over the past decade and there has not been power in the town for at least a year. Continued shortages of gasoline in Ekiti State have affected the availability of transport, which is either limited by lack of fuel or by the number of passengers who can pay the resulting high fares.[16] There is no telephone service. The infrastructural support which could allow townspeople to reduce their reliance on the labour of children (Robertson 1991), either their own or fostered, is only marginally present. As one older woman explained it:

> The present situation in the country doesn't give joy at all. Some people have children in schools and as a government worker, he may not receive salary for a year. How is he going to manage at home? A person who used a vehicle in the past as a private vehicle is now turning it into a commercial vehicle so that he can eat, is that a good life? No fuel again in the town, even if you have your money you can't get it to buy. This is no joy!
>
> (DI97-16, Ìtàpá-Èkìtì, 1997)

The importance of improving rural townspeople's day-to-day existence by rebuilding the town's infrastructure and making low-cost healthcare and family planning options available was noted by the Nigerian demographer, P. O. Olúsànyà (1985:52) over fifteen years ago.[17] He eloquently concluded that:

> It is unrealistic to expect illiterate and under-privileged families to impose a conscious limit on their childbearing on the grounds of rapid population growth. This has little or no meaning for the population. What matters is the people's own day-to-day existence and the immediate factor that impinge on it – health, food, shelter and so forth. Population growth, in other words, is far from their centre of interest. Their concern is with the improvement of their quality of life. And this is the most rational stance from their own view-point. What they need to be told, therefore, is that planning their families is part of the effort to improve their and their children's health and survival as well as their general living conditions. And the results of this effort must be clearly perceived in order to bring about the desired change in family size.

While the current national leaders may have the intention to make such improvements, they do not necessarily have the wherewithal, making it difficult for Ìtàpá and other towns and cities in Nigeria to repair a devastated infrastructure. What is more serious for the town's present progress is the problem of the sectional dispute – reflecting long-standing political claims as well as the short-term economic interests of some of its political leaders – that is threatening the townpeople's ability to work together. That some local politicians are immediately benefiting from what Chabal and Daloz (1999: xviii) refer to as 'the political instrumentalisation of disorder ... the process by which political actors in Africa seek to maximise their returns on the state of confusion, uncertainty, and sometimes even chaos' does not mean that such political leadership is inevitable.

Furthermore, this in-fighting is not the result of overpopulation and environmental degradation as some social analysts claim (Kaplan 2000). Rather, it reflects the particularities of historical events, political judgment and circumstance. For the men and women of Ìtàpá, the path they have taken leading to this impasse may still be reversed. With a certain amount of accommodation toward those with opposing views – understanding that one side 'can't just rest on traditions' and the other needs 'to be a bit patient with traditions', as the Ìtàpá lawyer A. O. Àkànle, explained – the unity of the town could be restored and its progress resumed. As the Yoruba say, *Ìgbà wo ni ọmọ náà á lè rìn* (It takes a period of time for a child to know how to walk); similarly, development does not 'start in a day.'

★ ★ ★

This chapter began with the death and funeral of a prominent citizen of the town and it will conclude with a brief description of another. Madame Julianah Dúrójayé Ọmọtóyìnbó died on 24 July 2000 and was buried in Ìtàpá on 30 September 2000. She had been ill since suffering a stroke earlier in the year after hearing of the February riots in Kaduna (Akinkuotu 2000; Onishi 2000a), where her son lived and owned property. The rioting, which broke out arose from arguments over the introduction of Sharia law in Kaduna State, led to 'at least 2,000' deaths (Maier 2000: 146) and she feared for his life. If Chief S. A. Dada was the 'father of development' in Ìtàpá who made it possible for many of its sons and daughters to attend school, it was Madame Ọmọtóyìnbó who, as one of the principal midwives in the town, made the existence of many of these people possible in the first place.

Madame Ọmọtóyìnbó worked as a traditional midwife in Ìtàpá all of her life and it was in this capacity that I first got to know her. She patiently explained how she cared for expectant mothers in her house and what was done during deliveries. Later, when I needed information about vital registration practices and views about local development, particularly regarding specific projects such as the maternity clinic, Madame Ọmọtóyìnbó was both eloquent and knowledgeable. When the clinic first opened, she worked there gratis for several years after which she went back to delivering children in her home. I often visited her on my return to the town and appreciated her outspoken, intelligent and sometimes hilarious comments. In 1997, for example, she demonstrated her disgust with the town's lack of electricity by 'removing all the lightbulbs in my house. This,' she explained, 'was because I was annoyed with the prolonged off-and-on light for almost a year. It was my daughter from Adó who forced me to put them back.'

On my visit to Ìtàpá in July 2000, I learned of her stroke and that she had been taken to Adó-Èkìtì to be cared for by her daughter. It was shocking to see her there, small and emaciated, lying on a bed. Only a year earlier, she compellingly explained to a visiting graduate student why women in the town continued to have their daughters circumcised. She was conscious, however, and even made the effort to greet me. Later, when I went to say goodbye, she pointed her finger at me, I was not quite sure why. But later, I remembered her admonishment from an earlier discussion of the problems of Ìtàpá-Èkìtì and Nigeria. 'When you get home, Òyìnbó, tell your people to come and help the problem ... let everything become normal again' (J. Ọmọtóyìnbó, 1 August 1997, Ìtàpá-Èkìtì). This book represents an attempt to honour her request.

APPENDIX I

RESEARCH METHODS AND MATERIALS

GENERAL DESCRIPTION OF RESEARCH METHODS

This study began in June 1991, when I moved into the house of Dr Michael Òjó, a retired university professor, who was living in Ìtàpá-Èkìtì. My selection of the town as a research site was largely based on its location: it was rural but on the main highway about midway between Adó-Èkìtì and Ìkọ̀lé-Èkìtì and at the intersection of several neighbouring towns (Ìjẹ̀lú, Osín, Ìrè, and Ìlúpéjú). While the town had some of the infrastructural characteristics of larger cities (for example, electricity, pipeborne water, a bank, police station and post office), its size made townwide mapping and surveys possible, which was a concern considering certain financial constraints. It was also a fairly typical town for the north-east Yoruba area in its social institutions, physical configuration and architecture.

Having obtained the permission of the Ọwátàpá and his council of chiefs to conduct research in the town and with the help of Dr Òjó, I was able to obtain the research assistance of Mr Káyọ̀dé Owóẹyẹ and Ms Comfort Àjàyí, who worked throughout the first year of the project. Together, we conducted a household census of the entire town, which included mapping all buildings. This was followed by open-ended interviews of a stratified sample of seventy women (aged fifteen to thirty-nine) and sixty-six men (aged twenty to forty-four), selected by age and availability. They were asked a range of questions about their attitudes toward family size and government population policies, marital relations, child-fostering, the use of birth-control methods and associated health concerns. These interviews were conducted primarily in Yoruba by Mr Owóẹyẹ and Ms Àjàyí, whom I alternately accompanied, and by myself. Brief notes were taken at the time of the interviews, and interviews were also recorded. They were then translated into English and transcribed by Mr Sunday Fálọdún and Mr Kẹ́hìndé Àjàyí.

Through these qualitative interviews I gained a general sense of the attitudes and vocabulary associated with fertility, childbearing, family planning and gender relations. This information was used to devise a survey that focused on family size, infant mortality, contraceptive use, the practice of dilation and curettage (D & C), reproductive health knowledge and spousal discussion of fertility intentions. The surveys for men and for women

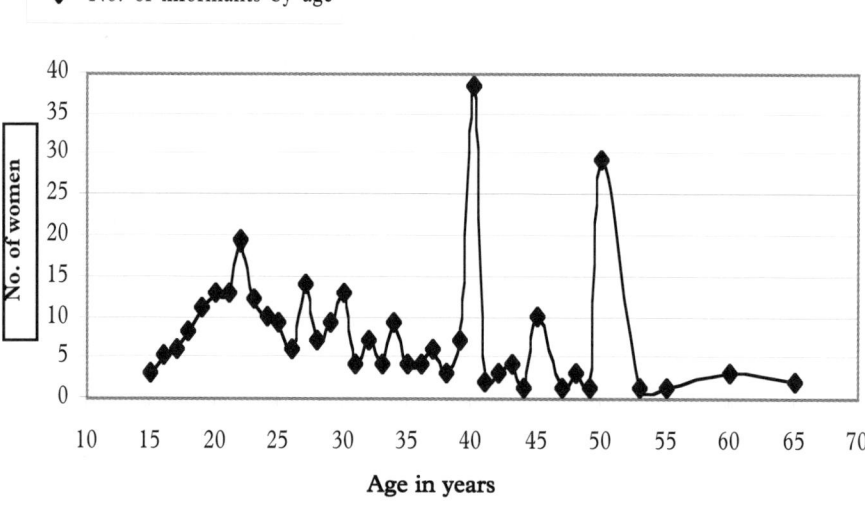

Figure App. 1.1 Age heaping by survey women's age, Ìtàpá-Èkìtì, 1997

were worded differently when appropriate but were essentially the same in content, with 294 women aged fifteen to forty-nine, and 302 men aged twenty to fifty-four questioned in the period from January–March 1992. People were randomly selected by household, with women (within the prescribed age ranges obtained from the census) living in every third house (selected from the map) and men living in every other house (as it was difficult to find men at home). These interviews were conducted in Yoruba and recorded on survey forms by Ms Àjàyí, Ms Adénìkẹ́ Ọ̀ṣọ́, Mr Owóèyẹ, Mr Fálọdún, and myself in the early part of 1992.

The survey results suggested several areas for further questioning. For example, while the survey documented the number of people in the sample who were presently fostering children, the reasons for their actions and their own experiences of child-fostering called for follow-up questioning. Similarly, information recorded in the survey about abortion, about the use of particular contraceptives, about age of first intercourse and about occupations was expanded through a series of long interviews on specific topics carried out over the next eight years (see below). Additionally, many of the men who had participated in the 1991 long interviews were re-interviewed in 1995 by Mr Owóèyẹ[1] and an identical five-year follow-up survey of the women participating in the 1992 survey was conducted in 1997 by Ms Ìyábọ̀ Arósọ, Ms Bọ́sẹ̀ Ayẹni, and myself.

Because these people questioned in these interviews and surveys were often selected on the basis of age, something needs to be said about numerical age, the accuracy of which may not be as compelling to some informants as it is to researchers. Thinking in terms of age may reflect, for some, a discomfort with quantifying such things as people, not simply a lack of familiarity. Furthermore, the heaping of ages given by women over forty suggests that ranking by seniority and status – 'so-and-so is older than ...' – has more cogency for many older women than actual numerical age (see Figure App 1.1).[2] However, younger, more educated women tended to know their exact birth dates as evidenced by the lack of heaping among younger cohorts. Nonetheless, numbers themselves conveyed certain meanings that even young, educated informants might want to disguise or were disinterested in relaying. For example, one man with a university degree whose age stayed the same over a period of three years explained to me that there are certain expectations, such as a good job (which he did not have) associated with age, hence his adjustment. Similarly, numerical age could be a source of embarrassment to women who were still schooling and still unmarried, or to those who did not want to admit that their childbearing days were over by giving a large number suggesting that they were old. Caldwell and Igun (1971: 299) observed this effect when comparing data from the 1963 Nigerian census with a follow-up study in 1969:

> We can conclude that there is a significant tendency amongst fifteen- to nineteen-year-old females for marital and parity conditions to affect age enumeration. The single have a somewhat greater chance of having their ages understated than overstated, while the married are much more likely to have their ages overstated.

Similarly, they found a tendency for women aged twenty to twenty-four who are single (and without children) to have their ages underestimated by interviewers.[3]

Figure App 1.2 gives an indication of this indifference to exact numerical age as evidenced by a comparison of women's responses to questions about their ages in the 1992 survey and the 1997 follow-up survey.[4] The variation in reported age in this study sometimes went in directions one might not expect – some women reported themselves to be three years younger than they were five years ago. This sort of variation may also be seen in responses to questions about their children's ages.[5] While more accuracy in age will probably occur as more women are educated (as Figure App 1.1 suggests), there is probably no way around numerical misrepresentation, in other words, in eliminating the social and political aspects of numbers.

In addition to these interviews and surveys, I collected local written materials relating to the history of Ìtàpá, including short histories as well as speech manuscripts and church and funeral programmes. Having attended Ìtàpá Day in 1994, I gathered materials from the day's celebration and from

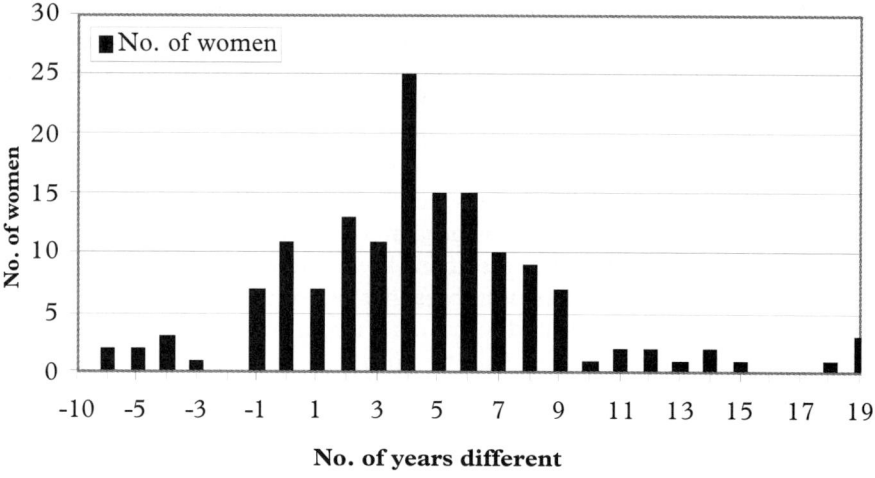

Figure App. 1.2 Comparison of ages reported in 1992 and 1997 surveys

subsequent Ìtàpá Days, as well as programmes from some of the various quarter days in the town. There are also numerous documents located in the Nigerian National Archives at Ìbàdàn pertaining to Ìtàpá-Èkìtì, including one file ('Matters affecting ItapaVillage, 1924–1952', Ekiti Div 1/1, File no. 278) that includes various correspondence as well as the Láyẹni history of Ìtàpá (see Chapter 2). (The wealth of papers in this file contributed to my decision to conduct research in Ìtàpá.) I also regularly read and kept clippings from local newspapers (*The Nigerian Tribune*, *The Guardian*, and more recently *Ekiti Now*) and from the national news journal *Tell*.

Along with conducting long interviews and survey interviews, amassing written materials and attending community events such as the commissioning of the Ìtàpá-Ìlúpéjú Hospital in 1991 and the Ìtàpá-Èkìtì Community Bank in 1995, I also participated in and observed various rituals (funerals, *Ìtàlè*, the Ògún Festival, prayers for a woman *olúbú*, among others) and more everyday affairs, such as trekking to the farm, making social visits and attending church. While I will always ultimately be a stranger for most townspeople as I am family-less there, we have shared experiences that give us some common ground, despite our different backgrounds and interests. This is one of the principle benefits of long-term anthropological research.

SPECIFIC INTERVIEW TOPICS AND DATES

After moving to Ìtàpá-Èkìtì in June 1991, I lived there (with brief intervals away) until April 1992. I then returned to Ìtàpá for shorter stays, usually during the summer when specific research questions could be pursued. These specific interview topics (and dates), brief descriptions of the types of questions asked and number of people interviewed, and where the interview findings are discussed, are listed as follows:

July–August, 1991: Long interviews, men, women (LIM, LIW): The findings from these interviews of women (n=70, ages fifteen to thirty-nine) and men (n=66, ages twenty to forty-four) mentioned above have been incorporated into several chapters of this book, including Chapters 3, 4 and 5, as well as in a published paper on gender relations (Renne 1993a).

September, 1991: Funeral interviews (FI): Twenty-five older men (n=18) and women (n=7) living in Ìtàpá (one woman actually lived primarily in neighboring Ìlúpéjú) of varying occupational and religious backgrounds were interviewed by Mr Owóẹyẹ about funeral practices and beliefs about the dead, with specific questions about what constitutes a 'big' funeral, how children participate in funeral performance, why funerals are important, what happens to the dead and where people should be buried (Chapter 6; Renne 1998a).

September 1991: Fostering interviews (FoI): Preliminary information about child-fostering was obtained both from the household census carried out in June and July 1991 and from the long interviews conducted in July and August, 1991. One hundred and fifteen foster parents (106 women and nine men) from the census list were revisited on the basis of informant availability and were questioned by Ms Àjàyí and myself in detail about the children they were fostering, a total of 166 children, from birth to nineteen years of age. The principal questions asked concerned the relationship of foster parent to birth parents, who initiated fostering, reason for fostering, amount of time with foster parent, and who paid for expenditures on a foster child. Foster parents were also asked about their experiences as foster children and their attitudes about fostering (Chapter 5; Renne 1993b).

October 1991: Interviews of ọmọ Ìtàpá (OI). Ninety-four men and women who had been born in Ìtàpá (ọmọ Ìtàpá, literally, children of Ìtàpá) but were living in one of three major urban areas – Adó-Èkìtì (n=42), Àkúrẹ́ (n=36), and Lagos (n=16) – were interviewed by Renne and Àjàyí (Adó-Èkìtì), Owóẹyẹ (Àkúrẹ́) and Àjàyí (Lagos) about the extent of their connections with town and their relatives (including child-fostering), participation in local Ìtàpá Progressive Union branches and burial preferences (Chapter 6).

November 1991: Time-study interviews. From the household census, I made a short list of thirty houses for the fostering time-study. Selection of a household was based on the presence of a least one foster child of school age and at least one non-foster child of comparable age and sex. I revisited these houses in order to verify foster children's presence and selected the final twenty households for the time-study. The activities of a total of 126 children aged from birth to nineteen were recorded on ten different hour-long periods for ten non-consecutive days by Mr Owóẹyẹ and Ms Àjàyí. To ensure a range of activities was represented, houses were visited at different times of the day at each of these visits. Of the 126 children observed, twenty-four were eliminated from analysis because they were under school age. Data from the 102 children was considered both at the house level and at the aggregate level. For each house, the foster-child was matched with a non-foster child of the same age and preferably sex. This was done in order to control for differences in the treatment of children in different houses.[6] From information on the thirty-three pairs, I classified activities ranging from fetching water, sleeping, attending school and going to the farm as either leisure, work or school-related, and then calculated percentages of time spent on each for every child in the study, based on the ten visits (Chapter 5; Renne 1995b).

December 1991–January 1992: Houseplot transaction interviews (LTS). A small survey of houseplot transactions was also carried out, which included information on land transfers for all houses in the western two-thirds of the town, based on the mapping done in June–July 1991. House-heads were asked questions about how the houseplot was obtained, from whom it was obtained, whether there was a written transaction, types of boundary markers, and whether the plot had been surveyed (Chapter 8; Renne 1995a).

January–March 1992: Women's and men's survey interviews (see above). These surveys followed the format of a standard demographic survey, the Demographic Health Survey (Nigeria, Federal Office of Statistics 1992), that is used by demographers and policymakers to measure demographic factors, contraceptive use, infant health and fertility change, although this particular survey was tailored to refer to local practices (such as including questions on bridewealth payment and other preliminary stages of marriage). This data (and the follow-up 1997 women's survey) was used in Chapters 3, 4 and 5; also Renne 1993a–d, 1996a, 1997a).

February 1992: Virginity interviews (LVI, SVI). Ninety-five women were interviewed jointly by Adéníké Ọ̀ṣọ́ and myself, primarily in Yoruba. Two groups of women were questioned, based on age and availability. Thirty-eight older women (aged thirty-five to eighty) were asked an extended set of open-ended questions about their experiences and perceptions of virginity while fifty-seven women (aged fifteen to thirty-four) were asked a shorter set of questions about virginity and whether they were (or would be) virgins when they married. Short notes were taken at the time of the interviews which were also taped and later translated and transcribed by Ms Ọ̀ṣọ́ (Chapter 4; Renne 1993b, 1996b).

March 1992: Abortion interviews. The long interviews conducted in July–August 1991 provided a good deal of information about the use of D&Cs and abortifacients. In these interviews, we did not directly ask about personal abortion histories, but rather asked women what they knew about other women who had done so. As a result of learning this information, I included questions about going for D&C and the use of abortifcaients in the large women's survey conducted in January–March 1992. Follow-up interviews of women were conducted based on their responses in this survey. Additionally, the personal abortion histories of five women were documented in open-ended interviews that were not recorded, although I took extensive notes at the time (see Renne 1996a).

April 1992: Handweaving interviews. Twenty-five weaving workshops were identified in Ìtàpá and four neighbouring Èkitì towns (Ìfàkì, Ìkọ̀lé, Ìlúpéjú, and Oyẹ́) and interviews of weaver–owners and apprentices were conducted by Ms Ọ̀ṣọ́ and by myself. These interviews consisted of a short series of interview questions about appenticeship education, about expenses and profits and about cloth production (see Renne 1997a).

October 1993: Cleanliness and IUD interviews (HPF). Mr Owóẹ̀yẹ conducted short interviews of twenty women and twenty men on health education in primary school, their experiences of this education and how they compared hygiene care they give their own children with the care they themselves received as children. They were also asked about child-fostering and the health effects of contraceptive use. This material was supplemented with archival documents, primary school health textbooks (Chapter 7) and with secondary source materials on IUDs (see Renne 1997b).

December 1994–January 1995: Census interviews (CI). In these interviews conducted by Mr Owóẹ̀yẹ and myself, twenty-five women and men (with a variety of backgrounds) in the town were asked a series of open-ended questions relating to the 1991 national census (Chapter 9; Renne 2000b).

January 1995: Re-interview of men (MRI): Of the sixty-six men previously questioned in the 1991 long interviews, forty were re-interviewed by Mr Owóẹ̀yẹ, with the same questionnaire, in order to ascertain any changes in their earlier answers, for example, on children wanted, on fostering, and on breast-feeding and sexual abstinence intervals (Chapter 5).

July–August 1997: Development interviews (DI97). These interviews included questions on comparisons of the past with the present in Ìtàpá and with neighbouring towns, major development initiatives in the town, the present situation in Ìtàpá, and questions on census-taking, vital registration and Ekiti State. Forty-seven women and men, selected by age and occupation, were interviewed by Mr Owóẹ̀yẹ, Ms Ìyábọ̀ Arósọ, and Ms Bọ́sẹ̀ Ayẹni, and myself (Chapters 6, 7 and 9).

1997–9 Menstrual regulation interviews (Renne 2001a).

1998: Road interviews (RI). These interviews of two older men living in Ìtàpá were conducted as follow-up interviews to the 1997 development interviews to clarify questions about building the main road through Ìtàpá (Chapters 2 and 10; Renne 2000a)

1998–9: Twins interviews (Renne 2001b).

1999: Bibeli Mímọ́ (Biblical stories and fertility) interviews (Renne 2002).

July 2000: Sanitation interviews (SI). Seven men and two women in Ìtàpá were interviewed by Mr Ọlaóyè Ìdòwú about general sanitation practices such as sanitary inspection and latrine building in the town (Chapter 7).

July 2000: Land transaction survey (LTS/2000). The owners of twenty-five houseplots with new construction on the western edge of the town were briefly questioned by Mr Ọlaóyè Ìdòwú on how the owners obtained the plots and what, if anything, was given for the land (Chapter 8).

INTERVIEW INFORMATION

The details on interviews cited in the text are given below in the order in which they appear in each chapter. They indicate who participated in the interview, the language in which it was conducted, who transcribed it in Yoruba or English and who translated the interview into English. Information about the interview series is given in the previous section of this appendix.

Chapter 1 interviews

DI97-3, Ìtàpá-Èkìtì, July 1997, conducted in Yoruba by Elisha Renne and Ìyábọ̀ Arósọ, transcribed in Yoruba by Ọlaóyè Ìdòwú, translated into English by Káyọ̀dé Owóèyẹ

DI97-35, Ìtàpá-Èkìtì, July 1997, conducted in Yoruba by Elisha Renne and Ìyábọ̀ Arósọ, transcribed in Yoruba by Ọlaóyè Ìdòwú, translated into English by Káyọ̀dé Owóèyẹ

DI97-14, Ìtàpá-Èkìtì, 1997, conducted in Yoruba by Elisha Renne and Káyọ̀dé Owóèyẹ, transcribed in Yoruba by Ọlaóyè Ìdòwú, translated into English by Káyọ̀dé Owóèyẹ

DI97-3, Ìtàpá-Èkìtì, 1997 [see above]

DI97-16, Ìtàpá-Èkìtì, 1997, conducted in Yoruba by Elisha Renne, Ìyábọ̀ Arósọ and Bọ́sẹ̀ Ayẹni, transcribed in Yoruba by Ọlaóyè Ìdòwú, translated into English by Káyọ̀dé Owóèyẹ and Elisha Renne

Chapter 2 interviews

S. A. Dada, Ìbàdàn, August 1997, conducted in English by Elisha Renne and Káyòdé Owóèyè, transcribed by Elisha Renne

Prince Alóngé, Ìrè-Èkìtì, August 1997, conducted in English by Elisha Renne and Káyòdé Owóèyè, transcribed by Elisha Renne

LTS-102, Ìtàpá-Èkìtì, January 1992, conducted in Yoruba by Káyòdé Owóèyè, translated into English by Káyòdé Owóèyè

S. A. Dada, Ìbàdàn, August 1997 [see above]

RI-1, Ìtàpá-Èkìtì, July 1998, conducted in Yoruba by Elisha Renne and Káyòdé Owóèyè, translated into English by Káyòdé Owóèyè

DI97-36, Ìtàpá-Èkìtì, 1997, conducted in Yoruba by Káyòdé Owóèyè, transcribed in Yoruba by Olaóyè Ìdòwú, translated into English by Káyòdé Owóèyè

Chapter 3 interviews

OI-23, Àkúré, 1991, conducted in Yoruba by Káyòdé Owóèyè, translated into English by Káyòdé Owóèyè

OI-2, Adó-Èkìtì, 1991, conducted in Yoruba by Elisha Renne and Comfort Àjàyí, translated into English by Káyòdé Owóèyè

LIM- JM13/10-66, Ìtàpá-Èkìtì, 1991, conducted in Yoruba by Elisha Renne and Káyòdé Owóèyè, translated into English by Káyòdé Owóèyè

LIM-AC13/8-19, Ìtàpá-Èkìtì, 1991, conducted in English by Káyòdé Owóèyè, transcribed by Elisha Renne

MRI-95: IC2/8-7, Ìtàpá-Èkìtì, 1995; conducted in Yoruba by Káyòdé Owóèyè, translated into English by Káyòdé Owóèyè

CBI98-YB, Ìtàpá-Èkìtì,1998, conducted in Yoruba by Elisha Renne and Ìyábò Arósọ, translated into English by Káyòdé Owóèyè

CBI98-TD, Ìtàpá-Èkìtì, 1998, conducted in Yoruba by Elisha Renne and Ìyábò Arósọ, translated into English by Káyòdé Owóèyè

CBI98-AO, Ìtàpá-Èkìtì, 1998, conducted in Yoruba by Elisha Renne and Ìyábò Arósọ, translated into English by Káyòdé Owóèyè

YT-5, Ìtàpá-Èkìtì, July 1998, conducted in Yoruba by Elisha Renne, Ìyábò Arósọ and Bósè Ayẹni, translated into English by Káyòdé Owóèyè

LIM-PC30/8-53, Ìtàpá-Èkìtì, 1991, conducted in Yoruba by Káyòdé Owóèyè, translated into English by Sunday Fálọdún

Chapter 4 interviews

All but last interview conducted in Yoruba by Elisha Renne and Adéníké Òṣó, translated into English by Adéníké Òṣó

LVI-7, Ìtàpá-Èkìtì, 1992
LVI-1, Ìtàpá-Èkìtì, 1992
LVI-4, Ìtàpá-Èkìtì, 1992
SVI-14, Ìtàpá-Èkìtì, 1992

LVI-10, Ìtàpá-Èkìtì, 1992
LVI-2, Ìtàpá-Èkìtì, 1992
LVI-10, Ìtàpá-Èkìtì, 1992
LVI-9, Ìtàpá-Èkìtì, 1992
LVI-11, Ìtàpá-Èkìtì, 1992
LVI-10, Ìtàpá-Èkìtì, 1992
LVI-4, Ìtàpá-Èkìtì, 1992
LVI-13, Ìtàpá-Èkìtì, 1992
SVI-17, Ìtàpá-Èkìtì, 1992
SVI-22, Ìtàpá-Èkìtì, 1992
SVI-26, Ìtàpá-Èkìtì, 1992
LVIa-27, Ìtàpá-Èkìtì,1992
LVIa-30, Ìtàpá-Èkìtì, 1992
LVI-35, Ìtàpá-Èkìtì, 1992
SVI-17, Ìtàpá-Èkìtì, 1992
SVI-6, Ìtàpá-Èkìtì, 1992
SVI-57, Ìtàpá-Èkìtì, 1992
SVI-42, Ìtàpá-Èkìtì, 1992
LVI-21, Ìtàpá-Èkìtì, 1992
SVI-30, Ìtàpá-Èkìtì, 1992
SVI-28, Ìtàpá-Èkìtì, 1992
LVI-22, Ìtàpá-Èkìtì, 1992
LIW-OC20/8-44, Ìtàpá-Èkìtì, 1991, conducted in Yoruba by Elisha Renne and Comfort Àjàyí, translated into English by Kẹ́hìndé Àjàyí

Chapter 5 interviews

HPF-F5, Ìtàpá-Èkìtì, 1993, conducted in Yoruba by Káyọ̀dé Owóèyẹ, translated into English by Káyọ̀dé Owóèyẹ
FoI-94b, Ìtàpá-Èkìtì, 1991, conducted in Yoruba by Elisha Renne and Comfort Àjàyí, translated into English by Comfort Àjàyí, with Elisha Renne
FoI-19b, Ìtàpá-Èkìtì, 1991, conducted in Yoruba by Elisha Renne and Comfort Àjàyí, translated into English by Comfort Àjàyí, with Elisha Renne
MRI-IA29/8-50, Ìtàpá-Èkìtì, 1995, conducted in Yoruba by Káyọ̀dé Owóèyẹ, translated into English by Káyọ̀dé Owóèyẹ
MRI-OA/FE31/8-57, Ìtàpá-Èkìtì, 1995, conducted in Yoruba by Káyọ̀dé Owóèyẹ, translated into English by Káyọ̀dé Owóèyẹ
HPF-M17, Ìtàpá-Èkìtì, 1993, conducted in Yoruba by Káyọ̀dé Owóèyẹ, translated into English by Káyọ̀dé Owóèyẹ
MRI-CS16/8-27, Ìtàpá-Èkìtì, 1995, conducted in Yoruba by Káyọ̀dé Owóèyẹ, translated into English by Káyọ̀dé Owóèyẹ
MRI-GC30/8-56, Ìtàpá-Èkìtì, 1995, conducted in Yoruba by Káyọ̀dé Owóèyẹ, translated into English by Káyọ̀dé Owóèyẹ
MRI-GC30/8-56, Ìtàpá-Èkìtì, 1995, [see above]

MRI-C81/8-5, Ìtàpá-Èkìtì, 1995, conducted in Yoruba by Káyọ̀dé Owóèyẹ, translated into English by Káyọ̀dé Owóèyẹ
FS5/8-8, Ìtàpá-Èkìtì, 1991
LIM-FS5/8-8, Ìtàpá-Èkìtì, 1991, conducted in Yoruba by Káyọ̀dé Owóèyẹ, translated into English by Káyọ̀dé Owóèyẹ
MRI-FC28/8-47, Ìtàpá-Èkìtì, 1995, conducted in Yoruba by Káyọ̀dé Owóèyẹ, translated into English by Káyọ̀dé Owóèyẹ
LIW-TG3/8-4, Ìtàpá-Èkìtì, 1991, conducted in Yoruba by Elisha Renne and Comfort Àjàyí, translated into English by Kẹ́hìndé Àjàyí
LIW-CK7/8-11, Ìtàpá-Èkìtì, 1991, conducted in Yoruba and English by Elisha Renne and Comfort Àjàyí, translated and transcribed into English by Kẹ́hìndé Àjàyí
LIM-JB13/10-67, Ìtàpá-Èkìtì, 1991, conducted in Yoruba by Elisha Renne and Káyọ̀dé Owóèyẹ, translated into English by Káyọ̀dé Owóèyẹ
LIM-IC14/8-21, Ìtàpá-Èkìtì, 1991, conducted in Yoruba by Káyọ̀dé Owóèyẹ, translated into English by Káyọ̀dé Owóèyẹ
LIW-LIC14/8-28, Ìtàpá-Èkìtì, 1991, conducted in English by Comfort Àjàyí, transcribed by Elisha Renne
LIM-EC27/9-61, Ìtàpá-Èkìtì, 1991, conducted in English by Káyọ̀dé Owóèyẹ, transcribed by Elisha Renne
MRI-CS16/8-27, Ìtàpá-Èkìtì, 1995 [see above]
LIM-SC27/7-1, Ìtàpá-Èkìtì, 1991, conducted in English by Káyọ̀dé Owóèyẹ, transcribed by Elisha Renne
MRI-FS5/8-8, Ìtàpá-Èkìtì, 1995, conducted in Yoruba by Káyọ̀dé Owóèyẹ, translated into English by Káyọ̀dé Owóèyẹ
MRI-PC6/8-9, Ìtàpá-Èkìtì, 1995, conducted in Yoruba by Káyọ̀dé Owóèyẹ, translated into English by Káyọ̀dé Owóèyẹ
LIM-FC28/8-47, Ìtàpá-Èkìtì, 1991, conducted in Yoruba by Káyọ̀dé Owóèyẹ, translated into English by Káyọ̀dé Owóèyẹ
MRI-AC16/8-28, Ìtàpá-Èkìtì, 1995, conducted in Yoruba by Káyọ̀dé Owóèyẹ, translated into English by Káyọ̀dé Owóèyẹ

Chapter 6 interviews

FI-2, Ìtàpá-Èkìtì, 1991, conducted in Yoruba by Elisha Renne and Káyọ̀dé Owóèyẹ, translated into English by Sunday Fálọdún
FI-23, Ìtàpá-Èkìtì, 1991, conducted in Yoruba by Elisha Renne and Káyọ̀dé Owóèyẹ, translated into English by Fẹ́mi Òjó
FI-25, Ìtàpá-Èkìtì, 1991, conducted in Yoruba by Káyọ̀dé Owóèyẹ, translated into English by Káyọ̀dé Owóèyẹ
FI-1, Ìtàpá-Èkìtì, 1991 conducted in Yoruba by Káyọ̀dé Owóèyẹ, translated into English by Sunday Fálọdún
FI-20, Ìtàpá-Èkìtì, 1991, conducted in Yoruba by Elisha Renne and Káyọ̀dé Owóèyẹ, translated into English by Káyọ̀dé Owóèyẹ

RI-1, Ìtàpá-Èkìtì, 1998, conducted in Yoruba by Elisha Renne and Káyọ̀dé Owóẹ̀yẹ, translated into English by Káyọ̀dé Owóẹ̀yẹ
FI-13, Ìtàpá-Èkìtì, 1991, conducted in Yoruba by Elisha Renne and Káyọ̀dé Owóẹ̀yẹ, translated into English by Sunday Fálọdún
DI97-15, Ìtàpá-Èkìtì, 1997, conducted in Yoruba by Elisha Renne and Iyabo Arósọ́, transcribed in Yoruba by Ọlaóyè Ìdòwú, translated into English by Káyọ̀dé Owóẹ̀yẹ
DI97-13, Àkúrẹ́, 1997, conducted in Yoruba by Káyọ̀dé Owóẹ̀yẹ, transcribed in Yoruba by Ọlaóyè Ìdòwú, translated into English by Káyọ̀dé Owóẹ̀yẹ
FI-12, Ìtàpá-Èkìtì, 1991, conducted in Yoruba by Elisha Renne and Káyọ̀dé Owóẹ̀yẹ, translated into English by Sunday Fálọdún
FI-25, Ìtàpá-Èkìtì, 1991 [see above]
FI-4, Ìtàpá-Èkìtì, 1991, conducted in Yoruba by Káyọ̀dé Owóẹ̀yẹ, translated into English by Sunday Fálọdún
FI-22, Ìtàpá-Èkìtì, 1991, conducted in Yoruba by Káyọ̀dé Owóẹ̀yẹ, translated into English by Káyọ̀dé Owóẹ̀yẹ
FI-9, Ìtàpá-Èkìtì, 1991, conducted in Yoruba by Káyọ̀dé Owóẹ̀yẹ, translated into English by Fẹ́mi Òjó
FI-17, Ìtàpá-Èkìtì, 1991, conducted in Yoruba by Elisha Renne and Káyọ̀dé Owóẹ̀yẹ, translated into English by Fẹ́mi Òjó
FI-20, Ìtàpá-Èkìtì, 1991 [see above]
FI-8, Ìtàpá-Èkìtì, 1991, conducted in Yoruba by Káyọ̀dé Owóẹ̀yẹ, translated into English by Sunday Fálọdún
FI-1, Ìtàpá-Èkìtì, 1991 [see above]
FI-14, Ìtàpá-Èkìtì, 1991, conducted in Yoruba by Káyọ̀dé Owóẹ̀yẹ, translated into English by Sunday Fálọdún
FI-17, Ìtàpá-Èkìtì, 1991 [see above]
FI-2, Ìtàpá-Èkìtì, 1991 [see above]
FI-22, Ìtàpá-Èkìtì, 1991 [see above]
FI-11, Ìtàpá-Èkìtì, 1991, conducted in Yoruba by Káyọ̀dé Owóẹ̀yẹ, translated into English by Fẹ́mi Òjó
FI-5, Ìtàpá-Èkìtì, 1991, conducted in Yoruba by Elisha Renne and Comfort Àjàyí, translated by Kẹ́hìndé Àjàyí
FI-10, Ìtàpá-Èkìtì, 1991, conducted in Yoruba by Káyọ̀dé Owóẹ̀yẹ, translated into English by Fẹ́mi Òjó
FI-17, Ìtàpá-Èkìtì, 1991 [see above]
FI-8, Ìtàpá-Èkìtì, 1991 [see above]
FI-19, Ìlúpéjú-Èkìtì , 1991, conducted in Yoruba by Elisha Renne and Comfort Àjàyí, translated into English by Fẹ́mi Òjó
FI-13, Ìtàpá-Èkìtì, 1991 [see above]
FI-8, Ìtàpá-Èkìtì, 1991 [see above]
FI-18, Ìtàpá-Èkìtì, 1991, conducted in Yoruba by Káyọ̀dé Owóẹ̀yẹ, translated into English by Fẹ́mi Òjó

FI-3, Ìtàpá-Èkìtì, 1991, conducted in Yoruba by Káyọ̀dé Owóẹ̀yẹ, translated into English by Sunday Fálọdún
FI-13, Ìtàpá-Èkìtì, 1991 [see above]

Chapter 7 interviews

SI-3, Ìtàpá-Èkìtì, 2000, conducted in Yoruba by Ọlaóyè Ìdòwú, translated into English by Ọlaóyè Ìdòwú
SI-5, Ìtàpá-Èkìtì, 2000, conducted in Yoruba by Ọlaóyè Ìdòwú, translated into English by Ọlaóyè Ìdòwú
SI-10, Ìtàpá-Èkìtì, 2000, conducted in Yoruba by Káyọ̀dé Owóẹ̀yẹ, translated into English by Káyọ̀dé Owóẹ̀yẹ
HPF-F5, Ìtàpá-Èkìtì, 1993, conducted in Yoruba by Káyọ̀dé Owóẹ̀yẹ, translated into English by Káyọ̀dé Owóẹ̀yẹ
HPF-M1, Ìtàpá-Èkìtì, 1993, conducted in Yoruba by Káyọ̀dé Owóẹ̀yẹ, translated into English by Káyọ̀dé Owóẹ̀yẹ
HPF-M16, Ìtàpá-Èkìtì, 1993, conducted in Yoruba by Káyọ̀dé Owóẹ̀yẹ, translated into English by Káyọ̀dé Owóẹ̀yẹ
HPF-F20, Ìtàpá-Èkìtì, 1993, conducted in Yoruba by Káyọ̀dé Owóẹ̀yẹ, translated into English by Káyọ̀dé Owóẹ̀yẹ
HPF-F19, Ìtàpá-Èkìtì, 1993, conducted in Yoruba by Káyọ̀dé Owóẹ̀yẹ, translated into English by Káyọ̀dé Owóẹ̀yẹ
HPF-F3, Ìtàpá-Èkìtì, 1993, conducted in Yoruba by Káyọ̀dé Owóẹ̀yẹ, translated into English by Káyọ̀dé Owóẹ̀yẹ
HPF-F14, Ìtàpá-Èkìtì, 1993, conducted in Yoruba by Káyọ̀dé Owóẹ̀yẹ, translated into English by Káyọ̀dé Owóẹ̀yẹ
HPF-M10, Ìtàpá-Èkìtì, 1993, conducted in Yoruba by Káyọ̀dé Owóẹ̀yẹ, translated into English by Káyọ̀dé Owóẹ̀yẹ
DI97-4, Ìtàpá-Èkìtì, 1997, conducted in Yoruba by Káyọ̀dé Owóẹ̀yẹ and Elisha Renne, transcribed in Yoruba by Káyọ̀dé Owóẹ̀yẹ, translated into English by Káyọ̀dé Owóẹ̀yẹ and Elisha Renne
HPF-M11, Ìtàpá-Èkìtì, 1993, conducted in Yoruba by Káyọ̀dé Owóẹ̀yẹ, translated into English by Káyọ̀dé Owóẹ̀yẹ
HPF-F2, Ìtàpá-Èkìtì, 1993, conducted in Yoruba by Káyọ̀dé Owóẹ̀yẹ, translated into English by Káyọ̀dé Owóẹ̀yẹ
HPF-F3, Ìtàpá-Èkìtì, 1993, conducted in Yoruba by Káyọ̀dé Owóẹ̀yẹ, translated into English by Káyọ̀dé Owóẹ̀yẹ
CI95-4, Ìtàpá-Èkìtì, 1994, conducted in Yoruba by Káyọ̀dé Owóẹ̀yẹ and Elisha Renne, translated into English by Káyọ̀dé Owóẹ̀yẹ
HPF-F14, Ìtàpá-Èkìtì, 1993 [see above]
HPF-M8, Ìtàpá-Èkìtì, 1993, conducted in Yoruba by Káyọ̀dé Owóẹ̀yẹ, translated into English by Káyọ̀dé Owóẹ̀yẹ
HPF-F9, Ìtàpá-Èkìtì, 1993, conducted in Yoruba by Káyọ̀dé Owóẹ̀yẹ, translated into English by Káyọ̀dé Owóẹ̀yẹ

HPF-M13, Ìtàpá-Èkìtì, 1993, conducted in Yoruba by Káyọ̀dé Owóèyẹ, translated into English by Káyọ̀dé Owóèyẹ
HPF-M11, Ìtàpá-Èkìtì, 1993, conducted in Yoruba by Káyọ̀dé Owóèyẹ, translated into English by Káyọ̀dé Owóèyẹ
SI-1, Ìtàpá-Èkìtì, 2000, conducted in Yoruba by Ọlaóyè Ìdòwú, translated into English by Ọlaóyè Ìdòwú
HPF-F18, Ìtàpá-Èkìtì, 1993, conducted in Yoruba by Káyọ̀dé Owóèyẹ, translated into English by Káyọ̀dé Owóèyẹ
SI-1, Ìtàpá-Èkìtì, 2000 [see above]
SI-4, Ìtàpá-Èkìtì, 2000, conducted in Yoruba by Ọlaóyè Ìdòwú, translated into English by Ọlaóyè Ìdòwú
DI97-38, Ìtàpá-Èkìtì, 1997, conducted in Yoruba by Káyọ̀dé Owóèyẹ, transcribed in Yoruba by Ọlaóyè Ìdòwú, translated into English by Káyọ̀dé Owóèyẹ
SI-10, Ìtàpá-Èkìtì, 2000 [see above]
DI97-3, Ìtàpá-Èkìtì, 1997, conducted in Yoruba by Elisha Renne and Ìyábọ̀ Aróṣọ, transcribed in Yoruba by Ọlaóyè Ìdòwú, translated into English by Káyọ̀dé Owóèyẹ
HPF-M16, Ìtàpá-Èkìtì, 1993, conducted in Yoruba by Káyọ̀dé Owóèyẹ, translated into English by Káyọ̀dé Owóèyẹ
HPF-M11, Ìtàpá-Èkìtì, 1993 [see above]

Chapter 8 interviews

DI97-36, Ìtàpá-Èkìtì, 1997, conducted in Yoruba by Káyọ̀dé Owóèyẹ, transcribed in Yoruba by Ọlaóyè Ìdòwú, translated into English by Káyọ̀dé Owóèyẹ
LIM-IC9/8-16, Ìtàpá-Èkìtì, 1991, conducted in Yoruba by Káyọ̀dé Owóèyẹ, translated into English by Káyọ̀dé Owóèyẹ
LTS-99, Ìtàpá-Èkìtì, 1992, conducted in Yoruba by Káyọ̀dé Owóèyẹ, translated into English by Káyọ̀dé Owóèyẹ
LTS-88, Ìtàpá-Èkìtì, 1992, conducted in Yoruba by Káyọ̀dé Owóèyẹ, translated into English by Káyọ̀dé Owóèyẹ
FI-5, Ìtàpá-Èkìtì, 1991, conducted in Yoruba by Elisha Renne and Comfort Àjàyí, translated into English by Sunday Fálọdún
LTS-84, Ìtàpá-Èkìtì, 1992, conducted in Yoruba by Káyọ̀dé Owóèyẹ, translated into English by Káyọ̀dé Owóèyẹ
LTS-101, Ìtàpá-Èkìtì, 1992, conducted in Yoruba by Káyọ̀dé Owóèyẹ, translated into English by Káyọ̀dé Owóèyẹ
LTS-200, Ìtàpá-Èkìtì, 1992, conducted in Yoruba by Káyọ̀dé Owóèyẹ, translated into English by Káyọ̀dé Owóèyẹ
LTS-31, Ìtàpá-Èkìtì, 1992 conducted in Yoruba by Káyọ̀dé Owóèyẹ, translated into English by Káyọ̀dé Owóèyẹ
OI-7, Lagos, 1991, conducted in Yoruba by Comfort Àjàyí, translated into

English by Sunday Fálọdún
LIW-CN1/8-1, Ìtàpá-Èkìtì, 1991, conducted in English by Elisha Renne, transcribed by Elisha Renne
FI-17, Ìtàpá-Èkìtì, 1991, conducted in Yoruba by Elisha Renne and Káyọ̀dé Owóèyẹ, translated into English by Fẹ́mi Òjó

Chapter 9 interviews

DI97-3, Ìtàpá-Èkìtì, July 1997 conducted in Yoruba by Elisha Renne and Ìyábọ̀ Arósọ, transcribed in Yoruba by Ọlaóyè Ìdòwú, translated into English by Káyọ̀dé Owóèyẹ
CI95-2, Ìtàpá-Èkìtì, 1994, conducted in Yoruba by Elisha Renne and Káyọ̀dé Owóèyẹ, translated into English by Káyọ̀dé Owóèyẹ
CI95-10, Ìtàpá-Èkìtì, 1994, conducted in Yoruba by Elisha Renne and Káyọ̀dé Owóèyẹ, translated into English by Káyọ̀dé Owóèyẹ
CI95-4, Ìtàpá-Èkìtì, 1994, conducted in Yoruba by Elisha Renne and Káyọ̀dé Owóèyẹ, translated into English by Káyọ̀dé Owóèyẹ
DI97-30, Ìtàpá-Èkìtì, 1997, conducted in Yoruba by Káyọ̀dé Owóèyẹ, transcribed in Yoruba by Ọlaóyè Ìdòwú, translated into English by Káyọ̀dé Owóèyẹ
DI97-25, Ìtàpá-Èkìtì, 1997, conducted in Yoruba by Káyọ̀dé Owóèyẹ, transcribed in Yoruba by Ọlaóyè Ìdòwú, translated into English by Káyọ̀dé Owóèyẹ
DI97-15, Ìtàpá-Èkìtì, 1997, conducted by Elisha Renne and Ìyábọ̀ Arósọ, transcribed in Yoruba by Ọlaóyè Ìdòwú, translated into English by Káyọ̀dé Owóèyẹ
DI97-36, Ìtàpá-Èkìtì, 1997, conducted in Yoruba by Káyọ̀dé Owóèyẹ, transcribed in Yoruba by Ọlaóyè Ìdòwú, translated into English by Káyọ̀dé Owóèyẹ
CI95-4, Ìtàpá-Èkìtì, 1994 [see above]
DI97-3, Ìtàpá-Èkìtì, 1997 [see above]
CI95-8, Ìtàpá-Èkìtì, 1994, conducted in Yoruba by Elisha Renne and Káyọ̀dé Owóèyẹ, translated into English by Káyọ̀dé Owóèyẹ
CI95-20, Ìtàpá-Èkìtì, 1995, conducted in Yoruba by Káyọ̀dé Owóèyẹ, translated into English by Káyọ̀dé Owóèyẹ
CI95-10, Ìtàpá-Èkìtì, 1994 [see above]
CI95-23, Ìtàpá-Èkìtì, 1995, conducted in Yoruba by Káyọ̀dé Owóèyẹ, translated into English by Káyọ̀dé Owóèyẹ
CI95-1, Ìtàpá-Èkìtì, 1994, conducted in Yoruba by Elisha Renne and Káyọ̀dé Owóèyẹ, translated into English by Káyọ̀dé Owóèyẹ
CI95-13, Ìtàpá-Èkìtì, 1995, conducted in Yoruba by Káyọ̀dé Owóèyẹ, translated into English by Káyọ̀dé Owóèyẹ
CI95-21, Ìtàpá-Èkìtì, 1995, conducted in Yoruba by Káyọ̀dé Owóèyẹ, translated into English by Káyọ̀dé Owóèyẹ

CI95-7, Ìtàpá-Èkìtì, 1994, conducted in Yoruba by Elisha Renne and Káyọ̀dé Owóèyẹ, translated into English by Káyọ̀dé Owóèyẹ
CI95-13, Ìtàpá-Èkìtì, 1995 [see above]
CI95-15, Ìtàpá-Èkìtì, 1995, conducted in Yoruba by Káyọ̀dé Owóèyẹ, translated into English by Káyọ̀dé Owóèyẹ
DI97-17, Ìtàpá-Èkìtì, 1997, conducted in Yoruba by Elisha Renne and Ìyábọ̀ Aróṣọ, transcribed in Yoruba by Ọlaóyè Ìdòwú, translated into English by Káyọ̀dé Owóèyẹ
DI97-22, Ìtàpá-Èkìtì, 1997, conducted in Yoruba by Káyọ̀dé Owóèyẹ and Elisha Renne, transcribed in Yoruba by Ọlaóyè Ìdòwú, translated into English by Káyọ̀dé Owóèyẹ
DI97-15, Ìtàpá-Èkìtì, 1997 [see above]
DI97-16, Ìtàpá-Èkìtì, 1997, conducted in Yoruba by Elisha Renne, Ìyábọ̀ Aróṣọ and Bọ́sẹ̀ Ayẹni, transcribed in Yoruba by Ọlaóyè Ìdòwú, translated into English by Káyọ̀dé Owóèyẹ and Elisha Renne
DI97-23, Ìtàpá-Èkìtì, 1997, conducted in Yoruba by Káyọ̀dé Owóèyẹ, transcribed in Yoruba by Ọlaóyè Ìdòwú, translated into English by Káyọ̀dé Owóèyẹ
DI97-14, Ìtàpá-Èkìtì, 1997, conducted in Yoruba by Elisha Renne and Káyọ̀dé Owóèyẹ, transcribed in Yoruba by Ọlaóyè Ìdòwú, translated into English by Káyọ̀dé Owóèyẹ
DI97-9, Ìtàpá-Èkìtì, 1997, conducted in Yoruba by Káyọ̀dé Owóèyẹ, transcribed in Yoruba by Ọlaóyè Ìdòwú, translated into English by Káyọ̀dé Owóèyẹ
DI97-43, Ìtàpá-Èkìtì, 1997, conducted in Yoruba by Káyọ̀dé Owóèyẹ, transcribed in Yoruba by Ọlaóyè Ìdòwú, translated into English by Káyọ̀dé Owóèyẹ
DI97-4, Ìtàpá-Èkìtì, 1997, conducted in Yoruba by Elisha Renne and Káyọ̀dé Owóèyẹ, transcribed in Yoruba by Káyọ̀dé Owóèyẹ, translated into English by Káyọ̀dé Owóèyẹ and Elisha Renne
DI97-27, Ìtàpá-Èkìtì, 1997, conducted in Yoruba by Káyọ̀dé Owóèyẹ, transcribed in Yoruba by Ọlaóyè Ìdòwú, translated into English by Káyọ̀dé Owóèyẹ
CI95-20, Ìtàpá-Èkìtì, 1995, conducted in Yoruba by Káyọ̀dé Owóèyẹ, translated into English by Káyọ̀dé Owóèyẹ
CI95-15, Ìtàpá-Èkìtì, 1995 [see above]
CI95-11, Ìtàpá-Èkìtì, 1995, conducted in Yoruba by Káyọ̀dé Owóèyẹ, translated into English by Káyọ̀dé Owóèyẹ
CI95-4, Ìtàpá-Èkìtì, 1994 [see above]
DI97-10, Ìtàpá-Èkìtì, 1997, conducted in Yoruba by Káyọ̀dé Owóèyẹ, transcribed in Yoruba by Ọlaóyè Ìdòwú, translated into English by Káyọ̀dé Owóèyẹ

Chapter 10 interviews

S. A. Dada, Ìbàdàn, 1997, conducted in English by Elisha Renne and Káyọ̀dé Owóèyẹ, transcribed by Elisha Renne

J. Ọmọtóyìnbó, 1 August 1997, Ìtàpá-Èkìtì, conducted in Yoruba by Elisha Renne, Ìyábọ̀ Arósọ, and Bọ́sẹ̀ Ayẹni, translated into English by Káyọ̀dé Owóèyẹ and Elisha Renne

APPENDIX II

IMPORTANT DATES IN ÌTÀPÁ AND NIGERIAN HISTORY

1876	Installation of Ọwátàpá, Ọba Arọ́wọ́gbádamú
1879–86	Kíríjì Wars
1891	Death of Ọwátàpá, Ọba Arọ́wọ́gbádamú
1891	Installation of Ọwátàpá, Ọba Ọ́lá I
1900	First meeting of the Èkìtì Ọbas Pelú-Pelú
1901–2	Introduction of Methodist Church to Ìtàpá
1911	The people of Ìtàpá, Ùsín and Ìkọ̀lé first saw the District Officer's bicycle in their town
1914	Creation of Ìkọ̀lé District
1915	Ekiti and Ondo Divisions merged under Ondo Province
1915	Establishment of a Grade C Native Court for Ìtàpá, Ìjẹ̀lú, Òmù and Osín
1915	Cocoa first grown in the District
1917	African Church introduced to Ìtàpá
1918	*Lùkúlùkú* (influenza) epidemic
1918	General poll tax introduced in Ìkọ̀lé District
1920	Poll tax levy (6s./adult) changed to income tax approved by Èkìtì Ọbas
1920	First service of African Church held at James Fálọdún's house
1921	Death of Ọwátàpá, Ọba Ọ́lá I
1921	Installation of Ọwátàpá, Ọba Adémilóyè
1921	National Census, township enumeration, provincial estimates
1922	First Methodist Church house built at Ìsálú
1922	Introduction of Islam to Ìtàpá by Pa Òjákànrìnkàn
1923	Methodist Church Primary School granted to Ìtàpá
1924	Motor road from Ìfàkì to Ìkọ̀lé constructed
1924	Catholic Church introduced to Ìtàpá
1929	Death of Ọwátàpá, Ọba Adémilóyè
1929	Installation of Ọwátàpá, Ọba Alli Atọ́batẹ́lẹ̀ I (Sanni)
1929	Methodist Church opens first school in Ìtàpá
1932	Methodist Dispensary built in Ìkọ̀lé-Èkìtì
1934	Ìtàpá-Ìjẹ̀lú Road constructed

IMPORTANT DATES IN ÌTÀPÁ AND NIGERIAN HISTORY

1935	Founding of Catholic primary school
1936	St Augustine Church changed to St James African Church
1936	Courthouse built in Ìtàpá
1937	Catholic Church roofed with iron sheeting
1942	Death of Ọwátàpá, Ọba Alli Atọ́batẹ́lẹ̀ I
1943	Installation of Ọwátàpá, Ọba Samuel Ọla II (Òjó)
1946	Ìtàpá Progressive Union established
1947	Nigerian Constitution introduced, federal system with three regions
1949	Palace roofed with iron sheeting
1950	First car bought for the Ọwátàpá
1952–3	National Census, first complete enumeration attempt
1955	Construction of first tarred road through Ìtàpá
1956	Queen Elizabeth visits Nigeria
1 Oct 1960	Federation of Nigeria established (as constitutional monarchy) under Tafawa Balewa
1961	Post Office building constructed
Oct 1963	Federal Republic of Nigeria established (as Commonwealth member)
1963	National Census retaken, substantial overcount
1964	Ìtàpá Community Development Committee established
Jan 1966	Tafawa Balewa's government overthrown; Tafawa Balewa killed; Gowon new head of government
May 1967	Gowon created the Mid-West Region from the Western Region, making four Regions, then restructured as twelve states
May 1967	Nigerian civil war begins
1969	Official opening of the Ìtàpá Maternity Centre
1970	Surrender of Biafran forces, civil war ends
1973	National Census, provisional results only
1976	Ìtàpá-Osín Secondary School established
July 1976	Gowon forced to resign; Murtala Muhammed heads government
1976	Murtala Muhammed creates seven new states
Feb 1977	Murtala Muhammed assassinated, Olúṣẹ́gun Obásanjọ́ becomes head of state
1977	Pipeborne water project begun from Ìtápàjì Dam
1977	Town Hall building project begun
1978	Death of Ọwátàpá, Ọba Samuel Ọla II (Òjó)
1 Oct 1979	Return to civilian rule, Shehu Shagari named president of Second Republic
1982	Currency exchange rate: ₦1=US$1.54
1983	Redeemed Church introduced to Ìtàpá

31 Dec 1983	Shagari deposed in bloodless coup, Muhammadu Buhari becomes head of state
Feb 1985	Currency exchange rate: ₦1=US$1
Aug 1985	Buhari overthrown in bloodless coup, Ibrahim Babangida becomes head of state
1986	Electrification of Ìtàpá commissioned
1986	Introduction of Structural Adjustment Programme, including devaluation of currency
Oct 1986	Currency exchange rate: ₦4.6=US$1
Sept 1987	Two new states (Akwa Ibom and Katsina) named
1987	Installation of present Ọwátàpá, Ọba Adéyẹyẹ Àmùdá Alli II
1988	First Ìtàpá Day celebrated
1988	Introduction of National Population Policy ('Four is enough')
1988	Establishment of Ọyẹ́ Local Government
1989	Attempted military coup by junior officers crushed
1991	Ìlúpéjú-Ìtàpá General Hospital opened
Aug 1991	Babangida names nine new states
Nov 1991	National Census, state results only
Dec 1991	Currency exchange rate: ₦14.50=US$1
May 1992	Fuel increase, national protests
Sept 1992	Presidential primaries held
12 June 1993	Election, Abíọ́lá assumed to have won
23 June 1993	Babangida, AFRC annul election results
Summer 1993	Widespread strikes against Babangida's annulment of election
Aug 1993	Babangida resigns; Ernest Shonekan named to head Interim National Government
17 Nov 1993	Abacha forces Shonekan to resign and takes over government
June 1994	Abíọ́lá claims presidential victory; arrested and imprisoned
July 1994	National petroleum workers and transporters strike; fuel shortages
1995	Ìtàpá-Èkìtì Community Bank opened
March 1996	First LGA elections held since 1993
August 1996	Abacha replaced twenty-seven out of thirty state military administrators
30 Sept 1996	Registration of five political associations as political parties announced, all others dissolved
1 Oct 1996	Ekiti State announced and five other new states (Bayelsa, Ebonyi, Nasarawa, Gombe, Zamfara) by Abacha
10 Feb 1997	Registration of voters for local government elections
Feb 1997	Abacha indicates he might run as political candidate in 1998
15 Mar 1997	LGA elections

June 1997   Currency exchange rate: ₦86=US$1
Sept 1997   Bomb blast at Ekiti State secretariat at Adó-Èkìtì
8 June 1998   Abacha dies
9 June 1998   Abdulsalami Abubakar takes over interim regime
7 July 1998   Abíọ́lá dies
Feb 1999   Olúṣẹ́gun Obásanjọ́ elected president
29 May 1999   Obásanjọ́ inaugurated president of the Fourth Republic
Feb 2001   Currency exchange rate: ₦123=US$1

Sources: Adeyẹmo 1997; Àjàyí and Igun 1963; Diamond et al. 1997; Maier 2000; Synge 2001.

APPENDIX III

CONTRACEPTION EVER USED BY ÌTÀPÁ-ÈKÌTÌ WOMEN, BASED ON 1992, 1997 SURVEYS

While the relatively high total fertility rate (TFR in 1997=5.3, that is, in 1997 a woman could expect to give birth to 5.3 children in her lifetime) may suggest that they do not attempt to manage their fertility, they actually use a range of substances and practices that allow them to control their childbearing to some extent. While not specifically discussed in this book, readers may refer to several published papers for more information on contraceptive use (for example, condoms: Renne 1993a; IUDs: Renne 1997a; Postinor: Renne 1998b), abortion (Renne 1996a), and the regulation of menstruation (Renne 2001a) in this Èkìtì Yoruba town.

These substances and practices fall into four general categories including: (1) substances taken or practices used before coitus; (2) substances taken or practices used after coitus; (3) intentional abstention practices; and (4) abortion practices. The first category includes Western contraceptives (such as family planning tablets, condoms, IUDs and Depo-Provera injections), traditional contraceptives (such as rings), and substances (such as decoctions made from ground roots and herbs) that are thought to cleanse the womb and promote fertility. The second consists of a range of local herbal remedies (such as the juice of *enupòkurè* (*Pedilanthus tithymaloides*) leaves, mixed with egg); patent medicines (such as B-codeine); commercial emmenagogue tablets (such as E. P.-Forte and Menstrogen); the postcoital contraceptive, Postinor; salt and water; and a range of combinations of lemony soft drinks, Andrew's Liver Salts and other substances. The third category includes practices such as safe period, withdrawal and, literally, long-term abstention, particularly by women after childbirth. The fourth category, abortion practices, is related to the use of substances taken after childbirth since many women believe that, by using a combination of various substances, they can 'bring a pregnancy down'. However, some women mentioned going for D&C (dilation and curettage; abortion) when asked about contraception, suggesting the way that all types of substances and practices that limit fertility – whether taken before or after coitus – are considered to be *oògùn bàjé* ('medicine that spoils'; see Renne 1996a).

In the following graph (see Figure App 3.1), an indication of the types of 'contraception' ever used by Ìtàpá women is shown in a comparison of the responses of 294 married and unmarried women (aged fifteen to forty-nine)

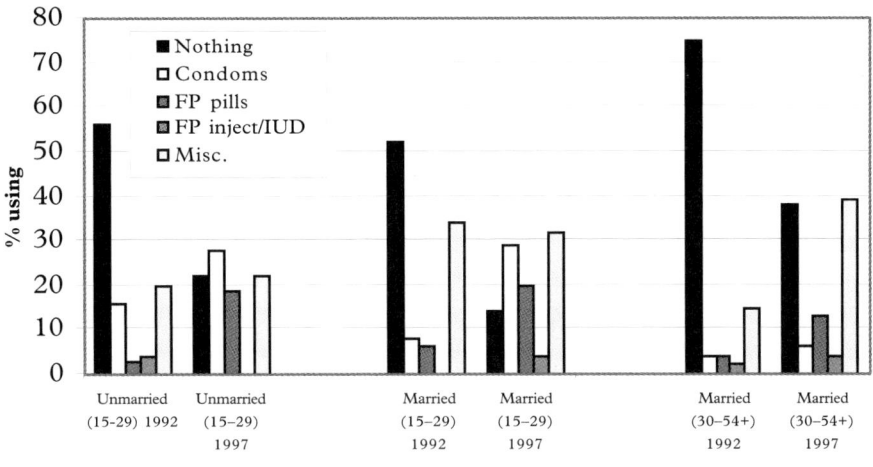

Figure App. 3.1 Comparison of contraception ever used, women's surveys, Ìtàpá-Èkìtì, 1992, 1997

to the 1992 fertility survey and 305 married and unmarried women (aged fifteen to sixty-five) to the 1997 survey. (For a comparison of contraceptive use by Ìtàpá women and men based on 1992 surveys, see Renne 1993d.)

The figure shows an increase in the use of Western contraception, particularly family planning pills (oral contraceptives) and condoms, among unmarried and married women in the 1997 survey responses. Only a few women used other types of Western contraception such as IUDs, injections (Depo-Provera) and Postinor (a hormonal post-coital contraceptive). The category 'Miscellaneous' includes safe period, salt and water, D&C, patent medicines and some traditional contraceptives, such as *kaun* (potash) and *ògògòrò* (gin). Some women mentioned using more than one method, in which case the contraceptive with longer-term and/or more effective protection was represented in the graph. Also women who said they used nothing and women who said they abstained were included together under 'Nothing used', not because there are unimportant differences in these responses but because the interviewers for the 1992 survey did not make this distinction (the 1997 interviewers did). Finally, some women mentioned the use of D&C as a form of contraception (which it is not); however, how contraception and abortion are perceived depend, in part, on beliefs about when life begins (see Renne 1996a).

NOTES

CHAPTER 1: INTRODUCTION: PARADOXES OF PROGRESS

1. In 'The Case for Ekiti State', the brief sent to the Armed Forces Ruling Council (AFRC) by Chief S. B. Falegan (1991), he argued that Ekiti State should be created out of Ondo State, in part, because the 1963 census figures showed that 'Ekitis constituted 52 per cent of the state and non-Ekitis 48 per cent' (1991: 16). Because Ekiti had fewer Local Government Areas (LGAs) (a miscarriage of justice in his view since 'the 1963 census holds as the authentic basis for decision-making'), they will be represented by fewer representatives (twenty-four) in the State House of Assembly compared with thirty-two members for the non-Èkitì area.
2. Indeed, these three factors parallel the criteria set forth by Coale (1973) as prerequisites for fertility decline, namely that the idea of controlling fertility comes to be considered within the 'realm of possibility', that modern contraceptive methods are available, and there are economic reasons for people pursuing these practices.
3. The term *y'ílé ọmọ padà*, 'turning the uterus', refers to a type of infertility that may be attributed to witchcraft (Renne 1997a: 1144).
4. The term *idíléde* refers to the ritual performed to identify the ancestral spirit of the child, according to one Èkitì diviner. It is also known as *l'ẹ̀sẹ̀ ní aiyé*, literally 'leg in the world', the name of the ritual performed to identify the spiritual ancestor reborn in a child, refers to the child stepping (with its leg) into this world from another. The idea of stepping into the world is mirrored in the naming ceremony known as *k'ọmọ jáde* or *ikọmọ*, performed eight days after birth. The child born inside the house goes outside (*jáde*) into public space where it is named.
5. Peel (1978: 144) notes that the verb *lajú*, formed from the verb *là* (to open, to separate) and *ojú* (eyes), implies separation, but is also related to discernment, with particular knowledge distinguishing one group from another.
6. For example, there have been several new economic programmes instituted by the government aimed at improving the lives of rural Nigerians. These include the War Against Indiscipline (WAI), Directorate of Mass Mobilization for Self-Reliance, Social Justice, and Economic Recovery (MAMSER), the Directorate of Food, Roads, and Rural Infrastructure (DFRRI), the Better Life for Rural Women programme (sponsored by Maryam Babangida), and the Family Support Initiative (sponsored by Mariam Abacha). With the exception of the DFRRI programme, which provided funds for a deep borehole in the town, the benefits of these programmes have not reached Ìtàpá residents.
7. These include two civilian regimes (Shehu Shagari (1979–83), Olúṣẹ́gun Ọbásanjọ́ (1999–present), two interim governments (Ernest Shonekan (August–November 1993), Abdulsalami Abubakar (June 1998–May 1999), and

three military governments (Muhammadu Buhari (1983–5); Ibrahim Babangida (1985–93); Sani Abacha (1993–8)). See Appendix II for a list of important dates in Ìtàpá and Nigerian history.
8. Free universal primary education was begun in south-western Nigeria in 1955 (Eades 1980: 149). With the implementation of a Structural Adjustment Programme in 1986 and the reduction in federal funding for education, school fees have been introduced. More recently, Ekiti State government withdrew these fees in 2000.
9. At the time this proposal was floated, the estimated national total fertility rate for women aged fifteen to forty-nine was 6.011 (Nigeria, Federal Office of Statistics 1992: 23). Some people who took this proposal literally wanted to know what those who already had five or six children were supposed to do with the surplus. Many nonetheless thought it was a good idea under the current economic conditions. The proposal was later supported by the Ministry of Health campaign 'Space Your Children' (see Figure 1.3). This promoted extended 'spacing' between births, both as a way of ensuring the health of mother and child and of limiting the number of children born.
10. Alternately, the introduction of family planning ('modern' contraception) is generally classified as ọ̀làjú because it is a practice introduced from outside (òde).
11. Some older siblings, however, are refusing to do this. One middle-aged Ìtàpá man recounted that when he was about to enter university and approached his senior brother for financial help, he was told, 'No, it is the responsibility of the parents.'
12. Such a perspective can help to explain how moral values figure into local thinking about fertility and development (Renne 1996b). Olúsànyà (1989b) pointed out the importance of people's assertion about bearing children as an unquestioned moral responsibility while Peel (1978: 158) observed that love (ìfẹ́) and cooperation (ìfọwọ́sọwọ́pọ̀) were critical for development to succeed.
13. References for this extensive literature, by both anthropologists and by demographers, may be found in these two edited volumes; see also Renne (1996c).
14. The term 'diagnostic things' is derived from Moore (1987: 730), who used the term 'diagnostic event' to describe behaviour and beliefs surrounding particular events that are distinctly different from prior thinking and practice.
15. 'Life More Abundant' was a campaign slogan for the Action Group (Peel 1978: 159), the political party headed by the popular Yoruba politician Chief Ọbáfẹ́mi Awólọ́wọ̀.

CHAPTER 2: HISTORICAL AND ANTHROPOLOGICAL ASPECTS OF ÌTÀPÁ: CENTRIPETAL AND CENTRIFUGAL TENDENCIES

1. This market was abandoned early in 1999, with traders moving to the site in front of the Ọwátàpá's palace next to the main road, which offers better access to travellers; it was changed back in 2000.
2. Igbó Afà – literally, the forest of afàrà trees (*Terminalia superba*, Abraham 1962: 16) – was a swampy densely forested area. It was uninhabited because it was believed that spirits (*iwin*, sprites) from the nearby Ijétí stream would come out at night.
3. Àorogún Hill is home to the imọlẹ̀ (nature deity) Àorogún to which an annual sacrifice of a cow is made. People travelling on the road as it wends its way upward along this hill may make special prayers to this deity for protection; despite the fact that there have been several motor accidents on this stretch of road, no one has been seriously injured.

4. Evidence of their stay in Aiyédé may be seen in 'place-names such as Omi Ìtàpá (Ìtàpá stream)' (Apter 1992: 53).
5. These raids, combined with the previous warfare, are believed to have taken a heavy toll on the local population. Indeed, it is said that the population of Ìtàpá formerly exceeded Ìkọlé-Èkìtì (now a local government area headquarters) (J. F. A. Àjàyí, personal communication).
6. However, an alternative explanation of the settlement of the north-eastern Èkìtì Yoruba area is given by Ọbáyẹmí (1976). He argues for a westward migration from the confluence area to the east, rather than for the more politically profitable migration from Ifẹ̀ to the south-west. I emphasise the Láyẹni (1935) account here as it is the version most commonly accepted in the town (e.g. Ayẹni 1991).
7. Some also believe that the baby tie that this mother used to carry the three sons as infants is still kept in Osín.
8. Migrants from the Kingdom of Ìkọlé to the east (see note 21 below) settled the eighth quarter, Oròkè.
9. Moore (1986), however, makes the point that they are not finally heading towards a continuity characterised by equilibrium but towards one characterised by continual contest.
10. For example, at Ilésà (Peel 1983), Ìrée (Berry 1985), Òkukù (Barber 1991), Aiyédé (Apter 1992), Ìgbòho (Matory 1994), and Ìkọlé (Rea 1998).
11. See Polly Hill (1977) on the economic and political implications of population in Northern Nigeria.
12. The political authority of kingdoms is not strictly speaking dependent on population for, as Òjó (1966: 126) has noted, their authority rests on their ranking as paramount chieftaincies, legitimated through the ownership of a beaded crown. For towns such as Ìtàpá without beaded-crown chiefs, power in the larger political sphere of current local and state governments depends on population and the strength of connections/advocacy by 'sons (and daughters) of the soil'.
13. While there is no written confirmation of this commission, Chief S. A. Dada – whose father was Obaàró Gabriel Dada, scribe to Ọwátàpá Samuel Ola II – believes that it was written at the Ọwá's behest (Dada, Ìbàdàn, August 1997).
14. 10 December 1934, Èkìtì Div 1/1, File no. 278, NNAI, p. 7.
15. 'Having completed this change, the people of the adjacent town of Ire heard that Apeju skipped over those with a Grade C oba (as was the Onire). So the people of Ire started to find a way to bring Onire to Grade B as well. Fortunately for them, an indigene of Ire now became the LGA chairman and they used the same system created by the Ilupeju people to bring their king to Grade B level, too … Owatapa has been sending petitions to the local government explaining his grade as stipulated in the chieftaincy declaration of 1958 where Owatapa and Onire were ranked Grade C. Since now Onire has moved from Grade C to B and Apeju from D to B … Fortunately for Itapa, an indigene came to power in 1997 as the chairman of Oye LGA who put the case of the Owatapa forward [to become a Grade B chief]. It has been ratified by the local government …' (Owóẹyẹ 1999: 60).
16. According to one Ìtàpá man, the initial agreement between the towns of Ìlúpéjú, Ìrè, Ìtàpá, Ìjèlú, and Osín to form a separate local government with Ìtàpá as its headquarters has unraveled. Presently, the town of Ìlúpéjú is lobbying to become the headquarters even though it is less than two kilometres away from Ọyẹ́-Èkìtì, the headquarters of Oye Local Government. A memo-writing campaign has begun to counter this request (see Owóẹyẹ 1999: 61).

17. Earlier, six chiefs formed the Ìràfà along with Owátàpá. Presently the Ìràfà chiefs include (in descending order of importance): Ọdòfin (Ògbọ́n Rẹ́mọ), Ọbaàró (Ògbọ́n Ẹgẹ̀tún), Ẹlẹ́mọ (Ògbọ́n Rẹ́mọ), Ọdẹdẹ (senior priest), Ọbasálú (Ògbọ́n Rẹ́mọ), Ọbaísà (Ògbọ́n Ẹgẹ̀tún), and Asába (Ògbọ́n Rẹ́mọ). Ọbaàró and Ọbaísà are kingmakers (Owolabi et al., no date).
18. For example, members of Oròkè Quarter, seeing themselves as being treated as second-class citizens of Ẹgẹ̀tún, have recently decided to disaffiliate themselves from this section. They now consider Oròkè to be a separate, unaffiliated quarter.
19. Some quarters have shrines for distinctive deities, for example the Ọmọba Quarter (where the Owátàpá and his family live) have a shrine to the deity Jiuju, while several quarters may have their own shrine to a commonly worshipped deity such as Ògún. For example, the sub-quarter of Egbè Quarter known as Ìdọ̀fin is associated with Umọlẹ̀ Ògún Idọ́fin. Furthermore, the entire town comes together to celebrate the Ògún Festival every September. A dynamic of distinctiveness and of unity, similar to that seen in the political sphere, is suggested by these different levels of religious followings (see Barber 1981). Later conversion to Christianity and the subsequent emergence of many separate churches suggests this process as well (Peel 1968b; Turner 1967; Webster 1964).
20. The Oròkè Quarter, according to Láyẹni (1935: 10), was founded by a chief, 'a Royal son from Ikole but [who] took refuge under the Owa of Itapa when he had a quarrel of chieftaincy with his brother princes of Ikole. The Owa of Itapa sheltered him and gave him land and named him with [the] title Baloke [Obaloke] which his successors used up till to-day's date.'
21. See Jackson 1977 on women's use of men's dress in ritual practice.
22. One song of abuse is translated as follows:
Àjà ìmùta omiye màá bó mi ye jà o kò The elders, relations will face relations!
Ééé ye – Òwà se rú eyi kokò Yes! Òwà has done this!
Ééé ye – Dèmí se rú eyi kokò Yes! Dèmí has done this!
Àjà ìmùta omiye màá bó mi ye jà o kò
23. Krapf-Askari (1966: 10) has argued (in response to Èkìtì (1962: 192)) about the likely presence of triadic political structures in Èkìtì: 'I should think it more likely that it [Adó-Èkìtì] is simply a more elaborate case of a triadic pattern which might profitably be sought in other Èkìtì towns.'
24. Rea (1998) discusses recent developments in masquerade performance in Ìkọ̀lé-Èkìtì where young men use masquerade as a way of attracting visitors and outside resources to the town.
25. See Berry (1985: 187–8) for a description of a similar event in Ìrée (currently in Oṣun State) and Trager (2001) for a description of Iloko Day.
26. See Guyer (1997: 39–40) (also Eades 1980; Fadipe 1970; Peel 1983) for a discussion of the importance of this aspect of social life. Ẹgbé are organised in ways similar to other town organisations, that is, with a head, officers and general members. They provide yet another avenue for the centrifugal and centripetal tendencies discussed elsewhere in this chapter.
27. On getting a ride back to Adó-Èkìtì myself after the 1991 Ìtàpá Day, I was told by the ọmọ Ìtàpá driving that he himself could not bear to spend a night in the town, with its lack of light and running water.
28. This is a common goal of Quarter Day fund-raisers. Additional funds will be used for sponsoring Ọmọ Rẹ́mọ at university and in making local sacrifices (sàráà) (Ayẹni, personal correspondence).
29. The difference in funds given to chiefs in these two ranks is considerable: a grade B chief receives a monthly stipend of ₦15,000 (US$175 in 1998).

30. Indeed, it was the presence of this main road and the market at Ìlúpéjú that allowed residents of Ìtàpá to see a motor vehicle for the first time, according to one older man. 'At Ilupeju, there was a building mainly for storing bags of cement. So there was a vehicle then that used to bring bags of cement to that building ... We closely watched it as if it were a wonderful miracle (*tiyanutiyanu*) – this vehicle was called "Reo"' (RI-1, Ìtàpá-Èkìtì, 1998).
31. However, in 1999, a sawmill was established in the town.
32. In early 2000, however, women traders were prevented by the town's young men from travelling to these other markets if their market days coincided with that of Ìtàpá.

CHAPTER 3: DEMOGRAPHIC DIMENSIONS OF ÌTÀPÁ ÈKÌTÌ

1. Men were not resurveyed because of the difficulties of locating sufficient numbers of them. However, twenty-one men questioned in 1991 about a range of fertility-related issues were reinterviewed in 1995.
2. The Nigerian census figures are also larger because *de jure* status was very broadly interpreted and could sometimes include family members living outside the town. It is also possible that my figures represent an undercount as people hesitated to give out full information to a foreigner (see Piot 1999: 114–16; see also Chapter 9).
3. When asked why women built house for themselves, one older man explained it this way:

    First and foremost, if the husband happens to marry more than one wife, and if [they are unhappy in their marriage], either of them may wish to build a building of her own to stay in to give room for peace to reign. Aside from this ... if a woman has enough money to decide to invest in a building, especially if she knows that her husband has got a building ... Some women decide to have a building of their own for privacy – they would want to have a special place to keep their properties outside the matrimonial place, this is common in polygynous homes. [And] many women do have their own buildings so that their children could inherit these when they died, particularly if it is a poly-gynous home. Some women wouldn't want their children to scramble for inheritance from their father because some children do harm themselves or even kill themselves because of inheritance.

    (BA-2002a, 2002, Ìtàpá-Èkìtì)
4. While this decline in women students may be due to economic constraints and increasing school fees, it probably also reflects the fact that during the 1992 survey, many younger women were at home because of various school strikes and closings (n=110). Only thirty-three women in the 15–19 age group were found in these houses in the reinterview in 1997.
5. According to Ògúntúyì (1979: 19), the number of pieces that the calabash is broken into represents the number of children the bride will bear.
6. Spousal discussions of family size preferences have become more common in recent years; formerly such matters were not discussed in many Yoruba communities (Mott and Mott 1985; Oyèmádé and Ògúnmúyiwá 1981; Renne 1993d).
7. The total fertility rates calculated from the 1990 NDHS data and 1986 Ondo State DHS were comparable to the 1992 Ìtàpá survey. In the 1990 NDHS the total fertility rate for the 15–49 age group for southwestern Nigeria (both urban and rural) was 5.461; the total fertility rate for the 15–49 age group countrywide was 6.011. For Ondo State, the total fertility rate for the 15–44 age group was 6.2. In the 1999 NDHS, the total fertility rate for the 15–49 age group for

south-western Nigeria (both urban and rural) was 4.50. The total fertility rate for the 15–49 age group countrywide was 5.15 (National Population Commission, Nigeria 2000: 36), comparable with the 1997 Itapa survey TFR.

8. For example, one man complained that his second son insisted on attending the same expensive private school that his older brother had attended.
9. Compared with US infant mortality figures (infant mortality for 1997 was six per 1,000 births; Hilts 1999: A24), these figures are high, but compared with countrywide infant mortality figures for Nigeria, they are low (in 1990 infant [under one year] mortality was 91.4 per 1,000 births, child [one to five years] mortality was 109.6 per 1,000 live births; Nigeria, Federal Office of Statistics 1992: 80). They are comparable with infant mortality figures from the Nigerian Demographic and Health Survey (Nigeria, Federal Office of Statistics 1992: 81) for women with secondary school education and higher (48.6 per 1,000 births).
10. The 1992 and 1997 survey formats were practically identical but the interviewers (myself excluded) differed. Since 151 women were reinterviewed in the 1997, it was possible to compare reporting of infant and child deaths. The respective assiduousness of the different interviewers is reflected in the number of deaths reported: the 1997 interviews include more complete reports, particularly for older women. However, the reports of younger women are very similar, and in some cases, these women gave more complete responses in the 1992 survey (see Appendix I).
11. Not surprisingly, such women often 'disapproved' of family planning contraceptives and were likely to give 'up to God' answers to questions about how many children they wanted. Some said that saying a number was an affront to God who ultimately would decide the number of children a woman would bear in any case. While women with secondary education would be likely to give a number when asked about desired family size, if they had lost children a sense of not wanting to presume God's will sometimes overrode their willingness to do so (cf. van de Walle 1992), suggesting that giving non-numerical answers may be more than a matter of schooling.
12. These uncertainties included fluctuating prices for goods and services, particularly transportation, retrenchment exercises, the late payment of salaries, infrequent electricity and piped water, and political uncertainty, reflected in transport and university strikes, irregularly-held elections and bombings (for example, at the Ekiti State Secretariat on 2 September 1997; Adeyẹmi 1997: 28).
13. Seven of these women also delivered children at clinics or hospitals during this five-year period; one woman actually delivered on the road on the way. All the women were married at the time of the survey and only one had not 'first cohabited' prior to the home birth of her child. With the exception of this one case, these were not premarital pregnancies and hence premarital status was not a likely reason for clinic non-attendance (see Gage 1998).
14. In the period from 1987–91, five infants born in the Ìtàpá Maternity Centre died soon after birth; four died within a day of birth, one within two days. It is possible that women were avoiding the Centre for fear that their infants would die as well.
15. The possibility that place of delivery might be affected by the characteristics of those 'remaining on the farm', so to speak, was suggested to me by A. Bánkọlé.
16. When compared with the movements of 1992 survey women in the older age groups (30–49), this pattern of out-migration by young women is statistically significant (p=0.000023, Yates corrected). Of the seventy-two women located in the older age groups, 83 per cent (n=60) were still in Ìtàpá while only 17 per cent (n=12) of these women had left the town.

17. Indeed, 48 per cent (n=38) of the 1992 survey women, aged fifteen to twenty-nine in 1992, now living outside Ìtàpá are reportedly living in these two cities.
18. In 1997, this included ₦100 for registration and medicines, ₦200 for delivery (normal), ₦50 for the birth certificate, and ₦100 for circumcision.
19. These items (in 1997) included cotton wool (sanitary pad; ₦60), packet of blades (₦40), olive oil (₦50), Lux or Joy soap (₦25), one gallon kerosene (₦55), thread (₦10), Dettol disinfectant (₦120), gloves (₦50), baby materials (powder, cloth; ₦80) and methylated spirits (₦30). The total for the items was ₦545.
20. One woman attributed several infant deaths at the clinic to one matron's cutting umbilical cords too short and their subsequently becoming infected; this nurse–midwife has since been transferred. The woman may have been referring to the five neonatal deaths of infants born in the Ìtàpá Maternity Centre during 1987–91.
21. This perception of risk is supported by 1997 Ìtàpá survey data: of the four neonatal deaths (infants who died within one month of birth), two were born at home and two were born in a clinic or hospital.
22. According to figures from the 1963 census, Ìtàpá had a population of 5,730 while the 1991 census reported a population of 11,392 for the town.

CHAPTER 4: WOMEN'S BODIES, VIRGINITY AND MARRIAGE

1. *Ìbálé*, defined as virginity by Abraham (1962: 87), is listed under the verb *bá*, to meet. The word *ibálé* might possibly be considered as a compounding of the words *bá* and *ilé*, meaning literally 'the meeting of someone (or something) in the house'.
2. The words *òbò*, *abẹ́*, and *ojú ara* refer to women's genitalia in general and are sometimes translated as vagina. *Ojú ara* is a polite way of saying *òbò* or *abẹ́* (the latter literally meaning 'below').
3. The association of the calabash with fertility in women is reflected in the derogatory names given to non-virgin brides such as *aíkàrágbá* (broken calabash) and *àjọdí ikòkò* (broken pot), implying they had broken or spoiled their fertility.
4. The birth canal is referred to in Buckley (1985: 71) by one Ọ̀yọ́ Yoruba diviner-healer as *okùn ọmọ*, the pipe of the child; another *babaláwo* translated this phrase as 'child's rope', which ties together the father's semen and mother's remaining menstrual fluid. I have not myself heard this phrase used either way in Èkìtì.
5. Before maternity clinic and midwife deliveries were introduced by the British during the colonial period, male diviner-healers (*babaláwo*) were likely to be present at childbirth, particularly during difficult births.
6. *Baálẹ̀* is 'village head' or 'local quarter head'. This is distinct from *baálé* 'head of the household'. With no tone marking or indication of vowel quality, the two words look the same.
7. A common theme in Nigerian popular fiction depicted the upwardly-mobile, educated man married to an uneducated 'bush wife', trying to dump her for a more sophisticated spouse (Obiechina 1973).
8. It is unclear whether this condition refers to *atresia vaginae*, closure of the vagina, a condition that may result from an unbroken hymen or the growing together of the vaginal walls (Kahn and Holt 1990: 32).
9. The space between premarital sex (as a prelude to subsequent marriage) and the social recognition of a marriage (usually by an agreement between two families), referred to elsewhere as the 'bio-social gap' (Gyepi-Garbrah 1985: 30), has led to an increase in premarital pregnancies. Since pregnancy results in automatic

suspension from secondary schools and an end to aspirations for salaried employment, young women may decide, along with their boyfriends, to abort a pregnancy rather than stop their education (Barker and Rich 1992; Nichols et al. 1986; Renne 1996a). This situation has led to another interpretation of the term *ibàjẹ́*, 'spoiling oneself' (i.e. one's fertility), not from premarital intercourse as it was earlier believed but from frequent abortion (see Chapter 1).
10. In their study of a small rural community in southern Ondo State in 1974, Mott and Mott (1985: 92) found that 72 per cent of all women surveyed said they did not discuss family size with their husbands.
11. The question asked was, 'Have you ever discussed with your husband/boyfriend the number of children you want to have in the future?' The difference in men's and women's responses may reflect gender ideals in which men are said to discuss and decide the number of children to be born while women are said to acquiesce to their decisions (see Renne 1993d).
12. According to an analysis of 1990 NDHS data (Nigeria, Federal Office of Statistics 1992), education was statistically significant in predicting whether a woman will discuss the number of children wanted with her spouse; it also appeared to be the underlying factor for predicting a lower ideal number of children (Renne and Bánkọlé 1996).
13. Delaney (1987: 47) has suggested that it is this ideational aspect of education – the sense of altering women's view of the world and their place in it – that is the key to lowering high rates of fertility in Turkey.

CHAPTER 5: CHILD-FOSTERING, BLOOD TIES AND PARENTHOOD

1. For example, see Bledsoe 1990a, 1990b (Sierra Leone); Bledsoe and Isiugo-Abanihe 1989 (Sierra Leone); Etienne 1979 (Cote d'Ivoire); Fiawoo 1978 (Ghana); Goody 1982, 1984 (Ghana); Hammer and Sutton 1988 (Nigeria); Isaac and Conrad 1982 (Sierra Leone); Isiugo-Abanihe 1985 (Nigeria); Moran 1992 (Liberia); Page 1989 (Sub-Saharan Africa); and Schildkrout 1973 (Ghana).
2. As one man explained, 'I can't allow my children to stay more than three weeks outside my control, I don't want anyone to help finance my children. This is why I want just three, if I have more, then I am looking for trouble' (MRI-FC28/8-47, Ìtàpá-Èkìtì, 1995).
3. The term 'social capital' may also be used to refer to community relations of trust and reciprocity, which some argue facilitate local development (see Widner 1998). For example, in Ìtàpá, when people say that 'a lack of love' is obstructing development in the town, they are talking about a lack of trust in the town's political leadership as well as social discord. However, preliminary findings based on a comparative study of particular characteristics of social capital in Uganda and Botswana found 'no clear relationship between social capital and the performance of local institutions' (Widner 1998: 2). Part of the problem with taking a social capital approach to the study of fertility decline and of local development is the assumption that what constitutes social utility is everywhere the same, but as Hocart observed many years ago: 'In the main it is doubtless true that men are guided in their activities by reasons of utility, but their conceptions of utility differ widely.'
4. This particular configuration of fostering was made clearer to me when one research assistant who had fostered her son to her own mother, was referred to by the child as 'aunty'. He only called his grandmother 'mama'.
   The problem of defining who is a foster child, either from survey data or in

field situations, is further complicated by the problem of deciding when a person's fostered status ends and adult status begins. Since fostering was defined as 'raising a child as one's own' in Ìtàpá, an individual could be twenty years old and still essentially be fostered, that is, raised with food, shelter, medical, and educational expenses provided by a foster parent. I limited foster children to completed age nineteen (omitting some, such as married women, who were clearly no longer fostered) because of demographic age-group conventions.

5. This definitional distinction of in-fosters as children raised within the town and out-fosters as children raised outside it by someone other than a biological parent somewhat distorts the situation. Some of the children raised as in-foster children within Ìtàpá represented in-town fostering – with biological parents residing in a different (or the same) house within the town. In order to prevent duplicate counts of foster children who might be counted as an in-foster in one household and an out-foster in another, I have only counted out-foster children as those living outside Ìtàpá. Ideally, these in-town foster children should have been linked in the preliminary census so that in-fostered children from within the town and those in-fostered from outside could be distinguished. This could be done by asking where an in-fostered child's parents are living. In the smaller foster survey of 166 children, this question *was* asked. Sixty-nine per cent of the in-foster children had both birth parents (or their mothers) living outside Ìtàpá (that is, they were inter-town fosters), while 26 per cent were intra-town foster children. However, this distinction can be messy especially when the birth-parents are intermittently resident in the town (see Schildkrout 1973).

6. However, the relatively low out-town fostering figures suggest that the presence of the Ìtàpá-Osín Community High School and a nearby 'Unity' secondary boarding school may affect the need to out-foster in order to obtain a secondary school education (see Hammer and Sutton 1988: 294).

7. Comparing research conducted in the state capital, Adó-Èkìtì, in 1991, with survey data collected in Ìbàdàn in 1973, Caldwell et al. (1992: 227) found 'no drop in the proportion of families fostering out at least one child, but a major decline in the proportion of all children fostered, from 29 to 14 per cent.'

8. For Sierra Leone, Bledsoe and Isiugo-Abanihe (1989: 471) argue that a deteriorating national economy is likely to lead to increased fostering of young children to rural grandmothers, in part because it provides insurance of sustained rural ties.

9. Fifteen men gave the same responses in both interviews to this question about the number of children wanted, giving credibility to these figures. Since these numbers are often subject to revision based on individual circumstances, they are taken with 'a grain of salt' by demographers. This point was clearly seen in the responses of men who had lost children, as they tended to revise the number wanted upward. Three men (7.5% of men reinterviewed) said they could not say how many children they wanted, some because they had lost children. Another artefact of this data is the comparison in the numbers wanted. For example, wanting fewer children in 1995 did not necessarily mean few children, as one man, who revised his preference from 15+ to 10–15 makes clear.

10. This man had said he wanted five children in 1991 as well; he presently has two children although he had lost two children prior to the 1991 interview.

CHAPTER 6: BURIAL, REBIRTH AND RELATIONS WITH THE DEAD

1. His death was announced first to the Ẹlẹ́kọ̀lé because his family was said to have originated from that town. Láyẹni (1932: 10), a local historian, described the Ọbalókè as 'a royal son from Ikole'. The late Ọbalókè, interviewed in November 1991 prior to his death, described the situation similarly.
2. While the burial of the Ọbalókè differed from the burials of other Ìtàpá chiefs as well as from the Ọwátàpá, the King of Ìtàpá, his burial reflects continuing ideas about the importance of representing the extraordinary qualities of chiefs by a symbolic inversion of the everyday social order. Prior to his burial, the town had been turned topsy-turvy by family members going through the streets, capturing all stray animals and threatening to kill them unless their owners paid ransom, a 'tradition', referred to as *A ń ságùn*, 'running around the town'. In a ritual mock fight (*àjà mùta*) performed just after his burial, women from the three Oròkè sub-quarters dressed as men warriors, each side blaming the other for the death of their king (see Chapter 2). Additionally, the Ọbalókè had been secretly buried in the bush, rather than in a church cemetery or under the veranda of his house, where as a Christian and a respected local government judge, he would otherwise have been buried. These special practices, relating to religious beliefs about the power of chiefs (Feeley-Harnik 1997), are maintained, in part, because they support a system of local political rule by 'traditional chiefs'. These individuals, invested with certain powers and responsibilities during the process of their installation, require an equal amount of effort to divest them of these attributes after death.
3. Until recently, cemetery burials were carried out entirely by church officials. This separation of the church cemetery gravesite (and all burial responsibilities) from the family house (and family responsibility) is consistent with Weber's (1946: 329) observation that religious communities centred around 'prophecies of salvation', making a conscious effort to separate individuals from their kin. His point is supported by the following passage from Matthew 10: 37–8: 'Whoever loves father or mother more than me; and whoever loves son or daughter more than me; and whoever does not take up the cross and follow me is not worthy of me.'
4. Since houses with unmarked graves inside or houses that were unoccupied would not have been counted, it is likely that the percentage of houses with graves is somewhat higher.
5. This placement of the grave away from the house distinguishes the inopportune deaths of those who die young. The discontented spirits of these people are also said to move about to other places where they appear as their former living selves (*àkú dààyà* (Abraham 1962: 46)). The entire novel *The Palm-Wine Drinkard and his Dead Palm-Wine Tapster in the Deads' Town* is about the tribulations of the palm-wine drinkard who is looking for the deceased palm-wine tapster who is believed to be living in another town (Tutuọla 1952).
6. Muslims in the town were generally buried near, but never in the floors of, their houses. The cloth-covered corpse would be carried to the gravesite on a wooden or woven palmfrond frame.
7. They could also be buried in rubbish heaps at the back of houses (Verger 1968).
8. During the colonial period, the relationship between chiefs and kings was somewhat altered. Kings were given more power than their chiefs, upsetting the 'balance' associated with this form of political organisation (Eades 1980: 103–4).

9. Láwuyì (1993: 234) makes a similar point about educated or wealthy children enhancing the prestige of the deceased.
10. The special ceremony, known as *ètùtù*, consists of a sacrifice led by a herbalist–diviner (*babaláwo*) or a prophet or prophetess associated with one of the *Aládurà* churches. Another such ceremony is known as *ó nlọ pè*, 'calling the dead', and it is only done for unusual deaths. It is not performed in Ìtàpá but rather in one quarter in Ìkọ̀lé to the east, as described by one man: 'We will tell that man (an expert, a *babaláwo*) the name of the dead person, that we have come to call. Then whatever is needed will be given to that expert. This man will then enter a particular place set aside for that purpose and will make the necessary sacrifices. He will shout that people have come for a request ... then that expert will call the name of the dead person and the dead person will answer from a very far place ... When the dead person arrives, whatever killed him or her, the person will say it' (FI-1, Ìtàpá-Èkìtì, 1991).
11. This ritual is performed around the same time as Id-el-Kabir, the Muslim celebration that commemorates Abraham's sacrifice of a ram as a substitute for his son Isaac. I do not know if there is a historical connection between these two practices.
12. Abraham (1962: 168) defines *ètùtù* as 'atonement'; other types of *ẹbọ* are referred to as offering or thanksgiving, stressing a Christian association.
13. The woman quoted was careful to make the distinction between seeing a dead person in a dream and in life, as some people believe that if one sees a living person one knows has died, this is a sign that one will soon die oneself. The idea behind this unnatural occurrence is that the person has committed some extraordinary offence against the deceased who appears on earth to beat the person to death as retribution (FI-16, Ìtàpá-Èkìtì, 1991).
14. See Gilbert (1988) for an example from Ghana that exemplifies this point.
15. This practice began in the early twentieth century in Ìtàpá. Prior to that, individuals were known by a range of single names.
16. There is some resistance to using the names Bàbátúndé and Yétúndé although there is also continued support for this practice, as the following incident indicates:

> For example, my mother died in 1973. She died on the fourth day and I had a child born on the seventh day (this was after my mother had died) and the child was a female. But rightly, I didn't want to give her just any name, so I named her Alfana (according to Muslim rites) but my family named her Yèyétúndé [Mother Returns], some called her Ìyábọ̀ [Mother Comes] just because immediately my mother had left the child came ... (FI-16, Ìtàpá-Èkìtì, 1991).

17. The complexity of these preparations has spawned several 'how-to' books on this subject (Akande 1976; Osuafor 1997).
18. This family probably did obtain a death certificate in order to keep the corpse in a mortuary and also because the death took place in a major urban centre. However, despite what one man claimed ('Nowadays, with the advent of civilization, wealth, and education, will-making is now a usual trend' (FI-18, Ìtàpá-Èkìtì, 1991)), for Ìtàpá residents who die at home, wills or death certificates are rarely used.

CHAPTER 7: PERSONAL HYGIENE, PUBLIC SANITATION AND WESTERN EDUCATION

1. A decree defining sanitary regulations was signed by the Ẹlẹ́kọ̀lé of Ìkọ̀lé on 17 May 1935 (Ondo Prof 1/2 OP565BA, 1929/37), suggesting that inspections began sometime after this date. This date also coincides with the fact that one Ìtàpá man stated that when sanitary inspectors first came to Ìtàpá, there was an outbreak of smallpox, and with the fact that a smallpox epidemic in Èkìtì for this period has been documented (Ondo Prof 1/1, File no. 521, 1934–46). Furthermore, according to Ògúntúyì (1979: 145), 'sanitary officers were few. They employed the services of their servants who often made the incisions [for smallpox vaccination] too deep. Some became deep sores and made people run away as soon as the presence of the sanitary officers was announced.'
2. In order to register for the two-year training course offered in Lagos in 1950, candidates needed a 'minimum educational requirement for Trainees is Secondary Class IV Certificate' (Ondo Prof 1/1, File no. 612, vol. II.).
3. This inspector is probably Mr S. O. Òṣiré, listed as a sanitary inspector for Èkìtì, some time between 1949–56 (Ondo Prof 1/1, File no. 612, vol. II).
4. The internalisation of social values associated with the French Enlightenment and the growth of the nation-state are discussed more fully in Foucault (1973), Vigarello (1988), and Turner (1984).
5. The term ọ̀làjú literally means 'opening the eyes'. Two critical aspects of ọ̀làjú include the association of 'enlightenment' with ideas and things from foreign places and the idea that knowledge is a limited commodity. Modern cleanliness practices reflect both of these aspects. One older man's use of the term ìgbàlódé may be translated as 'civilisation' or 'enlightenment' but with a specific reference to contemporary influences (SI-10, Ìtàpá-Èkìtì, 2000).
6. See Elias (1978) for an analysis of the ways that everyday body practice (in particular, table manners) related to a heightened sense of civility and national identity.
7. These ideas co-existed with others that associated the presence of dirt with spirituality, as in the case of àbíkú ('born to die') children who were intentionally kept dirty so as to dissuade their spirit-child friends from calling them back to the spirit world. See Douglas (1966: 35) on the distinctions made between sacred and secular ideas about dirt.
8. IBMINED 1/2, File no. 432, NNAI, 1945–50.
9. There are at least four primary health text series currently available (for example, Ayẹni, no date; Obogbaimhe 1983; Ọmọ́dára and Dáre 1984; Usua and Dada 1987). Hygienic practices are also included in primary texts for home economics and for social studies.
10. The Annual Report on the Medical and Health Services, 1932 (Session paper no. 5, 1934) describes these posters as follows:
    Two series of attractive coloured posters mounted on linen and with rollers, and printed in English and Hausa, English and Yoruba ... were completed and issued to schools throughout the Northern and Southern Provinces and three further series are almost completed. The cost was met by a grant from the Colonial Development Fund.
    The subjects of these posters are as follows:
    (i) Eat more fruit, (ii) This baby loves his bath, (iii) Bury your empty tins and bottles, (iv) Let the sun come into your house, (v) Keep the house clean.
11. Nigerian National Archives (Ibadan) documents on health propaganda films include: Cinema Van (Ekiti Div 1/1, File no. 922, vol. I); Cinematograph: Correspondence, 1933–55 (Ondo Prof 1/1, File no. 387, vol. I); Cinema shows,

films, etc. (IBMINED 1/2, File no. CIW 234); and Health Propaganda, 1935/ 1937 (CSO 26/2, File no. 30314).
12. Demographers have attempted to distinguish between whether it is the education of parents or the expense involved in raising educated children that causes parents to have smaller families. While Axinn (1993) concluded that it was the latter that led to reductions in family size in the Nepalese town where he worked, the material from Ìtàpá suggests that such a clear-cut distinction cannot be made. The childcare aspirations of parents who want to raise their children properly (through hygienic practices as well as schooling) were learned in school.
13. Sanitary inspectors were responsible for large areas and since they generally travelled by bicycle, their coverage would be intermittent at best. The sanitary inspector appointed by the Health Superintendent, Ondo Province, in 1951, was 'responsible for Ijero, Iddo, Osi, Otun, Ishan, Aiyede, Itaji, Oye, and Ikole' (Ekiti Div 1/1, File no. 995, p. 8).
14. The War Against Indiscipline programme was begun by the Buhari regime in 1983.
15. The version of the Public Health Ordinance signed by the Ẹlẹ̀kọ̀lé in 1935 included the following passage:
   The practice of committing nuisances in open spaces or in the bush adjoining compounds is prohibited. Heads of compounds will be held responsible that their families make use of the public latrines if such are provided, or if not some simple form of trench latrine and that no nuisance which is calculated to be harmful to the general public is permitted.
   (Ondo Prof 1/2 OP565BA, 1935)
16. In a month-long time-study conducted in Ìtàpá in 1991, of fifty-seven paired foster and non-foster children randomly surveyed for a month at ten different one-hour periods, over half (n=30) spent at least 10 per cent of this time fetching water.
17. The connection between politics, economics, and hygiene is illustrated quite literally in the naming of a skin disease after a former president of Nigeria, Ibrahim Babangida. His economic policies were blamed for people's inability to buy soap, as a result of rising prices (Alubo 1990: 1078).
18. Several demographic studies (Axinn 1993; Bledsoe et al. 1999; Caldwell 1977a; Lloyd et al. 2000) have found that primary schooling is a significant predictor of lower fertility, although the reasons proffered for this effect vary. Some have stressed economic factors, for example, that educating many children is costly (Axinn 1993) or that educated children are not good returns on parents' investment so they have fewer (Caldwell 1977b), while others focus on health factors, with lower child mortality associated with educated parents (Cleland and Wilson 1987).

CHAPTER 8: HOUSES, DESCENDANTS AND LAND TENURE

1. The Land Use Decree was renamed the Land Use Act during the subsequent civilian regime.
2. Household composition was documented in terms of relationships to the head of the household for the entire house as the people were generally related. Hence, I use the term household to refer to residents of a single house. See Netting et al. (1984) for discussions of the difficulties of defining the household as a social unit of analysis.
3. The symbolic implications of houses have been studied in several African societies:

for example, the Kaguru (Beidelman 1986), the Batammaliba (Blier 1987), and the Kuranko (Jackson 1977).
4. For example, Barber (1991: 231) describes this process in the Yoruba town of Òkúkù:

> Pakoyi [a successful farmer-businessman) did have a large family ('three wives and many children') but building houses had become almost as important as marrying wives: Pakoyi built two, apart from the compound where he lived, and one of them was a prestigious 'upstairs'. Whereas at the turn of the century a large house was a sign of wealth because it was evidence of the large human population inside of it, by 1950 bricks and mortar were valued in themselves.

5. This number is considerably less than the mean of 16.3 people per house found in a survey of 773 houses in Adó-Èkìtì in 1987 (Orubuloye, no date: 9).
6. Daughters are also included as inheritors of family houses, but since they usually marry out, they are not expected to continue living in it. They may also be buried with their husbands.
7. For example, the following items were given by one man who acquired non-family land in the town:

3 cartons of beer	₦80
1 goat	₦300
1 bag of salt	₦30
2 bottles of Schnapps	₦60 (January 1992 prices).

8. It is also possible that these chiefs believe that their roles in arbitrating land transactions will be undermined by cash.
9. In July 2000, twenty-five house transactions for houseplots on the western edge of the town (a growth area) were recorded. Cash was involved in eight of these transactions, including cash given in four transactions between family members.
10. $x^2=12.30$; $p<0.001$.
11. For example, sixteen people from Ìtàpá-Èkìtì indigenes living in Lagos reported paying rents ranging from ₦40 to ₦400 a month in 1992.
12. The course that rural land tenure practice has taken in Nigeria, with its emphasis on ultimate state control and on occupancy rather than on a legal system of ownership, has its roots in the British colonial policy of 'indirect rule' (see Beidelman 1971). Rather than establish a costly system of surveyance of land and registration of titles in rural areas, colonial officials opted for the cheaper method of vesting legal authority over land distribution to traditional chiefs. Thus the tendency toward individual ownership of rural land was played down in favour of communal ownership and 'customary' use rights, as individual ownership would have undermined the authority of chiefs over land distribution. The preference for customary land tenure practices, and particularly the prohibition of the sale of rural land was also a strategy for preventing expatriate interests from acquiring land for plantations. For a fuller discussion of British colonial land tenure policies and their legacy in postcolonial Africa, see Bohannan (1957), Chanock (1991), Colson (1960), Meek [1946] (1968).
13. See Myers (1990) for a discussion of a similar response to the Land Use Decree by Yoruba farmers in the Ìbàdàn area.
14. An examination of the family size of non-resident househead-owners of hometown houses, difficult as this would be, might clarify the relationship between commoditisation of houseplots and fertility.

CHAPTER 9: COUNTING BODIES: CENSUSES, VITAL REGISTRATION AND THE CREATION OF EKITI STATE

1. I was unable to find an example of òwìwí, since Chief Káyòdé had died before I knew about them and I was told that they were no longer being kept.
2. Cohn (1990: 250) argues that:
   The movement of objectification has moved by the 1930s from a small group of intellectuals in Calcutta searching for cultural tools with which to counter Western influences to the towns and villages of much of India. In this process of classifying and making objective to the Indians themselves their culture and society, the census played a key role.
3. According to the government report on the 1931 census in the Southern Provinces (which would have included Ondo Province of which Ekiti Division was part), 'no Census proper, except in Lagos itself, was sanctioned ... and the figures reported are rarely more than an estimate of population based on the number of adult males assessed to tax ... The adult male, therefore, is the unit on which the Census compilation for the Southern Provinces has been based' (Jacob 1933: 5).
4. Indeed, one local government objected to the inclusion of rules for death registration. Their version of the Bye-laws omitted the reference to deaths (Ekiti Div 1/1, File no. 1042B, 1953–7).
5. According to Adépòjù (1981: 31), the 1973 census, the first after the Nigerian Civil War, was part of the reform platform introduced by General Gowon when he took over the government in 1966. After provisional figures were released in May 1974, they were immediately disputed as inaccurate. The furore created by the 1973 census figures – they were seen as favouring certain ethnic groups and areas – contributed to the bloodless coup that brought down Gowon's government (Adépòjù 1981: 35).
6. The 1991 census results for Ìtàpá was 11,392 while Ayégbajú reported a figure of 8,685 (Department of Population Activities 1997: 31). These results differ considerably from the 1963 census results.
7. Babangida named nine new states in 1991, but Ekiti State was not one of them.
8. This lobbying included considerable publicity in the press, for example, Alade and Aromokunola (1992), Omoseebi (1991), Omotoso (1992), Orji (1992), Osifo-Whiskey (1992), *Sunday Sketch* (1992).
9. The reference here is to the Yoruba-wide response to the annulment of the election of Moshood Abíólá in June 1993 and the widespread dislike of Abacha in south-western Nigeria.
10. The naming of six new states was nonetheless criticised by some who viewed it as a political strategy to build local support for the military regime. It was justified by Abacha as ensuring a 'fair spread and balance within the geopolitical zones'. His opponents, however, claimed the move merely increased the level of bureaucracy and put still more patronage at the disposal of the head of state (Arnold 1998: 193). Others have criticised state formation as a means for the local elites to enrich themselves (Bach 1997: 344).
11. This Decree was officially launched on 20 October 1989 although it was introduced by the government on 1 April 1988 (Population Association of Nigeria 1990: 8; see Federal Republic of Nigeria 1988).
12. The implementation of the census and vital registration, however, come under the purview of the National Population Commission.
13. For example, it is believed that the widow of General Abacha and three of her children stole US$4 billion from the Federal Republic of Nigeria, which was

deposited in 'more than 130 bank accounts spread around the world' (Ọlórunfẹ́wa 2000: 13).
14. This man's comments were made in January 1995, after Abacha had become president and Abíọ́lá had been imprisoned.
15. He was making reference here to the intense competition between towns, states, and regions over census results that has contributed to the padding of census rolls, quarrelling over enumeration areas, and the cancellation of results (see Adépọ̀jù 1981; Ẹbigbọla 1981; Olúsànyà 1983).

CHAPTER 10: CONCLUSION: LOCAL DEVELOPMENT, POLITICS AND TWO FUNERALS

1. A road-building project, funded by the military-led Nigerian federal government, was also commissioned in 1997 (Ayọ̀ọlá 1997) although it did not affect Ìtàpá.
2. Several letters from S. A. Dada to the Ekiti District Officer may be found in the Nigerian National Archives, Ìbàdàn (for example Letter to District Officer, 1950; Letter, 22 February 1960, to the District Officer) in the file Matters affecting Ìtàpá Village, 1924–52, Ekiti Div 1/1, File no. 278.
3. Dada first attended the Methodist Primary School in Ìtàpá in 1936. He then went to Ìfàkì Methodist School, on to Government Teacher Training College and later to University College, Ìbàdàn (an affiliate of the University of London), where he obtained a BA in 1957 and a diploma (in Education) from the University of London (Dada 2000).
4. Letter, Chief S. A. Dada to the District Officer, Adó-Èkìtì, 22 February 1960, Ekiti Div 1, File no. 278, pp. 84–7:
    Sir: I am directed by the 'Ìtàpá Progress Union' to which I am a secretary to forward to the District Officer the following decisions arrived at ... The Union, at its general meeting of January the 4th at Ìtàpá-Èkìtì, made the following resolutions which I was asked to communicate to the District Officer.
    'Be it resolved that (1) the District Officer be thanked for his past efforts;
    (2) 'that the 'Show' [So] brook which was about to be improved by Government in 1948 and which project was abandoned, should be completed;
    (3) 'that the fact that Egosi has twice failed to maintain a Post Office should not be an excuse to deny us the use of one;
    (4) 'that the time is over-due that market stalls are erected;
    (5) 'that a local dispensary is our people's urgent need;
    (6) 'that the salary of the Owatapa be increased and the following Chiefs beside the Owatapa to receive pay: (a) Odofin (b) Obaro (c) Elemo (d) Obasalu (e) Obaloke (f) Obalawe (g) Olomodetapa.
    (7) 'and that lastly we put implicit faith in the District Officer, in that he would give this petition his deepest consideration and put the requests therein before the appropriate Authorities.
    I hope the District Officer – at his earliest convenience – shall communicate any reply to the Secretary of the above address.
    (Sgn) M. A. Jawolusi, President   S. A. Dada, Hon. Secretary
5. There are eight members of the Ọwátàpá's council, including the Ọwátàpá (see note 16, Chapter 2).
6. Letter to the District Officer, Ekiti Division, from Olomodakomo of Akoro Compound, Egetun Quarter, Ìtàpá-Èkìtì, 8 March 1950; Ekiti Div 1, File no. 278, Nigerian National Archives, Ìbàdàn; my italics.

7. 'Response of Acting DO, Owatapa-Obaisa Palaver. I went into this thoroughly ... I spoke very firmly to the Chiefs about their own misconduct in preventing the Obaisa from sitting in the court and on the council [of chiefs], and warned them that if I found any of them interfering with Obaisa's sitting in the court then that person would be liable to be suspended very readily (W. Simpson, 'Extract from Touring Notes,' Ìkọ̀lé, 4 March 1950, Ekiti Div 1, File no. 278, pp. 93–4, Nigerian National Archives, Ìbàdàn).
8. Piot (1999: 149) describes how dispute settlement has become an important source of income for chiefs in northern Togo.
9. See Guyer (1993) for a discussion of a shift at the national level away from the welfare state.
10. This claim is not entirely correct as two recent community projects have been carried out in recent years, including the town hall and the community bank.
11. For example, in a recent release by the comedian–social commentator Gbenga Adébóyè (aka 'Funwọntan') entitled 'Guess Who? A Call From Above' (1999), Abacha brags, 'No single kobo to run the democracy! ... No money left in the treasury!'
12. Boserup (1990) also argues that a large population is essential for this development.
13. The phrase 'governing on the cheap' (Beidelman 1971: 97) refers to the British colonial government's use of 'Native Authority' chiefs to conduct most local political affairs as part of the policy of 'indirect rule', without going to the expense of bringing in large numbers of British officials. This strategy is similar to the current use of family planning assistance as development, rather than financing (more expensive) infrastructural improvements and better terms of trade.
14. For example, the Ìtàpá market has been revitalised because one of the young men's associations imposed a system of fines on women who travelled out of the town to other markets on Ìtàpá's market day.
15. During this period there were five different national heads of state: Babangida, Shonekan, Abacha, Abubakar, and Obásanjọ́.
16. As of June 2000, refined petroleum continues to be imported because none of the refineries is functional – in this oil-producing country.
17. From 1999–2000, a community-based contraception distribution project, sponsored by the Packard Foundation, involved two women's ẹgbẹ́ (clubs) in Ìtàpá. Thirty-five Ìtàpá women members participated in the programme that made low-cost oral contraceptive tablets available.

APPENDIX 1: RESEARCH METHODS AND MATERIALS

1. The difficulties of finding men to re-interview in 1997 precluded conducting a follow-up survey. While I tried to document both men's and women's fertility experiences in this study, in order to counter the past tendencies to focus solely on women's fertility, men's work patterns and polygynous marriage made this plan particularly challenging.
2. Duru (1968: 74) also noted that the rural elderly in Nigeria may tend to inflate their ages for economic reasons, namely tax exemption.
3. Olúsànyà (1966: 145) also found problems with age estimates used in the 1952 Nigerian census: 'Males aged 15–49 years appear to have been shifted down to the 7–14 age group, while proportionally more females appear to have been shifted in the opposite direction, that is, from the age group 7–14 years to the reproductive age group 15–49 years.'

4. There were similar findings in the Ìlọrin re-survey earlier cited: of the 83 women who reported a specific age (out of 159 women re-interviewed), between 48–60 per cent gave consistent reports of age, plus or minus one year (Becker et al. 1995: 238.)
5. In a longitudinal study by Bánkọlé et al. (1996), Bánkọlé conducted follow-up interviews in 1993 of 725 women identified from the original 1990 Nigerian DHS survey interviews. They found considerable discrepancy in ages and number of children reported: '... Analysis of the consistency of the information reported for age and number of children ever born indicated that only for 247 of the 725 women re-interviewed was there a clear indication of matching the sample of women.'
6. The variation in the number of children reported may also reflect the different levels of patience and competence of the interviewers. In particular, women who had had infants and children die were not always forthcoming about mentioning them, and a certain amount of unpleasant prompting was sometimes necessary to encourage women to recall them.

BIBLIOGRAPHY

PRIMARY SOURCES: ARCHIVAL (NIGERIAN NATIONAL ARCHIVES, ÌBÀDÀN)

General files

Annual Report of the Medical and Health Department, 1931. Session Paper no. 23, 1932.
Annual Report of the Medical and Health Department, 1932. Session Paper no. 5, 1934.
CSO 26/2, File no. 15683, vol. I. Organisation to promote sanitary conditions throughout the Protectorate, 1925.
CSO 26/2, File no. 30314. Health Propaganda, 1935/1937.
Ekiti Div 1/1, File no. 857. Sanitation in Ekiti Division, Correspondence re: House to House Inspection, 1949–54.
Ekiti Div 1960. Matters affecting Itapa Village, 1924–52. Ekiti Division 1/1, File no. 278.
Ekiti Div 1/1, File no. 995. Government Sanitary Staff, Correspondence re: 1951–2.
Ekiti Div 1/1, File no. 922, vol. I. Cinema Van.
IBMINED 1/2, File no. CIW 234. Cinema shows, films, etc.
IBMINED 1/2, File no. CIW 3427A. Higher Elementary Revised Syllabus, 1951.
IBMINED 1/2, File no. CIW 432. Medical, Health and Sanitary Arrangements in Schools, 1945/50.
Ministry of Health, Ondo State. 1953. Minhealth 1/1, File 3189.
Ondo Prof 1/1, File no. 387, vol. I. Cinematograph: Correspondence, 1933–55.
Ondo Prof 1/1, File no. 521. Smallpox: Outbreak of in Ekiti Division, 1934–46.
Ondo Prof 1/1, File no. 612, vol. II. Training School for Sanitary Inspectors, 1949–56.
Ondo Prof 1/2, File. no. OP565BA. Health Rules: Ekiti Division, 1929/37.
Ondo Prof 1/3, File no. D. 21. Development Scheme: Sanitation, 1945–56.

Specific documents

Alexander, D. 1925. Scheme for Preventative Medicine and Hygiene in Nigeria; Travelling Officers. CSO 26/2, File no. 15216, vol. I.
Bromage, J. R. V. A. 1952. Annual Report 1952, Ekiti Division. Ondo Prof 1, File no. 120A.
Chambers, S. B. 1956. Population Census of the Western Region of Nigeria 1952. Lagos: Government Printer, Western Region, Nigeria. File no. PX/H2E.
Dada, S. A. 1960. Letter to the District Officer, Ado-Ekiti. Ekiti Division 1, File no. 278, pp. 84–7.
Davidson, J. 1925. Scheme for Preventative Medicine and Hygiene in Nigeria; Travelling Officers. CSO 26/2, File no. 15216, vol. I.

de la Mothe, H. D. 1921. 1921 Annual Report on Ekiti Division, Ondo Province. Ondo Prof 4/1.
Ekiti Division. 1945. Ekiti Division Annual Report 1945, Ondo Prof 120A.
Ekiti Division. 1952a. Census Instructions. Ekiti Division 1/1, File no. 918A.
Ekiti Division. 1952b. Census of Population Publicity. Ekiti Division 1/1, File no. 918B.
Ekiti Division. 1952c. Census of Population [1952 Census]. Ekiti Division 1/1, File no. 918D.
Ekiti Division. 1952d. Hints for Enumerators [1952 Census]. Ekiti Division 1/1, File no. 918F.
Ekiti Division. 1953/1957. Registration of Birth and Death Bye-laws: District Councils. Ekiti Division 1/1, File no. 1,042B.
Elékọ̀lé of Ìkọ̀lé. 1935. Health Rules: Ekiti Division, Ondo Prof 1/2 OP565BA, 1929–37.
Gavin, C. I. 1932. Ekiti District 1/1, File no. 214A.
Jacob, S. M. 1933. Census of Nigeria, 1931, vol. I. London: Government of Nigeria/Crown Agents. File no. PX/HIA.
Láyẹni, J. B. 1934–35. Miscellaneous correspondence. Matters affecting Itapa Village, 1924–52, Ekiti Division 1/1, File no. 278, NAI.
Láyẹni, J. B. 1935 A History of Itapa. Unpublished manuscript. Matters affecting Itapa Village, 1924–52, Ekiti Division 1/1, File no. 278, NAI.
Matthews, B. 1941. Handing over notes, Ekiti Division, 25/8/41, Ikole District. Ondo Prof 1/2, File OP37a.
Ọlọmọdakọmọ, Chief. 1950. Letter to the District Officer, Ekiti Division. Ekiti Division 1, File no. 278.
Simpson, W. 1950. Extract from Touring Notes, Ikole, 4 March 1950, Ekiti Division 1, File no. 278, pp. 93–4.
Swayne, A. C. C. 1935. Health Rules: Ekiti Division, Ondo Prof 1/2 OP565BA, 1929–37.

PRIMARY SOURCES: NEWSPAPER, MAGAZINE CLIPPINGS, UNPUBLISHED MANUSCRIPTS, AND RECORDINGS

Adébóyè, G. 1999. 'Guess Who? (A Call from Above), in: *Pasan Oro*, Lagos: G. Adébóyè Productions.
Adeyẹmi, W. 1997. 'Looking beyond NADECO', *Tell* (22 Sept), p. 28.
Ajaja, D. 2000. 'Samuel Ayoola Dada: the end of an era', 16 February 2000. unpublished manuscript.
Àjàyí, J., and I. Arowosoge. 1996. 'An address presented today 1 October 1996 at Ado-Ekiti Stadium to thank General Sani Abacha, the Head of State and congratulate Ekiti people for the creation of Ekiti State', unpublished manuscript.
Àjàyí, A. 1999. '12th Itapa-Day Celebration: An address of welcome', 2 October, 1999, unpublished manuscript.
Ajetunmọbi, Y. 2000. 'Ekiti to spend N. 55bn on roads', *Ekiti Now* 1(9), 1,4.
Ajiboye, S. B. No date. 'Memoires of Chief S. B. Ajiboye, in the Progress of Ilupeju-Ekiti, Ondo State and Nigeria as a Whole', unpublished manuscript.
Akinkuotu, A. 1998. 'Royalty for sale', *Tell* 3 (19 Jan), pp. 12–15.
Akinkuotu, A. 2000. 'A dangerous agenda', *Tell* 12 (20 March), pp. 12–16.
Alade, A. and T. Aromokunola. 1992. 'Honorable Oladeji Fasuan – Adherent of Ekiti State', *Supreme Magazine* (15 February), p. 30.
Ayoola, B. 1997. 'Federal government to construct roads in Ekiti', *The Guardian* (29 July), p. 5.

Dada, S. A. 1988. 'First Itapa Day – A call for unity, peace and progress', First Itapa Day, 8 October 1988, Ìtàpá-Èkìtì, unpublished manuscript.
Dada, S. A. 1999. 'An address to the Council of Obas', Oye LGA, Oyé-Èkìtì, 30 September 1999, unpublished manuscript.
Department of Population Activities. 1997. *Ekiti State of Nigeria: Population Projections by Towns and Villages (1996–2000)*, Population Compendium, vol. 1, Adó-Èkìtì: Office of the Military Administrator.
Ẹgètún Community. 1999. 'A memo for the restructure of the chieftancy institutions in Itapa Ekiti in Oye Local Government by Egetun Community in Itapa Ekiti', 25 May 1999, unpublished manuscript.
Ekiti State of Nigeria. no date. *Republic of Nigeria Policy on Population for Development, Unity, Progress and Self-Reliance, 1988*, Adó-Èkìtì: Department of Population Activities.
Elémùré, Chief O., and his New Dimensions. no date. *Ekiti State*, Lagos: Amoni Records.
Falegan, S. B. 1991. 'The case for Ekiti State', *Supreme Magazine* 1(1): 16–17.
Fasae, B. 1997. 'Where are the Ekitis?' *Nigerian Tribune* (22 July).
Federal Republic of Nigeria. 1988. *Republic of Nigeria Policy on Population for Development, Unity, Progress and Self-Reliance*, Lagos: Government Printing Office.
Hilts, P. 1999. 'Nation is falling short of health goals for 2000', *New York Times* (11 June), p. A24.
Ọbaléké, I. 1988. 'Putting a ceiling on procreation', *The Guardian* (17 February), p. 13.
Ọlanipẹkun, R. O. 1997. 'The role of policy makers/community leaders in improving vital registration', paper presented at a seminar organised by the Population Activities Department, Governor's Office, Adó-Èkìtì, 7 July 1997.
Ọlọ́runfẹ́wa, A. 2000. 'The wages of sleaze', *Tell* 30 (24 July), pp. 12–18.
Olowopọrọku, B. 1996. 'An open letter to the Head of State and Commander-in-Chief of the Armed Forces of the Federal Republic of Nigeria: General Sani Abacha', unpublished manuscript.
Ọmọsẹebi, T. 1991. 'State creation: agitation for Ekiti State continues', *Supreme Magazine* 1 (1; 31 December): 11–19.
Ọmọtọsọ, D. 1992. 'We want development too', *Tell* 38 (21 September), p. 16.
Onishi, N. 2000a. 'Nigeria: death toll rises', *New York Times* (25 February).
Onishi, N. 2000b. 'Faltering giant: a special report; Against tough odds, Nigeria bets on reform', *New York Times* (20 August).
Orji, U. 1992. 'Ekiti chiefs call for prayer and fasting to back state creation agitation', *The Guardian* (22 July), p. 3.
Orubuloye, I. O. No date. 'People, housing and living conditions in Ado-Ekiti and Akure in Ondo State, Nigeria', unpublished manuscript, Department of Sociology, Ondo State University, Adó-Èkìtì.
Osifo-Whiskey, O. 1992. 'New states: more knocks at the door', *Tell* 38 (21 September), pp. 10–18.
Owolabi, J., M. Meshe, J. Adesina, and S. A. Dada. No date. 'Memorandum in respect of Owatapa of Itapa Chieftaincy Declaration', unpublished manuscript.
Rẹ́mọ Community. 1999. 'Reactions from Remo, Itapa-Ekiti to the "Memo" of Egetun',7 June 1999, unpublished manuscript.
Renne, E. 1995c. 'Do foster children work more? Perceptions of work, education, and child fostering in Southwestern Nigeria', unpublished paper presented at the Population Association of America meetings, San Francisco.
Renne, E. and A. Bánkọlé. 1996. 'Gender relations and fertility decline in

Southwestern Nigeria', paper presented at the Population Association of America annual meetings, New Orleans.
Social Progressive Party. 1996. 'An address presented today 1 October 1996 by the Social Progressive Party Ekiti State to thank General Sani Abacha, the Head of State and to congratulate Ekiti people for the creation of Ekiti State', unpublished manuscript.
Sunday Sketch. 1992. 'Obas renew call for Ekiti State', *Sunday Sketch* (10 January), p. 5.

SECONDARY SOURCES

Abraham, R. C. 1962. *Dictionary of Modern Yoruba*, London: Hodder and Stoughton.
Adédèjì, A. and O. Otite (eds). 1997. *Nigeria: Renewal from the Roots?*, London: Zed Books.
Adépòjù, A. 1974. 'Migration and socio-economic links between urban migrants and their home communities in Nigeria', *Africa* 44: 383–95.
Adépòjù, A. 1981. 'Military rule and population issues in Nigeria', *African Affairs* 80 (318): 29–47.
Adépòjù, A. (ed.). 1993. *The Impact of Structural Adjustment on the Population of Africa*, Portsmouth, NH and London: Heinemann and James Currey.
Adétúnjí, J. 1992. 'Church-based obstetrics in a Yoruba community, Nigeria', *Social Science & Medicine* 35: 1,171–8.
Adétúnjí, J. 1995. 'Infant mortality and mother's education in Ondo State, Nigeria', *Social Science & Medicine* 40 (2): 253–63.
Adétúnjí, J. 1996. 'Preserving the pot and water: a traditional concept of reproductive health in a Yoruba community, Nigeria', *Social Science & Medicine* 43 (11): 1,561–7.
Adewuya, V. 1986. *Family Living: home economics for boys and girls in Nigerian primary schools*, vols. 1–4, Ìbàdàn: Onibonge Press.
Ahonsi, B. 1988. 'Deliberate falsification and census data in Nigeria', *African Affairs* 87 (349): 553–62.
Àjàyí, J. F. A. 1965. *Christian Missions in Nigeria 1841–1891*, London: Longman
Àjàyí, J. F. A. 1993. 'On the politics of being mortal', *Transition* 3 (59): 32–44.
Àjàyí, J. F. A. 2000. *Tradition and Change in Africa: the essays of J. F. Ade Ajayi*, ed. T. Falola, Trenton, NJ: Africa World Press.
Àjàyí, J. F. A., and A. A. Igun. 1963. *Population Census of Nigeria, 1963: lists of historical events for determination of individual ages*, Ìbàdàn: Regional Census Office.
Ajiṣafẹ, A. K. 1924. *The Laws and the Customs of the Yoruba People*, London: Routledge.
Akande, S. T. O. 1976. *What to Do When Someone Dies*, Ìbàdàn: Daystar Press.
Akintoye, S. A. 1971. *Revolution and Power Politics in Yorubaland, 1840–1893: Ibadan expansion and the rise of Ekitiparapo*, London: Longman.
Alonso, W., and P. Starr (eds). 1987. *The Politics of Numbers*, New York: Russell Sage Foundation.
Alubo, S. 1990. 'State violence and health in Nigeria', *Social Science and Medicine* 31.
Aluko, S. A. 1965. 'How many Nigerians: an analysis of Nigeria's census problems, 1901–63', *Journal of Modern African Studies* 3(3): 371–92.
Apter, A. 1992. *Black Critics and Kings: the hermeneutics of power in Yoruba society*, Chicago: University of Chicago Press.

Apter, A. 1998. 'Discourse and its disclosures: Yoruba women and the sancitity of abuse', *Africa* 68 (1): 68–97.
Apter, A. 1999. 'IBB=419: Nigerian democracy and the politics of illusion', in John Comaroff and Jean Comaroff (eds), *Civil Society and the Political Imagination in Africa: Critical Perspectives*, pp. 267–307, Chicago: University of Chicago Press, pp. 267–307.
Arhin, K. 1994. 'The economic implications of transformations in Akan funeral rites', *Africa* 54 (3): 308–22.
Arnold, G. 1998. 'Nigeria', in *The Africa Review 1998*, pp. 193–7, Essex: Walden Publishing.
Astone, N. M., C. Nathanson, R. Schoen, and Y. J. Kim. 1999. 'Family demography, social theory, and investment in social capital', *Population and Development Review* 25 (1): 1–31.
Axinn, W. G. 1993. 'The effects of children's schooling on fertility limitation', *Population Studies* 47 (3): 481–93.
Ayẹni, A. 1991. 'Itapa-Ekiti – a history: 1900–1985', unpublished BA thesis, Department of History, Ondo State University, Adó-Èkiti.
Ayẹni, E. O., No date. *Health Education for Primary Schools*, vols. 1–5. Ilorin: Omoniyi Ayeni Press.
Bach, D. 1997. 'Indigenicity, ethnicity, and federalism', in L. Diamond, A. Kirk-Greene, and O. Oyediran (eds), *Transition Without End: Nigerian politics and civil society under Babangida*, pp. 333–49, Boulder: Lynne Rienner.
Bánkọlé, A. 1995. 'Desired fertility and fertility behaviour among the Yoruba of Nigeria: a study of couple preferences and subsequent fertility', *Population Studies* 49: 317–28.
Bánkọlé, A., G. Rodriguez, and C. Westoff. 1996. 'Mass media messages and reproductive behaviour in Nigeria', *Journal of Biosocial Science* 28: 227–39.
Barber, K. 1981. 'How man makes God in West Africa: Yoruba attitudes toward the Orisa', *Africa* 51 (3): 724–45.
Barber, K. 1987. 'Popular arts in Africa', *African Studies Review* 30: 1–78.
Barber, K. 1991. *I Could Speak Until Tomorrow: Oriki, women, and the past in a Yoruba town*, Washington, DC: Smithsonian Institution Press for the International African Institute.
Barker, G., and S. Rich. 1992. 'Influences on adolescent sexuality in Nigeria and Kenya: findings from recent focus-group discussions', *Studies in Family Planning* 23 (3): 199-210.
Barnes, S. 1986. *Patrons and Power: creating a political community in metropolitan Lagos*, London: Manchester University Press for the International African Institute.
Bascom, W. 1984. *The Yoruba of Southwestern Nigeria*, Prospect Heights, IL: Waveland Press.
Becker, H. 1992. 'Cases, causes, conjunctures, stories, and imagery', in C. Ragin and H. Becker (eds), *What is a Case? exploring the foundations of social inquiry*, pp. 205–16, Cambridge: Cambridge University Press.
Becker, S., K. Feyisetan, and P. Makinwa-Adebusoye. 1995. 'The effect of the sex of interviewers on the quality of data in a Nigerian family planning questionnaire', *Studies in Family Planning* 26 (4): 233–40.
Beidelman, T. O. 1971. *The Kaguru*, New York: Holt, Rinehart, and Winston.
Beidelman, T. O. 1982. *Colonial Evangelism: a sociohistorical study of an East African mission at the grassroots*, Bloomington: Indiana University Press.
Beidelman, T. O. 1986. *Moral Imagination Among the Kaguru*, Bloomington: Indiana University Press.

Beidelman, T. O. 1997. *The Cool Knife: imagery of gender, sexuality, and moral education in Kaguru initiation ritual*, Washington, DC: Smithsonian Institution Press.
Bender, D. 1970. 'Agnatic or cognatic? A re-evaluation of Ondo descent', *Man* 5 (1): 71–87.
Bender, D. 1972. '*De facto* families and *de jure* households in Ondo', *American Anthropologist* 73: 223–41.
Berry, S. 1985. *Fathers Work for Their Sons: accumulation, mobility, and class formation in an extended Yoruba community*, Berkeley: University of California Press.
Berry, S. 1993. *'No Condition is Permanent': the social dynamics of agrarian change in Sub-Saharan Africa*, Madison: University of Wisconsin Press.
Bledsoe, C. 1990a. 'Differential care of children of previous unions within Mende households in Sierra Leone', in J. Caldwell et al. (eds), *What We Know About Health Transition*, pp. 561–583, Canberra: Australian National University.
Bledsoe, C. 1990b. 'No success without struggle: social mobility and hardship for Sierra Leonean children', *Man* (New series) 25: 70–88.
Bledsoe, C. 2002. *Contingent Lives: Fertility, time, and aging in West Africa*, Chicago: University of Chicago Press.
Bledsoe, C. and U. Isiugo-Abanihe. 1989. 'Strategies of child fosterage among Mende "grannies" in Sierra Leone', in R. Lesthaeghe (ed.), *Reproduction and Social Organization in Sub-Saharan Africa*, pp. 442–72, Berkeley: University of California.
Bledsoe, C., J. Casterline, J. Johnson-Kuhn, and J. Haaga (eds). 1999. *Critical Perspectives on Schooling and Fertility in the Developing World*, Washington, DC: National Academy Press.
Blier, S. 1987. *The Anatomy of Architecture: ontology and metaphor in Batammaliba architectural expression*, Cambridge: Cambridge University Press.
Boddy, J. 1989. *Wombs and Alien Spirits: women, men, and the Zar cult in Northern Sudan*, Madison: University of Wisconsin Press.
Bohannan, L., 1952. 'A genealogical charter', *Africa* 22: 301–25.
Bohannan, P. 1957. *Justice and Judgment Among the Tiv*, London: Oxford University Press for the International African Institute.
Boserup, E. 1965. *The Conditions of Agricultural Growth: the economics of agrarian change under population pressure*, Chicago: Aldine.
Boserup, E. 1990. *Economic and Demographic Relationships in Development*, Baltimore: Johns Hopkins Press.
Brackett, D. G., and M. Wrong. 1930. 'Notes on hygiene books used in Africa', *Africa* 3: 506–15.
Brown, S. 1992. 'Public health in Lagos, 1850–1900. Perceptions, patterns, and perspectives', *International Journal of African Historical Studies* 25 (2): 337–60.
Buckley, A. 1985. *Yoruba Medicine*, Oxford: Oxford University Press.
Burke, T. 1996. *Lifebuoy Men, Lux Women: commodification, consumption, and cleanliness in modern Zimbabwe*, Durham: Duke University Press.
Cain, M. 1985. 'On the relationship between landholding and fertility', *Population Studies* 39: 5–15.
Cain, M. 1986. 'Landholding and fertility: a rejoinder', *Population Studies* 40: 313–17.
Caldwell, J. C. 1976. *The Socio-Economic Explanation of High Fertility: papers on the Yoruba society of Nigeria*, Canberra: Australian National University.
Caldwell, J. C. 1977a. 'The economic rationality of high fertility: an investigation illustrated with Nigerian survey data', *Population Studies* 31 (1): 5–27.
Caldwell, J. C. 1977b. 'Towards a restatement of demographic transition theory', in

J. Caldwell (ed.), *The Persistence of High Fertility*, pp. 25–119, Canberra: Australian National University.

Caldwell, J. C. 1980. 'Mass education as a determinant of the timing of the fertility decline', *Population and Development Review* 6 (2): 225–55.

Caldwell, J. C., P. Caldwell and B. Caldwell. 1987. 'Anthropology and demography: the mutual reinforcement of speculation and research', *Current Anthropology* 28 (1): 25–43.

Caldwell, J. C., and A. A. Igun. 1971. 'An experiment with census-type age enumeration in Nigeria', *Population Studies* 25 (2): 287–302.

Caldwell, J. C., I. O. Orubuloye and P. Caldwell. 1991. 'The destabilization of the traditional Yoruba sexual system', *Population and Development Review* 17 (2): 229–62.

Caldwell, J. C., I. O. Orubuloye and P. Caldwell. 1992. 'Africa's new kind of fertility transition', *Population and Development Review* 18 (2): 211–42.

Callaway, H. 1980. 'Women in Yoruba tradition and in the Cherubim and Seraphim society', in O. U. Kalu (ed.), *The History of Christianity in Africa*, pp. 321–32, London: Longman.

Castro Martin, T. 1995. 'Women's education and fertility: results from 26 demographic and health surveys', *Studies in Family Planning* 26 (4): 187–202.

Chabal, P., and J.-P. Daloz. 1999. *Africa Works: disorder as political instrument*, Oxford: James Currey, and Bloomington: Indiana University Press for the International African Institute.

Chanock, M. 1985. *Law, Custom and Social Order*, Cambridge: Cambridge University Press.

Chanock, M. 1991. 'Paradigms, policies, and property: a review of the customary law of land tenure', in K. Mann and R. Roberts (eds), *Law in Colonial Africa*, pp. 61–84, Portsmouth, NH: Heinemann.

Cleland, J. and C. Wilson. 1987. 'Demand theories of the fertility transition: an iconoclastic view', *Population Studies* 41 (1): 5–30.

Coale, A. 1973. 'The demographic transition', in *International Population Conference Proceedings, 1973*, vol. 1, pp. 53–72, Liege: IUSSP.

Cohen, D. W. and E. S. Atieno Odhiambo. 1992. *Burying SM: the politics of knowledge and the sociology of power in Africa*, Portsmouth, NH: Heinemann.

Cohen, D. W. and E. S. Atieno Odhiambo. 1989. *Siaya, the Historical Anthropology of an African Landscape*, London: J. Currey.

Cohn, B. 1980. 'History and anthropology: the state of play', *Comparative Studies in Society and History* 22 (2): 198–221.

Cohn, B. 1990. 'The census and objectification in South Asia', in B. Cohn, *An Anthropologist Among the Historians and Other Essays*, pp. 224–54, New Dehli: Oxford University Press.

Cohn, B. and N. Dirks. 1988. 'Beyond the fringe: the nation state, colonialism, and the technologies of power', *Journal of Historical Sociology* 1 (2): 224–29.

Colson, E. 1960. 'The impact of the colonial period on the definition of land rights', in V. Turner (ed.), *Colonialism in Africa*, pp. 193–215, Cambridge: Cambridge University Press.

Comaroff, J. and J. Comaroff. 1992. 'Medicine, colonialism, and the black body', in Comaroff and Comaroff, *Ethnography and the Historical Imagination*, pp. 215–33, Boulder, Colorado: Westview Press.

Condorcet, M. [1795] 1970. *Esquisse d'un Tableau Historique des Progrès de l'Esprit Humain*, Paris: Librairie Philosophique J. Vrin.

Crook, N. 1997. *Principles of Population and Development*, Oxford: Oxford University Press.

Dada, S. A. 2000. *The Struggles of My Life: an autobiography*, Akure: Aowa Press.
Dada, S. A. No date. *The African Church: a decade of revolution*, Ìbàdàn: A. Ajayi & Sons.
Davis-Floyd, R. and C. Sargent (eds). 1997. *Childbirth and Authoritative Knowledge: cross-cultural perspectives*, Berkeley, CA: University of California Press.
Delaney, C. 1987. 'Symbols of procreation: implications for education and population planning', in S. M. Akural (ed.), *Turkic Culture: Continuity and Change*, pp. 41–8, Bloomington: Indiana University Press.
Demeny, P. 1988. 'Social science and population policy', *Population and Development Review* 14 (3): 451–79.
Denzer, L. 1992. 'Domestic science training in colonial Yorubaland, Nigeria', in K. Hansen (ed.), *African Encounters with Domesticity*, pp. 116–39, New Brunswick: Rutgers University Press.
Diamond, I., A. Kirk-Greene and O. Oyediran. 1997. 'Appendix I: Chronology: 31 December 1983–17 November 1993', in Diamond et al. (eds), *Transition without End: Nigerian politics and civil society under Babangida*, pp. 485–92, Boulder, Colorado: Lynne Rienner
Diamond, I., M. Newby, and S. Varle. 1999. 'Female education and fertility: examining the links', in C. Bledsoe et al., *Critical Perspectives on Schooling and Fertility in the Developing World*, pp. 23–48, Washington, DC: National Academy Press.
Dmochowski, Z. 1990. *An Introduction to Nigerian Traditional Architecture, Vol. 2: South-West and Central Nigeria*, London: Ethnographica.
Douglas, M. 1966. *Purity and Danger*, London: Routledge and Kegan Paul.
Drewal, H., J. Pemberton and R. Abiodun. 1989. *Yoruba: nine centuries of African art and thought*, New York: Center for African Art.
Durkheim, E. 1961. *Moral Education*, Glencoe: Free Press.
Duru, R. C. 1968. 'Problems of data collection for population studies in Nigeria with particular reference to the 1952/53 census and the Western Region', in J. Caldwell and C. Okonjo (eds), *The Population of Tropical Africa*, pp. 71–7, London: Longman.
Eades, J. 1980. *The Yoruba Today*, Cambridge: Cambridge University Press.
Ẹbigbọla, A. 1981. 'Politics and population enumeration in Nigeria, 1960–1973', *Odu* 21: 28–51.
Ekanem, I. 1972. *The 1963 Census: a critical appraisal*, Benin City: Ethiope Publishing Co.
Eke, I. I. 1966. 'Population of Nigeria, 1952–1965', *Nigerian Journal of Economic and Social Studies* 8 (2): 289–309.
Ekwempu, C. C., D. Maine, M. Olorukoba, and M. S. Essien. 1990. 'Structural adjustment and health in Africa', *The Lancet* 336: 56–7.
Elias, N. 1978. *The History of Manners*, New York: Pantheon Books.
Elias, T. O. 1951. *Nigerian Land Law and Custom*, London: Routledge and Kegan Paul.
Etienne, M. 1979. 'The case for social maternity: adoption of children by urban Baule women', *Dialectical Anthropology* 4 (3): 237–42.
Fadipẹ, N. A. 1970. *The Sociology of the Yoruba*, Ìbàdàn: University of Ìbàdàn Press.
Federal Republic of Nigeria. 1988. *National Policy on Population for Development, Unity, Progress and Self-Reliance*, Lagos: Government Printing Office.
Feeley-Harnik, G. 1991. *A Green Estate: Restoring Independence in Madagascar*, Washington, DC: Smithsonian Institution Press.
Feeley-Harnik, G. 1997. 'Death, mourning, and ancestors', in J. Middleton (ed.),

Encyclopedia of Africa South of the Sahara, vol. 1, pp. 406–16, New York: Charles Scribner and Sons.

Fiawoo, D. K. 1978. 'Some patterns in foster care in Ghana', in C. Oppong et al. (eds), *Marriage, Fertility and Parenthood in West Africa*, pp. 273–88, Canberra: Australian National University.

Fortes, M. 1963. 'Time and social structure: an Ashanti case study', in M. Fortes (ed.), *Studies Presented to A. R. Radcliffe-Brown*, pp. 54–84, New York: Russell and Russell.

Fortes, M. 1978. 'Family, marriage, and fertility in West Africa', in C. Oppong at al. (eds), *Marriage, Fertility, and Parenthood in West Africa*, vol. I, pp. 17–54, Canberra: Australian National University.

Foucault, M., 1973. *The Birth of the Clinic*, New York: Vintage Books.

Francis, P. 1984. '"For the use and common benefit of all Nigerians": consequences of the 1978 land nationalization', *Africa* 54: 5–28.

Francis, P. 1998. *Hard Lessons: primary schools, community, and social capital in Nigeria*, Washington DC: The World Bank.

Fricke, T. 1997. 'Culture theory and demographic process: towards a thicker demography', in D. Kertzer and T. Fricke (eds), *Anthropological Demography: towards a new synthesis*, pp. 248–77, Chicago: University of Chicago Press.

Gage, A. 1998. 'Premarital childbearing, unwanted fertility and maternity care in Kenya and Namibia', *Population Studies* 52: 21–34.

Gilbert, M. 1988. 'The sudden death of a millionaire: conversion and consensus in a Ghanaian kingdom', *Africa* 58 (3): 291–313.

Goody, E. 1982. *Parenthood and Social Reproduction*, Cambridge: Cambridge University Press.

Goody, E. 1984, 'Parental strategies: calculation or sentiment?', in H. Medick and D. Sabean (eds), *Interest and Emotion*, pp. 266–77, Cambridge: Cambridge University Press.

Goody, J. 1990. 'Futures of the family in rural Africa', in G. McNicoll and M. Cain (eds), *Rural Development and Population: institutions and policy*, supplement to *Population and Development Review* 15: 119–44.

Greenhalgh, S. 1988. 'Fertility as mobility: Sinic transitions', *Population and Development Review* 14: 629–74.

Greenhalgh, S. 1990. 'Toward a political economy of fertility: anthropological contributions', *Population and Development Review* 16: 85–106.

Greenhalgh, S. 1995. 'Anthropology theorizes reproduction: integrating practice, political economic, and feminist perspectives', in S. Greenhalgh (ed.), *Situating Fertility: Anthropology and Demographic Inquiry*, pp. 3–52, Cambridge: Cambridge University Press.

Guyer, J. 1993. '"Toiling Ingenuity": food regulation in Britain and Nigeria', *American Ethnologist* 20 (4): 797–817.

Guyer, J. 1994. 'Lineal identities and lateral networks: the logic of polyandrous motherhood', in C. Bledsoe and G. Pison (eds), *Nuptiality in Sub-Saharan Africa*, pp. 231–52, Oxford: Clarendon Press.

Guyer, J. 1997. *An African Economic Niche: farming to feed Ibadan, 1968–88*, Edinburgh: Edinburgh University Press for the International African Institute.

Gyepi-Garbrah, B. 1985. *Adolescent Fertility in Nigeria*, Boston: Pathfinder Foundation.

Hammer, M. and C. Sutton. 1988. 'The social world of the Yoruba child', in S. Salzinger et al. (eds), *Social Networks of Children, Adolescents, and College Students*, pp. 285–303, Hillsdale, NJ: Lawrence Erlbaum.

Hefner, R. 1993. 'Introduction: world building and the rationality of conversion', in R. Hefner (ed.), *Conversion to Christianity: Historical and Anthropological Perspectives on a Great Transformation*, pp. 3–44, Berkeley: University of California Press.
Hertz, R. [1907] 1960. 'A contribution to the study of the collective representation of death', in R. and C. Needham, trans., *Death and the Right Hand*, pp. 27–86, Glencoe, IL: Free Press.
Hill, A. 1997. 'Truth lies in the eye of the beholder: the nature of evidence in demography and anthropology', in D. Kertzer and T. Fricke (eds), *Anthropological Demography: toward a new synthesis*, pp. 223–47, Chicago: University of Chicago Press.
Hill, P. 1977. *Population, Prosperity, and Poverty: rural Kano, 1900 and 1970*, Cambridge: Cambridge University Press.
Hobsbawm, E. and T. Ranger (eds). 1983. *The Invention of Tradition*, Cambridge: Cambridge University Press.
Hocart, A. M. 1937. 'Kinship systems', *Anthropos* 32: 345–51.
Hocart, A. M. 1987. *Imagination and Proof*, Tucson: University of Arizona Press.
Hodgson, D. 1983. 'Demography as social science and policy science', *Population and Development Review* 9 (1): 1–34.
Hodgson, D. 1988. 'Orthodoxy and revisionism in American demography', *Population and Development Review* 14 (4): 541–69.
Hollos, M. 1992. 'Why is it difficult to take a census in Nigeria?' *Historical Methods* 25 (1): 12–19.
Hollos, M. and U. Larsen. 1997. 'From lineage to conjugality: the social context of fertility decisions among the Pare of Northern Tanzania', *Social Science & Medicine* 45 (3): 361–72.
Hunt, N. 1999. *A Colonial Lexicon of Birth Ritual, Medicalization, and Mobility in the Congo*, Durham, NC: Duke University Press.
Idowu, E. B. 1962. *Olodumare, God in Yoruba Belief*, London: Longman.
Iro, M. 1987. *The Population Censuses of Nigeria From Colonial Times – an evaluation of their coverage and accuracy*, Okigwe: M. I. Iro.
Isaac, B. and S. Conrad. 1982. 'Child fosterage among the Mende of Upper Bambara Chiefdom, Sierra Leone: rural-urban and occupational comparisons', *Ethnology* 21 (3): 243–57.
Isiugo-Abanihe, U. 1985. 'Child-fosterage in West Africa', *Population and Development Review* 11 (1): 53–73.
Jackson, M. 1977. *The Kuranko*, London: C. Hurst.
Jeffery, R. and A. Basu. 1996. 'Schooling as contraception?' in R. Jeffery and A. Basu (eds), *Girls' Schooling, Women's Autonomy and Fertility Change in South Asia*, pp. 15–47, New Dehli: Sage Publications.
Jewkes, R. and K. Wood. 1998. 'Competing discourses of vital registration and personhood: perspectives from rural South Africa', *Social Science & Medicine* 46 (8): 1,043–56.
Johnson, S. 1921. *The History of the Yorubas*, Lagos: CSS Bookshops.
Kahn, A. and L. Holt. 1990. *The A–Z of Women's Sexuality*, New York: Facts on File.
Kaplan, R. 2000. *The Coming Anarchy: shattering the dreams of the post Cold War*, New York: Random House.
Kawonise, S. 1997. 'Civil society in a mixed urban and rural area: Ijebu-Ode, Ogun State', in A. Adedeji and O. Otite (eds), *Nigeria: renewal from the roots?*, pp. 108–37, London: Zed Books.
Kertzer, D. 1995. 'Political-economic and cultural explanations of demographic

behavior' in S. Greenhalgh (ed.), *Situating Fertility*, pp. 29–52, Cambridge: Cambridge University Press.
Kertzer, D. and D. Arel (eds). 2002. *Census and Identity: the politics of race, ethnicity, and language in national census*, Cambridge: Cambridge University Press.
Kertzer, D. and T. Fricke. 1997. 'Toward an anthropological demography', in D. Kertzer and T. Fricke (eds), *Anthropological Demography: toward a new synthesis*, pp. 1–35, Chicago: University of Chicago Press.
Krapf-Askari, E. 1966. 'Time and classifications: an ethnographic and historical case-study', *Odu* 2 (2): 3–18.
Kuczynski, R. R. 1937. *Colonial Population*, London: Oxford University Press.
Kunitz, S. 1994. *Disease and Social Diversity: the European impact on the health of non-Europeans*, Oxford: Oxford University Press.
Laqueur, T. 1990. *Sexuality: from the Greeks to Freud*, Cambridge: Harvard University Press.
Láwuyì, Olatunde B. 1991. 'The social marketing of elites: the advertised self in obituaries and congratulations in some Nigerian dailies', *Africa* 61 (2): 247–263.
Láwuyì, Olatunde B. 1993. 'The dialogue with the living: biography in the order of a Christian's funeral service in Yoruba society', *Journal of Religion in Africa* 21 (9): 227–40.
Levine, R. 1982. 'Gusii funerals', *Ethos* 10 (1): 26–65.
Lloyd, C., C. Kaufman, and P. Hewett. 2000. 'Implications for fertility change of the spread of primary schooling in sub-Saharan Africa', *Population and Development Review* 26 (3): 483–515.
Lloyd, P. 1962. *Yoruba Land Law*, New York: Oxford University Press.
Lloyd, P. 1966. 'Agnatic and cognatic descent among the Yoruba', *Man* 1 (4): 484–500.
Lloyd, P. 1968a. 'Divorce among the Yorubas', *American Anthropologist* 70: 67–81.
Lloyd, P. 1968b. 'Conflict theory and Yoruba kingdoms', in I. M. Lewis (ed.), *History and Social Anthropology*, pp. 25–61, London: Tavistock.
Lloyd, P. 1970. 'Ondo descent', *Man* 5 (2): 310–12.
Lucas, A. O. 1980. 'What we inherited', in E. E. Sabben-Clarke, D. J. Bradley and K. Kirkwood (eds), *Health in Tropical Africa During the Colonial Period*, pp. 239–44, Oxford: Clarenden Press.
Maier, K. 2000. *This House has Fallen: midnight in Nigeria*, New York: Public Affairs.
Malthus, T. [1798] 1914. *An Essay on Population*, New York: E. P. Dutton.
Mann, K. 1986. *Marrying Well*, Cambridge: Cambridge University Press.
Marx, K. [1867] 1906. *Capital: a critique of political economy*, New York: The Modern Library.
Matory, J. L. 1994. *Sex and the Empire That is No More*, Minneapolis: University of Minnesota.
Mauss, M. 1973. 'Techniques of the body', *Economy and Society* 2: 70–88.
McCall, J. 1995. 'Rethinking ancestors in Africa', *Africa* 65 (2): 258–62.
Medick, H. and D. Sabean. 1984. *Interest and Emotion: essays on the study of family and kinship*, Cambridge: Cambridge University Press.
Meek, C. K. [1946] 1968. *Land Law and Custom in the Colonies*, London: Frank Cass.
Millman, W. 1930. 'Health instruction in African schools: suggestions for a curriculum', *Africa* 3: 484–500.
Moore, S. F. 1986. *Social Facts and Fabrications*, Cambridge: Cambridge University Press.
Moore, S. F. 1987. 'Explaining the present: theoretical dilemmas in processual ethnography, *American Ethnologist* 14: 727–36.

Moore, S. F. 1991. 'From giving and lending to selling: property transactions reflecting historical changes on Kilimanjaro', in K. Mann and R. Roberts (eds), *Law in Colonial Africa*, pp. 108–27, Portsmouth, NH: Heinemann Educational Books.

Moran, M. 1992. 'Civilized servants: child fosterage and training for status among the Glebo of Liberia', in K. Hansen (ed.), *African Encounters with Domesticity*, pp. 98–115, New Brunswick, NJ: Rutgers University Press.

Morton-Williams, P. No date. *Cinema in Rural Nigeria: a field study of the impact of fundamental education films on rural audiences in Nigeria*, Lagos: Federal Information Service.

Morton-Williams, P. 1960. 'Yoruba responses to the fear of death', *Africa* 30 (1): 34–40.

Mott, F. and S. Mott. 1985. 'Household fertility decisions in West Africa: a comparison of male and female survey results', *Studies in Family Planning* 16 (2): 88–99.

Myers, Gregory W. 1990. 'This is not your land: an analysis of the impact of the Land Use Act in Southwest Nigeria', unpublished PhD dissertation, Madison: University of Wisconsin.

National Automobile Chamber of Commerce. 1928. *Handbook of Automobiles*, New York: National Automobile Chamber of Commerce.

National Population Commission, Nigeria. 2000. *Nigeria Demographic and Health Survey 1999*, Calverton, MD: National Population Commission and ORC/Macro.

Netting, R., R. Wilk and E. Arnould. 1984. *Households: comparative and historical studies of the household group*, Berkeley: University of California Press.

Nichols, D., O. A. Ladipo, J. M. Paxman and E. O. Otolorin. 1986. 'Sexual behavior, contraceptive practice, and reproductive health among Nigerian adolescents', *Studies in Family Planning* 17 (2): 100-6.

Nigeria, Federal Office of Statistics, and Demographic and Health Surveys/Macro Systems. 1992. *Nigerian Demographic and Health Survey 1990*, Federal Office of Statistics and Macro Systems, Lagos and Columbia, MD.

Ọbáyẹmí, A. 1976. 'The Yoruba and Edo-speaking peoples and their neighbours before 1600', in S. Ajayi and M. Crowther (eds), *A History of West Africa*, vol. I, 2nd edn, pp. 196–263, London: Longman.

Obiechina, E. N. 1973. *An African Popular Literature: a study of Onitsha market pamphlets*, Cambridge: Cambridge University Press

Obogbaimhe, E. A. 1983. *Primary Health Education*, vols 1–6, Ìbàdàn: African Universities Press.

Ogbuagu, Stella C. 1991. 'Changing burial practices in Nigeria: some evidence from the obituaries', *Savannah* 12 (1): 21–33.

Ogunlesi, T. O. 1968. 'Before and after a population census operation in Nigeria', in J. Caldwell and C. Okonjo (eds), *The Population of Tropical Africa*, pp. 117–22, London: Longman.

Ògúntúyì, A. 1979. *History of Ekiti*, Ìbàdàn: Bisi Books.

Ọjọ́, G. J. A. 1966. *Yoruba Culture*, London: University of London Press.

Okediji, F. O. and W. Ogionwo. 1973. *Experiment in Population Education and Attitude Change: an evaluation of the film 'My Brother's Children' in two rural Nigerian communities*, Ìbàdàn: Africa Regional Council of the International Planned Parenthood Federation, London, and the Family Planning Council of Nigeria.

Okeem, E. O. and W. E. Okeem. 1987. *Health is Wealth*, Uruowulu-Obosi, Nigeria: Pacific Publishers.

Okri, B. 1991. *The Famished Road*, London: Vintage Press.

Ọlayinka, M. S. 1987. *Sex Education and Marital Guidance*, Lagos: Lantern Books.
Olupọna, J. K. 1991. *Kingship, Religion, and Rituals in a Nigerian Community*, Stockholm: Almqvist and Wiksell International.
Olúsànyà, P. O. 1966. 'Adequacy of existing census and vital statistics for demographic research and planning', *Nigerian Journal of Economic and Social Studies* 8 (1): 141–50.
Olúsànyà, P. O. 1967. 'Cultural barriers to family planning among the Yoruba', *Studies in Family Planning* 37 (1): 13-16.
Olúsànyà, P. O. 1970. 'A note on some factors affecting the stability of marriage among the Yoruba of Western Nigeria', *Journal of Marriage and the Family* 32: 150–5.
Olúsànyà, P. O. 1983. *Nigeria's Demographic Delusion: a critical examination of the census controversy*, Lagos: University of Lagos Press.
Olúsànyà, P. O. 1985. 'Some aspects of family planning programmes and fertility in selected ECA member states', African Population Studies Series, no. 9, Addis Adaba: UNECA.
Olúsànyà, P. O. 1988. 'Population with the context of family structure and function', in P. O. Olúsànyà and 'Lai Olurode (eds), *Developments in Introductory Sociology*, pp. 77–100, Ikeja: John West Publications.
Olúsànyà, P. O. 1989a. 'Evolution and status of family planning in Nigeria', in *Readings in Family Planning Policies and Programmes in Africa*, pp. 408–450, Legon: University of Ghana.
Olúsànyà, P. O. 1989b. 'Human reproduction in Africa: fact, myth and the martyr syndrome', *Research for Development* 6: 69–97.
Omídèyí, A. 1987. 'Status, cultural beliefs and fertility behaviour among Yoruba women', in J. Ẹbigbọla and E. van de Walle (eds), *The Cultural Roots of African Fertility Regimes: proceedings of the Ife Conference*, pp. 151–65, Ile-Ife: Obafemi Awolowo University and Philadelphia: University of Pennsylvania.
Ọmọ́dára, V. and T. Dáre. 1984. *Ilesanmi Health Education Course Book*, vols 1–5, Ilesa, Nigeria: Ilesanmi Press.
Ondo State, Ministry of Health. 1989. *Ondo State, Nigeria Demographic and Health Survey, 1986*, Columbia, MD: IRD/Macro International.
Onwudiegwu, U. 1993. 'The effect of a depressed economy on the utilization of maternal health services: the Nigerian experience', *Journal of Obstetrics and Gynaecology* 13: 311–14.
Orùbuloyè, I. O. 1981a. *Abstinence as a Method of Birth Control: fertility and child-spacing practices among rural Yoruba women of Nigeria*, pp. 22–41, Canberra: Australian National University.
Orùbuloyè, I. O. 1981b. 'Education and socio-demographic change in Nigeria', in H. Ware (ed.), *Women, Education, and Modernization of the Family in West Africa*, Canberra: Australian National University Press.
Osuafor, T. O. K. 1997. *A–Z of How to Organize a Funeral Ceremony*, Enugu: CECTA.
Owa J. A., A. I. Osinaike, and A. M. de L. Costello. 1992. 'Charging for health services in developing countries', *The Lancet* 340: 732.
Owóẹyẹ, K. 1999. *Events and History of Itapa-Ekiti*, Ann Arbor: Kolossos Press.
Owomoyela, O. 1988. *A ki I: Yoruba proscriptive and prescriptive proverbs*, Lanham, MD: University Press of America.
Oyèmádé, A. and T. Ògúnmúyiwá. 1981. 'Sociocultural factors in a rural Nigerian community', *Studies in Family Planning* 12 (3): 109–11.
Packard, R. 1997. 'Visions of postwar health and development and their impact on public health interventions in the developing world', in F. Cooper and R.

Packard (eds), *International Development and the Social Sciences*, pp. 93–115, Berkeley: University of California Press.

Page, H. 1989. 'Childrearing versus childbearing: co-residence of mother and child in sub-Saharan Africa', in R. Lesthaeghe (ed.), *Reproduction and Social Organization in Sub-Saharan Africa*, pp. 401–41, Berkeley: University of California Press.

Parrinder, G. 1953 *Religion in an African City*, Westport, CT: Negro University Press.

Peel, J. D. Y. 1968a. 'Syncretism and religious change', *Comparative Studies in Society and History* 10 (2): 121–41.

Peel, J. D. Y. 1968b. *Aladura: a religious movement among the Yoruba*, London: Oxford University Press for the International African Institute.

Peel, J. D. Y. 1978. 'Olaju: a Yoruba concept of development', *The Journal of Development Studies* 14 (2): 139–65.

Peel, J. D. Y. 1983. *Ijeshas and Nigerians*, Cambridge: Cambridge University Press.

Peel, J. D. Y. 1990. 'The pastor and the *babalawo*: the interaction of religions in nineteenth-century Yorubaland, *Africa* 60 (3): 338–69.

Piot, C. 1999. *Remotely Global: village modernity in West Africa*, Chicago: University of Chicago Press.

Popoola, D. 1993. 'Nigeria: consequences for health', in A. Adépòjù (ed.), *The Impact of Structural Adjustment on the Population of Africa*, pp. 92–7, Portsmouth NH: Heinemann, and London: James Currey.

Population Association of Nigeria. 1990. *Everybody's Guide to the Nigerian Census*, Ìbàdàn: PAN.

Rea, W. 1995 '"No Event, No History": The Masquerades of Ikole Ekiti', unpublished PhD thesis, University of East Anglia, Norwich.

Rea, W. 1998. 'Rationalising culture: youths, elites and masquerade politics', *Africa* 68 (1): 98–117.

Renne, E. 1992. 'Polyphony in the courts: child custody cases in Kabba District Court, 1925–1979', *Ethnology* 31 (3): 219–32.

Renne, E. 1993a. 'Condom use and the popular press in Nigeria', *Health Transition Review* 3: 41–56.

Renne, E. 1993b. 'Changes in adolescent sexuality and the perception of virginity in a Southwestern Nigerian village', *Sexual networking and HIV/AIDS in West Africa*, supplement to *Health Transition Review* 3: 121–33.

Renne, E.1993c. 'An anthropological approach to the demographic analysis of child fostering in Nigeria', *Proceedings*, vol. 4, pp. 327–42, IUSSP 1993 conference, Montreal.

Renne, E. 1993d. 'Fertility strategies and gender ideology in Ekiti Yoruba society', *Studies in Family Planning* 24 (6): 343–53.

Renne, E. 1995a. 'Houses, fertility, and the Nigerian Land Use Act', *Population and Development Review* 21 (1): 113–26.

Renne, E. 1995b. *Cloth That Does Not Die*, Seattle: University of Washington Press.

Renne, E. 1996a. 'The pregnancy that doesn't stay: the practice and perception of abortion by Ekiti Yoruba women', *Social Science & Medicine* 42 (4): 483–94.

Renne, E. 1996b. 'Virginity cloths and vaginal coverings in Ekiti, Nigeria', in H. Hendrickson (ed.), *Clothing and Difference: embodied identities in colonial and post-colonial Africa*, pp. 19–33, Duke University Press.

Renne, E. 1996c. 'Shifting boundaries of fertility change in Southwestern Nigeria', supplement to *Health Transition Review* 6: 169–90.

Renne, E. 1997a. 'Local and institutional interpretations of IUDs in Southwestern Nigeria', *Social Science & Medicine* 44 (8): 1141–8.

Renne, E. 1997b. '"Traditional modernity" and the economics of handwoven cloth production in Southwestern Nigeria', *Economic Development and Cultural Change* 45 (4): 773–92.
Renne, E. 1998a. 'History, anthropology, and traditions of burial' in N. Ejituwu (ed.), *The Multi-Disciplinary Approach to African History: essays in honour of Ebiegberi Joe Alagoa*, pp. 309–30, Port Harcourt: University of Port Harcourt Press.
Renne, E. 1998b. 'Postinor use among young women in Southwestern Nigeria: a research note', *Reproductive Health Matters* 6 (11): 107–14.
Renne, E. 2000a. 'Building the Itapa-Ikole Road in Southwestern Nigeria from a local perspective', *The Journal of the International Institute* 7 (2): 6–7, 22.
Renne, E. 2000b. 'Nigeria's "Demographic Delusion" and the 1991 census exercise in a Southwestern Nigerian town', in J. A. Ẹbigbọla and E. Renne (eds), *Population and Development Issues*, Ìbàdàn: African Book Builders Ltd.
Renne, E. 2001a. '"Cleaning the inside" and the regulation of menstruation in Southwestern Nigeria', in E. van de Walle and E. Renne (eds), *Regulating Menstruation: beliefs, practices, interpretations*, pp. 187–201, Chicago: University of Chicago Press.
Renne, E. 2001b. 'Twinship in an Ekiti Yoruba town', *Ethnology* 40 (1): 63–78.
Renne, E. 2002. Fundamentals of fertility: Cosmology and conversion in a Southwestern Nigerian town. *Journal of the Royal Anthropological Institute* 8(3): 551–69.
Richards, A. I. 1932. *Hunger and Work in a Savage Tribe*, London: Routledge.
Richards, A. I. 1935. 'The village census in the study of culture contact', *Africa* 8: 20–33.
Richards, A. I. 1940. 'Bemba marriage and present economic conditions', Rhodes-Livingstone Institute, Paper no. 4.
Richards, A. I. 1941. 'A problem of anthropological approach', *Bantu Studies* 15: 45–52.
Richards, P. 1996. *Fighting for the Rain Forest: war, youth & resources in Sierra Leone*, Oxford: IAI and James Currey, and Portsmouth: Heinemann for the International African Institute.
Robertson, A. F. 1991. *Beyond the Family: the social organization of human reproduction*, Berkeley: University of California Press.
Sargent, C. F. 1989. *Maternity, Medicine, and Power: reproductive decisions in urban Benin*, Berkeley: University of California Press.
Saro-Wiwa, K. 1985. *Sozaboy*, Port Harcourt: Saros International.
Schildkrout, E. 1973. 'The fostering of children in urban Ghana: problems of ethnographic analysis in a multicultural context', *Urban Anthropology* 2: 48–73.
Schneider, J. and P. Schneider. 1996. *Festival of the Poor: fertility decline & the ideology of class in Sicily, 1860–1960*, Tucson: University of Arizona Press.
Sembane, O. 1992. *Guelwaar*, New York: New Yorker Films.
Sen, A. 1994. 'Population: delusion and reality', *New York Review of Books* 41 (15): 62–71.
Sen, A. 1999. *Development as Freedom*, New York: Knopf.
Sharpless, J. 1997. 'Population science, private foundations, and development aid', in F. Cooper and R. Packard (eds), *International Development and the Social Sciences*, pp. 176–200, Berkeley: University of California Press.
Simmel, G. 1950. *The Sociology of George Simmel*, New York: Free Press.
Simpson, G. 1980. *Yoruba Religion and Medicine in Ibadan*, Ìbàdàn: Ìbàdàn University Press.

Smith, B. 1981. 'Federal-state relations in Nigeria', *African Affairs* 80 (320): 355–78.
Southon, Arthur. 1931[?]. *Ilesha & Beyond! The story of the Wesley Guild medical work in West Africa*, London: Cargate Press.
Ṣóyinká, W. 1988. *Ake: the years of childhood*. Ìbàdàn: Spectrum.
Ṣóyinká, W. 1989. *Isara: a voyage around Essay*, Ìbàdàn: Fountain.
Stokes, C. S. and W. A. Schutjer. 1984. 'Access to land and fertility in developing countries', in W. Schutjer and C. Stokes (eds), *Rural Development and Human Fertility*, pp. 195–215, New York: Macmillan.
Stokes, C. S., W. A. Schutjer and R. A. Bulatao. 1986. 'Is the relationship between landholding and fertility spurious?', *Population Studies* 40: 305–11.
Synge, R. 2001. 'Recent history', in *Africa South of the Sahara 2001*, 30th edn, pp. 864–75, London: Europa Publications.
Thomas, N. 1991. 'Land, fertility, and the population establishment', *Population Studies* 45: 379–97.
Townsend, N. 1997. 'Reproduction in anthropology and demography', in D. Kertzer and T. Fricke (eds), *Anthropological Demography: toward a new synthesis*, pp. 96–114, Chicago: University of Chicago Press.
Trager, L. 1997. 'Structural adjustment, hometowns, and local development in Nigeria', in R. Blanton, P. Peregrine, D. Winslow, and T. Hall (eds), *Economic Analysis beyond the Local System*, Monographs in Economic Anthropology no. 13. pp. 255–90, Lanham, MD: University Press of America.
Trager, L. 1998. 'Home-town linkages and local development in South-western Nigeria: whose agenda? What impact?', *Africa* 68 (3): 360–82.
Trager, L. 2001. *Yoruba Hometowns: community, identity and development in Nigeria*, Boulder, CO: Lynne Rienner.
Turner, B. 1984. *The Body and Society*, Oxford: Basil Blackwell.
Turner, H. W. 1967. *History of an African Independent Church* (vols 1–2), Oxford: Clarendon Press.
Turner, V. 1957. *Schism and Continuity in an African Society*, Manchester: Manchester University Press.
Tutuọla, A. 1952. *The Palm-Wine Drinkard and his Dead Palm-Wine Tapster in the Deads' Town*, London: Faber & Faber.
Udo, R. K. 1968. 'Population and politics in Nigeria', in J. Caldwell and C. Okonjo (eds), *The Population of Tropical Africa*, pp. 97–105, London: Longman.
Usua, E. J., and G. O. Dada. 1987. *Onibonoje Primary Health Education*, vols 1–6, Ìbàdàn: Onibonoje Publishers.
van Beusekom, M. 2002. *Negotiating Development: African farmers and colonial experts at the Office du Niger, 1920–1960*, Portsmouth, NH: Heinemann.
van de Walle, E. 1992. 'Fertility transition, conscious choice, and numeracy', *Demography* 29 (4): 487–502.
Vaughan, M. 1991. *Curing Their Ills: colonial power and African illness*, Stanford: Stanford University Press.
Vaughan, O. 2000. *Nigerian Chiefs: traditional power in modern politics, 1890s–1990s*, Rochester: University of Rochester Press.
Verger, P. 1968. 'La société *egbe orun* des *abiku*', Bulletin IFAN (Serie B) 30: 1,448–87.
Vigarello, G. 1988. *Concepts of Cleanliness: changing attitudes in France since the Middle Ages*, Cambridge: Cambridge University Press.
Vincent, J. 1986. 'System and process, 1974–1985', *Annual Review of Anthropology* 15: 99–119.

Weber, M. 1946. *From Max Weber: Essays in Sociology*, H. Gerth and C. W. Mills (eds), New York: Oxford University Press.
Webster, J. B. 1964. *The African Churches Among the Yoruba 1888–1922*, Oxford: Clarendon Press.
Widner, J., with A. Mundt. 1998. 'Researching social capital in Africa', *Africa* 68 (1): 1–24.
Yesufu, T. M. 1968. 'The politics and economics of Nigeria's population census', in J. Caldwell and C. Okonjo (eds), *The Population of Tropical Africa*, pp. 97–105, London: Longman.

INDEX

References in *italic* refer to illustrations.

Abacha, S., 10, 185–6, 187–8, 193, 205, 230–1, 248n10, 249n13, 250n11
àbíkú ('born to die' children), 66–7, 245n7
　burial of, 119–21
　decline in, 66
　rebirth of, 127
Abíọ́lá, M., 186, 248n9
abortion, 84–5, 240n8; *see also* virginity
Adépọ̀jù, A., 14, 248n5
Adó-Èkìtì, *22, 23*, 28, 37, 129, 191,199, 210, 247n5
　Adó kingdom, 26–7
　as colonial administrative centre, 77
　as state capital, 187, 188
　as trading centre, 46
age, 175, 213
　heaping, *212*, 213
　numerical, 175, 213, *214*, 250n3, 251n4, 251n5
　and birth registration, 176, 180–1, 195
　social, 175, 213
Aiyédé-Èkìtì, 22, 27, 29, 236n4
àjà mùta, 32, *32*, 237n22, 243n2; *see also* funerals, Ọbalókè
Àkànle, A., 203, 209
Àkúrẹ́, 28, 43, 129, 140, 141, 169, 187
antenatal health care, 65, 66
anthems, 36–7
anthropology, 15, 214
antisocial behaviour, 72, 81, 85; *see also* witchcraft
Àorogún Hill, 20, 235n3
Awólọ́wọ̀, Ọ., 194–5
　'Life More Abundant', 18, 235n15
Ayégbajú-Èkìtì *see* Ìtàpá-Èkìtì

baálé (house head), 7, 30, 46, 51, 74, 77, 182, 240n6
　authority undermined, 77
baálẹ̀ (village head), 182, 240n6; *see also* Bale
babaláwo (herbalist–diviner), 24, 62, 83, 118, 119, 120, 124, 125, 240n5

Babangida, I., 10, 11, 186, 187, 188, 190, 205, 246n17
Bale (*baálẹ̀*, village head), 28, 77, 182, 240n6
Bánkọlé, A., 53, 251n5
Barber, K., 34, 36, 160, 247n4
Barnes, S., 169
Beidelman, T., 250n13
Berry, S., 157, 174
'big man' *see* patron–client relations
'big woman' *see* patron–client relations
'bio-social gap', 240n8
birth *see* childbirth, Ìtàpá Maternity Centre
birth records *see* registration
　a ti marki (marks), *frontispiece*, 175
　birth certificates, 176, 180–1
　birth dates on walls, *158*, 175, *176*
　òwìwí (beads), 175, 176, 248n1
Bledsoe, C., 16, 99
blood
　and child-fostering, 92, 99, 103–5
　and kin relations, 67, 89, 91, 95, 103, 105, 110
　and kinship obligations, 91, 92, 99, 100, 103, 105, 110
　menstrual, 82–3
　and virginity, 73, 74, 82
bodies *see* census, fertility, hygiene, infertility, vital registration
　counting of, 176–9
　and houses, 33–4
　as houses of spirit, 116
　individual and body politics, connections between, 17, 74, 196
　as metaphors for social relations, 7
　as 'narrative of culture', 72
　and perceptions of social change, 14–15, 17, 72, 74, 81–2, 143–4
　and personal strategies of health, 137–8, 153–4
　and traditional hygiene, 138–40, 148
Boserup, E., 205
boundaries *see* child-fostering, houseplots

270   POPULATION AND PROGRESS IN A YORUBA TOWN

crossing of, 7
of Ìtàpá-Èkìtì, 20–2, 26
of land, 18, 77, 165–7, 170, 172
social, 18, 89, 91
burials *see* funerals, graves, houses, land
    tenure, Ọbalókè
    and beliefs about the dead, 114, 126–7
    bush, 114, 118–20
    cemetery, 114, 117–18, 243n3
    of chiefs, 31–2, 111, 118, 119
    Christian, 115–20, 122, 129
    and claims to land, houses, political
        office, 114, 116
    of diviners (*babaláwo*), 118
    and family unity, 116
    in hometown, 43, 118, 129
    and houses, 33, *115*, 115–18, 128, 161
    of hunters, 118
    Islamic, 114, 115, 122
    of a king of Ìtàpá (Ọwátàpá), 118–19
    as morally appropriate, 114, 129
    of objects, 111, 122–3
    and rebirth of spirits in children, 117
    as reflection of wealth, 115–16
    and retention of selected ritual practice,
        123–5, 129–30
    of Ṣàngó priests (*Onísàngó*), 118, 119
    of strangers, 129
    as symbols of progress, 129
    and urban–rural ties, 129
burial practices, changes in, 120–4
    and conversion to Christianity, Islam,
        114, 121, 122–3
    and decline in infant and maternal
        mortality, 120–1
    and diminution of traditional chiefs'
        power, 114, 121, 130

Caldwell, J. C., 13, 15, 110, 144, 153, 198
cemeteries (*ilé isinkú*) *see* burials, funerals,
    graves
census, 43, 177
    de facto, 43
    de jure, 43
census-taking, 176
    and access to development funds, 182–3
    associated with 1918 influenza epidemic,
        179
    and categorisation of population, 177
    during colonial rule, 177
    and development planning, 177, 183
    as example of development, 178
    as objectification of citizenry, 177
    and state authority, 177
    and taxation, 178–9
    value of, 177, 180–1, 195
centrifugal movements, 23, 26, 32

countering kinship ideals, 34
and out-migration, 41
centrifugal and centripetal tendencies in
    Ìtàpá, 33, 36, 39–41, 42, 199–200
    dynamics of, 31–3
    Ìtàpá Day and quarter days, 39
    movement of people, 23, 26
    need for children, 36
centripetal movements, 23, 26
    and Ìtàpá Day, 41
    and kinship ideals, houses, 34
Chanock, M., 171–2
'charter myths', 25
child custody, 51
child labour *see* child-fostering, labour,
    infrastructure
child mortality, 66
    and healthcare, 152
    and uncertainty, 67
childbearing preferences *see* children
    wanted
childbirth, 42, 58–66; *see also* Ìtàpá
    Maternity Centre, Methodist
    Maternity Centre, Ìkọlé
    and clinic staff, 60, 65
    during colonial period, 62–5
    and contigent events, 59, 60, 61–2
    decline in clinic and hospital deliveries,
        65–6
    expenses, 60, 65–6, 240n19
    home, 42, 58–62
    hospital as 'proper' birthplace, 60
    and maternal education, 58, 61
    and *ọ̀làjú* (enlightenment), 62
childcare, 'good', 54
    defined, 104–5
    and dress, 143, 152
    and educated parents, 103–4
    and good hygiene, 152–4
    by the 'real parents', 104, 105
    re-evaluated, 67
child-fostering (*gbàgbàbọ́ ọmọ*), 89–110,
    242n7
    and child labour, 89, 92, 100, 101–3, 105
    contested reassessment of, 89–92, 98–
        101, 103–10
    contradictory attitudes toward, 91, 105,
        106
    and crisis care, 90, 106–7, 110
    defined, 89, 95
    and discipline, 89
    and economic constraints, 105, 109
    and education, 90, 97, 98, 99, 103–4
    as exploitation of children, 90, 99, 100–1
    and fertility, 91–2, 109–10
    and food, 103, 104
    increase in, 106

and indulgent grandmothers, 90, 104
in-fostering, 42, 67, 96–7
and kin, 95–6, 104–5
as moral act, 91, 100
and moral development, 90
moral evaluation of, 92, 104–5, 110
out-fostering, 92, 97, 109
and population growth, 67, 91–2
reassessment of, 54, 67, 90–2, 99–100, 104–6, 107
rejection of, 90–2, 99–100
and social capital, 92, 241n3
and substitution of cash, 105
child-rearing practices
and education of parents, 103–4, 152
and hygiene, 135, 139, 152–4
children (ọmọ), 7; see also children of Ìtàpá (ọmọ Ìtàpá), names
and family name, 152
as source of pride, 152
children wanted
discussed with spouse, 87–88
by men, 52–4, 96, 106
'up to God', 53, 87, 239n11
re-evaluated, 67, 152–4, 170, 207
by women, 52–4, 170
child-spacing, 11, *12*, 87
'Space your children', *12*, 138, 191, 194, 235n9
Christianity *see* funerals, marriage, virginity
and churches in Ìtàpá, 19–20
and church-sponsored schools, 9
and conversion, 9, 10, 130, 161, 237n19
and maternity clinics, 42
and Western education, 9
civilian rule, 186, 205
civilisation (*ìgbàlódé*), 136, 245n5
cleanliness (*ìmọ́tótó*), 140; *see also* hygiene
and bathing, 138–9, 142, 143, 151
concepts of, 138–45, 147–52
and dental care, 138, 139, 140, 142, 143, 152
and dress, 138–9, 140, 142, 143, 152
and economic wherewithal, 140, 152
and food, 139, 140, 142, 143
and 'modern' forms of hygiene, 139, 140, 142, 143, 152–4
moral implications of, 137–8, 140, 142
and nail care, 138, 140, 141, 151, 153
and school inspections, 140–1, *141*
Coale, A., 5, 88, 234n2
coffins (*opósín*)
and Christian burial, 115
filled with cloth, 111
prices, 111
relaxing in, 116
and secret burial, 111

Cohn, B., 16, 177, 248n2
colonial court system, 51; *see also* Ìtàpá-Èkìtì, Customary Court
and customary court attendance, 77–8
and divorce, 51, 77–8, 87
and introduction of Native Authority courts, 77
and request for Native Authority court in Ìtàpá, 29
Colonial Development Fund, 141
colonial Native Authority *see* colonial rule
colonial officers, British
Alexander, D., 179
Bromage, J., 179, 182
Davidson, J., 179–80
Simpson, W., 29, 201, 250n7
Swayne, A. C. C., 27, 28–9
Tucker, R., 77
colonial rule, British *see* colonial court system, public health interventions, sanitary inspection
and implementation of census, 179, 181–2
and vital registration, 179–80
community labour (*àáró*), 156, 197
competition for resources, 39
complementary strategies
of fostering in but not out, 106–10
of houses and children, 170
Condorcet, M., 205–7
contingencies, economic and political, 59, 60, 61, 160; *see also* uncertainty
contraceptive use, 11, 65, 232–3, *233*; *see also* family planning
contradictions *see* state policies and programmes
Federal governmental policies retarding development, 159, 195–6, 208
conversion, 9, 10, 113, 120, 127, 130, 160; *see also* Christianity, funerals, Islam
cultural meaning of things, 16
customary (Native Authority) courts *see* colonial court system

Dada, S. A., 20–1, 23, 201–2
African Church leader, 198
criticism of, 199
education of, 198, 249n3
funding education of townspeople, 198–9
funeral of, 203–4, 210
Ìtàpá Day speech, 39
and Ìtàpá dispute settlement, 198, 203
and Ìtàpá Progressive Union, 198, 199
letter writing campaign, 199, 249n2, 249n4
and local development, 197–9, 210
on misuse of development funds, 201–2

death *see* burials, funerals, graves, rebirth
debt repayment, 205
delivery fees *see* childbirth
demographic–anthropological research, 14–17
   and cultural analysis, 15, 16
   distinctive disciplinary evidence, 15
   on fertility, 14–17
   and political economic perspective, 15, 16
   quantitative and qualitative studies, 15
   research methods, Ìtàpá study, 211–14
demography, 15, 42
dependence of the dominant, 7–8
development (*idàgbàsókè*) *see* education, 'Four is enough' policy
   'on the cheap', 250n13
   of children and the town, 10
   compared with *òlàjú* (enlightenment), 192
   defined, 3, 10
   and equitable distribution of funds, 195
   and fertility, 3, 5
   hampered by lack of love, 40–1
   and hygiene, 138
   and limiting family size, 192
   locally sponsored, 149, 197, 198–9, 207, 208
   and politics, 205, 206
   and population growth, 18, 199, 207
   and population programmes, 192–3, 195
   'take-off', 207
development philanthropy, 203; *see also* Dada, S. A.
diagnostic things, 16–17, 235n14
dirty (*òbùn*)
   defined, 138
   and lice-infested, 142, 153
   moral implications, 138, 140, 148
'disciplines of the body', 136
divorce, 35, 51; *see also* colonial court system, marriage, virginity
   and child custody, 52
   introduction of courts for, 77–8
   and polygynous marriage, 52
dress, 9; *see also* childcare, cleanliness, hygiene
   of corpse, 31, 111, 112
   of dignitaries, 37
   of women dressed as men, 32

economy, declining, 10
   and childbirth practices, 58–62, 65–6
   and currency devaluation, 152
   and failure of state programmes, 194
   and population policy, 193
   and state revitalisation schemes, 10, 234n6

education *see* child-rearing, child-fostering, hygiene, infant mortality, virginity
   and authority, 72, 86, 144
   of childbearing women, 57, 61
   and decline of virginity, 79–81
   and development of Ìtàpá, 10
   and economic constraints on fertility, 130, 191–3
   and employment opportunities, 5, 13
   and expenses, 11, 53, 153, 235n8
   and fertility decline, 4–5
   and family size, 54, 144–5
   moral implications of, 9–10
   and *òlàjú*, 62, 79–81, 88
   and personal hygiene, 140
   primary, 11, 14, 18, 55, 58, 79–81, 87, 91, 98–9, 136, 138, 140–4, 145, 149, 151–2, 180, 246n18
   and quality of schools, 102
   and school attendance, 9
   secondary, 13, 14, 20, 54, 55, 58, 62, 66, 67, 84, 87, 88, 98–9, 150, 176, 190, 239n9, 239n11, 240n8, 242n6
   and 'sibling chain of assistance', 13, 198
   and spousal discussion of childbearing, 87–8
egbé (clubs, age groups), 8
   and age, 175
   bàbá egbé (male group leader), 7
   and Ìtàpá Day, 36, 37
   ìyá egbé (female group leader), 7
Egètún *see* Ìtàpá-Èkìtì, town sections
Ekiti Division, 77
Ekiti Kete (Èkìtì Together), 186, 188, *189*
Ekiti North Local Government, 29, 40, 65
Ekiti State, 22, *23*, 197
   benefits of, 5, 186–7, 188
   creation of, 5, 177, 178, 186–90, 193, 195
   Department of Population Activities, 190–3, 194
   Ekiti Forum, 187
   lobbying efforts for, 187–8
   population as justification for, 5, 188, 194
   and road-building, 197
   and state-sponsored projects, 189
Èkìtì Yoruba, 3, 77, 236n6; *see also* Ìtàpá-Èkìtì, Ekiti State
Eléköle (King of Ìkòlé-Èkìtì), 27, 40, 111; *see also* traditional chiefs
   and Julius Láyeni, 27–9
   and public health ordinance, 145–6, 246n15
Èwí of Adó-Èkìtì (King of Adó-Èkìtì), 188

family (ẹbí) see burial, houses, land tenure, marriage
  division of property, 34
  extended, 3, 8, 92, 105, 110, 207
  houses as dynasties, 30, 116
  meetings, 34, 44
  obligations, 67, 91, 92, 95, 98, 99, 100, 105, 110, 131, 167, 172, 199, 207
  streets, 25, 30
  unity and conflict, 34
family planning (fètò s'ọmọ bíbí), 11; see also contraceptive use
family size, benefits seen in reducing, 191–3, 195
federal policies and programmes, contradictory
  and distrust of national government, 173
  and failure of infrastructural support, 136, 145, 150–9, 194
  and family planning, 178
  and Land Use Act (Decree), 158, 159, 170–2, 173, 246n1
  and national census, 178, 195
  and population policies, 190, 193, 194
  and public sanitation, 136, 145–9
  reinforcing need for children, 5, 159, 173, 194
  retarding development, 159, 195–6, 208
  undermining participation in government programmes, 194, 195
Feeley-Harnik, G., 14, 33
fertility see total fertility rate, virginity
  beneficial for development, 3
  changes related to, 17, 172–4, 207
  cultural vs. economic explanations of, 173–4
  delayed, 83
  double-bind, 13
  meanings of, 5, 6–7
  moral evaluations of, 15, 16
  'natural', 16
  and political economic factors, 5, 17
  and pregnancy, 71–2, 75–6, 78, 79, 80, 81, 86
  reassessment of, 10, 13, 17, 54, 67, 152–4
  as 'reproductive stigma', 15
  terms for, 6–7
  and urban–rural ties, 174
fertility decline see contraceptive use, education, infant mortality
  'collaborative' approaches to, 206, 207
  and economic concerns, 5, 54
  and fertility transition theory, 16
  and lack of development, 208
  'override' approaches to, 206–7
  reasons for, 11
  universal explanations of, 5
  and Western education, 4–5, 11, 54, 152–4
  'within realm of conscious choice', 5, 88
fertility strategies, 14
  attracting people to town, 41
  lower infant and child mortality, 67
  more children, not fewer, 14, 67
followers ('children of the back', ọmọ ẹ̀hìn), 3
  and leaders, 3, 7
food see child-fostering, funerals
  and funerals, 112, 129
  and hygiene, 139, 140, 142, 143
  and mistreatment of foster children, 100, 103, 104
  placement in graves, 122–3
  as representation of rights and obligations, 100
  ritual distributions, 121–2
  and social relations, 100, 103
foster parents, 89–96
foster child time-use study, 101–3, 215–16
'Four is enough' policy
  defined, 11, 143
  and economy, 191–3
  as political stop-gap measure, 192
  publicity by state, 191, 194
  reactions to, 11, 12–3, 14, 178, 190, 191
Fricke, T., 15–16
funerals see burial, graves, Ọbalókè
  changes in, 113, 114, 120–1, 129–31
  of chiefs, 119
  and children needed for proper burial, 113, 129, 131
  and children wanted, 130
  dressing deceased, 31, 111, 112
  expenses, 111–12
  funeral party (ìje), 32, 112, 114
  proper, 129, 130
  reasons for, 112, 113, 129
  and religious beliefs, 114

gender dynamics see 'Four is enough' policy
  affective ties overriding official ideology, 51
  and division of labour, 45–6, 47–9
  and family compounds, 33–4, 44–5
  hierarchy, 34–5
  and ideals, 34–6
  and inequality, 11
  and virginity, 81
Government Teacher Training College, Ìbàdàn, 198
graves (orórí) see burial, funerals
  cemetery, 117
  and date of burial, 128
  digging of, 31

as family claims to land, 128–9, 161
and houses, 33, *115*, 115–18, 128, 159, 161
and names, 128
secret, 111
as site of prayers and offerings to parents, 116
of town founders' mother (Ojú Èyé Osín), 24
Greenhalgh, S., 15
Guyer, J., 237n26

Harvest Day, 36
Hocart, A. M., 6, 153
home-birth, 58–62; *see also* childbirth, maternity clinics
hospitals 42, 57, 58–66, 138, 197, 206; *see also* childbirth, Ìtàpá Maternity Centre, Methodist Maternity Centre (Hospital), Ìkọ̀lé
  attendance by foster children, 98
  and birth certificates, 180
  and maternal and child mortality, 120, 121
  and proper childcare, 144, 153
houses (*ulé, ilé*) *see* burials, patrilineage
  associated with body, 33, 76, 116
  as alternative security investments, 157, 168, 170
  built in non-family quarters, 31, 164
  burial in, 161
  continuity of family and its name, 170, 174
  and division of property, 34
  as economic contribution, 157
  and ideal of patrilineage and descendents, 34, 160, 161, 162, 163
  and iron roofs, 33, 155–7, *156*, 164
  in Ìtàpá-Èkìtì, 19–20, 30
  as land tenure claim, 157–8
  as measure of individual status, 157
  and mobility of occupants, 33
  as monument of success, 117, 157
  and need for children, 157, 172
  and non-kin residents, 160, 168–9
  physical layout of, 31, 33–4, 160
  residents, mean number in Ìtàpá, 160
  as source of rental income, 168–9, 170
  as substitutes for children, 169, 170–1
  as symbol of family vitality, 33, 157
  terminology, 33–4
house residents, 33, 34
  kin, 160–1
  non-kin, 160
  tenants, 13, 167, 168–9, 172
house-heads, 30, 35–6
  de facto, women, 44–5, 51, 169

men (*baálé*), 30–1, 33, 34, 35–6, 50–1, 161
women, 35–6, 45, 51, 238n3
household composition, 33–4, 44–6, 51, 159, 160, 167–9
houseplots, 159
  adjoining road as 'centre of civilisation', 21
  ownership and economic security, 159
houseplot boundaries
  flexibility of, 165, 166
  reification of, 167
  and survey pillars, 167, 170
  surveyed, 159, 167, 169, 170
  and 'trespassing tactics', 166–7
  use of natural features, *165*
houseplot transactions
  and abandoned houses, 163
  commoditisation of, 167, 169
  family, 159, 161–5
  and household composition, 159, 160, 167–9
  ideals of, 165, 167
  and implications for fertility, 169
  non-family, 159, 164
  and regularisation of transactions, 172
  things used in, 162, 164
  and 'tradition', 174
  use of money in, 159, 161–3, 164, 167–9, 170, 172
  and use rights, 161–5
  and written titles, 157, 159
hygiene, 136
  and development, 137, 138, 149
  everyday practice of, 140–1, 151
  innovations, 139, 140–9, 152–4
  and labour, 151–2, 153
  personal, 137, 151
  public, 137, 140, 151
  traditional practices, 138–9, 153
  and Western education, 142–4, 152–4

Ìbàdàn, 13, 37, 41, 61, 129, 155, 169, 199
ibodè (meeting of chiefs), 25
ideals
  of family continuity, 114, 116, 128–30, 159, 161, 168, 173
  of hometown houses, 44–5, 155, 169, 173
  of tradition, 159–60, 169
idàgbàsókè see development
Ìféyẹwá Local Government *see* local government creation
Igbó Afà (bush), 20
Ìjèlú, 24, 30
Ìkọ̀lé-Èkìtì, 21, 26–9, 40, 41, 42, 65, 89, 111, 135, 145–6
  District, 29, 182

Kingdom of, 26, 27
Methodist Maternity Centre (Hospital), 62–4, *63*
Ilé-Ifẹ̀, 24, 25, 28, 155, 236n6
Ilésà, 41, 155, 157
  Ìjẹ̀sà Kingdom, 26
  Ìjẹ̀sà region, 77
Ìlọrin, 155
Ìlúpéjú-Èkìtì (Egosi), 19, 21, 26, 29, 39–41, 42, 60, 62, 65, 90, 190; *see also* Ìtàpá-Èkìtì
International Monetary Fund, 205
immunisation programmes, 66, 138
incinerators, *149*
'indirect rule', 77, 145
  compared with international development, 250n13
infant mortality, 42
  and health classes, 144
  and maternal education, 57–8, 144
  from perspective of mothers, 57
  and place of delivery, 57–65
  rates, in Ìtàpá, 56–8, 66
  rates, in Nigeria, 239n9
  rates, in US, 239n9
  reduction as development, 66
  and uncertainty, 67
infertility *see* fertility, virginity
  and abortion, 84
  and bodily disorder, 83
  diseases associated with, 72, 81–2
infrastructure
  deterioration of, 152, 193, 205, 207, 208, 209
  electricity, irregular, 13, 37, 195, 204, 208, 210
  fuel, lack of, 60, 205, 206
  lack of, 13, 150–1, 154, 194
  maternal and child healthcare, inadequate, 207
  and need for child labour, 13, 19, 152
  phone service, lack of, 13, 208
  pipeborne water, lack of, 13–14, 151, 195, 204
  and sewage disposal, 148, 151
  transport, lack of, 60, 61, 66, 208
institutionalisation of
  hygiene practice, 137–49
  public health care, 136
interest and emotion, 114
inter-generational relations *see* childcare, fostering, hygiene
  and authority, 9, 34–5, 74, 76–7, 86, 131, 144, 152–4
  and childbearing, 88, 131
  contests over moral grounds, 88, 92, 104–5, 110, 131, 145, 152–4

inter-generational relations and health criticisms
  by children, 142–4, 153
  by grandparents, 144, 153
  and hospital attendance, 144
  by parents, 139, 144
Ìràfà chiefs, 30, 111, 237n17
Ìrè-Èkìtì, 29, 42, 236n5
Islam
  conversion to, 122, 130
  introduction of, 9
  mosques, Ìtàpá, 20
Ìtàlè Festival, *123*, 124–6
  as appeasement (*ètùtù*) of deceased, 124–5
  reduction in observance by young, 130, 131
  and remembrance of deceased, 126
  and requests for children, 124–5
Ìtàpá Day, 36–8, 201–2, *202*
  boycott of, 203
  celebration, 1999, 201–2
  Committee, 36, 37
  disbanding of Ìtàpá Progressive Union, 202
  and local development, 36, 203
  as strategy to attract people, 14, 36, 41
  and suspect fund-raising, 201–2
Ìtàpá-Èkìtì *see* fertility, Ìfẹ́yẹwá Local Government, Ìkọ̀lé-Èkìtì, Ọyẹ Local Government
  compared with: Ayégbajú-Èkìtì, population of, 182, 185, 248n6; Ìlúpéjú-Èkìtì, development of, 26, 29, 39–41, 42, 62, 190
  Customary Court, Ekiti State Judicial, 20
  demography of, 43–62, 74–6, 86–8, 89–98, 106–10, 130–2, 167–70, 212–13
  Development Fund, 36
  disunity in, 39, 198–205
  founders of, 23–4
  history of, 9–10, 20–30, 77, 145–7, 178, 181–3, 199–201
  important dates, 228–31
  as local government headquarters, 29–30, 189, 236n16
  ọmọ Ìtàpá ('children of Ìtàpá'), 7, 10, 19, 22, 34, 35, 36, 37, 41, 43, 113, 129, 130, 208
  origins of, 23–6, 200
  physical description of, 19–20, 30
  population growth in, 21–2, 26, 184–5, 190
  post office, 20, 197, 199, 249n4
  praise poem (*oríkì*) of, 19–20, 22–3
  Progressive Union, 14, 36, 37, 198–9

quarter days, *38*, 38–9
Sanitation Committee, 147
sawmill, 197, *198*
shrines, 19
strategies of alliance and separation, 26–7
streams, 23, 25, 37, 149, *150*
total fertility rate, 14, 54–5, 67, 170, 208, 232, 238n7
town hall, 20, 30, 36, 38, 39, 197, 203, *204*
unity and separation, 4, 26–7, 33, 36–41, 199–203
Ìtàpá-Èkìtì research project, 211–14
interviews, 218–27
topics and dates of interviews, 214–18
Ìtàpá-Èkìtì, town dispute, 198–205, 207, 209
centripetal and centrifugal forces, 199–200
court case, 1950, 200–1
Ẹgètún and Rẹ́mọ memoranda, 203
and failure of political leadership, 201, 203, 204, 205
impeding progress, 198, 200–3, 204
and possibility of town division, 200, 203, 207
rooted in 19th century wars, 200
and unequal division of power, 200–1, 203
Ìtàpá-Èkìtì, town quarters (*ekù* or *àdúgbò*), 19, *20*, 25, 26
associated with specific in-migrating groups, 30
heads, 30–1
quarter dispute, 31–3
quarters, Ẹgètún: Akòró, 20, 30, 200; Ìlawè, 20, 30; Òkòòrò/Ìlárò, 20, 30; Orókè, 20, 25, 30, 31–3, 111, 237n18, 237n20
quarters, Rẹ́mọ: Egbè, 20, 25, 30; Ògbónmẹ́ta, 20, 30; Òkèlìjù, 20, 25, 30; Ọmọdékè, 20, 30
sub-quarters, 25, 30, 31
Ìtàpá-Èkìtì, town sections see Ìtàpá-Èkìtì, town dispute
Ẹgètún ('upper Ìtàpá'), 24, 30, 39, 200
Rẹ́mọ ('lower Ìtàpá'), 24, 30, 39, 200
Ìtàpá Maternity (Ọyẹ Local Government Health) Centre, 19, 42, *64*, 210
construction and opening of, 64, 65–6
as example of local development, 65, 66
and Ìtàpá Progressive Union, 64
and reduction of infant and child mortality, 66
and social service cuts, 65
Ìtàpá-Osín Secondary School, 20, 199, 242n6

Kertzer, D., 15
kinship
children from one mother, *ọmọ ìyá kan*, 34
ideology and practice, 34–5, 169
matrilateral kin ties, 35–6
patrilineage, children of, 34–5, 173
patrilineage and houses, 33–5, 160, 163, 164, 165, 173
patrilineal descent, 35, 36
patrilocal (virilocal) residence, 35, 36, 51, 161
knowledge and moral authority see education

labour see child-fostering, hygiene, infrastructure
child, 13, 152, 208, 246n16
manual, 151–2
shortage in Ìtàpá, 13
wage, 21
Lagos, 13, 37, 41, 61, 77, 102, 118, 129, 141, 151, 169
land reform policy, 171
'land security' hypothesis, 169–70
land tenure, 157–8, 170–2
and 'customary' practices, 171
and family houses, 160, 172–4
and fertility, 157, 159, 160, 169–70
and need for people, 157, 159, 169
and written titles, 157–8, 159
latrines, pit, 141, 142, 147–9
Láyẹni, J. B., 25–6, 27, 28–9
'History Researches on Ìtàpá', 28–9
Lloyd, P., 165–6
local government creation
Ifeyewa Local Government (with Ìtàpá as headquarters), 29–30, 41, 189
Oye Local Government, 29–30, 39, 203

Malthus, T., 205–7
markets
Ìkòlé, 41
Ìlúpéjú, 39, 41, 238n30
Ìtàpá, 19, 40, 41, 250n14
marriage see divorce, premarital pregnancy, virginity
arranged, 51, 71, 74–8, 86–7, 114
and fertility, 71–2, 75–6, 78, 86–7
for love, 77–8, 86–8
monogamous, 35
and patrilocal (virilocal) residence, 35, 36, 51, 161
payments: brideservice (*òwè*), 74; bridewealth (*ìdána*), 51, 71, 74, 77; virginity, 75
polygynous, 35

rituals, 51, 74, 75, 78, 238n5
and spousal communication, 87–8, 238n6
types: Christian, 51; Islamic, 51; traditional, 51, 74, 78
Marx, K., 205
maternal mortality, 42; *see also* childbirth, contraceptive use
maternity clinics (*ilé alábiyamọ*) *see* childbirth, Ìtàpá Maternity Centre, Methodist Maternity Centre (Hospital), Ìkọ̀lé
media
  influence of, 80, 103
  newspapers, 205
  radio, 186
  ridicule of military dictators, 205, 250n11
  television, 80
Medical and Health Department, 137; *see also* Federal Ministry of Health
medicalisation of childbirth, 60
men *see baálé*, gender dynamics, kinship, traditional chiefs
  and houses, 30–1, 33, 34, 35–6, 50–1, 161
  and marriage, 50, 51, 81
  and relation to children, 34–5, 52–4, 170
  and work, 45–6, 47
menstruation
  amenorrhea, 82–3
  and fertility, 82
  menarche, 74, 82–3
Methodist Maternity Centre (Hospital), Ìkọ̀lé, 42, 62–5, *63*
midwives (*agbẹ̀bí*), 62, 210, 240n5
migration, in-, Ìtàpá, 21, 25, 26, 28, 67
migration, out-, Ìtàpá, 4, 5, 13, 41, 42, 44, 61, 67, 130
  and Western education, 5, 13, 41, 61
military rule, 10, 205
Ministry of Health and Social Services, 136
modernisation theory, 16
money
  ban on use in houseplot transactions, 167
  devaluation of naira, 10, 11
  and houseplot transactions, 159, 161–3, 167–9
  and Ìtàpá Day donations, 37
  as morally inappropriate, 162, 167
  as substitute for fostering, 105
moral parenthood, 56, 106–10, 152–4
mortuaries, 112, 244n18

names, children's
  Christian/Muslim naming ceremonies, 128

and claims to property, titles, 129
family continuity, 128, 129
as honorifics, 130
and *oríkì orílẹ̀*, 128
and rebirth of parent's spirit, 128
and social status, 7
National Population Commission, 248n12
National Population Commission Decree, 12, 190, 248n11
National Population Policy, 11, 159; *see also* 'Four is enough' policy
Nigerian census, 1991 census in Ìtàpá *see* Ekiti State
  benefits of, 186, 188
  and enumerators, 184
  preparations for, 183–4
  uncertainty about, 185–6, 193–4
Nigerian censuses, 177, 178, 179, 182, 183–6, 194
Nigerian Land Use Decree (Act) of 1978, 158, 170–2, 173, 246n1

Ọbaísà, 200–1, 237n17, 250n7; *see also* traditional chiefs
Ọbalókè *see* burial, funerals, traditional chiefs
  and chieftaincy dispute, 31–3
  funeral of, 31–2, 111, *112*, 243n1, 243n2
  house of, 31
  on relations between living and dead, 126–7
Ògún Festival, 36, 237n19
Ògúntúyì, A., 22, 51, 178
ọlàjú (enlightenment), 9, 10, 62
  and childbirth limitation, 191–2
  and child-fostering, 106
  and education, 62, 79–81, 88
  as enlightened behaviour, 138
  family planning as, 235n10
  and hygiene, 138
  terms, 9, 234n5, 245n5
Olúsànyà, P., 3, 152, 170, 172–4, 209
Ọmọ Èyé Méta, 24; *see also* Ìtàpá-Èkìtì, founders of
Ọmọtóyìnbó, J., 210
oníṣègùn (herbalist), 72
oríkì (praise poems), 19, 22, 25, 116, 128
Orùbuloyè, I., 11
Osín-Èkìtì, 19, 20, 24, 29
Òṣogbo, 155, 157
Ọwátàpá (King of Ìtàpá) *see* Ìràfà chiefs, traditional chiefs
  Amọ́wá, first Ọwátàpá, 24
  Alli Sanni Atọ́batẹ̀lẹ̀ I, 27–9
  Amẹ́rìjoyè, 27
  Adéyẹyẹ Àmùdá Alli, Oguguleso II, 199
  authority of, 25–6

and council of chiefs, 30
and dispute settlement, 172, 200, 250n8
and funerals, 111, 118–19, 122, 124
and Ìtàpá Day, 36, 38
Ọwátàpá Òjó, 201
palace of, 20, 151, 201
and sanitary inspection, 135
Ọyẹ́-Èkìtì, 19, 29
Kingdom of, 26, 39
Oye Local Government, 29–30, 39, 203

paradoxes of progress, 4–5, 208
parental pressures for children, 88
parents as 'veritable props of childbearing', 152
parent–child relations
and human development, 8–9
and hygiene, 142–53
and knowledge, 136
metaphors of, 7, 34
patrilineage *see* kinship
patron–client relations, 3
'big men', 36
'big women', 36, 46
Peel, J. D. Y., 3, 39, 62, 234n5
people, importance of having, 3, 4, 14, 26, 207
politics
and development, 204–5, 208
and disorder, 11, 209
and foreign exchange manipulation, 209
and government credibility, 193
and misuse of development funds, 205
political corruption *see* politics
political economy
based on patron–client relations, 207
and deteriorating infrastructure, 207
and uncertainty, 11, 207
political legitimacy, 160
political resistance, 11, 60, 62, 66, 106, 186, 230–1
'politics of numbers', 5, 193–4, 234n1
population
conceptualisation, 43
de facto, defined, 43
de jure, defined, 43
and development, connection between, 3, 192
of Ìtàpá, 42, 43–5
policies, federal, supporting population growth, 5, 194, 195
programmes, 178
pyramid, Ìtàpá, 44–5, 45, 67
population growth and development hypotheses
capitalist production leads to unequal development, 205

development follows fertility decline, 206
economic and political problems impede development, 206
fertility decline follows development, 206
population impedes development, 3
postpartum abstinence, 11, 87; *see also* child-spacing
premarital pregnancy, 78, 79; *see also* virginity, marriage
and disease, 84–6
moral reassessment of, 83, 86
and sexuality, 7, 78, 80–1
primary school health classes, 136, 138, 140–5; *see also* cleanliness, hygiene
and lack of infrastructural support, 150–2
posters and textbooks, 140–1, 142
process (processual analysis), 14–15
of fertility decline and political context, 208
of land commoditisation, 159
of redefining blood ties and kin relations, 89
of reinterpreting virginity and marriage, 89
progress (*ilọsíwájú*), 3
proverbs, 3, 4, 7, 34, 35, 67, 75, 89, 98, 103, 111, 114, 129, 130, 155, 160, 167, 170, 172
public health interventions
development of 'health conscience', 137
Government Health Services, 137
health propaganda films, 141
Primary Healthcare Programme, 138
and social control, 137, 153
public sanitation *see* hygiene

rebirth *see àbíkú*
beliefs about, 114, 126–7
and kin relations, 114
and reincarnation, 117, 126
and resurrection, 127
rituals (*ìdíléde*̀), 128, 131
of spirit, 117, 126–7
'reborn' Christians, 81, 85
registration, of births
as beneficial, 180–1, 195
as development, 178
fees, 181
after hospital delivery, 180
and school attendance, 176
as unnecessary expense, 180
registration, of deaths, disapproval of, 177, 181
Registration of Births and Deaths Adoptive Bye-laws Order, 180
reincarnation *see* rebirth

relations between living and dead
  attenuation in beliefs about, 125, 131
  communication between, 124–5, 126
  and dreams, 125
  festivals commemorating (Ìtàlè, ìdílédè), 124–6, 127
  and presence of deceased spirit, 117, 161
  through sacrifice, 123–5
remittances, 14
Rémo see Ìtàpá-Èkìtì, town sections
rental property see houses
residence, indeterminate meaning of, 33; see also kinship, marriage
Richards, A., 16
roads
  and access to work outside, 21, 41
  and crossroads, 39
  and development, 40–1, 197
  in Ìtàpá, 19–20, 21, 24, 195
  Ìtàpá-Ìkòlé, 19, 197
  and motor vehicles, 40, 238n30
roofs see houses
'rotten children', 144, 153

sanitary inspection, 135–6, 145–7
  and extortion, 146–7
  and fines, 145–6
  and inspectors (wolé wolé), 135, 136, 145–6
  and political control, 145–7
  of schools and teachers, 136, 146
sanitation see hygiene
schism and continuity, 26; see also centrifugal and centripetal tendencies
Schneider, J., and P. Schneider, 15
schools see education
Sen, A., 206–7
shrines see Ìtàpá-Èkìtì
'sibling chain of assistance' see education
Simmel, G., 7
social capital, 92, 241n3
social structural positions, 6, 34–5; see also kinship, marriage
'social technologies', 177
songs of abuse, 32, 237n22
Soyinka, W., 34, 135, 157
state creation, 10, 186–90
state-sponsored economic reforms, 10, 234n6
  and fertility, 173
  and unworkable government policies, 173
Structural Adjustment Programme, 10, 11, 152, 235n8
surveys, Ìtàpá-Èkìtì
  fostering (1991), 43, 95, 103, 215
  household census (1991), 43, 211

houseplot transactions (1992), 43, 115, 161, 216
men's (1992), 43, 211–12
women's (1992, 1997), 43, 61, 62, 106–8, 211–12
surveys, Nigeria
  Adó-Èkìtì Survey (1991), 43
  Nigerian Demographic Health (1990), 43, 58, 238n7, 251n5
  Nigerian Demographic Health (1999), 238n7
  Ondo State Demographic Health (1986), 238n7
survey-taking, idiosyncracies of data collection, 251n6; see also age

thresholds
  front door (ojúulé, ojú ilé), 33, 74, 76–7
  vagina (ojú ara; òbò), 76–7
toilets and bathrooms, 37, 142, 151
total fertility rate see fertility, surveys
  Ìtàpá 1992, 14, 54–5, 67, 170, 238n7
  Ìtàpá 1997, 14, 54–5, 67, 232, 238n7
  Ondo State 1986, 238n7
  Nigeria 1990, 1999, 238n7
traditional chiefs see Elékòlé, Èwí-Adó, ibodè, Ìràfà chiefs, Obaísà, Obalókè, Owátàpá
  beaded crown kings, 28, 77
  and Ekiti State, 187–8
  'for sale', 10
  funerals of, 111, 118–19
  Grade B chief, 39, 236n15, 238n29
  ranking of, 25
traditional healers see babaláwo, onísègùn
traditional religion, 161
  imolè (umolè), 10, 25
  òrìsà, 24, 25
Trager, L., 204–5
Trott, Louise (Yèyé Tóró), Methodist Maternity Centre (Hospital), Ìkòlé, 62–4
Turner, B., 74, 138
Turner, V., 26

uncertainty
  and childbirth, 58–62
  and child-fostering, 56, 92, 106–7, 110
  and child survival, 57, 66–7
  and federal land reform, 173
  of marital fertility, 79
  political and economic, 10, 67, 152, 186, 207
Universal Primary Education (UPE), 1955, 11, 78, 99, 235n8; see also education
urban–rural ties see fertility

van de Walle, E., 239n11
venereal disease, 72, 82; *see also* virginity
virginity (*ibálé*), 71–86, 240n1; *see also* menstruation, marriage
    antisocial behaviour, 72, 81–2
    associated with disease, 72, 81–3
    and authority of fathers, 74, 76–7
    blood, 72, 73
    and Christianity, 81, 85, 86
    cloth (*aṣọ ibálé*), 73, 74
    and control of women's bodies, 74–7
    and decline in importance, 71–2
    and education, 79–81
    and fertility, 71–2, 78
    hymen, 72–3
    and infertility, 72, 75–6, 79, 81–3
    perceptions of, 72, 74–6, 81–3, 84–6
    reasons for, 79–81
    reinterpretations of, 71–2, 77–83, 84, 89
    spoiled (*ibàjẹ́*), 71–4
    as source of pride, 75, 84
    terms for, 72–3
vital registration, 130, 176; *see also* birth records, registration of birth, registration of deaths

war
    Ariba [Ìlọrin], 1875, 27
    Ekiti, 22
    and formation of Ogún Òsì, 25
    Itila (Hitler; World War II), 180
    Ogun Yinmiomo ('give me a child' war), 27
    and population loss, 27
    Yoruba, 22, 25
War Against Indiscipline (WAI), 147, 234n6, 246n14
water, 149–50, 151; *see also* infrastructure
Wesley Mission *see* Methodist Maternity Centre (Hospital), Ìkọ̀lé
Western education *see* education, Universal Primary Education
Western models of reproductive biology, *80*, 81
wills, 130, 244n18
witchcraft, 6, 234n3
womb (*ilé ọmọ*), 76
women *see* childbirth, gender dynamics, kinship, marriage
    and funerals, 31–2
    and houses, 35–6, 45, 51
    and property, 35
    and relations to children, 34–5, 52–4, 170
    and work, 45–6, 48–9
World Population Day, 191